Lincoln Christian College

D0936911

GREAT BRITAIN AND EUROPE
IN THE EIGHTEENTH CENTURY

*Oxford University Press, Ely House, London W.*1

GLASGOW NEW YORK TORONTO MELBOURNE WELLINGTON
CAPE TOWN SALISBURY IBADAN NAIROBI LUSAKA ADDIS ABABA
BOMBAY CALCUTTA MADRAS KARACHI LAHORE DACCA
KUALA LUMPUR HONG KONG TOKYO

GREAT BRITAIN
AND EUROPE
IN THE
EIGHTEENTH CENTURY

BY

DAVID BAYNE HORN

CLARENDON PRESS
OXFORD
1967

© Oxford University Press 1967

Printed in Great Britain by
Butler & Tanner Ltd, Frome and London

Dedication

To my daughter Hazel

PARKER & SON

38140

27180 11

PREFACE

FROM a deep conviction of the inadequacy of a purely or narrowly diplomatic approach to the relationship between Great Britain and the other states of Europe in the eighteenth century, I have tried to show in this book how British diplomacy was influenced by economic and ecclesiastical interests, strategic considerations, and social and cultural contacts—or the absence of them. The method adopted of treating British relations with Europe in this way, country by country, is novel and, I believe, useful. The conclusion attempts a synthesis which draws attention to the more general features of British foreign policy in the century.

Attention is concentrated firmly upon Europe. Colonial issues remain in the background unless they had a vital influence on diplomatic relations between Britain and the other European states. Similarly no attempt has been made to fill in the naval and military background of foreign policy during the periods when Britain was engaged in wars. An elementary knowledge of this must be assumed: otherwise the book, already larger than I like, would become much too long and much too diffuse.

My indebtedness to the printed works of many specialists in the political, economic and social relations between Britain and one particular country on the Continent will be obvious to the reader. This applies with especial force to the volumes published in the Camden Series on Anglo-French, Anglo-Danish and Anglo-Swedish diplomatic relations in the eighteenth century and to many other standard works such as Sir Richard Lodge's *Great Britain and Prussia* (Clarendon Press, 1923); Mrs. Jean Lindsay's *Trade and Peace with Old Spain 1667–1750* (Cambridge U.P., 1940); Marcus Meier's *Die diplomatische Vertretung Englands in der Schweiz im 18 Jahrhundert* (Basel, 1952); and Manfred Schlenke's *England und das friderizianische Preussen 1740–1763* (Freiburg/München, 1963). Even if my indebtedness is not always acknowledged as fully as I should wish in footnotes, which have been reduced to a minimum, these works are cited in the bibliographies: I would ask their authors to accept this general expression of my cordial thanks for their involuntary participation in the making of this book.

Greatly to its advantage, Professor Charles Wilson, Jesus College, Cambridge, was good enough to comment on chapter 4 in typescript. Professor Max Braubach of the Rheinische Friedrich-Wilhelms-Universität, Bonn, and Professor Walther Mediger of the Technical University of Hanover helped me in different ways in writing and re-writing chapter 7. Amongst my colleagues Dr. Stewart Oakley corrected many errors in the first draft of chapter 9 and Professor Denys Hay made valuable suggestions after reading the historical introduction to chapter 12. Any errors remaining after expert scrutiny in these chapters are my own. I should have liked to invite more of my friends' opinions on other chapters, but was restrained by the prudential consideration that this might prevent them from reviewing the book in learned journals. As always I owe a special debt to my friend and former pupil, Dr. Matthew Anderson of the London School of Economics, whose constructive criticism, not only of chapter 8 but of the whole book, has once again strengthened my respect for his profound scholarship and deepened my appreciation of his skill as a master of the art of historical composition.

Two sections of this book have already appeared, textually or in substance, in print. I am grateful to the Delegates of the Clarendon Press for allowing me to publish a version of chapter 2, somewhat extended and revised, in the April 1967 number of the *Journal of the Society of Archivists*. Messrs. Eyre and Spottiswoode generously gave me permission to reproduce the Conclusion (pages 378–384) which originally formed part of the introduction to volume 10 of *English Historical Documents* and is now reprinted with some alterations.

It is fitting that I should also acknowledge here my indebtedness to the authorities and staffs of the various archives and libraries in which I have worked, and especially to the Public Record Office, the British Museum, the Scottish Record Office, the National Library of Scotland, the National Central Library, the University of Nottingham Department of Manuscripts, and, above all, the Library of the University of Edinburgh. This is too often taken for granted by young scholars; I am old enough to remember a time when the bad traditions of the eighteenth century in regard to the opening of archives and libraries to scholars had not entirely died out.

Miss Elizabeth Whitelaw transformed an exceptionally indecipherable manuscript into a thing of beauty and accuracy which must have brought joy to a compositor's hard heart. The officials of the Clarendon Press made the transition from typescript to print as painless as possible for the author. My wife and daughter Hazel helped manfully with the chores of proof-reading and index-making: without their professional skill and willing support these tasks could not have been completed in the prescribed time.

D. B. HORN

Edinburgh, 23 November 1966

CONTENTS

xi

CHAPTER 1

English Foreign Policy 1603–1702

THE formulation and execution of foreign policy were usually regarded as one of the functions of a medieval English king: only when the policy he pursued affected adversely the economic interests of important sections of his subjects had there been even ineffective protests against royal monopoly of foreign policy. When England became Protestant and religion became a vital factor in the foreign policies of the leading European states, the pursuit of a foreign policy by the Crown which was not believed by Protestant Englishmen to protect and, if possible, advance the Protestant interest in Europe led to more general and better organized protests than had ever occurred in previous centuries. When Elizabeth was succeeded by the foreign house of Stuart, protest became still more articulate and much more widespread. Under James I it found expression both in the Apology and in the Protestation of the house of Commons. By denying supplies to Charles I successive houses of Commons at the beginning of his reign virtually prevented him from effectively pursuing any foreign policy at all during 'the eleven years' tyranny' from 1629 to 1640.

Although the Restoration left the royal prerogatives in foreign policy untouched, the Cavalier house of Commons, in the crisis of 1672–4 over the third Dutch war, used the power of the purse to show disapproval of the royal foreign policy and to force Charles out of the war. Even when the revocation of the edict of Nantes by Louis XIV in 1685 together with the widespread belief that James II would not hesitate to sacrifice the interests of his country to those of his faith, contributed to bring about the Revolution of 1688, no attempt was made to circumscribe the personal activities of the king in foreign policy.

William III was legally in the same position as James I with regard to the formulation and control of English foreign policy. Practically he was in a stronger position than his predecessor because he had already established an incontrovertible claim to be the leader of European Protestantism, whereas James I's pretensions to act as arbiter between Catholic and Protestant cost him the support of both. Moreover no unbiased Englishman could deny that William's grasp of European politics was incomparably superior to that of any of his ministers, let alone the rank and file of the two houses of Parliament. William became so used to getting his own way that he became careless of constitutional forms and at the very end of his reign ran into trouble over the Partition treaties.

The Act of Settlement, which provided for the succession to the English throne, also contained the first legislative restriction upon the Crown's control of foreign policy. When the house of Hanover came to the throne the king would be prevented from doing what the Tory Opposition contended William had done. No longer would the king of Great Britain be entitled to involve England in war for the benefit of the foreign territories in which he was interested.

While the practical importance of this declaration proved to be nugatory, it marked the clear emergence of the idea of national as distinct from royal policy in foreign affairs. By implication at least it indicated that future sovereigns would be expected to direct their foreign policy not according to their own personal interests and ambitions but in accordance with the wishes and the interests of their English subjects.

Instead of appearing as one of the minor powers subsidized by Louis XIV, though not above occasionally blackmailing her paymaster by a threat to change her 'system', England became in 1689 an equal partner with the Emperor and the Dutch in a Grand Alliance directed against the aggression of Louis XIV. While it would be obviously untrue to say that England had never before 1689 played the part of a Great Power on the west European chessboard, her appearances in this role had usually been involuntary, short-lived and ineffective. From 1689, for better or worse, is dated the continuous story of British intervention on the Continent and in the non-European world as a Great Power.

Needless to say, this change of approach to foreign policy was very unpopular with many of William III's new subjects and indeed constituted one of the dividing lines between parties in his reign. Most Whigs were prepared to accept William III's assurances that England's security and prosperity depended upon their vigorous support of his continental campaigns. Instead of accepting subsidies from France, England became, along with the Dutch, a payer of subsidies to several minor powers which could thereby be induced to take part in the war against France.

The attitude of the Tories was less decided. Those who put loyalty to the Stuarts before attachment to the Church of England were well aware that France was the Great Power most likely to be able and willing to give effective support to the exiled James II. Even those Tories who identified Toryism with fervent support of the Church of England looked askance at the new policy. It was ruinously expensive and much of the expense fell upon the Tory squires who paid most of the land tax, while Whig financiers and contractors, who made vast profits from the war, escaped their fair share of war taxation. The Tories therefore protested against the burden and expense of continental war. If war was necessary, why could the government not wage it at sea? A large and powerful navy was in itself sufficient for national defence and any ships which could be spared should be used to protect our merchant shipping and destroy that of our competitors. This basic difference continued to influence English attitudes to foreign policy and wars long after the death of George II.

There may be some slight doubt as to whether William III was his own prime minister; but he certainly was his own foreign minister. The Revolution, which attempted to define royal powers in domestic affairs, did nothing to limit the royal prerogative in foreign affairs. William III believed that he possessed the sole right to declare war or make peace and to conclude any treaties he pleased with foreign powers. Acting on this belief he brought the war of the English Succession to an end by the treaty of Ryswick in 1697, and this was in fact the last occasion upon which a British government made an important treaty of peace without formally communicating to Parliament the terms of the settlement. No voice seems to have been raised in protest in either house of Parliament in 1697; but when William proceeded to make the two Partition treaties with France, entirely upon his own authority, the Tory majority in the house of Commons raised a furious outcry, demanded and secured the production of the text of both treaties, and impeached the leading Whig ministers who were held to be, by a more than usually transparent constitutional fiction, responsible for the conclusion of the treaties.

William acted as he did during his reign because control of British foreign policy and the enhancement of his personal status were the objects he had most at heart in risking an invasion of England. As stadholder of the United Provinces he was merely the chief executive officer of a republican federation of sovereign provinces. It was only after his establishment in England that he secured admission to the select circle of crowned heads of states and he was fully resolved to retain every legitimate prerogative of the monarchy for himself and his successors. His determination was reinforced by the practical consideration that only by drawing from England as much support as could be obtained could he hope to defeat decisively Louis XIV and consolidate politically the economic leadership which the United Provinces had already acquired in Europe.

Such a foreign policy could hardly be openly avowed in England without arousing the suspicions of Englishmen who had already lived through three Dutch wars. In any case William had a supreme contempt for the understanding of continental politics and diplomacy possessed by even the closest of those associated with him in England in carrying on his foreign policy. Early in his reign when his wife was still alive he left her behind in England as head of a Regency Council with limited powers and advised her, if really difficult problems of foreign policy arose which could not be referred to him in the Low Countries for settlement, then she was to take the advice of the Spanish ambassador at London.

When he was in England he treated the secretaries of state, whom he had chosen, and who had to accept responsibility for his foreign policy, as mere clerks. They were all so impressed by the superiority of the king's experience and ability in this field that they made no protest—some of them even thanked the king for reducing them to ciphers. Not only was foreign policy the king's: it was he who chose the subordinate agents who had to carry out this policy at foreign courts. The execution of his policy, even in matters vitally affecting England, was often entrusted to the diplomatic agents of the United Provinces. When he did accredit an English diplomatic agent to a foreign court he often chose a Dutchman, a French Huguenot refugee or a Swiss Protestant. And William deliberately retained in his own hands the decision whether it was either necessary or desirable to send a minister at all to a particular court at a particular time—there was as yet no fixed establishment for the foreign service. Enough has been said to show that, at least down to the closing months of his reign,

England's foreign policy was both formulated and executed by the king, almost uninfluenced by his ministers and virtually unimpeded by Parliament, if we except its traditional reluctance to vote supplies for a war.

CHAPTER 2

The Machinery for the Conduct of Foreign Policy in the Eighteenth Century

WHILE there was little, if any, change in theory under Queen Anne, control of foreign policy in practice was passing from the queen to her ministers, Godolphin and Marlborough, and to the party leaders. Anne had neither the specialized knowledge of European politics nor the intellectual grasp required to formulate and control foreign policy. Had her husband Prince George of Denmark been abler and more energetic, he might possibly have inherited the mantle of William III. Had England been at peace during her reign a possible solution would have been not to have a foreign policy at all; but the outbreak of the Spanish Succession war excluded this possibility. For most of Anne's reign the critical decisions were taken by Marlborough and Godolphin, working in close harmony. Anne's habitual acceptance of their advice not only shifted effective control of foreign policy, at least for the time being, from the sovereign to her ministers: it accentuated the earlier tendency for foreign politics to be one of the problems upon which English political parties tended to divide. War-weariness, and perhaps still more dissatisfaction with Whig conduct of the war was a powerful factor in the Tory victory in the general election of 1710.

Harley and St. John, with the acquiescence of the queen, took the decisions for the last four years of Anne's reign. Thus for more than a decade—and a decade in which war kept the problems of foreign policy continually in the public eye—the critical decisions had been taken by the ministers of the Crown. The secretaries of state now directed more and more effectively the day-to-day execution of policy in foreign affairs, while they and the other leading ministers met regularly in a Cabinet which, under the guise of preparing business for the queen's decision, formulated the major issues of foreign policy in a way which often predetermined royal decisions.

Almost the only thing which Whigs and Tories shared in their approach to foreign policy under the first two Georges was a determination to preserve the gains of Anne's reign and to prevent the Hanoverian kings from reverting to the practices of William III. The objectionable clause in the Act of Settlement was formally revoked; but its spirit inspired most of the protests made by Whig and Tory alike against the foreign policy of the Hanoverian kings. Indeed the authors of some speeches recorded in the parliamentary debates seem to have believed that the clause in the Act of Settlement had never been repealed. Pelham in 1726 was better informed. As Walpole's henchman he moved and carried in the house of Commons an address pledging the house to stand by the king &c. although his foreign dominions were attacked.[1]

George I was no William III. He lacked William's breadth of mind and outlook as well as his acute perception of political realities; but in the more circumscribed sphere of a German prince, whose colleagues regarded him with some justification as an upstart elector, he had shown ability both as administrator and diplomatist. Lord Chesterfield placed his finger unerringly upon the new king's weakness. 'His views and affections were singly confined to the narrow compass of the Electorate; England was too big for him.' Lady Mary Wortley Montagu described him patronizingly but with less than her usual insight as an honest blockhead. He showed a pragmatical approach to English politics and seems to have realized that he must accept in form, though he could safely try to undermine in practice, the influence attained over foreign policy by the English party leaders under his predecessor. The strength of his position lay in the fact that no one in 1714 questioned his right to choose his own ministers for foreign affairs and to cease to employ them if they diverged from the line of foreign policy which he himself prescribed. One of the reasons why virtually all George I's ministers were Whigs was that the ideas on foreign policy, of which the Whigs had become the protagonists under Anne, accorded closely with the views of the new ruler. By ditching the Emperor, sacrificing the interests of the Dutch and drawing close to France and its satellite Spain, the Tory ministers of Anne's last years convinced George that they could not be trusted. George, whose troops had fought on the Rhine as part of an Imperial army paid for by English subsidies, ostentatiously refused to follow the lead of his paymaster when the

---

[1] *Parliamentary Diary of Sir Edward Knatchbull*, ed. A. N. Newman (Camden 3rd series, XCIV. 52).

British armies ceased to fight against France and he openly protested against British betrayal of the Emperor. Not until the summer of 1714 did he, as a loyal member of the Holy Roman Empire, make peace with France.

George had contracted a marriage in 1682 with his cousin Sophia Dorothea with a view to the eventual reunion of the duchies of Lüneburg (with its capital at Celle) and Kalenberg (with its capital at Hanover). Although the primary objective was achieved and two children were born, the union soon proved unhappy. George I charged his wife with adultery, secured a divorce from her, and shut her up in a Hanoverian fortress. When George came to England in 1714, Sophia Dorothea was left behind; but he brought with him to England all his mistresses and some of his ministers. He found already firmly established at London Count Bothmer who had served him ably as Hanoverian envoy in the closing years of Anne's reign. George I, unlike most contemporary sovereigns, retained his mistresses for life and his two leading ladies, the Baronesses Schulenberg and Kielmansegge, were already in their forties when they reached England. Much Cockney wit was exercised at their expense. Schulenberg's height and her scrawny figure earned her the sobriquet of the 'hop-pole', while Kielmansegge's bulk, which terrified Horace Walpole as a boy, seemed to justify her nickname the 'Elephant and Castle'. Both ladies became peeresses in their own right, the former duchess of Kendal and the latter countess of Darlington, but neither seems to have appreciably influenced British foreign policy. Sir Robert Walpole did indeed declare in 1720 that the duchess of Kendal 'was, in effect, as much queen of England as ever any was', and that 'he did everything by her'. These statements must refer to her influence over the exercise of royal patronage, in which field her venality soon became notorious. She may have had some voice in the appointments made by the new king in the British diplomatic service, though this would seem to rest on presumption rather than on proof.

It is a completely different story when we consider the influence upon foreign policy of the new king's German ministers. At first the most influential was Bernstorff, an experienced administrator, who had successively served the dukes of Mecklenburg and Celle, before entering the Hanoverian service. Now that his master had become king of England, Bernstorff saw no reason why he should not advise him as freely on all aspects of British as of German politics. Hardly less influential than Bernstorff was his slightly younger rival Bothmer, formerly Hanoverian minister at the court of Queen Anne. In the early months of the reign Bernstorff and Bothmer were reported to meet every night at Bothmer's house with Marlborough and Townshend. And during the protracted crisis of the Jacobite rebellion some foreign ministers in London believed that George I's English ministers were so preoccupied with domestic difficulties that they had no option but to transact their business with the king's Hanoverian advisers.

Much inferior in official position to Bothmer and Bernstorff was Robethon, who had left his native country after the revocation of the edict of Nantes and attached himself as private secretary to the arch-enemy of Louis XIV, William III. Subsequently Bernstorff found him a job at Hanover and as private secretary to the king he accompanied George I to England in 1714. This position naturally gave him opportunities to serve the interests of applicants for positions abroad as well as at home. More important, the breadth of his experience and the subtleness of his mind caused the king and Bernstorff to value his advice on much more important matters of foreign policy. Diplomatists abroad also attached much value to keeping in touch with Robethon and through him with the king. Some, including Lord Polwarth at Copenhagen, confessed that without their regular correspondence with Robethon they would not have known how to conduct themselves at foreign courts.

Had George I and his German advisers foreseen the political development of eighteenth-century England they might well have adopted the maxim of 'divide and rule'. The nearest approach to this was Bothmer's advice that the king should not appoint a lord treasurer who might become troublesome to the sovereign by stressing or even expanding the traditional claims of this high office. Neither Bothmer nor Bernstorff seems to have advised George I to entrust responsibility for the various branches of administration to different English ministers, and to restrict each English minister to the work of his own department. This would have reserved to the king and his German advisers the final decisions on matters of policy, and particularly of foreign policy. The Cabinet, as an unpopular recent innovation, could have been allowed to wither away, if it was not to be abolished by a formal decision.

Though George I did indeed almost cease to attend meetings of the Cabinet after the opening years of his reign, there seems to be no evidence that he entertained any ideas of limiting its influence or preventing inter-departmental discussions between his English ministers. The virtual withdrawal of the king, even if it did not make necessary the growth of the office of first minister, must certainly have made it much easier for the English ministers to have full and free discussions of the outstanding issues of foreign policy. And this was also facilitated by another of George I's decisions— the exclusion of Tories from office.

In any case it may well be doubted whether the policy of 'divide and rule' would have been practicable in the political conditions of the years immediately after 1714. George consistently preferred not to divide his favours even amongst the leading Whigs. From 1714 to 1717 he placed his chief reliance upon Townshend, succeeded by Stanhope, the leading minister until his death. After a brief interlude during which Sunderland held sway, Walpole became and remained the leading minister until George I's death.

Before George I set foot in England he had appointed Townshend to be secretary of state. Townshend, although at the outset of his diplomatic career he had been described as 'by much the most shining person of all our young nobility', had hardly justified this encomium. He had failed to conclude peace with France at Gertruydenberg, and the Barrier treaty of 1709 which he had signed with the Dutch had been repudiated by the Tory administration of 1710. He owed his appointment in fact to the recommendations of Bothmer and Robethon, both of whom he had been careful to cultivate in the last years of Anne's reign.

His grasp of foreign affairs was much inferior to that of his colleague Stanhope, who was the son of a career diplomat. Born at Paris in 1673, 'he never had a fixed home in England until he was past forty'.[1] Whereas Townshend as the eldest son of a Restoration peer enjoyed every possible advantage, Stanhope had had to make his own way in the world. At the beginning of the Spanish Succession war he was already a colonel and a member of the house of Commons. Placed in supreme command of the British troops in Spain in 1708, Stanhope conquered Minorca and gave Britain a secure base in the Mediterranean; but two years later his military career came to a premature end at the battle of Brihuega

---

[1] Basil Williams, *Stanhope*, p. 2.

when Stanhope himself was taken prisoner and his army virtually destroyed.

Although this disaster removed the last possibility of carrying out what had become the central tenet of Whig war aims—no peace without Spain—Stanhope, when he returned to England after nearly two years as a prisoner-of-war, was accepted as one of the leaders of the Whig party in the house of Commons. Recognizing that the making of peace and war at Utrecht lay within the prerogative powers of the Crown, he held that it was preposterous to say anything for or against it. But the separate commercial treaty with France, also concluded at Utrecht in April 1713, included two clauses which undoubtedly required the co-operation of Parliament to bring them into force. The eighth clause provided that Britain and France should give mutually most-favoured-nation treatment in trade to each other. The ninth clause was intended to revoke the system of prohibitions and restrictions which had gradually been built up since 1664 upon Franco-British trade. Any alteration of custom duties to give effect to these clauses clearly required legislation.

Moreover it was generally believed by the trading and manufacturing classes that to free the shackles imposed on Anglo-French trade would lead to exchange of French luxuries and fripperies for English manufactures of solid worth. Indeed, since the French market for English exports was a very limited one, the result would almost certainly be to bring about export of bullion, open or concealed, to pay for luxuries imported from France. Worse still, if possible, to a mercantilist, the native English industries laboriously built up by prohibition and restriction of French imports in the preceding decades, would be destroyed. There was also the specific objection that the eighth clause was contrary to the stipulations of the Methuen treaty of 1703 with Portugal, in accordance with which the duties on import of Portuguese wines into England should never exceed two-thirds of those on French wines. The prosperous Iberian 'lobby' saw the whole basis of the flourishing trade they had built up about to be destroyed.

Stanhope therefore believed that the best hope of securing rejection of the Utrecht treaties was to concentrate attack on their economic aspects. This was the more attractive because the Whigs were by tradition the spokesmen of the mercantile and industrial classes, and his belief proved justified. The Spitalfields silk-weavers and the woollen-manufacturers in a dozen counties petitioned the house of Commons and after a fierce debate the objectionable clauses were rejected by 194 votes to 185. For the next seventy years, until the conclusion of the Eden treaty of commerce with France in 1786, Britain and France did everything in their power to damage and restrict the overseas trade of the other.

Although the return of Walpole to the house of Commons must have reduced Stanhope's pre-eminence there, he seems to have been almost as prominent and active in the first Parliament of George I as he had been in Anne's last Parliament. George I's German advisers, apparently prompted by the Walpoles, made the right decision when they offered him, instead of the post of commander-in-chief in Ireland, the secretaryship of state for the northern department. Here he would be working in double harness with Townshend, already appointed to what was still regarded as the senior post of secretary of state for the southern department. Since Townshend was a peer, Stanhope would have to present to the house of Commons the foreign policy of the government and share with Walpole responsibility for winning its support both for the foreign and the domestic policies of the new Whig administration.

The Walpoles probably expected Stanhope to produce original ideas on foreign policy which would be vetted, and if necessary vetoed, by Townshend. They certainly erred in thinking that he would remain for long contented with a position of inferiority in the ministry, although the brother-secretaries co-operated closely and without any sign of tension for some time.

Much has been written about the defects of the machinery for the conduct of British foreign policy in the eighteenth century. In particular, using their characteristic hindsight, historians have condemned the division of responsibility between two or occasionally three secretaries of state. For nearly the whole of the eighteenth century there were two secretaries who shared on a geographical basis executive control of British foreign policy. The secretary of state for the northern department dealt with the affairs of the Empire, the United Provinces, Scandinavia, Poland, and Russia. His colleague in the southern province corresponded with British diplomatists resident in France, the Iberian peninsula, Switzerland, the Italian states, and Turkey. British diplomacy was as yet confined for all practical purposes to Europe, with an extension to the Barbary states on the African coast of the Mediterranean and the Atlantic. The Barbary states fell naturally into the southern province.

Whereas in the seventeenth century the secretary for the southern department was regarded as the senior of the two, after the accession of the house of Hanover and the rise to Great-Power status of Russia and Prussia, superiority passed to the northern secretaryship. In practice in the early years of the century, so long as the king was able to retain effective control in his own hands, the division was not very important. Both Stanhope and Townshend were well aware that when they gave detailed instructions to a British minister abroad or conducted negotiations with a foreign minister in London that they must stick closely to the brief which they had received from the king. Occasionally their correspondence reveals examples of instructions given by one of the secretaries to a diplomatist at a foreign court which had to be hurriedly countermanded when the king took a different line from that anticipated by the secretary of state. Similarly when the secretary of state wrote that the king had disapproved some action taken by a British diplomatist at a foreign court this was almost certainly literally true in the opening years of the reign.

But by the middle years of the century, although the formula had remained unaltered, its meaning had changed. More often than not it now meant disapproval by the Cabinet with the concurrence of the king. Carmarthen finally threw the old formula overboard during the Ochakov crisis.[1] Lord Auckland, British ambassador at The Hague, had been deliberately giving the pensionary wrong impressions of British foreign policy and seeking thereby to thwart his superior. Leeds then ordered him brusquely to change his attitude at once. 'My own opinion,' Leeds wrote, 'however insignificant in itself, happens to be that of the Cabinet'; and he did not even mention the attitude of the king.

As effective royal direction of British foreign policy diminished, the drawbacks of division of ministerial responsibility between two secretaries of state became more obvious and more serious. It was bad enough when the secretaries were personally incompatible and each was intent on increasing his personal influence over foreign affairs at the expense of the other. This normally led them to become the champions in Closet and Cabinet of alternative policies,

---

[1] See below, chapter 8, pp. 223–31.

as when, at the end of the Austrian Succession war, Newcastle advocated subsidy treaties and active intervention in continental politics, whereas Bedford became the recognized leader in the government of the policy of leaving the Continent to stew in its own juice and concentrating British resources in exclusive pursuit of colonial and maritime expansion.

In the 1760's the secretaries of state could nearly all be classified as advocates of alliance with either Prussia or Austria, and when a Prussophil and Austrophil were yoked together conflict was inevitable. Professor Michael Roberts has recently shown that in the early 'seventies, during the crisis over Gustavus III's *coup d'état* in Sweden, Rochford intrigued for an *entente* with France while his brother-secretary Suffolk 'was prepared to face France alone and scramble along in Europe as best he might'.[1]

Occasionally throughout the eighteenth century, when conflicts between the two secretaries were acute, each secretary tried to secure the appointment of a nominee of his own to a court where the British government was already represented by a supporter of the other secretary. Such appointments were however rare, especially if compared with the numerous occasions when France was represented not merely by two but sometimes even three accredited representatives, each pursuing a line of policy independently of his colleagues. A main cause of this was the pursuit of Louis XV of a private system of foreign policy with objects sometimes diametrically opposed to the foreign policy recommended by his ministers and officially approved by the King. None of the Hanoverian kings made a serious attempt to by-pass the secretaries of state and send instructions directly to British diplomatic agents abroad, although the secretaries occasionally suspected that their subordinates had sometimes been privately briefed by the king at a personal audience.

It was George III, who had had some experience of the bad effects of conflicts between the secretaries of state, who took the initiative in arranging in 1782 for the separation of home from foreign affairs and established the Foreign Office. Although the adoption for political administration of Adam Smith's principle of the division of labour was certainly the most important change in the machinery for the conduct of British foreign policy during the

[1] 'Great Britain and the Swedish Revolution 1772–73' in *The Historical Journal* VII. 1 (1964), 45–46.

eighteenth century, its immediate effects can easily be exaggerated. Charles James Fox, who became the first secretary of state for foreign affairs, no longer had a rival foreign minister sitting in the same Cabinet, but he was still by no means the final authority either in the formulation of foreign policy or even in the day-to-day conduct of affairs. After 1782 the foreign secretary, under the supervision of the king and his prime minister, conducted the foreign policy of Great Britain. In the last resort appeals could still be made to the Cabinet. The relations between Pitt and his foreign minister, Carmarthen, in the 'eighties probably show the high-water-mark of direct control of foreign policy by a prime minister.

It was natural that the leading minister of the Crown, whether or not he was styled 'premier' by his colleagues, should insist upon making his voice heard and his influence felt in decisions upon foreign as well as on domestic policy. Indeed when quarrels between the two secretaries became acute he was almost compelled to act as arbiter between them. Thus it was Pelham who decided the conflict between Newcastle and Bedford, though the actual decision to dismiss Bedford seems to have been the king's.

The first lord of the Treasury, whether recognized as prime minister or not, had other means of influencing foreign policy. The making of appointments to posts in the foreign service came under the general heading of patronage and hence the first lord had an unquestioned right to be consulted. Indeed on some occasions the head of the Treasury forced his own nominee upon a reluctant secretary of state. Once appointed, diplomatists abroad almost invariably kept in touch with the Treasury lords not only with an eye to favours to come but also in the hope of securing reasonably prompt and generous payment of the various allowances to which they were, or at least considered themselves to be, entitled. In war-time especially, Treasury control of the purse gave the first lord an even closer direction over war aims, alliances with foreign powers, subsidy treaties &c. While conflict between the secretaries, personal and political, was endemic in the eighteenth century, it could always be ended for the time being by a decision of the king or his chief minister. Since most eighteenth-century secretaries of state were ambitious politicians, and very few were willing to be merely clerks directed by their brother-secretary, the release of tension was not likely to last long.

Another defect of the machinery for conducting British foreign policy which however has attracted little attention is the fact that the two secretaries, even working in harmony, were distracted by a multiplicity of other duties having no necessary connexion with foreign affairs. Home affairs, the army and navy, Scotland and Ireland and the colonies took up much of their time. Nor did they have exclusive control of the whole field of foreign affairs. The Board of Trade enjoyed the right or duty of being consulted about commercial treaties and negotiations, the appointment and instructions to be given to consuls &c. And the joint postmaster generals controlled the operation of the secret office which intercepted the letters of the foreign ministers at London and provided the secretaries of state with data upon which a system of foreign policy could be securely based. Even after the creation of the Foreign Office the Barbary consuls continued to be supervised by the newly established Home Office until the middle of the nineteenth century.

Finally it should be emphasized that the weaknesses of British machinery for conducting foreign policy were not in any way peculiar to Britain, but were shared by the most important and the most advanced continental states. Even in France, which had gone further than most states towards creating specialized ministries, and which was certainly regarded by contemporaries as a model to be copied for diplomatic techniques, the secretaries of state for foreign affairs neither controlled every aspect of foreign policy nor were responsible solely for foreign business. For example, down to the Revolution French consuls were under the direction of the ministry of Marine and the successive secretaries of state for foreign affairs were each responsible for the affairs of a group of French provinces.

The key position of the secretaries of state in British diplomacy depended upon the recognition by the beginning of the eighteenth century that they were the only official channel of communication between the British government and its diplomatic and consular agents abroad. Most British diplomatists contented themselves with carrying out to the best of their ability the instructions they received from time to time from the secretary of state and sending back home such information as they could collect about the court at which they resided. Few showed much initiative and fewer still seriously attempted to exert influence on the general direction of British foreign policy.

Only less vital was the intermediary position of the secretaries of state between the British government and the foreign ministers accredited to it. Normally the members of the diplomatic corps at London transacted the business entrusted to them by their own courts at personal interviews with the appropriate secretary of state or one of his subordinates. In the absence or incapacity of one secretary there was nothing to prevent the other discharging his colleague's duties either by corresponding with British ministers abroad or by conducting current business with the foreign ministers in London. This practice was based on the old legal theory that there was only one office of secretary of state, though its functions could be divided amongst two or more holders. It proved as a rule an administrative convenience, though there were occasions when it further embittered disputes between the two secretaries concerned with foreign affairs.

The reader who is accustomed to the present-day conduct of British foreign policy may be surprised that no mention has hitherto been made of the place of Parliament. This can be justified because in constitutional theory neither house of Parliament in the eighteenth century had any share either in formulating or in executing foreign policy. It was agreed that one of its most important aspects, the making of all treaties with foreign powers, lay entirely within the prerogative of the Crown. Equally the declaration of war was a royal prerogative. Even if the Crown had consulted Parliament before going to war, it remained within the legal rights of the Crown to bring the war to an end by signing a peace treaty without consultation with Parliament.

But already before 1714 there was a wide gulf between legal theory and actual practice. Seventeenth-century Parliaments repeatedly asserted their right to discuss foreign policy and in particular to criticize *ex post facto* the actual conduct of foreign affairs by the king's ministers. This was already being claimed in the reign of James I and after the Restoration the house of Commons, greatly helped by the increasing effectiveness of its control of the purse, did not hesitate to make known its views on the policy to be pursued in future as well as to censure ministers for doing what they had already done. Its intervention was most effective when England was actually at war or about to enter a war, since, without the supplies needed for the conduct of the war, the Crown could only escape imminent bankruptcy by either remaining at peace or making an immediate peace on any terms which the enemy would grant.

Under these conditions the exclusive royal prerogative of making war and concluding peace became a figment of the imagination of constitutional lawyers. As early as the third Dutch war Charles II had to yield to the dictates of the house of Commons. William III, who had not hesitated to arrange Partition treaties without even the pretence of consultation with Parliament, knew that only with the prior approval of the house of Commons could he hope to wage war with France. And if the Crown had to consult Parliament before engaging in war, and to secure the concurrence—indeed the active support—of the house of Commons in the conduct of military operations and diplomatic negotiations designed to attain war aims, it was impossible to prevent members of both houses of Parliament from criticizing these war aims and seeking to impress upon the government their own ideas of what objects should be secured and of the priorities between them. The extension of war aims during the war of the Spanish Succession, culminating in the famous resolution 'no peace without Spain', was due more to parliamentary feeling, backed by the course of events, than to a voluntary change in royal and ministerial policy.

Once the Crown had tacitly accepted advice on peace-making from members of Parliament and in fact tried to base its conduct of war on such resolutions, it could hardly deny to Parliament a voice in the actual making of peace. No one suggested that the Crown should share its executive functions with Parliament; but, once peace had been made by the agents of the Crown and had been formally ratified and approved by the king-in-Council, the practice began of submitting important peace treaties to both houses of Parliament. Whereas William III in 1697 merely intimated that he had made peace with France at Ryswick without communicating the actual terms to Parliament, Anne's ministers submitted the text of the treaties of Utrecht to both houses.

It may at first sight seem surprising that Harley and St. John, the leaders of a party traditionally believed to be upholders of prerogative, should have deliberately reversed the peace-making precedents of 1697 and earlier years. Their reasons for so doing were not based on constitutional theorizing but were entirely pragmatical. The conclusion of peace had come to be the main controversial issue between the Tory government and the Whig

Opposition led by Stanhope. French suspicions that the Tory ministers could not carry the houses with them in a Francophil policy must be set at rest by a vote. And Harley and St. John believed that once the treaties had been formally approved by both houses, Whig threats to impeach the responsible ministers would lose much of their force. Ministers whose efforts to bring peace to a war-weary country had been approved by Parliament could hardly be impeached for high treason.

The precedent of 1713 was not entirely comprehensive or conclusive. Pelham, supported by the authority of Lord Chancellor Hardwicke, argued in 1748 that preliminary treaties of peace should not be submitted to Parliament on the ground that they were liable to alteration. The royal prerogative of peace-making had not been exercised until the Crown had agreed with the heads of foreign states concerned on a definitive treaty. He added for good measure the practical argument that debate on a preliminary treaty might well encourage foreign powers to press for changes in the agreement and in extreme cases to reopen the war. He was careful not to point out that by the time a definitive treaty had been signed and ratified there was not much a dissatisfied Parliament could do about it, except possibly to compel the king to dismiss the minister responsible for it.

Naturally the Opposition were not convinced by Pelham's arguments and a succession of speakers contrasted his conduct of the Aix-la-Chapelle negotiations in 1746–8 with the behaviour of his Tory predecessors at the end of the Spanish Succession war. Harley and St. John had taken, or at least pretended to take, Parliament into partnership with them in negotiating peace, whereas Pelham had excluded Parliament from knowledge of the negotiations and reduced to a minimum its participation in the final treaty of peace.

In practice, ministers during the eighteenth century had little difficulty in securing approval for successive peace treaties. Not until 1783 were Shelburne's preliminaries with the American colonies rejected by the house of Commons. About this time, too, the lawyers introduced a further refinement. It came to be accepted that although the Crown could by prerogative cede in a peace treaty any territories conquered during the war, its prerogative did not permit it to make cessions to foreign powers of what had been British territory at the beginning of the war. Any such cessions were legally valid only if expressly approved by Parliament. Thus a further restriction was introduced on the peace-making prerogatives of the Crown.

Treaties of peace, although the most important, were not the only ones which in practice required to be approved by Parliament. Any treaty containing clauses which required new legislation or the repeal of an existing law to give legal effect to them obviously must be submitted. Commercial treaties which required alterations in customs or excise duties were an important type of such treaties. So too were the numerous treaties of subsidy concluded with foreign, and especially German, states during the eighteenth century. Except on the rare occasions when the king could afford to pay a tiny subsidy from the civil list, a vote of the house of Commons was required. This afforded members an opportunity not merely to discuss whether the subsidy should be voted but to canvass the whole record of the government and expound their own views on foreign policy.

Perhaps more important in the long run than the actual communication of certain kinds of treaty to Parliament was the growth of the practice of submitting selected and edited extracts from the official correspondence between the secretaries of state and British diplomatic agents abroad or foreign ministers in London. Sometimes this was done on the initiative of the government in the hope of convincing the houses that the resulting treaty was the best that could be obtained or that war was the only way of securing vital British interests. More often the Opposition took the initiative and demanded the production of diplomatic correspondence to enable them to assess the motives and effectiveness of the government's foreign policy.

Such a demand soon came to be regarded as a routine step in an attack upon the government, and as such ministers usually rejected it. If they yielded or if the independent country gentlemen had doubts and supported the Opposition a full-dress debate on foreign policy followed almost automatically. At first the Opposition was modest in requesting access to diplomatic correspondence; but before the middle of the eighteenth century it was asking for and sometimes obtaining the production of long series of dispatches and instructions relative to British relations with several foreign states. This added substantially to the burdens of the clerks in the offices of the secretaries of state and sometimes made demands upon the secretaries of state themselves, who had to edit the correspondence selected by their subordinates for submission to the houses of Parliament.

It was partly to avoid the risk of secret intelligence and confidential assessments of the situation being made public through the demands of the house of Commons that something like a regular practice developed by which such information and assessments were not included in the official correspondence, but were reserved for private letters between the diplomatist and the secretary of state. The most the Opposition could hope to get was the 'office letters'. Walpole in 1727 argued that royal letters between sovereigns could not be produced 'without indecency to the Crown'[1] in spite of the fact that such letters were usually as much the responsibility of ministers as was the drafting of the king's speech at the opening of a parliamentary session.

[1] *Parliamentary Diary of Sir Edward Knatchbull*, p. 62.

CHAPTER 3

Great Britain and France

THE basic problem of British foreign policy in the eighteenth century was the attitude which should be adopted towards France. It is customary to speak of the years between 1689 and 1815 as the period of the second Hundred Years war between Britain and France and to add up the number of years when Britain and France were actually at war or at least engaged in supporting by auxiliary and subsidiary troops armed opposition to the other. Since no eighteenth-century treaty succeeded in removing the fundamental causes of conflict between Britain and France the short periods of peace between actual wars are best described as truces. And the only peace treaty with France which lasted much longer than a decade was the treaty of Utrecht, which was unique in another respect, since it alone was followed by a genuine and determined effort by both parties to solve outstanding problems and by diplomatic co-operation to impose their will upon the rest of Europe.

That the pursuit of such a policy was practicable in the early eighteenth century is probably the most fundamental reason for Franco-British hostility for the rest of the century. It certainly shows the marked development of British prestige and influence upon the Continent after the Revolution of 1688. A contemporary yardstick, often employed to test claims to what would now be called Great-Power status, required that such a power should have the material and moral resources to wage a major war without being dependent on other powers. In the opinion of many contemporaries only Britain and France could do this with any prospect of success.

Austria after 1720 was an ineffective power. Eugene's victories against both France and the Turks and the territorial gains made by Charles VI at the beginning of his reign had led contemporaries to over-rate her. Some of them even anticipated a return to the great days of Charles V. They neglected to observe that it had required massive financial support from the Maritime Powers to keep Austrian armies in the field during the war of the Spanish

Succession. When that support was withdrawn the Emperor had had reluctantly to make peace with France on what he regarded as outrageous terms. Not until he had secured a promise of substantial subsidies from Spain was he able to resume the struggle. When the Austro-Spanish alliance collapsed and the Maritime Powers refused to support Charles VI against the Bourbons in the Polish Succession war, Austria became in the late 'thirties a satellite of France.

Spain, too, in spite of some signs of economic and maritime revival under the Bourbons, was no more capable than Austria of waging a major war from her own resources. Alberoni, and still more Ripperda, realized that the over-ambitious foreign policy to which they were committed could only be realized with the active support of at least one Great Power. Hence their successive approaches to France, Britain, the Baltic powers, and finally Austria. Later in the century Spain linked herself to France by successive Family Compacts. These agreements may have helped to preserve the Spanish territories in Europe and America, but they indicate clearly that Spain no longer felt able to pursue a completely independent line in foreign policy.

The international position of the United Provinces after the treaty of Utrecht was quite different from that of Austria and Spain. William III had probably overstrained the resources of the Dutch republic, great and resilient as they were in the late seventeenth century. Heinsius continued his master's policy but with increasing difficulties during the Spanish Succession war and had to make peace at Utrecht on terms much less favourable than had seemed to be in his grasp earlier in the war. Disillusionment over the results of Orange foreign policy revivified the burgomaster or 'patriot' party with its headquarters in Amsterdam. They rejected the Orange conception of France as the bogeyman of Europe and either saw no need for a land-barrier in the Netherlands against France or believed that this had been sufficiently secured by the Utrecht settlement.

There is little evidence of Dutch economic decline in the early eighteenth century; but the rate of growth had certainly slowed down. Rivals, particularly Britain and France, were now forging ahead and the general set-up of European commerce and the development of large-scale industries no longer favoured the United Provinces. Britain and France, with their much greater natural resources, were adopting techniques pioneered by the Dutch in the seventeenth century, and the manifold pressures of war upon their economies accelerated economic developments. The Dutch, on the other hand, declined to take any part in these wars and hoped to make commercial profit out of a policy of wavering neutrality. The sudden disappearance after the Utrecht settlement of the United Provinces as a Great Power must be attributed not to failure of economic strength but to paralysis of the will.

If Austria, Spain, and the United Provinces, in spite of their ancient traditions and present pretensions, could no longer be placed in the first rank of Great Powers by a clear-sighted political realist, this is even more clearly the case of Sweden under Charles XII. The battle of Poltava had finally overthrown Swedish predominance in the Baltic: after years of exile and imprisonment the young king returned to the scenes of his early triumphs older but no wiser. He imposed intolerable sufferings on his people without procuring any advantages either for them or for himself. For two generations after his death the dominant feeling in Sweden, as in Holland, was to avoid any policy of adventures which might bring involvement in a major war.

In the years immediately after 1713 the nearest approach to a really independent Great Power, apart from Britain and France, was to be found in Russia under Peter the Great; but this was more important as a portent for the future than it was for its immediate effect upon European diplomacy. For one thing the politicians of western Europe hardly regarded Russia as being an integral part of their political system; and they had this measure of justification that it had been feasible to have two major wars, one between the Baltic powers, the other in south-west Europe, running concurrently for a decade, each with only minimal influence on the course of the other. Contemporaries were certainly impressed by Peter the Great's crushing military defeat of Charles XII and his equally crushing diplomatic defeat of his *quondam* allies at Nystad. Yet his personal attempts to secure admission to the inner circle of Great Powers had been rebuffed, though for different reasons, both by France and Britain. Indeed a divergent attitude to Russia and her Prussian satellite was one of the earliest symptoms of diplomatic *malaise* in the attempted collaboration between Britain and France after 1713.

It is unnecessary to discuss at this stage in the argument the position of any of the minor powers. A brief Cook's tour of political Europe has shown that Britain and France alone stood forth as first-class Great Powers. Since Britain had achieved Great-Power status mainly by her contribution to the defeat of Louis XIV the two outstanding powers of Europe were already rivals. The normal attempts made by minor powers to secure changes in the Utrecht settlement favourable to their interests by appealing either to France or to Britain for support contributed to, but certainly was not the prime cause of, tension between the would-be partners.

Had the basic political rivalry been between Britain and, say, Russia it would have been blunted by distance and more easily counteracted by other considerations, political as well as economic and ecclesiastical. The physical difficulties of contact between Britain and Russia in peace-time were bad enough; but under eighteenth-century conditions war between them was virtually impossible. It could be declared, but not carried on effectively and with any likelihood of a decisive result being attained by either side. But France was Britain's closest neighbour and propinquity had produced a dominant tradition of hostility dating from the Middle Ages and little modified by more recent recollections of short-lived and usually ineffective attempts to co-operate against Spain or the Dutch. As the Abbé le Blanc wrote, 'the bulk of the English nation bear an inveterate hatred of the French, which they do not always take the pains to conceal from us'.[1] No historian has tried to assess the influence of this surviving tradition upon Franco-British relations: it seems to have been assumed that with so many contemporary reasons for conflict it was otiose to delve into the past for an explanation.

In the later seventeenth and early eighteenth centuries Francophobia was rooted psychologically in fear. The Abbé le Blanc summed up admirably the prevailing English attitude.

By their continual uneasiness, they seem to believe that we are in regard to them what the Persians were to the Athenians; that the king of France is the great King: hence this invincible aversion to the people who obey him, whom they suppose that they alone prevent from giving laws to the rest of Europe. . . . They fear and yet despise us: we are the

[1] *Letters on the English and French Nations* (London, 1747), p. 25. I am indebted to Dr. Matthew Anderson for calling my attention to this work.

nation that they pay the greatest civilities to, and yet love the least: they condemn, and yet imitate us: they adopt our manners by taste, and blame them through policy.[1]

Not until the wars of the mid-century did national ambition and economic imperialism become dominant in England. As long as France remained a naval power of the first class, British governments rushed or blundered into war with her only to discover that they lacked adequate means of self-defence. Again and again the protection of Britain against a French threat of invasion had to take priority over offensive strategy which might have ended the war with promptitude and in triumph. In successive wars men-of-war which might have been used to acquire coveted sugar islands in the West Indies had to be employed on convoy duty to protect British trade from French privateers. Looking back, it is astonishing that successive French invasion plans produced so little result. Only in Scotland and Ireland, where special factors were at work, was anything tangible achieved and this mainly by native resources.

Even the elder Pitt, in developing the war strategy of a powerful 'Western squadron', had to compromise, to some extent, between home defence and overseas conquests. At the same time his reorganization of the English militia was a valuable pioneering experiment which was to be developed and extended by his successors. It strengthened morale and reduced the risk of widespread and catastrophic panic: perhaps fortunately its material efficacy against a foreign invader was never put to the test. Yet even in Pitt's time it was universally agreed that Britain was not strong enough to resist France—let alone a combination of the Bourbon courts—without the help of foreign powers.

This idea, which survived the conditions which gave rise to it, was largely based on the fashionable calculations of political arithmetic. The population of France was usually reckoned to be at least three times larger than that of England. The richness of her soil, the development of her agriculture, the advanced state of her industries, the pre-eminence she had gained in the arts and sciences, all contributed to her greatness. And her system of government, as reorganized by Louis XIV, brought all these resources, material and moral, under the immediate direction of an absolute monarch, who had used them to build up an army

[1] *Letters on the English and French Nations* (London, 1747), p. 27.

capable of defeating any other army in Europe and of resisting successfully any combination of powers which could be organized to oppose it.

At the same time he had spared from his main objective sufficient resources to make France a first-class naval power and a competitor on equal terms with the Dutch and the English for commercial and colonial ascendancy over the known world. It is true that a European coalition of hitherto unknown size and complexity had succeeded in reducing somewhat the stature of Louis XIV during the Spanish Succession war; but events soon showed that the bases of French power remained unimpaired. And this formidable state, greatly superior to England, lay just across the Straits of Dover.

Louis XIV had given France another advantage which his successors exploited for the rest of the eighteenth century. His lavish building, his patronage of the arts and sciences, his careful cultivation of the *mystique* of monarchy, and suppression of potential or actual threats to royal absolutism, all made him a model to be admired, and, as far as their lesser resources allowed, followed, by European sovereigns. French became the language of all civilized Europeans as well as of diplomacy. Paris became the capital of Europe in a sense in which Valladolid, Madrid, or even Rome, have never been. And the cultural ascendancy of France was at its greatest in Germany, the country to which Britain must mainly look for support if she were to have any chance of defeating France in diplomacy and war.

Moreover Louis XIV had been ready to strengthen his influence beyond the borders of France by well-directed money grants to influential sovereigns and statesmen. Subsidy treaties and bribes were already firmly established adjuncts of French foreign policy in time of peace almost as much as in war, whereas Englishmen groaned over the cost of subsidizing their allies in war and refused absolutely to make such payments between wars. In 1706 France paid subsidies to Bavaria, Cologne, Hungary, and Sweden, amounting in all to over 3,400,000 livres. Later in the eighteenth century much larger sums were paid.

It has been calculated that Austria alone received between 1757 and 1769 nearly 75 million livres. Sweden drew over 30 million in French subsidies between 1750 and 1762 and a further 16 million between 1762 and 1773. Insignificant German princes, Württemberg, Zweibrücken, and the ecclesiastical elector of Cologne each received millions of livres from the French government,[1] though they did virtually nothing in exchange for these subsidies. Successive French sovereigns dipped lavishly into the apparently bottomless purse of an absolute ruler of a wealthy and prosperous state. The Hanoverian kings of England depended on grudging supplies doled out by Parliament in time of war and had to incur debts on their already over-burdened civil list if they wished to cultivate the favour of an influential minister at a key court.

So far as subsidies and bribes could determine foreign policy all the advantages rested with France, which right down to the French Revolution continued to enjoy the reputation of being a good paymaster, especially in the German and Scandinavian courts. It has also been pointed out that Britain always required action from a court she subsidized, whereas France often paid subsidies to sovereigns who had merely to remain passive and to follow the line of policy which they would probably have adopted in any case. It is not surprising when all these considerations are taken into account that eighteenth-century Englishmen were often despondent about their chances of competing successfully with France in foreign courts.

The fact that British governments, as Castlereagh informed the eastern European despots of the Holy Alliance, were based ultimately on the Revolution of 1688 was a source of weakness rather than of strength in the eighteenth century to the conduct of British foreign policy. Englishmen were often regarded on the Continent as king-killers and republicans; and, especially in the early years of George I's reign, the belief that his government was unstable was widespread in Europe and vitally affected the attitude towards England of some powerful continental states. This attitude persisted to a less extent as long as Jacobitism remained an active political force.

Since few continental sovereigns grasped the political realities of English politics at any time in the eighteenth century, they naturally exaggerated the strength of Jacobitism. As late as the 1750's Frederick the Great sought to alarm and intimidate the timorous duke of Newcastle by posing as the friend of the Jacobites. But what was mere play-acting in the 'fifties was in deadly earnest in the early years of George I's reign, when France, Spain,

---

[1] Details in F. Weiss, *Histoire des fonds secrets sous l'ancien régime* (Paris, 1940), pp. 151–62. I am indebted to Dr. Matthew Anderson for calling my attention to this book.

Russia, and Sweden, successively or in concert, countenanced the Jacobites and engaged in serious negotiations with their chiefs, while one or two of the Italian states actually broke off diplomatic relations with the Hanoverian king.

The danger seemed so great to contemporaries that the most enterprising Whig leader of the day, Stanhope, carried through a Diplomatic Revolution to counter it, with the unfortunate result that for some years after 1717 Englishmen were not only divided into Jacobites and Hanoverians but the latter were also divided against themselves—some supporting Stanhope's reversal of traditional Whig foreign policy,[1] others led by Townshend and Walpole trying to cling for a time to the ancient ways. Stanhope triumphed in the end, not so much by his own ability and resource, great though they were, but because France happened to be almost as divided as England between adherents of Louis XIV's system on the one hand and supporters of the Regent, Philip of Orleans, on the other.

Englishmen had good reason to suspect and fear political developments within France which made her king the prototype of absolute monarchy. The greater the concentration of power within France and the extension of French culture and prestige over Europe the more dangerous did France become to a weaker and, above all, divided neighbour. Against the fashionable concepts of absolutism, Englishmen tried to impress upon continental thinkers an image of Britain as the land of liberty where under a constitutional king, guided and advised by Parliament, the laws were enforced by an independent judiciary.

Voltaire and Montesquieu were only the best known of a whole school of writers who subscribed to this view and did their best to popularize it on the Continent. But in an age of enlightened, and sometimes not so enlightened, despotism the pragmatic directors of continental foreign policies showed no interest in such speculations. Indeed the source of such theories in writers who were essentially anti-Establishment was sufficient to condemn them in the eyes of most continental autocrats. Frederick the Great, for example, was just as hostile to 'mixed government' on the British model as Bismarck, a century later, was to any attempt to modify the administration of Prussia in the direction of a Gladstonian liberal system of party government.

[1] As defined below, pp. 44 ff.

Nor, to be quite honest, is there much evidence that the British secretaries of state made any serious attempt to win friends on the Continent and influence foreign powers by presenting the image of Britain which was to become current in the subsequent age of enlightenment and make a real impact upon Europe in the nineteenth century. Even in the Palmerstonian era support of constitutional states never became an end in itself—it was at most a concurrent influence upon British policy along with other and more decisive practical considerations. The nearest that secretaries of state came to putting forward such views in the eighteenth century was when they tried to win allies against France by arguing that the political supremacy of France was a danger to the 'liberties of Europe'; and in this phrase they were certainly thinking not of the internal organization of the component states, but of the risk of a French domination of Europe on the model of Louis XIV's ascendancy. Nor did they foresee that Napoleon Bonaparte, the next French dictator of Europe, would, partly by attraction and partly by repulsion, exert such a decisive influence upon the constitutional and political development of the individual states of Europe.

So far an attempt has been made to consider the relations of Britain and France from a purely political aspect; and the conclusion has been reached that at the beginning of the eighteenth century they were, as contemporaries phrased it, 'natural enemies'. Ancient tradition and present political rivalry, physical propinquity and mob psychology combined with ideological divergence to make Franco-British rivalry and hostility the most persistent and stable factor in the politics of eighteenth-century Europe. Louis XIV had become the personification of everything that eighteenth-century Englishmen hated just as Napoleon was to be a hundred years later. The very fact that Jacobitism depended on French support was sufficient to doom the cause of the Stuarts in England. Even when the balance of political forces in Europe changed fundamentally in the mid-eighteenth century the bulk of English politicians refused to alter their system of foreign policy to meet the new conditions. Some of them appreciated that the only chance of overthrowing the domination exercised since 1763 by the three eastern powers lay in co-operation between Britain and France but they believed that opinion in Britain was too hostile to France to make this a practical proposition. In any case few British politicians before the closing years of the century believed that the control of eastern Europe by Russia, Austria, and Prussia was sufficiently adverse to British interests to justify the expense and danger of intervention against them.

This purely political or, at most, politico-ideological explanation of the hostility between Britain and France is, in my opinion, the basic factor in their relationship in the early years of the century. This is not to deny the significance of other factors, above all religious and economic; but both of these reinforced and in no way ran counter to the prevailing political considerations. Hatred of popery was at least as potent a force in bringing about the Revolution of 1688 as the suspicion that James II, with the support of Louis XIV, was hell-bent on destroying English liberties. Until George I was securely established on the throne, English Tories believed that their church was still in danger. Much as they disliked the wars waged against France in the reigns of William III and Anne, in their heart of hearts most Englishmen had to admit that these wars were necessary to secure the national church as well as national independence of French domination. These fears found confirmation when the Old Pretender refused to accept the throne of his fathers on condition that he would protect the Church of England and confirm its ascendancy. His adherence to the position that it was not worth giving up the Mass to reign in London cost him so much support that a Jacobite restoration could henceforth be expected only as a result of large-scale foreign intervention.

Since France was the only power able and likely to intervene to support James III, France continued to be regarded as the political embodiment of popery even when its government was in fact upon the worst terms possible short of actual war with the Pope. Memories of the revocation of the edict of Nantes were kept alive during the Spanish Succession war by the Protestant revolt in the Cevennes and, long after it had petered out, by the survival in various parts of England and Scotland of communities of Huguenot exiles. In the middle years of the century it was still possible to whip up English opinion over the grievances of 'the poor Palatines' and other religious minorities. Substantial sums of money were raised for their relief and they were allowed to settle on advantageous terms in some British colonies. Even when in the second half of the eighteenth century France and the Papacy came to an open breach over the suppression of the Jesuit order, Englishmen continued to think of the French king as the embodiment in politics of popery.

If attention be directed from British opinion to British foreign policy it becomes much more difficult to assess, at least after 1714, the influence of religious considerations. Their influence was however in one respect increased by the accession of George I. To make himself eligible for the Polish crown Augustus II, elector of Saxony, had been converted in 1697 to Roman Catholicism. Since the early days of the Reformation his predecessors as electors of Saxony had been generally recognized as the leaders of German Protestantism. Augustus saw no incompatibility between leading German Protestantism and reigning as a Roman Catholic in Poland; but his rivals in the *corpus evangelicorum*, chiefly Brandenburg-Prussia and Hanover, seized the chance to edge Augustus out of his former position and take over jointly the defence of the interests of Protestantism in central Europe.

Especially in the early years of George I's reign, when he was on bad terms with the Emperor and on comparatively good terms with Frederick William of Prussia, the rulers of Brandenburg and Hanover combined to thwart Hapsburg proselytism and persecution. This they sometimes achieved by the threat of persecuting their Roman Catholic subjects if the Emperor persisted in attacks on German Protestantism. A more serious crisis arose in 1720 when sectarian rioting in the Polish town of Thorn was followed by the execution of some of the Protestant leaders. The kings of Great Britain and Prussia protested vigorously and a long and acrimonious dispute followed. The political significance of this incident was that it made more difficult the attempts to reconcile Britain and Austria, and in the long run the British government subordinated the defence of German and Polish Protestantism to the need to secure allies against France.

The days when religion dominated international politics, if indeed they ever existed outside of the imagination of historians of the sixteenth and seventeenth centuries, had long since gone. By 1714 there just were not enough Protestant states in Europe with the resources to form a viable league against France. Indeed the very attempt to organize one would have been foolish, since it must have strengthened the hands of the politicians at Versailles and Vienna, who wished to arrange a reconciliation between Hapsburgs and Bourbons which would give the law to Europe.

Nevertheless there were occasions in the eighteenth century when British secretaries of state expressly appealed to their common Protestantism in attempts to secure co-operation from continental states. Indeed the Protestant cause and the liberties of Europe runs like a refrain through their dispatches; but this appeal rarely produced the desired effect and, when it did, it succeeded because of more important interests than Protestantism. Prussia and Denmark did not join the league of Hanover in 1725 because they were Protestant states. Protestant Sweden did not scruple to attach herself at the beginning of the Seven Years war to the Roman Catholic coalition against Prussia and Britain.

Yet the Pope himself had advised Austria and France to proceed with great caution lest their attack upon Prussia should be misrepresented as a religious crusade; and during the Seven Years war Frederick the Great was regarded as a Protestant hero in Britain. Even as late as the 1770's some Englishmen looked with favour upon the first Partition of Poland because it weakened a reactionary and Roman Catholic state, which was still engaged in persecuting Protestants during the European enlightenment. That this was accompanied by a diplomatic defeat for France, still regarded by them as the leader of the Roman Catholic cause, was a further cause of satisfaction. Other writers declared themselves to be Russophils because Russia as a Christian power was fighting the Turks. At the very end of the century hostility to the French Revolution was partly motivated by the godlessness ascribed to it by Burke and other commentators.

At no point in the century did the cause of religion determine the foreign policies of the European states. Yet in Britain at least the influence of religious feeling can be traced in the prevailing approaches to policy, and sometimes in the reasons actually given for supporting the foreign policy adopted by the government of the day for other reasons. Naturally enough, governments sought to enlist support both at home and abroad by representing their policies as being in accord with religious prepossessions of their own subjects and of certain foreign powers. I do not know of any case after 1714 where British foreign policy ran counter to the dominant religious feeling in the country. It would be equally difficult to find a British government adopting a concrete policy on any important question primarily because that line of policy would appeal to the religious prepossessions of its subjects.

It may be suggested that the importance of religion as a factor in foreign policy diminished during the eighteenth century. The converse would certainly be true of the other factor which has still to be considered—economic interest. Just as hostility to popery buttressed and sometimes intensified the political causes of hostility between Britain and France, so did conflicts of economic interests. These remained fairly constant in character and intensity but the economic growth of both countries gave them added significance for both as the century went on.

Colonial trade had played a quite minor part in the economic conflicts of William III's reign. Many merchants believed that our trade with Old Spain in George I's reign was far more valuable and important than any profit to be gained from trade with America. The massive build-up of population and resources in North America and the developing trade of the East India Company altered the balance between Britain's continental and colonial trades and led to the organization of various 'lobbies'—nabobs, planters, &c.—which sought to exert influence upon British foreign policy in the economic interests of their members. Changing fashions in the approach to colonial trade, e.g. whether colonies should be valued as export markets for British manufactured goods or as producers of primary materials which could be used to compete with foreign powers in continental markets, further complicated the attitude of economic groups to questions of foreign policy. The classic instance of how such interplay of economic interest could complicate and influence British foreign policy is the debate during the Seven Years war over the advantages to be secured for Britain by the retention of Guadeloupe as compared with those anticipated by keeping Canada. Pitt declared in the house of Commons in 1760 that some were for keeping Canada and others for keeping Guadeloupe. 'Who', he added, 'will tell me which I shall be hanged for not keeping?'

The whole pamphlet literature of the eighteenth century—and pamphlets were the normal method of discussing issues of foreign policy likely to interest the political nation—must be read in the light of the economic advantage or sectarian prejudice of the authors, who were almost invariably spokesmen of interested groups, if they were not merely eccentric individuals. The cynic may well doubt whether anything approaching 'public' opinion on foreign policy existed in eighteenth-century Britain. The nearest approach to it was certainly the howl of execration which arose at the mere mention of France. If anything this became stronger as the century advanced.

Stanhope and Townshend, aided by widespread fears of Jacobitism, had been able to make and maintain an *entente* with France. Walpole killed Jacobitism in England and it was buried in 1745–6. As we have seen, Jacobitism had made a contribution to Franco-British hostility, but its final disappearance from the political stage did nothing to improve relations between these two powers. It did however contribute to modify the British attitude to France. The house of Hanover, the Church of England, and the union of the Parliaments of Scotland and England, were now securely established. Fear of what France might do to English liberty and the Protestant cause, though still alive in the background and liable to cause national panic at successive threats of a French invasion, ceased to dominate the British attitude to France.

Many Englishmen were still anxious to avenge upon France the insults she had inflicted and alarms she had caused; others, and especially the mercantile classes, were now chiefly influenced in their attitude to France by consideration of economic advantage. With the decline of the Dutch as a trading power and their failure to develop industries on a scale adequate for the support of their existing commerce, under eighteenth-century conditions of international trade, France was now regarded as Britain's number one economic rival.

If Stanhope and Townshend had aimed primarily at self-defence, the elder Pitt was the outspoken advocate of British imperialism. And eighteenth-century imperialism was far more nakedly economic in inspiration than that of the nineteenth and early twentieth centuries, when the philanthropist, the missionary, and the colonial administrator all did something to restrain the uninhibited economic lust of the trader. Virtually the only acceptable reason for acquiring colonial territory in the eighteenth century was that it would increase British trade and improve her competitive position against France or some other colonial power.

The strength of this force and its influence upon British foreign policy is perhaps best seen in the years between the Austrian Succession and the Seven Years war. While the British and French governments were both genuinely anxious to observe the terms of the peace of Aix-la-Chapelle, and to reach a lasting settlement on the outstanding problems which that treaty had not settled, the American colonists and their mercantile allies in Britain did everything they could to prevent a comprehensive settlement being reached by the two governments. The East Indian traders went one better—they waged a private war upon their French rivals in India. Newcastle, whose worst weakness as a foreign minister was the excessive deference he showed to what he believed to be public opinion, was driven step by step along a path which led inevitably to the renewal of war against France. For the first, but unfortunately not for the last, time in European history a timid, peace-loving statesman had been forced into wars by self-interested advocates of economic imperialism.

The economic causes of Franco-British hostility in the later eighteenth century were not confined by any means to the colonies. Their political rivalry and pre-eminence in Europe led them to wage alike in peace and in war economic conflicts with each other. As Andrew Anderson explained 'the expense of modern wars is become so excessive, that the potentates of Europe are indispensably obliged to endeavour at an increase of their revenues by all possible means, money, and not merely multitudes of men, as in olden times, being now the great measure of power'.[1] Since for those states which did not control the precious metals of the New World the most practicable method of gaining possession of additional money depended on extending their foreign commerce, international trade was not usually regarded as a mutual benefit to all states which engaged in it. The balance of trade came to be regarded primarily as an adjunct to the balance of power. Indeed the conception of international trade was still in its infancy. Theoreticians were inclined to concentrate upon trade between two countries without paying sufficient attention to the whole network of international trade of each country. It was often assumed that if two countries traded with each other, one of them would benefit and the other lose, or at least gain much less than its trading partner.

Applying these principles to the particular case of trade between Britain and France, it was generally agreed that France stood to gain by its development far more than Britain. The arguments that

[1] *An Historical and Chronological Deduction of Commerce* (London, 1764), I. xxi.

had enabled Stanhope and the Whigs to demolish the commercial treaty of Utrecht which Bolingbroke had concluded with France were still held to be valid. Indeed the partial success which tariffs designed against French imports had attained in developing luxury industries, such as silk manufacture, in England, reinforced older arguments based on the frivolous nature of French exports and the undesirability of allowing France to import wool from England, manufacture it, and then use it to undermine Britain's position in foreign markets where we were in competition with France.

It was in vain that those in a position to know pointed out that the restrictions on export of wool were defeated in practice by a flourishing trade in smuggled wool conducted from the Channel ports. Not until the younger Pitt's first administration was the decision of 1713 reversed, and a commercial treaty signed between Britain and France in 1786, to the advantage of both countries in the short time that was to elapse before the renewal of war in 1793. At the same time Pitt conducted negotiations for similar treaties with several other countries; but in no other case was he successful. Earlier in the century Britain had of course concluded commercial treaties, notably with Russia in 1734 and 1766, and with the four Barbary states on the North African coast, Morocco, Algiers, Tunis, and Tripoli. Trade with Russia was vital if the British navy was to rule the seas, and without supplies of grain and cattle from North Africa Britain could hardly maintain her garrisons in Gibraltar and Minorca.

Thanks partly to these commercial treaties with Russia, Britain had greatly strengthened her position as a trading nation in the Baltic, largely at the expense of the Dutch, whereas France had made little commercial progress in this sea. Apart from colonial produce, and luxury goods which only the nobles could afford to buy, France had little to offer in Baltic markets. On the other hand every expansion of the Russian or Prussian armies created a potential and often an actual demand for English cloth for uniforms and saltpetre for armaments.

In the Mediterranean, on the contrary, the balance of advantage during the eighteenth century was clearly with French commerce. There was a general lack of interest in this area on the part of British merchants. Colonial, above all American, trade was booming and naturally attracted the more enterprising traders. Even in time of peace Britain found it difficult to do more than maintain

her position in the Iberian peninsula and the hopes entertained in
the early years of the century of a fruitful commercial *entente* with
Savoy and some other Italian states soon faded. Only with Tuscany,
through its free port at Leghorn, was there much development of
British commerce. After the Seven Years war Franco-British
commercial rivalry reached a new peak. Though France failed to
gain as much commercial advantage as she had hoped from the
favourable political climate in Spain after the signature of the third
Family Compact in 1761, she was able to thwart British hopes of
improving her position in the overseas commerce of the Iberian
peninsula.[1]

Successive wars with France, when British naval forces had to
be withdrawn from the Mediterranean, periodically reversed such
gains as were made by British trade during the intervals of peace
and sometimes brought British trade there to a total standstill. The
French acquisition of Corsica in 1768 and the final British loss of
Minorca in 1783 weakened British control of the western Mediterranean. In the war of American Independence British fleets had
been completely withdrawn from the Mediterranean, and Britain
had only with great difficulty been able to maintain a garrison in
Gibraltar.

At the very beginning of the century the prospects of worth-
while expansion of British trade with the Levant had seemed
promising but the peak had been reached about 1720. For the
greater part of the century French merchants from Marseilles,
vigorously supported by their government, dominated the Levant
trade. Not until the attention both of France and Britain was
diverted towards Egypt was this tendency reversed. Britain's
friendly relations with Russia, by this time the arch-enemy of the
Turks, and in particular her open partiality in aiding a Russian
fleet to sail from the Baltic to the Mediterranean and attack the
Turkish coasts during the first Russo-Turk war of Catherine the
Great's reign, damaged British prospects, commercial as well as
political, at Constantinople. The Franco-Russian *rapprochement* of
the 1780's and the threatened war between Britain and Russia over
the Ochakov incident in 1791 contributed to the revival of British
commercial interests in the eastern Mediterranean.

It is unnecessary to trace the commercial rivalry between Britain
and France elsewhere in Europe. It existed throughout the

[1] Details below, chapter 10, pp. 302–3.

century, and the progress of the industrial revolution in Britain merely intensified it. The 'new, powerful, rich class', who were the successful pioneers of large-scale industries, lost no time in making their voices heard and their wishes known in the field of foreign policy. Josiah Wedgwood and the Chamber of Manufactures were portents of what was to happen in the next century not only in Britain but all over the world.

2 THE COURSE OF FRANCO-BRITISH DIPLOMACY

In the preceding section an attempt has been made to isolate and weigh against each other the factors which determined the British attitude to France in the eighteenth century. No one factor can be regarded as decisive by itself and the importance to be assigned to each varies appreciably from decade to decade. Anglo-French hostility was strong because it could be compared to a rope composed of various strands, each closely interwoven with the others. The greater the tension the more closely the strands came together and the longer the strain lasted the more difficult it became to separate the strands and, by cutting one or more of them, to snap the rope.

Yet it must not be argued that the strength of the chain of Anglo-French hostility was no greater than that of its weakest link. Had France by some historical freak of chance become a Protestant state in the eighteenth century, it seems wildly unlikely that this would have been sufficient to break the chain of hostility and restore cordiality to the relationship between Britain and France. Similarly had Louis XVI on his accession summoned the States-General and handed over the government to Anglophil followers of Voltaire and Montesquieu, this would hardly have prevented France from intervening on the colonial side in the war of American Independence.

The Paris embassy was regarded by contemporaries as the most important, though certainly not the most profitable, post in the British diplomatic service. It was held by a succession of great noblemen who would have scorned to accept any other diplomatic appointment. Since so many of them were essentially playboys, the practice grew up, in the second half of the eighteenth century, of appointing the secretary of embassy as minister plenipotentiary. This additional appointment enabled its holder to negotiate with the French government during the absence of the ambassador from the French court—and indeed sometimes when he was physically present but mentally incapable of discharging his duties with sufficient assiduity and skill to ensure success.

Most of the ambassadors were 'outsiders' with no previous diplomatic training or experience. Robert Liston, when appointed in 1783 to a minor post abroad, wrote: 'I shall never be ambassador to France, which would literally be at the top of my profession.'[1] So important was the Paris embassy that in the formation of governments in the second half of the century it was usually treated as equivalent to a Cabinet post. To have held it even for a short period gave one a claim to be considered for one of the secretary-ships of state at a suitable vacancy. It was indeed the nerve-centre of British diplomacy and ought therefore to have been filled by a diplomatist of ripe experience and proved skill.

It is difficult to assess the actual damage done to Franco-British relations by the incompetence and frivolity of many of the ambassadors. Instead of taking Chesterfield's advice and forming discreet liaisons with married women of good family who had a secure position at court and some means of access to political secrets, they ran up gambling debts and squandered their money on opera singers and ballet dancers. The duke of Dorset caused public scandal when he allowed the Baccelli to dance at the opera wearing his garter ribbon. He and his like then added insult to injury by trying to include payments to these ladies on his expense account or at least by arguing that the cost of living at Paris exceeded the emoluments of the post.

All ambassadors to France were not of course playboys. Stair fulfilled with distinction the duty of presenting a firm front to Louis XIV in his last days and then supervising the execution by Orleans of his bargain with George I. Though accused of rashness and ostentation, he proved a worthy representative of his master, whose dignity and interests he secured at the expense of some personal unpopularity at the French court. He and Waldegrave, one of his successors under George II, specialized in organizing an efficient intelligence service from the embassy. Horatio Walpole was perhaps the outstanding man of business in the roll of eighteenth-century British ambassadors to France, but his position was exceptional, since he was not only ambassador but

---

[1] Dalzel, *History of the University of Edinburgh* I. 41.

also chief adviser on foreign policy to his brother, the leading minister of the Crown.

On the whole there is no reason to suppose that more skilful and assiduous British diplomacy at Versailles could have established friendship between Britain and France in the eighteenth century. Nothing but a fundamental change of attitude both in London and Paris could have altered the pattern which persisted for more than a century. Wars, which diplomatists seemed unable to avert, broke out between Britain and France. Ambassadors patched up peace and made more or less determined efforts to settle the outstanding questions. Gradually hopes of reaching agreement were relinquished and the British ambassadors concentrated on convincing the French government that they were negotiating from strength. When the French ministers remained unconvinced, hopes of a permanent settlement faded. Old points of friction became acute and new ones would often be added, while the British diplomatists at Paris papered over the cracks. Before long diplomatic relations would be broken off and Britain and France would find themselves again at war.

The main issue in William III's war against France was the maintenance of the Protestant succession and the most important clause, from the English point of view, in the treaty of Ryswick was Louis XIV's recognition of William III as king of England. It was not the breakdown of William III's negotiations with Louis XIV for the partition of the Spanish empire, and Louis XIV's decision to accept the will of Charles II, which brought about the war of the Spanish Succession. Both England and the United Provinces were willing to recognize a Bourbon prince, so long as he was not also king of France, as ruler of Spain rather than involve themselves in a war with France to avert his accession. What forced them into the war of the Spanish Succession was Louis XIV's recognition of James, the Old Pretender, as king of England on the death of his father James II. This annulled his reluctant recognition of William III by the treaty of Ryswick and placed the Church of England as well as the Protestant succession and national independence in dire jeopardy. England formed the Grand Alliance and went to war in 1702, not to place the Archduke Charles on the throne of Spain, but to defend the succession to the Crown of England as laid down in the Act of Settlement of 1701.

The battles won by Marlborough at Blenheim and subsequently

in the Netherlands raised the military reputation of England to a
height it was not to reach again until Waterloo. These victories had
been won by close co-operation with large bodies of Dutch troops,
mostly supplied by arrangements with mercenary princes, and with
armies raised by the Emperor and commanded by Eugene of
Savoy. These successful campaigns against France in the Spanish
Succession war did not merely avert the menace of Louis XIV:
they provided the most practical argument for the restoration in
the 1730's of the old system of British foreign policy.

French diplomatists were quick to seize the chance to argue that
the defeat of France meant that she was no longer a danger to the
balance of power. On the contrary, British aggressiveness on the
Continent, her abuse of her near-monopoly of sea-power, her
seizure of French colonies and establishment of Mediterranean
naval bases, the unpredictability and unreliability of her policy
were all represented as proofs of British ambition which, taken
together, made Britain a real danger to the peace of Europe. The
moment peace had been made with Austria, Louis XIV despatched
an ambassador to the court of Vienna to propose a reconciliation
between the Bourbons and the Hapsburgs, which would have
anticipated the Diplomatic Revolution of 1756. Louis XIV, for all
his pride and obstinacy, was more capable than some of his
successors of learning from experience: convinced that France
could not defeat what was the nearest approach yet known to a
European coalition, he set about detaching Austria from her allies.
At the same time he took up, more seriously than had proved
possible in the course of a great European war, the use of the
Jacobites to threaten George I's throne.

The peaceful succession of George I had been a great blow to
him, especially when it was followed by the triumph of the Whigs,
who had inflicted upon France her worst defeats since the Hundred
Years war. By extending British war aims at a time when the
country was already weary of a continental war, and refusing to
make peace on terms which would have adequately secured the
interests which had forced Britain to take up arms in 1702, the
Whigs had brought about their own fall in 1710. The Tories, who
were in power during the last four years of Anne's reign, having
secured what they regarded as the essential interests of England by
a secret bargain with France, deserted their allies and withdrew
from the war by the treaty of Utrecht.

Apart from the manner of its negotiation, which was clearly contrary to British undertakings by the Grand Alliance, the chief criticism of this treaty is that the Tories had placed themselves in a position which compelled them to accept French promises, some of which soon proved illusory. If Dunkirk, that nest of pirates, was ultimately destroyed, the building of the new port at Mardyke threatened to defeat the objectives both of the Tory ministry which had made the treaty and of their Whig successors who had to enforce its terms upon a reluctant France. Similarly promises intended to disarm the Jacobites sat so lightly on Louis XIV that he was soon giving active help to them. The gains anticipated from the *asiento* and the annual ship by which England was to trade directly with Spanish America were never to be realized. Worst of all the Tories had accepted a paper renunciation by Philip V of his claims to the French succession, which was doubtless invalid in Bourbon house-law and soon proved almost worthless in practice.

The treaty of Utrecht did however give Britain more substantial gains, notably the exclusion of France from the Netherlands, the consolidation of British naval supremacy in the western Mediterranean with bases at Port Mahon and Gibraltar, and the prospect of increasing trade with her colonial acquisitions in North America and the West Indies. Other commercial clauses were intended to promote direct trade between Britain and France to their mutual advantage: they anticipated in essentials the famous Eden commercial treaty of 1786, but the Whigs proved strong enough to prevent their ratification. For the next seventy years France and Britain, instead of benefiting from mutual trade, fought with each other an economic war, without any of the intermissions afforded by periods of truce in their political struggles.

Apologists for the treaty of Utrecht are therefore entitled to claim that it was English repudiation of what was intended to form the economic basis of a political *entente*, if not an actual defensive alliance between Britain and France, that destroyed the substructure of Bolingbroke's work. They can claim with equal justification that Bolingbroke's moderate views on the line to be followed in tracing the north-eastern frontier of France secured in essentials a permanent settlement of a particularly thorny question.

Bolingbroke was less successful in his hopes of establishing an equilibrium in Europe which would make unnecessary English military intervention on the Continent. It was for this reason that he attached such importance to naval predominance in the Mediterranean and to promoting the interests of the house of Savoy which would be bound to Britain alike by gratitude and self-interest. Bolingbroke too showed a grasp of the shape of things to come when he encouraged the fitting out of an expedition to challenge French control of the St. Lawrence basin. Stanhope and his Whig successors loudly denounced Bolingbroke's conduct of foreign policy and war and yet made his peace settlement, and even his alliance with France, the basis of their own activities.

Just as the Tories disingenuously argued that their abrupt change of policy was due to the death of Leopold I and the accession of the Archduke Charles to the throne of the Holy Roman Empire, so did the Whigs contend that their reconciliation with France was due to the death of Louis XIV, and the claims of the Regent Orleans to succeed Louis XV on the throne of France, if the boy king should die without issue. These claims rested on the Utrecht treaty, as did, from the French point of view, those of George I to be king of Great Britain. Even before the death of Louis XIV, George I had tried to strike a bargain with Orleans and when this failed he reinsured himself by signing the defensive treaty of Westminster with Charles VI. Partly for this reason, partly because the suppression of the Jacobite rebellion strengthened his hands, George I was able to impose his will upon the Regent and the terms of the Triple Alliance of 1717 were remarkably favourable to Britain.

No attempt was made to vamp the commercial treaty of 1713 which was anathema to Whig merchants. Not only Dunkirk but also Mardyke must actually be demolished. The Pretender and his friends must be excluded from France, if not compelled to reside south of the Alps at a safe distance from the Channel ports. Britain and France would co-operate diplomatically to maintain the Utrecht settlement and to persuade or compel these powers, notably Spain and the Emperor, which were still at war with each other, to make peace on terms to be proposed jointly by France and Britain. George I believed also—and this was one of his principal reasons for concluding an alliance with France—that the treaty entitled him to expect diplomatic support from France for the ambitious policy which he was pursuing in the Great Northern war.

The Franco-British alliance from the day of its signature was uncertain and precarious. The astonishing thing is not that it broke down, but that it lasted as long as it did. It had no basis of popular support in either country. In France it was widely regarded, especially by politicians and generals who had made their reputations under Louis XIV, as a betrayal of France to secure purely personal advantage for the Regent. In England the Whig rank and file were just as suspicious of the new departure in foreign policy. Some raised what was to become the stock cry of Opposition that George I was betraying the interests of his kingdom to the advantage of his electorate. More important, Townshend and Walpole were at first hesitant to accept responsibility and their dilatoriness contributed to the Whig schism of 1717. If the alliance with France strengthened George I's government in its external relations, for a time it weakened it internally.

George I would probably have been better advised not to have pressed his advantage so far at the expense of the Regent. Orleans' unpopular foreign policy weakened his already uncertain control of the French administration; and the weaker his position, the less he could achieve to the advantage of George I and the more doubts he entertained about the wisdom of his own policy. While Stanhope and Dubois achieved a close partnership, neither George I nor the Regent ever came to feel confidence in the other. It was an added difficulty to the smooth working of the alliance that George I felt entitled to take the initiative and expect French support in the two main questions which were causing disturbance in European politics. These questions were the restoration of peace in the Baltic and in the Mediterranean. In both areas France had a much longer and more effective tradition of diplomatic activity than Britain, and naturally resented George I's assumption of leadership.

George I and Stanhope—it is hard to apportion responsibility between them—had devised before the end of 1716 a scheme to settle and ensure peace in the Mediterranean. Charles VI must recognize Philip V as king of Spain and the Indies. Philip V must abandon any claim to the former Spanish territories in Italy. Charles VI would then be allowed to exchange Sardinia, which had been awarded to him as a consolation prize by the Utrecht settlement, for Sicily which he coveted. Philip V's son by his second marriage with Elizabeth Farnese, Don Carlos, would receive Parma and Piacenza, to which his mother had claims. The house of Savoy would be awarded Sardinia and retain the title of king, if Victor Amadeus surrendered Sicily to the Emperor Charles VI.

The Regent, who was being visited by the Tsar in 1717, was at first more concerned with the other problem of how to end the Great Northern war. His bright idea was to enrol Prussia in the Triple Alliance and then arrange a peace with Peter the Great which would leave Sweden in possession of some of her Baltic provinces. But Spain's attack on Sardinia diverted attention to the Mediterranean and forced Charles VI to depend on British naval power. To please the Regent and conciliate his opponents in France, Tuscany was now added to the Italian territories which would eventually be ruled by Elizabeth Farnese's sons. Engaged in simultaneous wars against Spain and the Turks, Charles VI yielded to British pressure and accepted the plan in principle; but he absolutely refused to tolerate Spanish garrisons in Parma and Tuscany during the lives of their present rulers. This stipulation, in the opinion of the Regent and of Elizabeth Farnese, made the Emperor's agreement almost valueless, since he would be in a position to change his mind altogether, or at least to impose additional conditions, when the successions in the duchies actually opened.

Stanhope first tried to overcome this difficulty by hinting at the restoration of Gibraltar to Spain if Philip V would accept the Emperor's stipulation and, when this failed, he proposed the admission to the Italian duchies of British and Swiss troops which would offer effective guarantees to Elizabeth Farnese's sons without giving immediate cause for alarm to Charles VI. Stanhope undertook in vain a personal mission to Spain to seek Philip V's acceptance of this solution and had barely crossed the French frontier on his return journey when news arrived of the destruction of the Spanish armada, which was engaged in the conquest of Sicily, by a British fleet under the command of Admiral Byng.

After further futile negotiations at Madrid, which merely showed up the differences between Britain and France, war followed. French troops took some of the Border fortresses of Spain and occupied the neighbouring provinces, while a British fleet landed troops in Galicia. A joint war against Spain was the high-water-mark of Franco-British co-operation. It was at this time that the Regent actually offered to provide George I with fifteen regiments for the defence of his kingdoms against a Spanish invasion and to supply 1,500 French seamen for service with the British navy. Once Philip V had agreed to make peace and had thrown over the upstart Cardinal Alberoni, who was deliberately made a scapegoat both by the British and French governments, the Regent insisted that his British ally should now implement Stanhope's offer to restore Gibraltar to Spain. Though Stanhope finally convinced the Regent that to insist on this immediately would mean the overthrow of the Whig government, he was still prepared to surrender Gibraltar, which he described as 'useless and dangerous' to Britain, in exchange for adequate compensation, at some future date.

Franco-British co-operation proved even more difficult in the Baltic than in the Mediterranean. Sweden was traditionally the ally of France and Peter the Great was anxious to conclude an alliance with her. England in the seventeenth century had played a quite minor part in the politics of the Baltic Sea. The accession of George I added two new aims to her seventeenth-century objective of keeping open in war, and extending in peace, her commercial connexions with Baltic ports. George I deliberately used English prestige and resources to consolidate his precarious possession of Bremen and Verden, former Swedish territories adjacent to his ancestral lands, and to set limits to the domination of the Baltic by Russia. He was particularly sensitive to Russian infiltration into Mecklenburg which adjoined Hanover and over which he had hopes of acquiring authority as the vicar of the Emperor. These ambitions made George I the bitter enemy both of Sweden and Russia, whereas France was bound to Sweden by ancient ties of friendship, and to Russia by the prospect of securing an advantageous agreement with what was now the leading power in north-eastern Europe. The wavering policy pursued by Frederick William I of Prussia put further strains upon the Franco-British alliance. While the Regent offered his 'good offices' in patching up British relations with Russia and mediating between George I and Charles XII of Sweden, he was not prepared to give to Britain the unqualified support which George I regarded as his due.

The death of Charles XII helped to close the gap between George I and the Regent since both were now anxious to support the new government in Sweden against Peter the Great. Even now the Regent refused support to George I's unrealistic plans for a northern coalition, which should deprive Russia of a large part of the conquests she had made in the Northern war. Dubois was prepared to accept Russian conquests in the eastern Baltic and sought to bolster up Sweden by insisting on the return to her of her former provinces within the Holy Roman Empire. As these included Bremen and Verden, George I was naturally indignant at what he regarded as the treachery of his ally. French historians on the other hand argue that the Regent's alliance with Britain hampered France in pursuing her traditional and advantageous line of policy in the north. In particular an alliance of France with Sweden, Russia and Prussia could have saved Sweden much of the loss which George I's endeavours proved powerless to avert at the treaty of Nystad. But such an alliance would have meant the overthrow of the Utrecht settlement and in all probability a renewal of war between France and the Anglo-Dutch-Imperial coalition which had brought Louis XIV to his knees.

In spite of divergence between British and French policies in the north and the Regent's secret alliance with Spain in 1721, the Franco-British alliance remained the basis of Stanhope's foreign policy until his death. Townshend and Walpole had by this time rejoined the ministry; and Stanhope's death was followed by a bitter struggle between them and Stanhope's political heirs, Sunderland and Carteret. The rival factions in 1723 sent members of their own group to occupy simultaneously the Paris embassy. Dubois, who was tired of playing second fiddle to Stanhope, saw his chance to regain for France and himself the leading position in European politics. To isolate Austria, he arranged to admit Britain to the Franco-Spanish alliance of 1721 at a very moderate price. George I wrote a personal letter to Philip V in which he expressed willingness to restore Gibraltar and promised to propose to the British Parliament, at the first favourable opportunity, that the fortress should be returned to Spain.

A clumsy attempt by Townshend to extort from Dubois a promise that France would never invade the Low Countries, even if she were attacked by Austria from the Netherlands, was hurriedly disavowed by his colleagues, when Dubois pointed out that the formal presentation of such a demand would inevitably be followed by a French declaration of war upon Britain. The final settlement of the north by the treaty of Nystad, and the Regent's refusal to give any support to George I's futile attempts to secure its modification, was a more serious cause of coldness between the ostensible allies. While Orleans and Dubois were eager to effect a reconciliation of George I with Peter the Great, they insisted that there must be give and take on both sides. George I, on the other hand, considered that the services he had rendered to the Regent entitled him to the unquestioning support of France. Any attempt by the Regent to settle matters with Russia and then bring Britain in later on aroused his indignation, since he realized that this method of procedure would involve concessions to Russia which he was unwilling even to consider. By concluding the treaty of Charlottenburg (1723) with Prussia, George I secured the co-operation of Frederick William I in exchange for support of Prussian claims to Jülich and Berg. This combination was likely to attract Sweden. France was as reluctant to accede to this pact as Britain was to accept without criticism the terms of an agreement between France and Russia. Orleans gave up the idea of an exclusive Franco-Russian accord to secure the peace of the Baltic which had embittered the relations of Britain and France; but he and his successors firmly resisted at Constantinople British attempts to rouse the Turks to oppose Russian aims more actively both in Europe and Asia.

By this time Horatio Walpole was firmly entrenched at the Paris embassy and Carteret had been succeeded as secretary of state by Newcastle. After the death of the Regent and the accession to power of the duke of Bourbon, Horatio Walpole speedily realized that Louis XV's former tutor, Fleury, was now the real power behind the throne. Fleury and Walpole were at first sight an even more ill-assorted pair of allies than Dubois and Stanhope; but they had in common the desire to maintain the peace of Europe and the conviction that this end could be attained only by close co-operation between Britain and France. It is not too much to say that they transformed an alliance, originally based on dynasticism, into a political agreement which satisfied for nearly a decade the basic interests of the two nations.

Bourbon had inherited from Orleans the problem of Louis XV's marriage, but he approached the question from a diametrically opposite angle. Since Orleans was the destined successor should the young king die without issue, he had arranged a paper marriage between Louis XV and the infant daughter of Elizabeth Farnese and Philip V. Bourbon's jealousy of his Orleanist cousins may have motivated his reversal of Orleans' policy; but it cannot be denied that the national interests of France pointed in the same direction. As long as the succession to Louis XV remained an open question, so long would it bedevil Franco-Spanish relations. Doing evil that good might follow, Bourbon broke the marriage contract and sent the child bride back to her mother.

Spanish indignation broke off the futile congress of Cambrai, which had been attempting to find a solution for the Italian duchies problem, and contributed to the celebrated reconciliation of Philip V with his rival, the Emperor Charles VI. Since the main object of the congress of Cambrai had been to arrange such a reconciliation, Britain and France might have been expected to receive the news of the first treaty of Vienna (1725) with satisfaction, if not indeed with acclamation. Newcastle at first saw no cause for alarm; but his brother-secretary Townshend believed that secret clauses, attached to the public treaties, constituted a menace both to Britain and Hanover. Not content with treating the Austro-Spanish alliance as foreshadowing the restoration of the Empire of Charles V and constituting an immediate danger to the balance of power, he represented Spanish support for Charles VI's Ostend East India Company as a major threat to the commercial supremacy of the Maritime Powers.

The death of Peter the Great brought to the throne of Russia his widow Catherine I, who rejected approaches from France and Britain, organized a naval demonstration in the Baltic against George I and his allies, and concluded an alliance with Austria. The renewed threat to Britain's interests in the Baltic and to George I's position as elector in Germany reinforced popular alarms for Britain's Mediterranean outposts and commercial fears of rivalry from Ostend. Britain joined with France and Prussia in the league of Hanover, which included a mutual guarantee of their possessions and trading privileges, and a defensive alliance binding the other partners to provide troops to assist their ally, if attacked by the confederates of the Vienna alliance. George I and Frederick William I accepted thankfully a French guarantee of the treaties of Westphalia. This is the only time in the eighteenth century when a British government recognized in a formal document the legitimacy of France's Westphalian role in Germany. The closeness of Franco-British contact is perhaps even better indicated in the dynastically minded Bourbon's offer, promptly rejected by George I, to arrange the marriage of Louis XV to a daughter of the prince of Wales.

The rival leagues of Hanover and Vienna spent the next two years trying to secure recruits. Russia's adhesion to Vienna was balanced by the tardy accession of Sweden and Denmark to Hanover in the spring of 1727. Bavaria, the Palatinate and the Rhenish ecclesiastical electors adhered to the Emperor's side. Worse still the Protestant duke of Brunswick-Wolfenbüttel followed their example, while the king of Prussia transferred his allegiance from Hanover to Vienna by the treaty of Wusterhausen. British naval operations were limited to blockades in the Mediterranean and a futile attempt by Admiral Hosier to prevent the sailing of the Spanish treasure fleet from America. On land Spain laid siege to Gibraltar; but Fleury, who saw that Charles VI was already regretting his bargain with Spain, refused to allow Britain to involve him in war both with Spain and Austria.

It was Fleury who struck a bargain with the Emperor in the preliminary treaty of Paris. The Ostend Company was to be suspended for seven years, while all other outstanding questions were referred to a congress. Fleury was now determined to reach a similar settlement with Spain and resented British refusal to fall in with his plans. At this point Chauvelin, who was already known to be no friend to Britain, became keeper of the seals. Henceforth Horatio Walpole's influence with Cardinal Fleury waned. In spite of his signature of the preliminaries of Paris, the Emperor was still backing Spain in her hostility to Britain, and showed overt hostility to George II by transferring from Hanover and Wolfenbüttel to Prussia the powers of administration over Mecklenburg, which they had exercised by Imperial commission. Finally, Spain was induced to give up the siege of Gibraltar by the bribe that France and Britain would force the Emperor to allow immediate occupation of Parma and certain Tuscan ports by Spanish garrisons. This was the essential basis of the treaty of Seville (1729): the Spanish-Imperial alliance had been destroyed more by its own insufficiency than by Fleury's cautious diplomacy. Townshend's bellicose anti-Hapsburg policy had failed to win support and had merely prolonged the crisis.

Though the treaty of Seville bound Britain and France to secure the admission of the Spanish garrisons to Italy, they failed to agree on a plan of campaign to overcome the resistance of Charles VI. France advocated an invasion of the Austrian Netherlands which was anathema to Britain, which would have liked a French invasion of northern Germany, with the protection of Hanover from Austrians and Prussians as its main objective. France naturally preferred a direct attack upon Austria through Bavaria and down the Danube to Vienna.

Chauvelin's intractability and the closeness of Franco-Spanish relations convinced the British government that a direct approach to Austria offered better chances of securing basic British interests. Townshend's proposal that Britain should pay subsidies to German princes in order to build up opposition to Charles VI in Germany in accordance with Chauvelin's ideas was unhesitatingly rejected by Robert Walpole, who came to appreciate, belatedly, the need for ultimate direction of British foreign policy by the prime minister.

Townshend's resignation was followed by the conclusion of the second treaty of Vienna (1731) which appears, at least in retrospect, as the decisive turning point in Franco-British diplomatic relations. Instead of continuing to support France in her anti-Hapsburg policies, both in Italy and Germany, the two Walpoles and their satellite, Newcastle, preferred to strike a bargain with Charles VI on terms which they knew would be unacceptable to their French ally. Against the advice of Horatio Walpole, no attempt was made to keep France informed of the negotiation and win her concurrence.

The way in which the second treaty of Vienna was concluded was as insulting to France as its terms were injurious to her interests. Newcastle argued that secrecy was necessary since France, if informed of the negotiations, would have made certain that they failed. In defence it may also be argued that France had frequently engaged on secret and separate negotiations with continental powers, e.g. Spain, Russia, and Prussia, which were carefully kept secret from Britain. In fact both Britain and France, during the currency of the alliance, behaved in such a way that mutual confidence could never develop. This was the basic cause of the breakdown of the alliance of 1716.

The rise of Chauvelin was a sympton rather than a cause of Franco-British divergence, but it undoubtedly intensified mistrust. One of the difficulties which had always threatened the alliance was the unwillingness of French diplomatists at foreign courts to carry out the instructions they received from their home government, when these were in conflict with the traditions of Louis XIV. This became more serious when, from intercepted dispatches at London and Hanover, the British government was convinced that Chauvelin was responsible for the lack of effective co-operation. Unwilling to believe that their old friend Fleury was letting them down, they made Chauvelin a scapegoat.

The birth of a dauphin (1729) removed on the French side the original dynastic reason for a Franco-British alliance: the way was clear for the Family Compacts with Spain, which were, under eighteenth-century conditions, the natural outcome of the accession of a Bourbon king to the Spanish throne. Even had the Walpoles not drawn away from France, France would have drawn away from them. Twenty years of peace had been sufficient to restore the French economy and to revive national self-confidence. Chauvelin was merely the standard-bearer of French public opinion, with its demand that French foreign policy should be directed to achieve the permanent interests of France, unhampered by any consideration of the views of 'perfidious Albion'. If the English would not follow where France led, so much the worse for them: Chauvelin, when belatedly informed of British negotiations with Vienna, at once hinted that war with France might result.

It was above all the guarantee of the Pragmatic Sanction, contained in the second treaty of Vienna, which infuriated France. But Britain's defection and Fleury's bad relations with the Spanish sovereigns seemed to expose France to the dangers of isolation and this helps to explain the violence of the French reaction. There were acrimonious squabbles about the position of Dunkirk and rows about the West Indies and Nova Scotia. Chavigny, the French ambassador at London, behaved more like 'a Jacobite conspirator than the representative of a friendly power'.[1] Chauvelin asserted that Britain was bound by treaties to support the candidature of Stanislaus Leszczyński for the Polish crown.

Once France had escaped isolation and replaced Britain by Spain and Sardinia in her system of alliances, Fleury continued to give worthless assurances to Britain, while Chauvelin proceeded to threaten her. Having failed to avert war between Austria and the Bourbon alliance, Walpole refused to take any part in it. So ineffective was his diplomacy that he convinced France, his old ally, of his partiality for Austria, his new one, and his new ally of his partiality for the old one. Since he knew that any suggestion of British mediation would be treated by Chauvelin as equivalent to dictating terms of peace to France, he first offered 'good offices'

---

[1] *British Diplomatic Instructions*, ed. Legg, VI. xxi.

for the restoration of peace both to France and Austria. For a time it seemed possible that the Walpoles might reach agreement with Fleury, behind Chauvelin's back, on acceptable terms for the restoration of peace, which would then be presented to France's allies and to the Emperor. When this failed, Britain, in conjunction with the United Provinces, offered their mediation to the belligerents.

Charles VI had contended from the beginning of the Polish Succession war that he was entitled to the succour stipulated by his treaty of 1731 with Britain and had shown no inclination to accept anything less. His isolated position and military weakness made him susceptible to direct offers from France. Such a bargain might well include the surrender of the Austrian Netherlands to France in exchange for abandonment of Bourbon claims elsewhere against Austria. In view of the much greater importance attached to the Netherlands by the Maritime Powers than by Austria, this bargain would enable the Emperor to punish the Maritime Powers for their lack of support in the war. Though France and Austria reached a provisional agreement in 1735, British alarm about an exchange of the Austrian Netherlands proved unfounded.

The end of warlike operations eased the tension between Britain and France. Fleury actually proposed the revival of Franco-British alliance, since this alone could ensure peace in Europe by restraining the ambitions both of Austria and Spain. Chauvelin was dismissed early in 1737. There were suggestions that Britain and France might combine to protest against Spanish 'depredations' at their expense in the West Indies. When it came to negotiating actual terms for the renewal of the alliance, there were wide divergencies between Fleury's project and the British counterproject. Any chance that they could be reconciled was removed when the British government allowed a bill to become law which made it a capital offence for an Irishman to enlist in a foreign army.

Once he had reached a definitive agreement with the Emperor by the third treaty of Vienna (1738), signed an alliance with Sweden and mediated peace between Austria and the Turks on terms which gave important advantages to the Turks, Fleury had no need of a British alliance. On the other hand, the fact that Fleury was now clearly the arbiter of Europe revived all the old British suspicions of France and gave them added force. Instead of alliance with France, the British government now sought for allies against her with the avowed object of restoring the balance of power. It was partly because they believed that France was egging on Spain that the British government finally declared war on Spain in 1739. For a time they thought that the cardinal's timidity and genuine love of peace might keep France out of the war. Fleury warned them that if they conducted the colonial war in a way which did damage to the overseas interests of France he would be forced to interfere. When George refused to give him any assurances, France mobilized her fleet and despatched a squadron to the West Indies in 1740 with the avowed intention of preventing the British fleet from making conquests or settlements there.

Diplomatic relations between Britain and France continued in form until 1744, but in effect ceased four years earlier. The British government decided to give to Maria Theresa the support they had refused to her father. France became the leader and paymaster of a powerful coalition designed to partition the territories of the house of Hapsburg and prevent Maria Theresa's husband from securing the Imperial title. British and French troops even fought against each other as auxiliaries at Dettingen. Yet it was not until France refused to expel the Young Pretender, as required by the treaty of Utrecht, from France, where he was arranging for a Jacobite invasion of Britain, that diplomatic relations were finally broken off.

While this incident provided the occasion for a renewal of the struggle between France and Britain, its causes lie much deeper. It is significant that as long as Walpole and Fleury retained office, and with office some influence upon the policies followed in Britain and France, the declaration of war was postponed. What contributed most to it was the 'meddle and muddle' policy pursued by Carteret in Germany. With the ultimate aim of uniting Germany against France and thereby destroying the basis of Bourbon ascendancy in Europe, Carteret sought to reconcile Austria and Prussia, bribe some of the adherents of France to transfer their support to Austria, and to make the Bavarian elector, whom France had placed on the Imperial throne as Charles VII, the puppet of Britain, not of France and Prussia. His policy has only to be reduced to its essentials to show how little Carteret deserved his reputation in England as a master of German politics.

Yet the vigour with which he pursued it, and the attempted invasion of Alsace by a German army, alarmed France. In self-defence she adopted the traditional method, used by all continental powers in the first half of the eighteenth century when on bad terms with Britain, of threatening the Protestant succession and the reigning house by giving support to the Jacobites. Moreover France countered the Austrian threat to Alsace by invading the Netherlands and thus at one and the same time endangering the political security and economic interests of Britain. A contributory but not unimportant cause of the declaration of war was the insistence of Philip V of Spain that France, now linked with Spain in the second Family Compact (1743), should openly take his side in the Anglo-Spanish war of 1739.

The Pelhams, who took over control of British foreign policy from Carteret, were saddled with his legacy. They contrived to defeat the Jacobite threat at home in 1746; and they abandoned, as quickly as George II would allow them, Carteret's active policy in Germany by forcing Maria Theresa to sign the treaty of Dresden (1745) with Prussia. The war continued in the Netherlands and in Italy, as well as in India and North America, where the important fortress of Louisburg, commanding the St. Lawrence estuary, was taken by a joint British and colonial task force.

Failing to detach Spain from France by making a separate peace with her (1746–7), the war-weary majority in the British Cabinet conducted negotiations with France, in conjunction with the Dutch, at Breda. Louis XV and Madame de Pompadour were as weary of the war as Henry Pelham. Belated British naval successes and the virtual cessation of French trade with her colonies balanced the more spectacular military victories of Marshal Saxe in the Netherlands. When the new stadholder, William IV, confessed that he could no longer make a substantial contribution to the defence of the United Provinces, Newcastle at last saw the necessity for peace, which was signed at Aix-la-Chapelle.

The terms of this treaty corresponded closely to the stalemate which had been reached, so far as Britain and France were concerned, in the war. Britain had failed to undermine French domination in Germany and was quarrelling with Austria. Whereas in the last war Marlborough had threatened the north-eastern frontiers of France, Saxe had conquered the Austrian Netherlands. Britain, by making peace, in effect admitted the inadequacy of her resources for the defence of the United Provinces as well as the futility of the Barrier treaty.

France's military record, except in self-defence and in the Netherlands, was not impressive. Even aided by Prussia and most of the other princes of Germany, she had not succeeded in her war aims. Maria Theresa at the end of the war was much less of a French satellite than her father had been at the beginning. In Italy, partly because Sardinia had adhered pretty consistently to Austria, the combined armies of France and Spain had at the end of the day achieved little. At sea British naval superiority had finally been asserted over French and Spanish power. Partly for this reason, but also because of the accession of Ferdinand VI in Spain, France no longer felt confident of continued Spanish support.

If we disregard the territorial clauses, whose importance proved to be transient, in the treaty of Aix-la-Chapelle, the effects of the Austrian Succession war upon France and Britain become clearer. Any idea of alliance between them had disappeared by the end of the war: both sides regarded the settlement as a mere truce. Henceforth colonial issues were to bulk much more largely in determining Franco-British relations with each other. Britain had gone to war with Spain in 1739 largely over the danger to her West Indian interests and Newcastle, in the hope of retaining Louisburg with its implied threat to French Canada, had postponed the end of the war with France until 1748. But other colonial controversies had not been allowed to prevent the signature of peace in that year: they had either been ignored or referred to commissaries for subsequent settlement.

Within Europe, if Britain and France faced each other in irreconcilable opposition much more clearly in 1748 than in 1740, each was having difficulties with its allies. The Maritime Powers had not acted as a unit in the war and the Dutch were less inclined than ever to support Britain against France. Maria Theresa was indignant at the way in which Britain had treated her during the war and was quite likely to follow her father's example and become a satellite of France. Louis XV's main allies, Spain and Prussia, were just as unreliable as those of Britain. Ferdinand VI had abandoned his predecessor's ambitions in Italy and was soon to sign a treaty to establish the *status quo* there. Frederick the Great had behaved during the war in such a way that no reliance could be placed upon him by anybody.

The lesson drawn from the war by Louis XV was that French naval power must be developed without impairing her military superiority on the Continent. Newcastle concluded that the best chance of intimidating France and postponing a renewal of the struggle was to organize a European coalition under British leadership. He had not the slightest wish to renew the war: all his diplomatic preparations were designed to preserve peace by placing France in political quarantine. He argued that the stronger the British-led combination of powers the less likely France would be to risk a renewal of war. He failed to appreciate that British diplomatic activity, especially in Germany, was certain to accentuate French hostility and unlikely to achieve its object. The treaty of Aranjuez virtually excluded British influence from Italy. His attempt to add Russia to his system failed. Worse still, his best efforts did nothing to restore the old system of alliances, fatally impaired by Dutch lethargy and Austrian dissatisfaction. Only with Spain did he make progress; and the accession of Charles III in 1759 soon undid all that he had achieved.

Meantime the overseas controversies between Britain and France, which the negotiators of the Aix-la-Chapelle treaty had left over for subsequent settlement, became increasingly acute. Neither side showed any inclination to compromise; and the method, insisted upon by the French, of referring particular questions to commissaries, would in any case have made compromise difficult. All the issues were kept open and local agents in the colonies, by taking matters into their own hands, constantly added new problems. The most serious of these was the erection of forts designed to prevent expansion of the British colonies on the North American mainland, which provoked a demand from the British government for the evacuation by the French of the Ohio valley. To reinforce its diplomacy General Braddock was sent out early in 1755 to strengthen the Virginian troops already operating unsuccessfully against the French.

When Albemarle, the British ambassador to France, died at his post, he was not replaced. Contrary to the usual practice, Newcastle seems to have preferred to negotiate at London with the French ambassador, Mirepoix, instead of sending to Versailles a British ambassador capable of convincing Louis XV and his ministers that the British government was in deadly earnest over these American disputes. Though Albemarle's record was not inspiring and Newcastle may reasonably have thought that the available English noblemen were unlikely to do much good at

Paris, failure to replace him promptly may well have helped to bring about war.

Newcastle himself was pessimistic, almost fatalistic, in his approach. He had pinned his faith in building up a system of alliances strong enough to intimidate France and to convince her that she had nothing to gain by renewing the maritime and colonial struggle with Britain. By 1755 his failure was manifest to others, if not yet to himself. The weakness of his government in the house of Commons and his own inability to stand up to criticism made it impossible for him to adopt the Walpolean path of appeasement. The slightest concession to France would have been denounced by Pitt and probably by Fox. Yet Newcastle's desperate attempts to strengthen Britain's position against France on the Continent were likewise denounced by his many enemies as mere pandering to Hanover. Rightly convinced that the French were the aggressors in America, he was more concerned to prove that they were in the wrong than to avoid another war with France.

Arguing that France must not be allowed to reinforce her American garrisons, Newcastle despatched Boscawen to intercept French reinforcements. Braddock's force was overwhelmed and Boscawen could only capture two of the French ships, the *Alcide* and the *Lys*. Henceforth France could argue that British provocation at sea justified her in declaring war, whatever might be the rights and wrongs of their American disputes. From 18 May 1756 Britain and France were formally at war.

Disputes between British and French East India Companies between the Austrian Succession and Seven Years wars need not be discussed here. The recall of Dupleix, an energetic but over-ambitious French soldier who had visions of a French empire in India, ended the critical stage in August 1754. Conflict in India was not a direct cause of the Seven Years war, though it may have contributed to it by intensifying mutual hostility and making compromise more difficult.

Newcastle tried to avoid having to wage a continental war by signing the convention of Westminster with Prussia in January 1756. Austria had refused to help him defend the low Countries against France and was already seeking the French alliance. Newcastle's bargain with Frederick II to neutralize Germany, and incidentally bar France from attacking Hanover, ensured the success of Kaunitz's negotiations at Versailles (May 1756) and well-nigh destroyed British influence at St. Petersburg upon which Frederick had pinned his hopes of avoiding continental war. Ostracized by France and threatened by Austria and Russia, Frederick began the war on the Continent by invading the strategically placed electorate of Saxony, which had continued to be at one and the same time a satellite of France and of the Austro-Russian allies. He thus forced France against her better judgement to fight simultaneous wars at sea and in the colonies against Britain and (as Austria's ally) on the continent of Europe against Prussia.

The double war began disastrously for Britain. France threatened to invade England and the British fleet retired from the Mediterranean, leaving Minorca to be captured by the French. Newcastle hurriedly retired from office and trembled for his head. After a protracted ministerial *interregnum* the Pitt–Newcastle ministry was formed. While Newcastle managed patronage and raised unprecedentally large supplies of money, Pitt swept the French fleets from the seas, conquered French Canada, contributed to establish British supremacy in India, and contrived to save Hanover, or most of it, from French occupation.

France was hampered by the obligations in Europe which she had undertaken by her alliance with Austria, since the resources of France were inadequate to carry on successfully a European land war and a naval and colonial war. The sensational British successes overseas so alarmed Charles III of Spain that he joined France; but Spanish participation in the naval war merely gave Britain new lands to conquer beyond Europe.

By this time war-weariness affected the victorious as much as the vanquished power. Pitt claimed to have conquered Canada on the banks of the Elbe: he refused to make peace until France had been stripped of her colonies and forced to recognize that colonial competition with Britain was henceforth impracticable. Criticism was directed mainly against continued British participation, on a steadily increasing scale, in German campaigns. It was already widespread both within and without the ministry when Pitt was forced out of office in October 1761. George III lacked his grandfather's interest in Hanover, and his mentor Bute, well aware that he would never shine as a war-minister, had personal as well as national reasons for ending the war. With the aid of Bedford at Paris and Fox as manager of the house of Commons, they succeeded in making peace with France and Spain by the treaty of Paris (1763).[1]

As a settlement of the issues between Britain and France the treaty of Paris may be described as reasonable and moderate. Anderson, the author of *An Historical and Chronological Deduction of the Origin of Commerce*, published in 1764, concluded that the treaty brought enormous advantages to England, indeed 'such advantages (more especially in a commercial sense) as this kingdom never knew or experienced'.[2] Pitt's criticisms which, alone among politicians, he expressed in economic and strategic terms were in effect limited to the restoration to France of some West Indian islands and the allowing her to retain fishing rights off Newfoundland which would be advantageous to her naval power.

More serious was Pitt's contention that the treaty was negotiated without much regard for the interests of Prussia, our ally in the war. Frederick the Great's resentment, though largely unjustified, along with Austria's refusal to renew her former alliance with Britain, deprived successive British governments of any real hope of winning the support of a powerful continental state against France. This proved to be important, since the moderation of the treaty did nothing to moderate French resentment at its terms. Choiseul[3] and his successors set themselves systematically to rebuild the shattered naval and colonial power of France and maintain the system of alliances which would reduce British influence on the Continent to a minimum. Free of any danger from Britain's 'continental sword' and assured of peace on the Continent, France looked forward to renewing the colonial struggle with better prospects of success. It was for this purpose that Choiseul reconstructed the French navy and consolidated France's alliance with Spain. The Carthaginian peace advocated by Pitt could not have been more resented than were the terms imposed on France by the moderation of Bute and Bedford. French secret service agents swarmed across the Channel to study the prospects of a successful invasion of Britain while technologists reported on the development and organization of British industries in the 1760's. Victory

[1] On Franco-British peace negotiations during the war, Z. E. Rashed, *The Peace of Paris* (Liverpool, 1951), should be consulted.

[2] Postscript (not paginated) to Vol. II. Anderson also gives a useful analysis of the differences between the preliminary and the definitive peace treaties.

[3] Choiseul's attitude is admirably explained in J. F. Ramsey, *Anglo-French Relations, 1763–1770* (Berkeley, 1939).

in the Seven Years war had made Britain the leading World Power; but the peace of Paris had destroyed the foundations of the influence she had exerted over Europe since the Glorious Revolution.

The instability of British governments in the first decade of George III's reign, and the distraction of attention from European politics by internal disorder and difficulties in governing the territories Britain had acquired beyond Europe by the treaty of Paris, further weakened Britain *vis-à-vis* France. This was shown very clearly when France annexed Corsica in 1768-9. The Corsican question had already produced exchanges between Britain and France in the 1730's and George III's ministers protested repeatedly against Choiseul's establishment of French control over the island. Yet in the end Britain tamely acquiesced in the acquisition by France of a new naval base in the Mediterranean, which most Britons believed would neutralize the British base at Port Mahon and undermine British predominance in the western Mediterranean.

Yet, when Britain stood firm, France usually gave way. The best illustration of this is provided by the Falkland Islands crisis[1] which contributed to the fall of Choiseul in December 1770. In this year British threats prevented France and Spain from interfering with the Russian fleet which sailed through the Mediterranean to attack France's Turkish ally. French desires to support Gustavus III against Russia by despatching a fleet to the Baltic were thwarted, when Britain threatened to send her fleet into the Baltic to counteract French influence. And when Louis XV proposed to transfer his squadron to the Mediterranean, where it could aid the Turks in a diversion against Russia, British protests caused him to abandon the idea.

The crisis over Gustavus III's *coup d'état* and the almost contemporaneous alarms and excursions over the first Partition of Poland tended to bring about a slackening of tension in Franco-British relations. The dominant role of Russia in both crises made clear that the centre of gravity in European politics had moved far to the east. Neither Britain not France could exert much influence upon the settlement, least of all when they spent most of their time and energies in neutralizing each other's activities. In the governing circles of both countries there appeared rather self-conscious and half-hearted advocates of Franco-British *rapprochement*.

[1] See chapter 10, pp. 297-8.

George III was prepared, at the time of the first Partition of Poland, to consider making an alliance with France, but as a possibility in the future rather than as an immediate object. He suggested as a first step the conclusion of a commercial treaty between the two countries and negotiations followed, although no treaty was concluded. Choiseul's successor, D'Aiguillon, coming into office in 1771, deliberately set himself, by a policy of 'graceful concessions' in the colonies, to take the sting out of Franco-British relations and, if possible, bring about a genuine reconciliation with Britain. Rochford, the secretary of state for the southern department, though eager for the commercial treaty, declined absolutely to consider a Franco-British alliance as a practical possibility in view of the state of British public opinion. He continued in public to threaten France rather than to attempt to co-operate with her; but while carefully avoiding written commitments, he indicated his readiness to collaborate with France on an *ad hoc* basis, and especially to prevent Russia from imposing her will upon the Swedes. His conversations with a secret French agent in London in 1773 prove that he was ready to 'connive at a swift French expedition to the Baltic, which should do its business and return before England had put the navy on a war footing'.[1] Neither George III nor Rochford dared actually to work openly with France: the most they could offer was a secret undertaking to postpone acting against her until such action would be certain to prove ineffective.

When Louis XVI succeeded Louis XV, D'Aiguillon's place was taken by Vergennes. The new foreign minister was a career-diplomatist, who had served mainly at courts where Franco-British opposition was acute. In any case the practical results achieved by his predecessor's approaches to Britain were hardly encouraging. Vergennes reverted to the policy of Choiseul, but with a rather more limited view of what was required in the way of revenge against Britain. He no longer anticipated the recovery by France of her position as a World Power, such as it had been at the opening of the Seven Years war. He would be content if Britain could be deprived of her near-monopoly of colonial and maritime power and a balance achieved between British and Bourbon commercial and colonial empires. Even then he believed that colonies should be regarded not as subject states but as allied provinces. Certainly

---

[1] Michael Roberts, 'Great Britain and the Swedish Revolution 1772–3' in *Historical Journal* 7 (1964), 32.

Vergennes was no Pitt—to impose a Carthaginian peace upon his enemy formed no part of his plans and he regarded Britain as a useful makeweight in the continental balance of power. But as soon as he came into power 'graceful concessions' ceased. France's legal rights were vigorously defended and widely interpreted.

Even when the outbreak of the American war of Independence gave France her chance, opinion in France was divided. Louis XVI, eager to revenge the treaty of Paris, had scruples of conscience about supporting rebels and republicans and wondered whether colonial success against Britain would be followed by similar risings against other colonial powers, especially his ally Spain. Might it not pay France better to assist Britain in suppressing the American rebels, if Britain would pay France's price for assistance—the surrender of Canada? Once convinced that Britain was not interested in such a bargain, French sympathies with the rebels became more and more overt.

American privateers were given encouragement well beyond the limits imposed by international law upon a neutral power. A French expedition was to be fitted out, ostensibly for the protection of French interests in the West Indies. French volunteers were allowed to make their way to America, sometimes assisted by the French ambassador at London. Burgoyne's surrender at Saratoga (October 1777) brought the French out openly on the side of the colonists. France allied herself with the Americans in March 1778 and sent a fleet to co-operate with them on the American coast. Loss of command of the sea compelled Cornwallis's surrender at Yorktown (1781) to a combined French and American army. The fall of Lord North forced George III to grant independence to the colonists, but Rodney's victory over the French at the battle of the Saints saved the British West Indies and restored British command of the seas.

Shelburne signed a peace with the colonists which virtually broke up the alliance of France and the Americans. Peace was then made with France without much difficulty by a complicated series of exchanges of colonial territories and rights which need not be described here. Britain admitted that France was now free to fortify Dunkirk: the prohibition by the treaty of Utrecht and the limitation imposed by the treaties of Aix-la-Chapelle and Paris had never been fully effective and were now wisely abandoned. Still more significant of less bitterness in Franco-British relations was their agreement to negotiate a commercial treaty, as had been suggested by Rochford nearly twenty years earlier. Equally significant, France put pressure upon her continental allies, Spain and Holland, to reduce their claims to what Britain was ready to accept.

But for the outbreak of the French Revolution it seems likely that Franco-British hostility might have died away after 1783. Not content with sending their sons on the Grand Tour, English families were now settling in French provincial towns. Voltaire and Montesquieu had propagated English social and political ideas among the educated classes of France. Even during the war of American Independence British subjects had been allowed to move freely about France. English fashions in clothes and sports were all the rage, with a prince of the blood royal setting the example. Pitt himself spent a month in 1783 at Rheims in the hope of polishing his French, and met Talleyrand. Yet it must be admitted that such intellectual and social contacts had continued throughout the eighteenth century without contributing anything to mitigate mutual political and economic hostility. Francophil Englishmen and Anglomaniac Frenchmen were perhaps more numerous in the 'eighties than in previous decades, but they seem to have exercised little more influence than their predecessors upon the political relations between their respective countries.

Pitt and his foreign minister, Carmarthen, agreed that peace was the greatest of British interests and that, until Britain had recovered her strength and prestige, there was little hope of either securing an alliance with Austria or counterbalancing in any other way the superiority of the house of Bourbon. Their fears were confirmed when renewed approaches to Austria and Russia in 1784-5 were politely but decisively evaded. This was the more serious because France was still actively interested in India and engaged in intrigues against the position of the East India Company. Included in these was the attempt, in which Vergennes took a personal interest, to establish French influence in Egypt, gain commercial access to the Red Sea and perhaps use Egypt as a base for recovering French military and political ascendancy in India.

A nearer and more immediate danger was the position in the Netherlands. The war between Great Britain and the United Provinces had made very difficult the position of the Anglophil stadholder, William V, and increased French influence in the Provinces. William V was opposed not only by the old aristocratic republican party, but by a democratic and widespread 'patriot' movement, which drew its inspiration largely from French precept and American example. French ascendancy was further increased by the belief in the United Provinces that it was the attitude of France which had prevented Joseph II from seizing Maestricht, opening the Scheldt to international navigation, with disastrous results to Dutch commerce, and exchanging the Austrian Nether-lands for Bavaria.

If France could give effective protection to the United Provinces and had openly abandoned her natural desire to destroy the Barrier treaty, even supporters of the house of Orange tended to gravitate into the French camp. The Dutch concluded in 1785 a formal treaty of defensive alliance with France and it was believed in London that henceforth the French and Dutch East India Companies would pool their resources against the British company.

To try to rebuild English influence in the Low Countries, Pitt dispatched to The Hague an experienced and Francophobe envoy, James Harris, who reached The Hague on 7 December 1784. Harris's instructions tied his hands so tightly that success seemed impossible. Pitt thought the loss of the Netherlands to the French a lesser evil than the immediate renewal of war with France. He steadfastly resisted Carmarthen's suggestions that now or never the domination of France in the Low Countries must be checked. Not until Prussia had committed herself (before the completion of her negotiations with Britain) to military intervention in the United Provinces, and had pricked the 'patriot' bubble, did Pitt take the initiative (September 1787). Then, and not until then, Carmarthen was allowed to warn the French foreign minister, Montmorin, that French intervention against the Prussian army would bring in Britain. This threat was reinforced by naval mobilization; but internal divisions and the acute financial crisis probably determined French action, or rather inaction. Not content to get his own way, Pitt compelled France to eat the leek in public. Montmorin was forced to sign a statement in which he disavowed the notorious intention of the king of France to support the Dutch 'patriots' and consented to disarm.

Pitt's conduct of British foreign policy, because he had virtually superseded Carmarthen, in this crisis may best be described as an essay in brinkmanship. Its justification depends upon its success and it should be noted that it succeeded because of factors which

Pitt could not have foreseen and did not fully appreciate even after they had occurred. A more experienced diplomatist would have avoided such a public humiliation of France, expecially as he badly needed French co-operation to give effect to his policy in eastern Europe.

Against the failure to improve the political relationship between Britain and France may be set the conclusion of the treaty of commerce, usually referred to by the name of its chief negotiator as the Eden treaty of 1786. It is customary to regard this agreement, with its novel approach to international trade, as the child of Adam Smith. While it is certainly in accordance with the enlightened precepts of *The Wealth of Nations*, it stands in a closer relationship with the views repeatedly expressed by Vergennes to the effect that a rich country will not get richer by cutting itself off from prosperous neighbours but by trading with them to mutual advantage. Certainly it was Vergennes who pressed for the conclusion of the treaty. The British government hung back and had to be continually prodded by the French negotiators. The conclusion of the Franco-Dutch alliance, which included commercial as well as political clauses, may have helped to awaken Pitt to the desirability of securing similar advantages for Britain; but it was not until Vergennes prohibited the import of certain textiles and other goods, largely drawn by France from British sources, that Pitt took the negotiations seriously.

After much hard bargaining the treaty was signed on 26 September 1786. It granted to Britons and Frenchmen freedom of trade and navigation within the European territories of Britain and France, as well as complete religious liberty while visiting the other country. Based on reciprocity and what had come to be called the most-favoured-nation principle, the British customs duties on French wines were to be reduced to equality with those levied on Portuguese wine. Maximum *ad valorem* duties were fixed for imports of British manufactured goods into France, e.g. 10 per cent. on hardware and 12 per cent. on cottons, woollens, and cambrics. Other clauses sought to avoid disputes about contraband, privateering, smuggling, &c. which had caused so much bad feeling between the two countries. It was expressly stated that a belligerent power was entitled to confiscate goods of a power with which it was at war if found on an enemy merchantman.

In defending the treaty in the house of Commons, though Eden

thought him half-hearted, Pitt had much the better of the argument with the leader of the Opposition, Charles James Fox, who
voiced once again the old Whig shibboleth that France was the
natural enemy of Britain. By signing the treaty Pitt had sacrificed
our ancient ally Portugal, limited his freedom to manœuvre, and
made it difficult to conclude the alliances which might prove
necessary to defeat the designs of France. Pitt denounced the
notion that one country could be unalterably the enemy of another
as 'weak and childish', and thus concealed the doubts he must have
felt about the anti-British direction of French policy in the
Netherlands and the still more sinister activities of French agents
in Egypt and India. The marked discrepancies between the
professions of a French foreign minister at Versailles and the
conduct followed by French agents at the periphery, which had
contributed to the failure of the Anglo-French *entente* of 1716, still
plagued British relations with France.

In defending the commercial treaty of 1786 Pitt publicly asserted
that it offered greater advantages to Britain than to France. This
was foolish since it gave a handle to the many opponents of the
treaty in France, ranging from disgruntled courtiers, who had formerly made profits from royal licences to import English manufactured goods in defiance of the laws, to the textile manufacturers of
northern France who had built up their industry behind barriers of
total prohibition of British imports and now found the French
market flooded with superior British goods selling at competitive
prices. In fact the Eden treaty may be regarded as the first large-
scale device of the British government to find foreign markets for
the torrent of goods produced by the Industrial Revolution. What
he had done with France he tried to repeat with Spain, Russia and
other countries. While Pitt clearly appreciated the close connexion
between politics and economics in international relations, his aims
in concluding the treaty were primarily economic and only in a
minor degree did he anticipate political advantage for his country.[1]

The onset of the French revolution at first markedly improved
the relations of Britain and France. In diplomatic circles there was
a general feeling of relief—internal troubles would prevent France
from throwing her weight about in Europe. Britain, at the head of
a new Triple Alliance with Prussia and the Dutch, felt more secure

---

[1] The preceding paragraphs are based on J. Ehrman, *British Government and
Commercial Negotiations with Europe 1783–93*, chapter 2.

than she had done since 1764. And the apparent weakness of France made it easy for the Triple Alliance to take on the role of France and seek to protect the former clients of France, Sweden, Poland, and Turkey, from Russia and Austria. Pitt even expressed the hope that France would give active support to the Triple Alliance.

In English political circles it was generally believed that France had set out to copy the English constitution. This would not only be a graceful and well-merited compliment, which might lead to more friendly co-operation in European politics. Even if it did not at once do this, France, with the limitation of her monarchical absolutism and the weakening of dynastic ties with other Bourbon states, would become a less potent enemy to Britain. And as long as French finances were in disorder, Pitt need not fear the revival of French designs in Egypt and India, which had rightly made him suspicious of the liberal and friendly professions of Vergennes. France had become an 'object of compassion' to Pitt. Fox, who had declared himself in the debates on the commercial treaty as the eternal enemy of France, now poured out his sympathies with the Revolutionaries and rejoiced in the fall of the Bastille.

France's failure to support Spain, on terms acceptable to Charles IV, contributed to the triumph of Pitt in the Nootka Sound crisis,[1] which occupied most of his attention in the summer of 1790. Since absolutist France had not always been eager to come to the assistance of Spain in the past, this failure in co-operation should not be attributed entirely to the effects of the French Revolution. But it is impossible to deny that the weakening of the bonds between France and Spain, directly caused by the Revolution, contributed as much to Pitt's success against Spain as the support of his allies in the Triple Alliance.

Towards France Pitt held firmly to a policy of non-intervention. He carefully abstained from making, or at least committing to paper, value-judgements on the progress of the Revolution. He had no more intention of supporting the revolutionaries against the king than of backing the émigré princes in their crusade against the Revolution. Burke's eulogy of the French monarchy no more excited his sympathies than Paine's defence of the mob. Yet impelled more by disorder in England than by revolutionary excesses in France, he drifted slowly into the reactionary camp.

Intent on increasing the revenue and diminishing the national

[1] See, for this crisis, chapter 10, pp. 304–5.

debt through the operation of his sinking fund, and thus laying a solid foundation for national prosperity, he ventured, as late as 1792, to look forward to fifteen years of peace. When Talleyrand came on an unofficial mission from the French revolutionary government to London, he received assurances from Pitt and his foreign minister, Grenville, that, far from thinking of intervention in France, they were anxious to maintain strict neutrality between *émigrés* and revolutionaries, and, should war unfortunately result, between France and the German powers which were now openly hostile to the revolutionary government of France. These assurances encouraged the Girondins to send Talleyrand back to London to explain that France in self-defence must occupy Belgium temporarily and probably overthrow the stadholderian régime in Holland. They hoped Pitt would abstain from intervention and offered him the alliance of France. Constitutional Britain and revolutionary France, acting in concert, could become the arbiters of peace and war for the whole world. Pitt refused to make public the assurances of neutrality he had already given, since he believed this would encourage France to attack Austria. Grenville also pointed out that Britain was bound by honour, treaty obligations, and national interest to preserve the Low Countries from conquest by France.

French victories soon showed the hollowness of these French professions. They were followed by the annexation of Savoy to the French republic, the unilateral opening of the river Scheldt to international commerce and navigation, and other measures which proclaimed French intentions to subvert the constitution of the United Provinces. Instead of merely defending herself against attack and implementing her formal undertaking not to make conquests, France offered to assist all peoples which wished to recover their liberty. Pitt saw in these measures 'a concerted plan to drive us to extremities, with a view of producing an impression on the interior of the country'.[1] What changed Pitt's attitude of neutrality was not merely his conviction of the illegality of French actions and the damage done to British interests on the Continent, but his belief that the French revolutionaries had now set themselves, with the avowed aid of British sympathizers, to revolutionize Britain. In November 1792 Pitt assured the stadholder that Britain would assist him against a French attack or a 'patriot' rising inspired by the French. This decision had been taken and communicated to

[1] Quoted by J. Holland Rose, *William Pitt and the Great War*, p. 73.

the Dutch government before the news of the French declaration of the unilateral opening of the Scheldt was known in London.

Before war was actually declared Pitt received some reassurance that Britain was less divided against herself than he had feared. The parliamentary Opposition split asunder and the majority rallied to the support of Pitt's government. Fox could muster only fifty votes in the house of Commons against 290 when he denounced Pitt's handling of the crisis. In the long run it was perhaps unfortunate for Pitt that the new recruits to his side included Burke, since Burke's oratory tended to muddle the issues which were the true cause of the war and to misrepresent it as a crusade against the atheistical and immoral French republic. Outside Parliament, though the Corresponding Societies continued what Pitt regarded as their treasonable activities, middle-class opinion also moved in his favour. It seemed to many people that it was becoming difficult to reconcile the precepts and the practices of the French revolutionaries. Under a smoke-screen of concern for humanity and the rights of man, they were intent on pursuing to the detriment of Britain the traditional aims of the Bourbon kings in foreign policy. New Jacobin was nothing but old Louis XIV writ large.

Fox's attempt to make Pitt responsible for the war with France because he would not recognize the French republic has no basis in fact; but after November 1792 war could have been averted only by French withdrawal of their armies from all conquered territory, the revocation of any laws passed by the revolutionaries to the detriment of other states, and a formal undertaking by them not to stir up trouble in future against foreign governments. In view of the temper of Paris, a French government prepared to give such assurances could not have survived a single day. Instead of withdrawing, the Convention in December 1792 codified and extended the revolutionary decrees which had forced Pitt to change his attitude to the Revolution.

The die had been cast in November 1792. Subsequent incidents, the execution of Louis XVI, the controversy over the Aliens Bill, the stoppage of corn ships bound for France, the misrepresentations of the French emissaries at London, were all at most occasions, not causes of the war. Britain joined the First Coalition. Her aims diverged widely from those of her allies; and two of her allies, Austria and Prussia, soon paid more attention to Poland than they did to France. Pitt assumed that all he need do was to follow the traditional recipe for fighting wars against France, i.e. concentrate on naval and colonial warfare and hire a sufficient number of continental mercenaries to check French aggression on the Continent.

Pitt and his associates reckoned that France could be driven to her knees once again by economic pressure, the loss of her colonies, the ruination of her overseas trade, the destruction of her navy and merchant shipping. Even in waging such an imperialist war they proved incompetent strategists. The French navy in the early years of the war was unprepared for action, disorganized and divided against itself. Yet the British fleets failed to win decisive victories: at the most they weakened the opposing French squadrons and drove them back to their bases where they could refit and, when it suited them, resume the struggle. Instead of contenting themselves with seizing France's West Indian harbours, they tried to conquer and hold the interior of the islands. The regular army was practically wiped out by pestilence and disease in such campaigns when it should have been deployed on the continent of Europe to prevent France from breaking out from her frontiers and exploiting the economic resources of the neighbouring lands in a way which counteracted the economic pressures Pitt and Dundas hoped to bring to bear on her by colonial and maritime defeat.

Such troops as were spared for the Continent were too few to achieve the strategic objectives which justified their employment and as usual it proved very difficult to secure effective co-operation between the army and navy in such combined operations. The military science of logistics was still in its infancy and Pitt showed no understanding of its fundamental laws. British Intelligence proved much less efficient than it had been in earlier wars against France. In particular far too much weight was attached to the optimistic and self-interested estimates by émigrés in London of the support that British expeditionary forces might expect to receive in such operations.

It is only fair to add that in some cases these estimates may have been correct at the time they were made, but were falsified by delay in taking action for which Pitt and Dundas must accept responsibility. Indecision and administrative fumbling at London cost Britain the chance of winning the war before the republicans could take complete control of France, overthrow the established order in adjacent areas and dominate the west of Europe. Once there were 'hordes of ragged republicans swaggering over western

Europe, roaring the Marseillaise and lighting their pipes at the altar candles',[1] even Pitt, who never understood ideological war, had, to some extent, to rethink his ideas on the conduct of the war.

The clearest evidence of this was the Wickham mission to Switzerland from 1794 to 1797. The swing to the right in France which began with the overthrow of Robespierre culminated under the Directory in the election to the Legislature of a majority composed of royalists and fellow-travellers. If a moderate government pledged to make peace on what Pitt regarded as reasonable terms, emerged or could be helped into power in France, this would be a much cheaper and more satisfactory way of attaining the war aims of the British government than to continue the war with half-hearted continental allies more interested in extracting a high price for their help than in using British subsidies to wage effective war against the French republic.

One difficulty in the pursuit of this policy was that French royalists were split into sections which found it almost impossible to co-operate successfully with each other. While the constitutional royalists were as opposed as the republicans to the resurrection of the old régime, the ultras would be content with nothing less. The British government's refusal to recognize Louis XVII, and later Louis XVIII, as the legitimate ruler of France was therefore a stumbling block to co-operation between them and the French royalist right wing.

The royalists were in fact divided in their attitude to peace. Some saw in peace between France and her enemies the end of royalist hopes of a restoration since peace would probably enable the republic to consolidate its position and stabilize the achievements of the Revolution. Others believed that the end of the war would reduce the *tempo* of revolutionary politics and drive a wedge between the republican government and the mass of the French people. They therefore saw in international peace the best chance of overthrowing the existing government of France.

As long as the British government believed that the First Coalition was destined to defeat French aggression while it looked on civil war within the bounds of France merely as a useful but subsidiary diversion of the republic's efforts, little attention was paid to the Counter-Revolution and no serious effort was made to assist *émigré*, royalist, clerical, or peasant resistance to the republic. It

[1] A. B. Rodger, *The War of the Second Coalition* (Clarendon Press, 1964), p. 2.

was not until 1794 that Wickham was sent to Switzerland to see whether the moderates who were gaining ground in France were prepared to make peace on reasonable terms. Failing in this, Wickham attempted to organize armed insurrection on the eastern borders of France while the British War Office financed a combined expedition with some of the *émigrés* to Quiberon Bay. Both schemes miscarried, but by this time Wickham was in contact with a group of royalist politicians at Paris, usually referred to as the Paris agency. This body repudiated as futile the old royalist tactics of secret conspiracy and armed insurrection. They were ready also to work along with the advocates of constitutional monarchy in open but constitutional and legal opposition to the Directory. Using all the resources of propaganda to influence the electorate and lavishly subsidized by the British government, the royalists managed to secure control of the legislature.

By this time the First Coalition had collapsed: even Austria had made peace with the French republic leaving Britain to carry on the war alone. Britain hoped that the royalist majority in the legislature would be strong enough to compel the Directory to conclude peace on reasonable terms and sent its top-ranking diplomatist, Lord Malmesbury, to negotiate with France. As soon as the Directory outmanœuvred its opponents, who were orators rather than men of action, and purged the moderates from the Legislature, the British government had to admit that the only choice they now had was between complete capitulation to the Directory on the one hand and continuing the war unaided on the other.

Undeceived though not discouraged by the speedy collapse of the First Coalition, Pitt tried again with the Second. Britain's position in 1796–7 was much less favourable than it had been in 1793. Spain and Holland were now the allies of France and their navies were under French control. The British fleet had had to retire from the Mediterranean at the end of 1796, though it was increasing the effectiveness of its blockade of the Atlantic coast of France. Pitt had been willing to make peace both in 1796 and 1797 on terms which would have given France all that she could reasonably desire from Britain. Each time the dominant party in Paris had contemptuously brushed aside his offers.

Bonaparte's campaign in Italy in 1796 shows clearly, at least in retrospect, the transition from a defensive war to protect the integrity of France and the unity of the French nation, to a war of imperialist French aggression. French soldiers now boasted that given adequate supplies of bread, iron, and gunpowder they could march from Paris to Kamchatka. And Britain was the only power still in arms against the French republic. While she might defend herself single-handed, she could only hope to achieve a peace which would secure her honour and national security by re-creating a continental coalition. This was a much more difficult task than it had been in 1793 when the Prussian and Austrian armies were already engaged in a campaign on French soil. Also the three eastern courts had shown in the years between 1793 and 1797 that they were all much more interested in making individual gains in central Europe than in combining together to destroy the Jacobins of France. The adjustment of their competing territorial claims to Poland by the third Partition somewhat eased tension between them, and the accession of Paul I to the Russian throne in 1796 at first increased the chances of effective Russian intervention in western Europe against the French republic. A spectacular success for Britain at sea seemed the most probable event which might clinch matters and enable Pitt to rebuild the continental coalition upon which a British victory over France depended.

Bonaparte and the Directory gave Pitt his opportunity by launching their invasion of Egypt with quite inadequate naval protection. This stroke was decided upon after Bonaparte early in 1798 had advised the Directory that a direct attack upon the south coast of England would be suicidal as long as British squadrons commanded the Channel. The Egyptian campaign was a natural continuation of the interest taken by the French monarchy in the Levant in the preceding centuries. The Bourbons had used the Turks in their diplomatic combinations and had then exploited their influence at Constantinople to develop French trade. The trading connexion had at the same time contributed to and buttressed the Franco-Turkish political alliance.

In the last days of the monarchy, when French trade in the Levant had lost its earlier buoyancy, French consul-generals in Egypt had urged upon their government the value of Egypt as a source of colonial produce. Cotton, rice, coffee, and sugar could be grown in the Nile delta or else secured by organizing the exchange of French exports with the Arabian and Persian merchants who already frequented Egyptian markets. Equally important, Egypt was the key to the short sea-route to India: in French occupation it at once threatened Britain's position in India and might conceivably even be used as a base in conjunction with Mauritius for an attack on British India. Such an attack would be supported by all the elements in India hostile to British influence, such as Tippoo Sahib, the sultan of Mysore. At the lowest calculation French occupation of Egypt would compensate France for the colonies and trading posts she had lost in the West and East Indies to Britain: at the highest it might lead to a reversal of the decision of 1763 and make France once again the leading colonial and mercantile power.

The feeble monarchy of Louis XVI was too weak and too pre-occupied with problems nearer home to respond to such sugges-tions. Not so the triumphant Jacobins who would stop short at nothing to bring to her knees the only power which dared to con-tinue her single-handed resistance to the French Revolution. One thing which had hampered the monarchy had been its respect for the ancient links, diplomatic and commercial, binding France to Turkey which still exercised a somewhat shadowy suzerainty over Egypt.

The new controllers of French foreign policy had no such scruples and they calculated that Turkey was so weak that the occupation of Egypt was devoid of military or diplomatic risk. Talleyrand, although essentially a man of the old régime, was so anxious to reduce the pressure of French imperialism upon her neighbours that he favoured letting off steam beyond Europe. France should occupy Egypt and then bargain with Austria and Russia for the partition of the Ottoman Empire. If the eastern em-pires were recalcitrant, France could ally herself with Turkey against them. 'By establishing France in Africa we shall guarantee the peace of Europe' he told the Prussian ambassador.[1] Bonaparte was as zealous an advocate of the Egyptian expedition as Talley-rand, but for totally different reasons. He was uninfluenced by Talleyrand's desire to preserve as much as possible of the old régime and heedless of Talleyrand's diplomatic calculations. What he wanted was war and its profits. Where the war was fought was unimportant so long as it yielded victories and spoils. If a direct invasion of Britain was impossible, 'then by all means let us attack her indirectly in Egypt'. The glamour of the east and thoughts of playing the role of a second Alexander the Great may have contri-buted to this decision, but it was based essentially on calculations

[1] Quoted in A. B. Rodger, op. cit., p. 19.

of personal advantage. Impressed by their military and diplomatic advisers, the Directory sanctioned the expedition to Egypt as the best means available of pursuing their vendetta against the British government.

Pitt and his colleagues reacted immediately. Their reaction was not simply or solely due to the French threat to British interests in India and the Levant. Even before news came of Bonaparte's preparations there had been signs in Britain of a more aggressive spirit. The naval mutinies had been ended without disaster. The Dutch and the Spanish fleets had been defeated. The old generation of admirals had been almost eliminated and aggressive young sea-captains, who sneered at Lord Howe's victories because they left the enemy fleet in being, were taking their places. Nelson and his peers resented the stalemate as much as Bonaparte and were anxious to re-enter the Mediterranean in the hope of breaking it. British diplomatists calculated that a dazzling naval victory offered the best chance of bringing about a Second Coalition. Believing that 'the presence of a British squadron in the Mediterranean is a condition upon which the fate of Europe may also be said to depend'[1] the Cabinet authorized a powerful naval squadron to re-enter the Mediterranean.

Nelson seized his chance and annihilated at the battle of the Nile the French fleet which had convoyed Bonaparte to Egypt (August 1798). By this time Bonaparte had made himself master of the Nile delta and early in 1799 marched through Syria to Acre. Failing to take this fortress he returned to Egypt and thence to France. The immediate results of Nelson's victory at the Nile more than justified the calculations of the British government. Instead of temporizing as they had hitherto done the Turks declared war upon France and negotiated an alliance both with Britain and Russia. Austria already had ample reason to reopen the war with France which she had reluctantly concluded at Campo Formio, and the battle of the Nile influenced the timing of her decision. Nelson himself visited Naples after the battle and the Neapolitan sovereigns, equally influenced by fear and hatred of French Jacobinism, rashly attacked the French occupying forces in the Papal states. The war of the Second Coalition had begun.

It was soon apparent that the Second Coalition had learned none of the lessons which it might have learned from the total failure of

[1] Quoted in A. B. Rodger, op. cit., p. 30.

the First. Apart from a vague idea of reducing French power it had
no common purpose: and each of its members had joined in pursuit of particular interests which it had no thought of subordinating
to the general good of Europe or of its allies in the coalition. Even
at the diplomatic level it was somewhat slow to form, while an overall plan of combined operations against the common enemy was
never concluded at all.

The Russian Tsar, after a few months' experience of what he
had fondly hoped would be a crusade, not only retired from the
struggle convinced that Britain and Austria had let him down, but
soon showed an inclination to join his forces with those of France
and fight against his former allies. The Austrians were as dilatory
and incompetent as ever, the Neapolitan army contemptible. Pitt
had squandered the bulk of the trained British army in the war of
the First Coalition and such troops as Britain contributed to the new
continental struggle were mostly still being trained on the model
of Frederick the Great's armies. While Bonaparte was revolutionizing both strategy and tactics, British generals, with the exception
of Sir John Moore, were still fighting the last war but one. Any
chance they may have had of defeating the French was taken from
them by the politicians who gave them 'vague orders, imprecise
information, insufficient artillery, cavalry and transport', told them
'to carry out operations planned on small-scale maps without any
allowance for logistics and the friction of war—and then warned
them that they must at all costs avoid losses, which we could not
afford, and for which they would be held responsible'. No wonder
the ablest of them, Sir Ralph Abercromby, remarked that 'no one
who had not held responsible command under the Pitt–Dundas
Cabinet knew what the risks of war could be'.[1] On the other hand
it may be argued that Pitt in reopening the war, re-establishing
British predominance in the Mediterranean, flinging Napoleon
back upon Europe, and subsidizing and encouraging the continental powers had done all that could reasonably be expected of a
British war minister. His critics are prone to ignore, or at least to
underestimate, the difficulties, internal and international, under
which he had to attempt an impossible task.

At Christmas 1799 the British foreign secretary, Lord Grenville,
in rejecting French feelers for peace, told Bonaparte that the restoration of the Bourbons in France, if not a necessary pre-condition

[1] A. B. Rodger, op. cit., p. 149.

of peace between Britain and France would certainly provide the most satisfactory evidence that France was ready to abandon the policy of subversion and aggression which, in his view, was the root cause of war between the two countries. After the defection of Paul I to France and the organization of the Armed Neutrality, the crushing defeats of Austria at Marengo and Hohenlinden, followed by Austria's withdrawal fron the war by the separate peace of Lunéville (1801), the overrunning of Switzerland, the consolidation of French control over the Netherlands, and the conquest of Naples by French armies, Pitt sued vainly for peace.

A short spell of brilliant successes had been followed by total collapse. France was reassembling her forces for a cross-Channel thrust. The Armed Neutrality closed the Baltic to Britain, forced her to relax the stringency with which she asserted her belligerent rights at sea and deprived her of the naval stores upon which her maritime ascendancy ultimately depended. While these results would be cumulative, the most serious immediate effect of the Armed Neutrality was to deprive Britain of grain imports from the Baltic, without which her increasing population could hardly be fed. Between 1798 and 1801 the price of grain trebled. Sporadic bread riots occurred and the trading classes came to believe that a speedy and lasting peace could alone save them from ruin. In spite of Pitt's best efforts, France was a greater danger to the balance of power in 1800 than she had been a hundred years earlier. The height of Bourbon ambitions had been exceeded; and, had Napoleon Bonaparte known where to stop, French ascendency in Europe might have been established at least for a generation, if not on a lasting basis.

Yet Britain still held valuable cards in any negotiation for peace with France. The stalemate between a dominant sea and a dominant land power which had been established on the collapse of the First Coalition remained unresolved. At sea Britain had clearly strengthened her position. If access to the Baltic was now threatened she once again controlled the Mediterranean. In September 1801 the last French soldier left Egypt. The most important French and Dutch colonies were securely in British hands. The new generation of naval officers had won decisive victories. The Dutch fleet had been almost eliminated and the French and Spanish weakened and demoralized. Nelson and his fellow captains were ready to enter the Baltic and test the fighting strength of the

Armed Neutrality. The naval battle of Copenhagen (March 1801) and the assassination of Tsar Paul removed for the time being the immediate threat of the Armed Neutrality.

Pitt's resignation, not itself due to issues immediately connected with the war, transferred to his successors, headed by Addington, responsibility for ending the war of the Second Coalition. The day before news of the surrender of the French at Alexandria reached London Pitt's successors signed a preliminary treaty of peace with France. Overseas Britain retained Ceylon and Trinidad; but she gave up all her other conquests in the East and West Indies while, by returning the Cape of Good Hope to the Dutch and Malta and Egypt to their former owners, she abandoned control of what were now coming to be recognized as alternative routes to India.

Even so, such surrender of colonial conquests might have been justifiable had Addington's government used them to purchase a European settlement in accordance with British desires and interests. In Bonaparte's view the British government had no right even to be consulted about the reconstruction of Europe, upon which he was already busily engaged, and the clauses in the preliminary treaty which dealt with these issues were so vague as to be valueless.

In the negotiation leading up to the definitive peace treaty of Amiens (March 1802) the British government failed to remedy the faults of the preliminaries and even made further concessions to France in regard to Malta. Britain failed also to secure the restoration of her rights under the Franco-British commercial treaty of 1786, still less any recognition by France of her belligerent naval rights of search and blockade. A British government so powerless to assert its own cherished interests could not be expected to do anything effective for its continental allies, still less for exiled protégés, notably the Savoyard ruler of Piedmont and the stadholder of the United Provinces.

By signing the definitive treaty Addington's government came near to recognizing that while Bonaparte was free to seek commercial and colonial gains for France, Britain was debarred from interference with his reconstruction of Europe to consolidate French hegemony. When this was tardily recognized there was an immediate reaction in London against the treaty of Amiens and the men who had negotiated it. Partly under this pressure, and partly because they had allowed themselves through indecision and inexperience to be pushed further by the French negotiators than they had intended or indeed realized at the time, Addington's government almost at once began to argue that the treaty of Amiens contained an implied guarantee by France of the existing state of affairs in Europe. Any alteration as a result of French action gave Britain a right of intervention either to prevent change or to secure compensation for any advantage gained by France.

The diametrically divergent interpretations of the clauses of the treaty of Amiens held at Paris and in London rendered certain a speedy renewal of the war. The disappointment of the British commercial classes with the immediate consequences of the peace treaty tended in the same direction. Bonaparte advanced French military domination and economic exploitation of western and central Europe and at the same time resumed the policy of overseas expansion which had been temporarily stopped by British victories in the war of the Second Coalition. The British government on the other hand not only ordered the evacuation of its colonial conquests but reduced the navy and abolished income tax. Sebastiani's mission to North Africa and the Levant and the publication of a report in which he expressed the opinion that an army of 10,000 men would be sufficient to reconquer Egypt, caused a sensation in London. Addington had to change his policy and decided not to evacuate Malta but to treat it as a French pledge for the restoration on the Continent of the conditions which had prevailed when the treaty of Amiens had been signed. While the attitude of Addington's government was no doubt morally justifiable it was legally indefensible. After charging Bonaparte repeatedly with breaches of the peace treaty, which they then condoned, they now unquestionably violated one of its most important clauses. By May 1803 Britain and France were again at war.

It is needless to trace the later vicissitudes of the struggle against Napoleonic domination of Europe in which Britain played so distinguished a part. It is sufficient to remember that memories of the struggle were to overshadow the relations of Britain and France in the nineteenth century even more than the shadow of Louis XIV had done in the eighteenth. In foreign affairs as in other spheres the early promise of the French Revolution, with its fraternal slogans, was not to be fulfilled. In dealing with each other the national governments of the nineteenth century stepped into the shoes of the enlightened despots. The emergent peoples of Europe associated themselves with the foreign policies of *ci-devant* rulers.

That Britain and France under the changing conditions of the nineteenth century contrived to avoid war with each other was due neither to lack of hostility nor to a deliberate reversal of eighteenth-century traditions, but to changed internal and international conditions which affected both countries.

A. *Primary Sources*

Annals and Correspondence of the Viscount and the First and Second Earls of Stair, ed. J. M. Graham (2 vols., Edinburgh and London, 1875)

British Diplomatic Instructions, ed. L. G. Wickham Legg (4 vols., Camden Society, 1925–34)

Colonel St. Paul of Ewart, Soldier and Diplomat, ed. G. G. Butler (2 vols., 1911)

Correspondence of John, Fourth Duke of Bedford, ed. Lord John Russell, (3 vols., 1842–6) [especially useful for the negotiation of the peace of Paris, 1763]

Despatches of Earl Gower, ed. O. Browning (Cambridge, 1885)

Despatches from Paris 1784–89, ed. O. Browning (Camden Series, 1909–10)

H.M.C. Polwarth MSS., vols. 1–4 (1911–42) [especially for Polwarth's correspondence as British representative at the Congress of Cambrai]

Journal and Correspondence of William Eden, Baron Auckland from 1771 to 1814, (4 vols., 1861–2) [especially for the negotiation of the commercial treaty of 1786]

Memorials and Correspondence of Charles James Fox, ed. Lord John Russell, vol. 4 (1857) [for negotiations at end of the war of American Independence]

Recueil des Instructions données aux ambassadeurs et ministres de France . . . Angleterre, vols. 2–3 (Paris, 1929, 1965)

B. *Secondary Authorities*

Andrews, C. M., 'Anglo-French Commercial Rivalry 1700–1750' in *AHR* 20 (1914–15), 761–80

Ballot, C., *Les Négociations à Lille* (Paris, 1910)

Bamford, P. W., 'French Shipping in Northern European Trade 1660–1789' in *JMH* 26 (1954), 207–19

Bardot, J., 'Essai d'une définition psychologique de la diplomatie britannique et de la diplomatie française' in *RHD* 41 (1938), 292–315 [almost entirely on the 19th and 20th centuries]

Bemis, S. F., 'British secret service and the French-American Alliance [1775–83]' in *AHR* 29 (1923–4), 474–95

Bourguet, A., 'Le duc de Choiseul et l'Angleterre' in *RH* 71 (1899), 1–32 [Bussy's mission to London]

— 'Le duc de Choiseul et l'Angleterre' in *RHD* 17 (1903), 456–68 and 541–56 [deals with negotiations in Seven Years war]

Bowden, W., 'The English Manufacturers and the Commercial Treaty with France' in *AHR* 25 (1919–20), 18–35

Bowman, H. M., *The Preliminary Stages of the Peace of Amiens* (Toronto, 1899)

Brandt, O., *England und die napoleonische Weltpolitik* [1800–3] (Heidelberg, 1906)

Bromley, J. S., 'The French Privateering War 1702–13' in *Essays Presented to David Ogg*, ed. H. E. Bell and R. L. Ollard (1963)

Brown, Vera Lee, *Studies in the History of Spain in the second half of the 18th century*; no. 2, 'Anglo-French Rivalry for the Trade of the Spanish Peninsula 1763–83' (Northampton, Mass., 1930)

Burner, A., 'Le Poète Destouches diplomate. Sa mission à Londres (1717–1723)' in *RHD* 43 (1929), 183–217 and 278–96

Cahen, L., 'Une nouvelle interprétation du traité franco-anglais en 1786–87' in *RH* 185 (1939), 257–85

Caudrillier, G., *L'Association royaliste de l'Institut philanthropique à Bordeaux et la conspiration anglaise en France pendant la seconde coalition* (Paris, 1908)

Cobban, A., 'The Beginning of the Channel Isles Correspondence, 1789–1794' in *EHR* 77 (1962), 37–52

— 'British Secret Service in France, 1784–1792' in *EHR* 69 (1954), 226–61

Coquelle, P., *Napoléon et l'Angleterre* (1904, transl. G. D. Knox, London, 1904)

— 'L'espionnage en Angleterre pendant la guerre de Sept-Ans' in *RHD* 14 (1900), 508 ff.

— 'Les projets de descente en Angleterre' in *RHD* 15 (1901), 433–52, 591–624, part 2 (1902), 134–57

— 'Les Responsabilités de la Rupture de la Paix d'Amiens en 1803' in *RHD* 15, part 2 (1902), 267–302

Corwin, E. S., 'The French Objective in the American Revolution' in *AHR* 21 (1915–16), 33–61

Cottin, P., *Toulon et les anglais en 1793* (Paris, 1898)

Doniol, H., 'La Première Négociation de la Paix entre la France et le Grande-Bretagne [1783]' in *RHD* 6 (1892), 56–61

— 'Tentatives de l'Angleterre en 1781 et 1782 pour amener la France à traiter de la paix' in *RHD* 14 (1900), 161–98

Dureng, Jean, *Le duc de Bourbon et l'Angleterre (1723–1726)* (Paris, 1911)

Eves, C. S., *Matthew Prior* (New York, 1939)

Faguier, B. du, 'Le duc d'Aiguillon et l'Angleterre' [1771–73] in *RHD* 26 (1912), 607–27

Fryer, W. R., *Republic or Restoration in France? 1794–1797* (Manchester, 1965) [based on William Wickham's papers]

Gabory, E., *L'Angleterre et la Vendée* (2 vols., Paris, 1930–1)

Gill, Conrad, 'The Relations between England and France in 1802' in *EHR* 24 (1907), 61–78

Godechot, J., 'Le Directoire vu de Londres' in *Annales historiques de la Révolution française* 21 (1949), 310–36.

Gooch, G. P., 'Europe and the French Revolution' in *Cambridge Modern History* VIII (1904), 754–90

Grant, W. L., 'Mission de M. de Bussy à Londres en 1761' in *RHD* 20 (1906), 351–66

— 'Canada versus Guadeloupe' in *AHR* 17 (1911–12), 735–43

Grose, C. L., 'England and Dunkirk' in *AHR* 39 (1933–4), 26–27

Henderson, W. O., 'The Anglo-French Commercial Treaty of 1786' in *EcHR* 10 (1957–8), 104–12

Hotblack, Kate, 'Peace of Paris 1763' in *TRHS* 3rd series, 2 (1908), 235–67

Hutt, M., 'Spies in France 1793–1808' in *History Today* 12 (1962), 158–67

Jollivet, M., *Les Anglais dans la Méditerranée: un royaume anglo-corse, 1794–1797* (Paris, 1896)

King, A., 'The Relations of the British Government with the Émigrés and Royalists of Western France, 1793–95' (unpublished London Ph.D. thesis, 1931)

Lebon, A., *L'Angleterre et l'émigration française de 1794 à 1801* (Paris, 1882)

Legg, L. G. W., *Matthew Prior* (Cambridge, 1921)

Lodge, Sir Richard, 'The Anglo-French Alliance, 1716–31' in *Studies in Anglo-French history during the eighteenth, nineteenth and twentieth centuries*, ed. A. Coville and H. Temperley (Cambridge, 1935)

— *Studies in Eighteenth Century Diplomacy* (1930) [especially for Franco-British peace negotiations at the end of the Austrian Succession war]

Lord, W. F., *England and France in the Mediterranean* (1901)

Mantoux, P., 'French Reports of British Parliamentary Debates in the Eighteenth Century' in *AHR* 12 (1906–7), 244–69

Mitchell, H., *The Underground War against Revolutionary France 1794–1800* (Oxford, 1965)

Morison, M. C., 'The Duc de Choiseul and the Invasion of England 1768–1770' in *TRHS* 3rd series, 4 (1910), 82–115

Pallain, G., *La Mission de Talleyrand à Londres en 1792* (Paris, 1889)

Patterson, A. Temple, *The Other Armada* (Manchester, 1960) [for the Franco-Spanish invasion project of 1779]

Philippson, M., 'La paix d'Amiens' in *RH* 75 (1901), 236–318 and ibid. 76 (1901), 47–68

Pinon, R., 'Vergennes et la grande Lutte contre l'Angleterre (1774–1789)' in *RHD* 43 (1929), 37–64

Ramsey, J. F., *Anglo-French Relations 1763–70: a Study of Choiseul's Foreign Policy* (Berkeley, California, 1939)

Rashed, Z. E., *The Peace of Paris* (Liverpool, 1951)

Reinhard, M., 'Les Négociations de Lille et la Crise du 18 fructidor d'après la correspondance inédite de Colchen' in *Revue d'histoire moderne et contemporaine* 5 (1958), 38–56

Rich, E. E., 'The Hudson's Bay Company and the Treaty of Utrecht' in *CHJ* 11 (1953–5), 183–203

Richards, N. F., 'British Policy and the Problem of Monarchy in France, 1789–1802' (London Ph.D. thesis 1954, unpublished)

Robitaille, G., 'Les preliminaires diplomatiques de la guerre de sept ans' in *Proceedings and Transactions of the Royal Society of Canada* 3rd series, XXXIII (1939), 109–26 and XXXIV (1940), 91–99 [historically worthless but offers interesting sidelights on French Canadian nationalism]

Savelle, M., *Diplomatic History of the Canadian Boundary 1749–63* (1940)

Schorer, H., 'Der englisch-französische Handelsvertrag von Jahre 1713' in *HJ* 21 (1900), 353–87, 715–42

Sutherland, L. S., 'The East India Company and the Peace of Paris' in *EHR* 62, 179–90

Thomson, Mark A., 'Louis XIV and the Grand Alliance 1705–10' in *BIHR* 34 (1961), 16–35

— 'Louis XIV and William III' in *EHR* 76 (1961), 37–58

Trevelyan, G. M., 'The "Jersey" Period of the Negotiations leading to the Peace of Utrecht' in *EHR* 49 (1934), 100–5

Vaucher, P., *Robert Walpole et la Politique de Fleury 1731–42* (Paris, 1924)

Wiesener, Louis, *Le régent, l'abbé Dubois et les Anglais d'après les sources britanniques* (3 vols., Paris, 1891–9)

Williams, D., 'The Missions of David Williams and James Tilby Matthews to England (1793)' in *EHR* 53 (1938), 651–68

Williamson, A., Mrs. (*King* is her maiden name *supra*), 'Jersey, centre d'espionnage au début de la période révolutionnaire' in *Revue d'histoire moderne* 9 (1934), 423–54

Wilson, A. M., *The Foreign Policy of Cardinal Fleury 1726–43* (Cambridge, Mass., 1936)

Note. A key to the abbreviated titles of periodicals mentioned above and in the other bibliographies printed in this book will be found below on p. 390. Sources and works on Anglo-French cultural and social contacts are excluded. They are listed in Pargellis and Medley's bibliography (see below, p. 385).

CHAPTER 4

Great Britain and the Dutch

IF France was the natural enemy of Britain in the eighteenth century, few Englishmen before the second half of the century doubted that the United Provinces were designed by Providence for the role of Britain's friend. Without Dutch help William III could hardly have forced Louis XIV to recognize him at Ryswick as king of Great Britain. Nor without Dutch contributions, belated and inadequate as they were felt to be in the later stages of the Spanish Succession war, could Marlborough and Eugene have brought Louis XIV's triumphal career to an inglorious close. As long as the shadow of the sun-king fell across Europe, so long were Britain and the United Provinces forced willy-nilly to co-operate in diplomacy and war.

William III's foreign policy as stadholder of the United Provinces has been criticized by some Dutch historians precisely on the ground that he taught the Dutch to depend upon British co-operation instead of relying upon their own resources. His foreign policy as king of Great Britain was criticized at the time in England on the ground that his continental wars were waged in the interests of the United Provinces and were proving so expensive that they would soon bring about the ruin of England. Some Tories may well have believed that William's continental wars were deliberately intended by him to secure this latter object and thereby to remove a growing menace to Dutch commercial supremacy.

Indeed close and harmonious diplomatic and military co-operation could hardly be expected between two states which had fought three wars against each other in the generation before the Glorious Revolution, especially as the peace treaties at the end of these wars had done little to decide the basic Anglo-Dutch conflicts which had brought about the wars. If Dutch commercial supremacy in Europe could hardly be questioned, England had seized considerable tracts of colonial territory in America, which were so located as to be of great strategic and economic value, from the Dutch, who nevertheless retained important footholds in the West Indies. In the east something like a division of spheres of interest had been attained, though such informal agreements are always liable to be overturned either by a change of heart on the part of the participants or by external forces. Britain was now tending to concentrate her eastern trade upon India, while recognizing tacitly the exclusive rights of the Dutch in the spice islands of Indonesia.

Even in the heyday of the Anglo-Dutch alliance under William III there were acute tensions, which were kept in restraint only by the personal authority of the king-stadholder. Tory opposition to his involvement of Britain in continental diplomacy and wars was hardly more vocal in England than the covert resistance of the Amsterdam burgomasters and other commercial oligarchies in the United Provinces to the wars waged by the stadholder with France. The murder of the republican leader John de Witt and the Orange *coup d'état* of 1672 was neither forgiven nor forgotten by Dutch opponents of Orange.

The rich merchants of Amsterdam resented the contributions to war costs which William III's policy imposed upon them just as much as the Tory squires in England hated a war-time land tax at four shillings in the pound. Indeed the Dutch burghers had more cause for complaint than English landlords, who must have benefited to some extent when the English economy was placed on a war footing. In spite of resolute attempts on the part of the Dutch to carry on business as usual during wars, enemy action and restrictions imposed by their own government inevitably limited the amount of foreign trade and reduced the profitability of what was left. If some Dutch republicans felt themselves to be insulted by the mere existence of the stadholderate, they certainly believed that the policy of William III and Heinsius was injurious and contrary to their interests.

The outstanding achievements of the Dutch republic in the sixteenth and seventeenth centuries were precarious and unlikely to be maintained in the changing Europe of the eighteenth century. In comparison with their neighbours and rivals the Dutch were a tiny people. At the beginning of the eighteenth century France had a population of about 18 million, Britain 6 million, and the United Provinces less than 2 million. The Dutch were poorer in natural resources and their territories were more vulnerable. It is more surprising that they played the part they did in international politics for so much of the eighteenth century than that they should finally have sunk into insignificance. Had they allowed themselves to be dragged into successive crises of power politics and resulting wars by interventionist British governments, they would merely have rushed to meet disaster. Non-intervention, and neutral wiles and stratagems, if they made the Dutch unpopular with both sides, at least helped postpone the day of final reckoning.

It is customary to find the key to Dutch internal politics in the struggle between the house of Orange, depicted as the consistent advocates of centralization, and the merchant oligarchies of the leading towns, above all of Holland itself, regarded as the champions of devolution and the defenders of local privileges, which gave them political importance and enabled them to advance their economic interests. From the point of view of foreign policy this traditional view is reinforced by the generalization that the regent party were isolationists and friends of France, while the supporters of the house of Orange favoured active intervention in European politics and believed that a close alliance with Britain was the condition of Dutch national security and independence.

It is easier to criticize this view, and show that there are many exceptions to it, than to substitute any other generalization as helpful to the foreign student of Dutch politics in the eighteenth century. Even when there was a stadholder there is remarkably little evidence that he sought to use his constitutional position to link the seven united provinces more closely together. William III had never used his pre-eminent authority to effect constitutional changes, but had preferred to use what would have been called in England 'influence' to reduce the regents to a position of dependence upon himself. It was in the stadholderless period, immediately after the end of the war of the Spanish Succession that the only serious attempt was made to reform the constitution and it was made by Simon van Slingelandt, a member of the burgher oligarchy, who a few years later was elected grand pensionary of Holland.

William IV, before his *coup d'état* in 1747, had shown himself to be skilled in using constitutional forms and local privileges to obstruct in Friesland the policy of the grand pensionary of Holland. After 1747 he made no attempt to counteract provincial particularism, far less to transform the United Provinces into a modern unitary state. His successor, William V, described himself as no friend to innovations: it was his duty as stadholder to preserve everyone in his established rights and privileges. By the closing years of the eighteenth century the Orange and regent parties, both basically conservative, had been forced to co-operate by the rise of the 'patriot' movement, inspired by the French Revolution. The more extreme 'patriots' were as much a threat to local oligarchies of regents as to the position of the house of Orange. And what finally brought about unity and centralization in the provinces was conquest by the armies of revolutionary France.

Professor Geyl has rendered a valuable service by insisting that the division between 'Orangists' and 'Statists' was less fundamental than used to be thought; though he would be the last person to deny its existence. The stadholders, and the supporters they attracted from the classes below the republican autocracies, were the only political force capable of resisting and counteracting the preponderance of these local oligarchies both in Dutch politics and social life. On the other hand he denounces the myth that the stadholders did anything effective to reform the constitution or to strengthen such central authority as existed, far less to offer such a political education to the lower orders as might have enabled them to play an effective role in the local estates or even perhaps in the States-General. The lower middle class served as civic guards, usually under officers with Orange sympathies; but their role in politics was that of the ventriloquist's dummy. Neither Orangists nor Statists, under normal conditions, were prepared to have their duologue interrupted by popular tumult. At the very end of the eighteenth century, inspired and aided by foreign troops, burgher democracy overthrew the stadholderian system and the Holland regent régime, which had flourished in its shadow.

Until this happened in 1795 sovereignty was vested in the Estates of each of the seven provinces. These were composed of delegations from privileged towns and provincial nobility. The Estates of Holland, for example, consisted of delegations from eighteen towns and a committee of noblemen. Each of these towns was controlled by a corporation, the members of which, known as 'regents', were appointed for life, vacancies being filled by co-optation. The burgomasters and other officials were appointed annually by the regents without reference to their fellow citizens.

So long as there was no stadholder, i.e. from 1702 to 1747, the 'regents' in the seven independent provinces virtually controlled the foreign policy of the United Provinces. Each province sent representatives to the States-General, which sat in permanent session at The Hague. All questions of foreign policy were discussed by a special committee of the States-General, the *Secreet Besogne*. The leading member of the deputation sent by the province of Holland to the States-General was a permanent member of this committee, as was also the Greffier, who was appointed for life to act as secretary to the States-General. The other members of the committee were one representative of each province; and they were liable to be changed frequently. If the committee reached agreement, its recommendations were discussed by the States-General. Then, if there was disagreement or if some members felt that their instructions did not cover the particular case, the decision had to be referred back to the Estates of the seven provinces and even, in the case of some provinces, to the towns which were represented in the provincial Estates.

The only hope of short-circuiting these protracted deliberations was to persuade the grand pensionary to exert his personal influence to secure approval from his colleagues in the Estates of Holland. Then, backed by the support of the leading province, the recommendation stood some chance of being accepted by the *Secreet Besogne* and in its turn by the States-General. Diplomatists therefore tended to treat the grand pensionary almost as foreign secretary of the Union. Next to him the Greffier was usually the most influential Dutchman, so far at least as foreign affairs were concerned. Even when the stadholderate was restored in 1747, the importance of these two officials was not greatly diminished.

William's death, and the increasing strain which the Spanish Succession war imposed on both countries, brought these barely concealed tensions more and more into the open. The Dutch decision to take part in this war was almost as dilatory and reluctant as the English. Just as Louis XIV's recognition of the Old Pretender with its threat to English national security and the Anglican Church eventually brought England into the war, so did his highhanded actions in the Spanish Netherlands and implied threats to the European balance of power force the Dutch to take part.

Both England and the United Provinces were motivated also by commercial ambitions in the Netherlands and more particularly in Spain and Spanish America. The various measures of the new government of Spain, clearly inspired from France, in favour of French merchants and capitalists were equally alarming to the

Dutch and English commercial classes. But while they could combine to thwart the commercial hopes of France, they failed to reach agreement on the division of mercantile profits which were expected to accrue to both on a successful conclusion of the war.

Against the plea that the war was damaging Dutch trade, upon which the solvency of the United Provinces rested, British statesmen found it harder and harder to extract from the Dutch what they regarded as the minimum acceptable contribution to the waging of successive campaigns and the maintenance of the fleets which were required to support the armies in the field and even launch expeditions against the French in Canada. The Dutch, on the other hand, clearly felt that as the war had developed and war-aims had expanded far beyond the modest claims of 1702, Britain stood to gain much more than the United Provinces. This increased the normal reluctance of a commercially minded people to continue the war.

The British government resorted to threats and promises. If the Dutch persisted in their attitude and withdrew from the war then Britain would take for herself all the commercial advantages to be obtained from France. Concurrently they made more and more extensive promises, notably in the Townshend treaty of 1709, of economic advantage for Holland if the Dutch would continue to take their fair share of the burdens of war. But they inwardly agreed with the view to be expressed by Canning a century later that 'in matters of commerce the fault of the Dutch is offering too little and asking too much'.

When peace was finally made, the Dutch were awarded a reasonable Barrier in the Netherlands[1] and some prospect of commercial predominance there; but Bolingbroke had gone back on the promises of his Whig predecessors to do considerably more than this for the Dutch burghers. In particular Britain had secured for herself exclusive trading privileges with Spanish America which, according to previous agreements, she was bound to share with her Dutch ally. These advantages proved in the long run derisory and even dangerous; but at the time both the British who gained them and the Dutch who were excluded from them believed that they would become the substructure of a vast and lucrative trade with the south seas.

[1] See P. Geyl, *The Netherlands in the Seventeenth Century, Part II, 1648–1715* (London, 1964), for maps showing the Barriers of 1678–1701, 1709, and 1715.

Nor was the way in which these terms were first adjusted between Britain and France, and only then communicated to the Dutch on a 'take them or leave them' basis, likely to recommend them to a power which had been accustomed to play a leading role in international politics for more than a century. Although the United Provinces, unlike Austria, decided to accept the proffered terms and made peace side by side with Britain at Utrecht, the terms of the treaty and the way in which it was negotiated did almost as much damage to Britain's relations with the Dutch as it did to her alliance with Austria.[1]

The course of war affected the prevalent English attitude to the Dutch in other ways. When the war began in 1702 it seemed that the Dutch alliance offered the best, if not the only, hope of preserving English Protestantism from destruction. Once this threat had been removed by Marlborough's victories many Englishmen, like Swift, saw in Protestant dissent a more dangerous enemy to the Anglican Church than the declining Roman Catholic minority in England. The Dissenters were not content with the limited toleration granted to them in 1689: they wanted religious equality and quoted the United Provinces as an illustration of the practicability and national advantages to be derived from full religious freedom. The more English Dissenters and Low Churchmen appealed to Dutch precept and example, the more hostile High Church Tories came to be to the Dutch. Religious freedom such as the Dutch enjoyed was often regarded as the first step towards infidelity and immorality.

In politics the Dutch had persistently resisted the Tory policy of making peace with France and restoring peace to war-worn Europe. 'Dutch-hearted' Whigs ought to be rooted out as a fifth column from English political life. Tory pamphleteers did not explain how the Dutch, who had had to be heavily bribed by their Whig allies in 1709 to continue in the war at all, had suddenly become bellicose warmongers in 1710.

When peace had been concluded, it was followed by a marked improvement in Anglo-Dutch relations. The successes of the Spanish Succession war had been won by the co-operation of Marlborough and the Whigs in England with Heinsius and his friends in the United Provinces. The return of the Whigs to power

[1] See, for a full and authoritative study of the relations between Great Britain and the Dutch before and during the Spanish Succession war, P. Geyl, op. cit.

in England in 1714 was naturally greeted by the Dutch as a good augury for the future.

Townshend, at first the leading minister of George I's English team, was well known at The Hague as the negotiator of the treaty of 1709 and in spite of the failure of that treaty he continued to be popular and respected. Stanhope, although his father had served for a time as ambassador to the United Provinces, was less known; and what was known about him was not thought to be much in his favour. He was thought of as a professional soldier whose military career had come to an inglorious end at Brihuega—a battle which had also contributed to the fall of the Whigs from power. And after Stanhope's transfer from a military to a political career the policies which he advocated and followed made the Dutch even more suspicious of him. He was regarded as one of the 'furious Whigs', of whom Peterborough was a notorious example. If he was not actually intent on reopening the war with France, he was certainly advocating a policy which might well have this result. And the thought of another war with France sent a *frisson* of fear and dismay through the stoutest of the not-too-stout Dutch hearts.

More important in determining the course of Anglo-Dutch relations than these personal considerations was the personal union of Great Britain and Hanover which followed the death of Queen Anne. As elector of Hanover George I had many contacts with the United Provinces. Geographical propinquity, common Protestantism, a shared suspicion of French political and military aggression leading to military co-operation against France in the campaigns of the Spanish Succession war, all tended to bring them together. And both states were becoming uneasy at the ambitions in their immediate neighbourhood of Brandenburg-Prussia, which had acquired part of Gelderland as a reward for her services in the Spanish Succession war and would clearly not remain satisfied for long with such a modest acquisition.

On the other hand, when George I showed that he was determined to put into operation his predecessors' schemes to acquire from Sweden the secularized bishoprics of Bremen and Verden and thereby gain for Hanover a share in control of the lower Elbe, the Dutch commercial classes feared interference from Hanover with their trade in central Germany. Even this suspicion was counteracted to some extent by the reflection that Bremen and Verden were actually in the possession of the Danes, who were clearly a more dangerous commercial rival of the Dutch than Hanover could ever be. From the point of view of Dutch trade, Hanover was a better custodian of Bremen and Verden than the rightful owner, Sweden, or the rival claimant, Denmark.

At the beginning of the new reign in England, the king himself, his English ministers and his Hanoverian advisers were all agreed on the importance of the United Provinces for their foreign policy. This belief was strengthened by the outbreak of the Jacobite rebellion in 1715, when the Dutch gladly and promptly fulfilled their treaty obligation to supply 6,000 troops to uphold the Protestant succession in England. It is true that the political effectiveness of this gesture was somewhat diminished by subsequent discussions over its financial implications.

Another force helped to restore cordial relations between the two countries. The Northern war was still going on and reached a protracted climax after the return of Charles XII from exile in the Ottoman empire. Swedes and Russians sought by every means in their power to wage economic as well as military and naval warfare against each other. Restrictions culminating in a total embargo upon neutral trade with their enemies were imposed and their imposition attempted by rival naval squadrons. Britain found herself for once in the position of a neutral power which fiercely resented belligerent attempts to restrict her commercial activity in the Baltic.

The Dutch were at first prepared to co-operate by sending joint naval squadrons into the Baltic sufficiently strong to beat off attacks either by Sweden or Russia and to convoy British and Dutch merchant vessels to the Baltic ports where they wished to trade. But unfortunately George I deliberately exploited the presence of a British fleet in the Baltic to influence the course of the war in the interest of Hanover, and represented to his allies that the help indirectly afforded them by the British fleet justified him in demanding Bremen and Verden for Hanover. The Dutch absolutely declined to become involved in these Hanoverian schemes and ceased to send convoys into the Baltic. Even in defence of trade they had become sluggish and uncertain in action.

But the touchstone of Anglo-Dutch relations for a year or two after the treaty of Utrecht continued to be the negotiation of the terms of a new Barrier treaty. Here the Dutch were in a strong position in so far as they now controlled most of the former

Spanish Netherlands. Before they would admit Austrian troops they insisted upon three conditions. Austria must hand over some strategically important fortresses to be garrisoned by Dutch troops, settle the relationships between the commanders of these troops and the Austrian authorities and, out of the revenues of the former Spanish Netherlands, appropriate funds sufficient for the upkeep of the garrisons or at least make a substantial contribution towards it. On this question Townshend was on the whole sympathetic to the Dutch point of view.

But the Dutch also insisted that the Barrier treaty must include clauses which would perpetuate, if not further improve, the trading advantages which they already enjoyed in the Netherlands under former treaties with Spain. Austria pointed out that she was not very anxious to rule the Netherlands and would have preferred to exchange them for some German territory, preferably Bavaria. If she must in the end accept the Netherlands under the heavy burden of maintaining the Dutch garrisons in the Barrier fortresses, then she should be free to develop the industries and foreign trade of her new subjects without artificial restrictions imposed for the benefit of the Dutch. Here the British government was rather undecided. As the leading commercial rival of the Dutch, she might have been expected to join with Austria in protesting against Dutch exploitation of the Netherlands. On the other hand she was tempted to side with the Dutch and to demand a share in the advantages they hoped to secure for themselves.

Once the Barrier treaty was signed in November 1715 and ratified by the Dutch, with their customary hesitancy, in January 1716, it became possible to try and restore what British politicians and diplomatists of the mid-eighteenth century loved to call 'the old system' of alliances, i.e. a coalition of Britain, Austria and the United Provinces against France. Townshend had set his heart on this as soon as he came into office, and the death of Louis XIV in September 1715 at first made no difference to his plans. Though the Barrier treaty was usually regarded as an essential step towards the restoration of the old system, the methods used by Townshend to secure Charles VI's signature, and the humiliation the Emperor felt over its terms made the attainment of his ultimate aims more, rather than less, difficult.

For one thing it had become clear during the Barrier negotiation that many Dutchmen would have preferred a tripartite treaty of guarantee of the Netherlands with Austria and France to the solution forced upon them by British pressure. This would have given the United Provinces better security than they in fact obtained and would have been much less costly. Austria might even have been able to develop the economic resources of the Netherlands without rousing to frenzy the commercial classes of the two Maritime Powers. France would not have felt as a grievance a régime in the Netherlands to which she had freely consented, whereas she was constantly tempted to pull down a Barrier that she was well aware was too weak to resist her armed might.

Moreover, it soon became clear that the Barrier treaty, instead of strengthening the links between the Maritime Powers and Austria, by giving them a common interest in the defence of the Netherlands against France, was in fact to prove a source of weakness and division between them. Austria regarded herself as the legitimate successor of Spain as sovereign in the former Spanish Netherlands. Charles VI and Maria Theresa bitterly resented the imposition of restrictions upon their rights of sovereignty and were determined to reduce them to nullity in practice, if not in international law. The Maritime Powers were bound to resist such attempts tooth and nail. As the duke of Newcastle put it, they believed that the Netherlands were now a kind of common country in which all three powers—Austria, Britain, and the United Provinces—were equally interested.

Even between the two Maritime Powers there was genuine agreement on only two points, one political and the other economic, with regard to the Netherlands. France must be prevented from dominating them and Austria must be prevented from reviving their commercial prosperity; and for a generation after the treaty of Utrecht the second problem caused far more international tension than the first. It was Austria's persistent attempts to develop economically the territories she had acquired in the Low Countries that did something to hold the Maritime Powers together when the changing attitude of France was tending to make them drift apart. Common dislike of Austria's economic policies helped to conceal the real divergence of interest between Britain and the United Provinces in the Austrian Netherlands.

The death of Louis XIV changed the diplomatic situation before Townshend had made any progress in his attempts to bring together the Dutch and the Emperor in a new league against France.

Followed as it was five years later by the death of Heinsius, pensionary of the province of Holland and the political heir of William III, it made possible a relaxation of tension between France and the United Provinces. In this changing atmosphere, the Dutch commercial oligarchies could now openly press their mercantile interests, which no longer conflicted with overriding considerations of political security and national independence. They had no doubts that Britain was a more dangerous competitor than France in what was already becoming for some purposes a world economy; and they saw means by which the basic political and economic conflict between Britain and France could be exploited to their own commercial advantage.

By blackmailing France with the threat of co-operation with Britain and Austria, they hoped to keep the French out of the Netherlands. By threatening to co-operate with France or at least to remain neutral, they believed they could maintain their economic stranglehold over the Austrian Netherlands and force Britain, when she was at war with France, to tolerate the extension of Dutch trade by connivance with France. The practical application of these ideas is seen most clearly in the opening years of the Austrian Succession and Seven Years wars, but they existed throughout the period.

The extent to which such Dutch threats could influence British foreign policy is not always realized by students who read back into the eighteenth century the international situation of their own day. In Europe generally, until the mid-century at least, the Dutch were still thought of as a Great Power. As late as Adam Smith's day, and even by such an acute observer as Smith himself, they were regarded as the leading mercantile state. Economic theorists deplored the backwardness of England and constantly held up the example of the Dutch for imitation. Their shipbuilding techniques, their commercial regulations, their exploitation of other people's fisheries, their development of banking, insurance and foreign exchange, their successful avoidance of war, their exportation of capital, gained by international trade, for investment in politically stable but economically under-developed countries, notably Britain, were all held worthy of respect and imitation.

In retrospect economic weaknesses may be detected, but they either escaped notice or were not regarded as important by contemporaries. As international trade developed quantitatively the tendency was to cut out the Dutch middlemen and for the rising industrial and commercial countries to trade directly with each other and merely adjust balances by bills on Amsterdam. Even in the seventeenth century the industrial basis for the Dutch extended system of commerce had been relatively weak: by the mid-eighteenth century it hardly existed. Dutch success in avoiding war had indirect results not appreciated by contemporaries who thought of war as the enemy of economic development. Much of the industrial strength of Britain and France by the end of the eighteenth century was a direct product of the needs of a war economy. On the contrary there was a marked decline in Dutch textile industry and shipbuilding. Wages in Holland, partly owing to heavy excise duties on the working man's food, were higher than in either France or Britain, the main competitors with Dutch industry and commerce. Excessive labour costs were pricing the Leyden cloth manufacturers out of international markets, while the high cost of shipbuilding and the rise in seamen's wages were depriving the Dutch of the competitive advantages they had formerly enjoyed in international trade. No wonder it seemed to the Dutch burgomasters that war was a luxury their country could not afford. Even in the long period of peace which they secured between 1713 and the war of American Independence there was a rise in state expenditure and public debt which imposed heavy burdens upon an economy that was no longer buoyant if not actually declining.[1] And as the century went on, less and less Dutch capital was devoted to enterprises with a substantial element of risk but which, if successful, would yield fantastic profits. Many Dutch merchants preferred to devote themselves to banking or insurance or even to become bondholders with heavy stakes in the British national debt.

Another weakness was the virtual disappearance of Dutch naval power after the Spanish Succession war. This was not due to deliberate policy, although it was no doubt partly due to the determination of the burgher oligarchies not to be dragged by England into another war. Even in England as soon as one of the wars of the eighteenth century ended the navy was allowed to fade away. Sailors were dismissed, their officers put on half-pay, the warships were allowed to decay and the dockyards were placed on a care and

[1] Charles Wilson, 'Taxation and the decline of empires' in *Bijdragen en Mededelingen van het historisch genootschap* 77 (Groningen, 1963), 14–21.

maintenance basis. If peace lasted only for a decade, it took a tremendous administrative and financial effort to provide once again a fleet-in-being at the beginning of the next war. Several years were almost bound to elapse before reluctant seamen and rusty officers and hastily patched-up ships could become an efficient fighting force.

Now, in the case of the United Provinces, they took no active part in any war between the Utrecht settlement and the later stages of the American war of Independence. They retained a certain number of vessels, primarily for commerce protection, and occasionally fitted out convoys when other powers were fighting each other; but the commercial classes who now ruled the roost in the United Provinces resolutely refused to provide the finances necessary to restore their country to the position of a first-class naval power which it had held in the preceding century. And the longer this attitude lasted without producing a catastrophe the longer it was likely to continue and the more difficult it became to reverse the policy. Even if it were to be reversed, years of administrative effort would be required to bring into existence once again a fleet which was not limited to a *guerre de course* but which could play an effective part in naval conflicts between the capital ships of Britain, on the one hand, and of the Bourbon powers on the other.

Even during the Spanish Succession war it took the Dutch all their time to keep 50 ships-of-war at sea, whereas in the crisis of 1721 Britain had available 124 ships-of-the-line and 105 smaller vessels. By 1783 Britain had 174 ships-of-the-line and 294 smaller vessels. The French navy, which had almost disappeared in the closing stages of the Spanish Succession war, included by 1780 81 ships-of-the-line while her ally Spain possessed almost as many. Even had the Dutch devoted the same proportion of their resources to their navy at the end as they had at the beginning of the eighteenth century they could not have kept pace with the leading naval powers.

In the wars in which Britain and the United Provinces had co-operated against France during the reigns of William III and Anne, they had both preferred to depend mainly upon foreign mercenaries, just as the Romans in the ancient world had relied upon native auxiliary troops and had tried as far as possible to reserve the legions, composed of Roman citizens, for military emergencies. Hence neither Britain nor the United Provinces ever became a first-class military power in the eighteenth century. It paid them better to reserve their manpower for economic activities and use the resultant profits to hire foreigners when war proved unavoidable.

In this way, both British and Dutch governments minimized the opposition to a standing army which was equally common amongst Dutch merchants and Tory squires. But when war did come, it seems to have been much easier for the British government than it was for the Dutch to extract from their subjects the cash necessary to hire foreign mercenaries. The classic example of this difference came in the concluding year of the Austrian Succession war. The restoration of the stadholderate in the United Provinces had been hailed with delight in Britain. Presumably the influence of the burgher oligarchies over Dutch policy was at its lowest ebb with the triumphant restoration of the house of Orange in the person of William IV to the place in the Dutch republic held by his great predecessor, William III. The Pelhams were entitled to expect that at last the United Provinces would take a part in the war against France in accordance with tradition and commensurate with their still great resources. Instead, Charles Bentinck was sent to London in 1748 to explain that the promises made by the stadholder a few months previously could not be honoured. The Dutch government confessed that without a large loan to be raised for their benefit in England they could not continue to take part in the war.

This traumatic shock may be regarded as the decisive turning point in Anglo-Dutch relations in the eighteenth century. Down to 1748 practically every British statesman, Stanhope almost as much as Townshend, Walpole as much as Newcastle, over-rated the importance of the United Provinces in the European state-system and therefore devoted a disproportionate amount of time and effort to seeking their alliance and their active co-operation. Walpole had not been wholly insincere when he adopted during the war of the Polish Succession as his guiding maxim, and forced George II to accept it also, that without the active concurrence of the Dutch Britain could not take part in the struggle.

The duke of Bedford was quick to grasp the change: he quoted the current quip about France being a live body tied to a dead one, Spain, and applied it to the relationship between Britain and the United Provinces. His successful rival for the control of British foreign policy after the treaty of Aix-la-Chapelle, Newcastle, was much slower to learn the lesson. One of the many serious charges to be brought against Newcastle's conduct of British foreign policy is his persistent over-rating of the United Provinces as a factor in the European balance of power he was eager to establish. When Maria Theresa and Kaunitz had virtually written off the Dutch, Newcastle still fancied that they could be persuaded or coerced to play the part in European affairs that they had taken under William III. And the conduct of the Dutch in the opening months of the Seven Years war convinced even Newcastle that the Dutch were a broken reed. No help could be obtained from them.

Whereas in 1715–16 they had at once sent to George I the succour promised by treaty, forty years later they declined to provide the stipulated help, even when Newcastle, in an attempt to overcome Dutch reluctance, had ordered transports to sail to Dutch ports and await the embarkation of the troops. Now that the *status quo* in the Austrian Netherlands had apparently been secured by the Diplomatic Revolution, the Dutch would do nothing to antagonize France. Indeed they were determined to exploit the Franco-British naval war to develop their colonial trade and this they could only hope to do by maintaining a formal neutrality.

There was also feeling in the United Provinces that the situation in Britain had completely changed since 1715. George I had been a newcomer to England, threatened by an armed rising of his subjects; but by 1756 Jacobitism was dead, even in Scotland; there was no rival to George II; and the Protestant succession was not in danger. Confessional politics had been replaced in Holland as elsewhere in Europe by the economics of expediency.

Another factor contributed to the marked alienation between Britain and the United Provinces after the middle of the century. Even in earlier years the United Provinces had oscillated between Britain and France, and the political alliance of France with Austria, which survived the strains of the Seven Years war and lasted to the French Revolution, increased the French field of force and strengthened the older tendency to Franco-Dutch reconciliation. The Dutch had learned once and for all in the war of the Austrian Succession that the Netherlands were militarily indefensible against a determined French attack, even when Britain and Austria were trying their hardest to support the Dutch.

Austria's transfer from the British to the French alliance in 1756

Lincoln Christian College

made the idea of the military defence of the Netherlands, with the Barrier fortresses in ruins and help available only from Britain, quite ludicrous. Even the few Dutchmen who remained faithful to the British connexion saw the need for an alternative policy. And France made it easy for the Dutch by explicitly abandoning the aggressive policy of Louis XIV in the Netherlands and by offering the Dutch commercial classes valuable advantages for their trade if they remained neutral during the struggle.

In another way the Diplomatic Revolution contributed to the alienation of the Maritime Powers from each other. As the Seven Years war proceeded, Britain was forced into diplomatic and military co-operation with Prussia. While it is true that there were many links between the reigning Hohenzollerns of Prussia and the house of Orange, the strength of these links had been diminished by the decline of 'confessional politics'. It should also be remembered that the partial survival of these dynastic and political connexions automatically made the Dutch opponents of the house of Orange almost as hostile to Prussia as they already were to Britain.

Apart from her anomalous outpost in the Netherlands, Austria was a distant power with numerous preoccupations much nearer home, whereas the central core of Prussia was almost a neighbour and the Prussian duchy of Cleve had a common frontier with the United Provinces. Even earlier in the century the Dutch had their doubts about Prussian land-hunger, and these came to a head with the accession of Frederick the Great, especially when four years later he established himself in the duchy of East Friesland, immediately to the north-east of the United Provinces. This acquisition gave Frederick control of the port of Emden which he hoped to develop in competition with the leading ports of Holland. While it would be going too far to suggest that Frederick the Great had stepped into the shoes of Louis XIV, his territorial acquisitiveness, aggressive mercantilism and restless energy made him in the eyes of the Dutch burghers more dangerous to their interests than the supine Louis XV.

In another way the course of the Seven Years war worsened Anglo-Dutch relations. As long as the Dutch had fought side by side with the English, they had almost been forced to connive at, without necessarily approving, Britain's use of the belligerent rights she claimed to exercise in time of war not only to sweep enemy commerce off the high seas, but narrowly to restrict the maritime trade of all neutral powers. As late as the war of the Austrian Succession, when the Dutch had not actually declared war on France but had acted as auxiliaries of Austria and Britain, they had been treated in this respect less rigorously than some other powers such as Prussia. This distinction rested partly on expediency, and partly on commercial treaties, dating back to the reign of Charles II, between the English and Dutch governments.

When the Dutch absolutely declined to support Britain in the Seven Years war, the British government tried to coerce them by interfering with their overseas trade, especially when the Dutch, by agreement with France, took over a large part of the trade with the French colonies from which they were rigidly excluded by the French in time of peace. The resulting disputes occupied much of the time of British and Dutch diplomatists during the Seven Years war; they should, however, be regarded as a result, rather than a cause, of the growing alienation between the two countries. The league of neutrals and the Armed Neutrality organized by Catherine II during the war of American Independence were however to some extent anticipated by Dutch activities in the preceding war.

The restored stadholderate could do little to counteract the prevailing political and economic tendencies. The restoration of the house of Orange in 1747 had been consciously—even conscientiously—modelled on William III's *coup d'état* of 1672; but it was apparent almost at once that William IV could not achieve what his great predecessor had managed to do. The basic explanation does not lie in the personal insufficiency of the new stadholder in comparison with the intellectual and political greatness of his distinguished predecessor. The United Provinces and Europe had changed during the half-century in which there had been no stadholder. Had William IV been able to continue the war and had the Dutch had to try desperately to stem a French invasion in 1748, he might have gathered around him national support and have become a genuine national leader. In fact he destroyed any possibility of this when he hurriedly scuttled out of the war and forced his allies by his defection to make peace too. Henceforth he could never be more than the leader of a party—and of a party discredited by the obvious gap between its professions in opposition and its performance while in power.

Orange influence, combined with the economic advantages to be derived from Dutch neutrality by the Amsterdam burgomasters, kept the Dutch neutral in the Seven Years war. That the United Provinces took part against Britain in the war of American Independence was not due to any change in Dutch attitudes or interests, but to increased opposition from the neutral powers, headed by a self-confident Russian Empress, to the assertion of Britain's maritime rights. By forcing the Dutch into belligerency, Britain hoped to deprive them of the economic advantages of neutrality and to limit in practice the operation of the principles of international law proclaimed by the armed Neutrality powers. The Dutch took hardly any part in the war either on land or sea and had to grant to Britain when peace was signed in 1784 the trading station of Negapatam in Ceylon and the right of navigation among the Indonesian islands which they continued to rule.

The naval base of Trincomalee, lying to windward of India and affording a safe harbour during seasonal monsoon changes, which had proved useful to Britain both in the war of the Austrian Succession and in the Seven Years war, had been promptly seized by Britain in 1782 as soon as the Dutch joined the coalition against her in the war of American Independence. Trincomalee was soon lost to the French but was restored to the Dutch by the peace of 1784. When the French republicans overran the Low Countries Britain again seized this port and continued to use it mainly as a stores base in the later stages of the Napoleonic wars.[1]

Both William IV and William V were in fact feeble and ineffective political figureheads. British diplomatists at The Hague sometimes went the length of speculating whether they lacked the will as much as they clearly lacked the power to swing the United Provinces back into the British orbit. William IV died in 1751 leaving a posthumous son. His widow Anne, daughter of George II, became regent for her son; but her position was so weak and her stock of statesmanship so slender that her best friends often despaired for her. Quarrelling with William Bentinck, the acknowledged leader of the Orange party, she attempted to conciliate the republicans and had often to defer to their views in foreign as in domestic affairs. Her son William V came of age in 1766. His main asset proved ultimately to be his marriage with the niece of

---

[1] This paragraph is based on H. A. Colgate, 'Trincomalee and the East Indies Squadron 1746–1844' (unpublished London thesis, summarized in *BIHR* 33 (1960), 238–41).

Frederick the Great in 1767; but, as long as Frederick the Great lived and Prussian influence was resolutely directed against Britain, this marriage did nothing to bring about a *rapprochement* between Britain and the United Provinces. By the time Frederick the Great died in 1786, the restored stadholderate had sunk so low that its continued existence offered no threat to republican domination of the United Provinces. Out of the seven provinces only one, Gelderland, was entirely loyal to William V and, when the 'patriots' deprived him of his command of the garrison at The Hague, he took up residence at the provincial capital, Nimeguen.

Why, in these circumstances, the republicans determined to liquidate the stadholderate is not entirely clear. No doubt they were anxious to pay off old scores and they may well have felt that as long as an institution so opposed to their domination of the United Provinces existed, no matter how powerless it was at the moment, their régime lacked security. There is evidence also that they were egged on by France, which regarded the stadholderate as a symbol of British influence in the Netherlands and, as such, the last barrier to complete French control of the Low Countries.

It shows how successful France had been in supplanting Britain as the protector of the United Provinces that when the Dutch found themselves threatened by Joseph II's schemes to reform the Austrian Netherlands and give them a chance of economic revival, the dominant republican party turned for support not to Britain but to France. In the days of Charles VI, Austrian projects in the Netherlands had been thwarted by the combination of Britain and the United Provinces. Under Joseph II the Dutch turned to France, offered to make a commercial and political treaty with her and begged Vergennes to bring pressure upon his Austrian ally. Instead of contributing to the reconciliation of Britain and the United Provinces, the economic threat from Joseph II forced them further apart than ever.

In the end the Republicans overplayed their hand, good though it was. The provincial Estates of Holland suspended the stadholder from the exercise of his offices as stadholder and captain general. The French ambassador asserted that 'a hereditary stadholder was of too new a creation to have acquired a constitutional sanction' and encouraged the 'patriots' to organize themselves in an association pledged to destroy the last trace of monarchy in the United Provinces. The French government had already in 1786 formally and publicly undertaken to resist any foreign interference in the internal affairs of the republic.

James Harris, the active and enterprising British envoy to the United Provinces, was already organizing associations whose members pledged themselves to defend the constitutional rights of the stadholder; but he knew well that his master Pitt would never allow the defence of the stadholderate to bring about a war with France. He failed early in 1787 to convince Pitt that it was safe to call Vergennes's bluff. Later in the year, after his sister Wilhelmina, wife of William V, had been arrested on the frontier of Holland and sent back to Nimuegen, the new king of Prussia, Frederick William II, mobilized his troops in the Rhineland and demanded satisfaction from the provincial Estates of Holland and the punishment of the offenders.

Once assured of the co-operation of a Prussian army Pitt's attitude changed: he warned France that she must either give up the position of predominance she had usurped in the Netherlands or fight for it. The Prussian invasion of Holland proved to be a mere military parade. The 'patriots' fled, William V and his wife returned in triumph to The Hague and the provincial Estates of Holland, purged of its aggressive republican members, rescinded its previous measures and offered an abject apology. France in the preliminary throes of the Great Revolution neither could nor would do anything to help her friends in the United Provinces.

The natural sequel to the stirring events of 1787 was the revocation of the treaty of Fontainebleau, concluded by the republicans with France in 1785 during their period of ascendancy. The United Provinces concluded a formal defensive alliance with the two powers which had restored the stadholder and rescued them from France (April 1788).

The treaty between Britain and the United Provinces promised mutual assistance if either power was engaged in war and specifically military and naval co-operation in the east. Britain none the less refused to restore to the Dutch Negapatam, which she had conquered and retained at the end of the American war of Independence. Britain undertook to maintain the stadholderate 'against all attacks and enterprizes, direct or indirect, of whatsoever nature they might be'. Harris could assure the secretary of state that the Dutch Revolution was as complete as it had been in 1747. His hope that it would be as lasting was destined not to be realized.

The Triple Alliance of 1788, which grew out of joint intervention in Holland, played a great role in European politics for only
a year or two before it split apart in the cataclysm of the French
Revolution. The place Vergennes had hoped to win by diplomacy
for France in the Low Countries was secured by his revolutionary
successors by military might and brutal repression. It was the
threats of the French revolutionaries to the independence of the
United Provinces and their established rights in the Austrian
Netherlands, above all the closure of the Scheldt, which compelled
Pitt to change his attitude of neutrality to the French Revolution.

Pitt put his trust in the Austrian and Prussian armies which,
when Britain entered the war, were already using the Low Countries as the base for an attack upon France. When his allies found
that what they had intended to be a military demonstration against
the French republic had well-nigh united France and provoked a
revolutionary upsurge against the established order in Europe,
their enthusiasm waned. Worse still both Austria and Prussia made
it clear that they put the advancement of their interests in central
Europe, and especially in Poland, before the defence of the Low
Countries from the attacks of France which they had themselves
provoked. Most of the Prussian troops were withdrawn in the
summer of 1794 and the Austrians who remained were defeated
at Fleurus.

Antwerp and the Barrier fortresses in the Netherlands surrendered and in the winter of 1794–5 the armies of the French republic conquered the United Provinces almost without resistance.
Most of the inhabitants were republican and Francophil in sympathy and welcomed the invaders. The most Orange element in
the country, the Dutch fleet, was frozen in the ice and captured by
the French cavalry. For the next few years, until eliminated by
British naval victories, it constituted a serious threat to British
control of the seas. At first organized as the Batavian republic,
most of the Low Countries were soon annexed directly to France.

Prussia, which was bound by the Triple Alliance of 1788 equally
with Britain to defend the United Provinces from France, recognized French annexations in, and domination of, the Low Countries by the treaty of Basel (1795). French control of the Dutch
fleet and the Belgian coast, especially Antwerp, certainly intensified
the naval and commercial threat which the French republic already
offered to Britain, though its immediacy was somewhat reduced by

Admiral Duncan's defeat of the Dutch ships off Camperdown in 1797. Driven out by the French invaders, William V took refuge in England and sanctioned British occupation of the Cape of Good Hope and other Dutch colonies which could be used as bases against the French overseas. This naturally increased Dutch resentment against Britain, due mainly to what Orange partisans were not alone in regarding as the futility and incompetence of Pitt's diplomatic and military attempts to protect the United Provinces from France. Anti-British feeling was also aroused by the pillaging to which the inhabitants had been subjected during the retreat of demoralized British troops under the duke of York. There was a great upsurge of Dutch democratic feeling in sympathy with the French Revolution and hostile to the old order represented by the stadholder and his British backers. The Dutch Revolution of 1795 according to Professor Geyl, 'created a new government, a new order and a new law'.

Pitt hoped in 1796 to persuade France to purchase peace by surrendering Belgium; but with the crushing defeats which Austria, his only important ally in the war, suffered in 1797 such hopes became chimerical. As soon as Pitt recovered the alliance of Austria and Russia and had some hopes that Prussia too might follow the example of her more powerful neighbours, he decided to send a British expeditionary force to Holland. It was believed in London that a landing on the Dutch coast would be followed by a national rising against the French army of occupation. Even if this failed, it would give the pro-Orange crews of the Dutch war-ships a chance to escape to Britain where they would provide a useful reinforcement for the naval blockade of France. If it succeeded Holland might become an allied base of operations for a direct assault upon north-eastern France modelled upon Marlborough's campaigns.

Tsar Paul readily agreed to supply a corps of Russian troops to join with the British force. It was hoped that Prussia too might be induced to take part in the operation, but Frederick William III preferred to adhere to his policy of wavering neutrality. The expedition landed in 1799 and seized some Dutch war-ships, but then bogged down. The duke of York, who was nominally in command, avoided disaster by arranging terms with the French which assured the unmolested withdrawal of his forces.

From first to last there had been no sign of Dutch readiness to rise for the house of Orange. Indeed Dutch troops had largely composed the army which forced York's evacuation. The only results of this costly and undignified operation were to lower the morale of the British army and to lead to recriminations between Britain and Russia. In spite of this fiasco Pitt and his successors persisted in their attempts to restore the exiled stadholder with the object of depriving France of her control of the coasts of the Netherlands. And in 1815, thanks largely to British support, the house of Orange did eventually return to rule over both the United Provinces and the former Austrian Netherlands in the new and more fashionable capacity of constitutional kings.

A. *Primary Sources*

Archives ou Correspondance inédite de la Maison d'Orange-Nassau [1552–1789] (27 vols., Leyden, 1835–1917)
Correspondence of John Churchill and Anthonie Heinsius, 1701–11, ed. B. van't Hoff (The Hague, 1951)
Historical Manuscripts Commission MSS. of the earl of Buckinghamshire, Report XIV, Appendix 9 (1895) [includes correspondence of Robert Trevor while envoy to the United Provinces]
[An] Honest Diplomat at The Hague, ed. J. J. Murray (Indiana University Publication, 1955) [correspondence of Horace Walpole the elder from The Hague]

B. *Secondary Authorities*

Bindoff, S. T., *The Scheldt Question to 1839* (1945)
Carter, Alice, see Wilson, Charles
Clark, Sir George, *The Dutch Alliance and the War against French trade, 1688–97* (Manchester, 1923)
Cobban, A., *Ambassadors and Secret Agents* (1954) [deals with Harris's mission to The Hague]
Coombs, D., *The Conduct of the Dutch. British Opinion and the Dutch Alliance during the War of the Spanish Succession* (The Hague, 1958)
Coquelle, P., *L'alliance franco-hollandaise contre l'Angleterre, 1735–88* (Paris, 1902)
Geikie, R., and Montgomery, Isabel A., *The Dutch Barrier, 1705–19* (Cambridge, 1930)
Geyl, P., *The Netherlands in the Seventeenth Century, Part II, 1648–1715* (1964)
— 'Holland and England during the War of the Austrian Succession' in *History* 10 (1925–6), 47–51
— 'William IV of Orange and his English Marriage' in *TRHS* 4th series, 8 (1925), 14–37

Hatton, Ragnhild, *Diplomatic Relations between Great Britain and the Dutch Republic, 1714–1721* (1950)

Hertz, G. B., 'England and the Ostend Company' in *EHR* 22 (1906), 255–79

Lodge, Sir R., 'The Maritime Powers in the Eighteenth Century' in *History* 15 (1930–1), 246–51

Palmer, R. R., 'Much in Little: The Dutch Revolution of 1795' in *JMH* 26 (1954), 15–35

Rose, J. H., 'Great Britain and the Dutch Question in 1787–88' in *AHR* 14 (1908–9), 262–83

— 'The Missions of William Grenville to The Hague and Versailles in 1787' in *EHR* 24 (1909), 278–95

Van der Haute, G., *Relations Anglo-Hollandaises au début du XVIIIe siècle d'après la Correspondance d'Alexandre Stanhope, 1700–1706* (Louvain, 1932)

Wilson, C. H., *Anglo-Dutch Commerce and Finance in the Eighteenth Century* (Cambridge, 1941)

— Review article on Mrs. Carter's published work on Dutch investment in England in *EcHR* 12 (1959–60), 434–9

Note. The sectional bibliography for Austria includes items relating to the Austrian Netherlands which are also relevant to Anglo-Dutch relations.

CHAPTER 5

Great Britain and Austria

DIPLOMATIC relations between the British islands on the fringe of western Europe and landlocked Austria, with its main preoccupation in the defence of central Europe against the Turkish menace, had been casual and unimportant in the earlier seventeenth century. England was much more directly concerned with the Spanish than with the Austrian branch of the Hapsburg family. Unless Protestant solidarity caused resentment in England at the treatment of German Protestant princes by the Hapsburg emperors, notably on the expulsion from Bohemia and subsequent deposition of the elector Palatine and his wife, 'the winter queen', England and the Austrian Hapsburgs might almost have belonged to unconnected diplomatic systems.

What really brought Britain and Austria together was Louis XIV's exploitation of the successes won by Richelieu and Mazarin. The two cardinals had presented to Europe an image of France as Catholic at home but Protestant abroad. They succeeded at least to the extent that European Protestants identified France's enemy Spain with the cause of the Papacy. The Dutch depended largely on France in their efforts to shake off the hateful yoke of Spain. Sweden became the executive instrument of France in the Empire during the Thirty Years war. Cromwell, disillusioned with his earlier idea of a Protestant and republican league between England and the United Provinces, concluded an alliance with France which was directed primarily against the Spanish Hapsburgs.

Louis XIV's temporary support of Gallicanism and his political quarrels with the Papacy helped to keep alive for a time the idea that France was a more natural ally than Spain for Protestant powers; but Louis XIV finally threw away this valuable political capital by his revocation of the edict of Nantes, support of the Roman Catholic Stuarts, and personal dependence on Jesuit advice in the later years of his reign. Earlier the Spanish Hapsburgs had been so successful in persecuting religious minorities that they had virtually eliminated them from Spain: the complaints of Protestant states henceforth had to be limited to objections about the treatment of their own Protestant subjects while temporarily resident in Spain. Hence, especially with the rise of Jansenism, France seemed a more active persecuting power than Spain. The Huguenot *émigrés* certainly did their best to give currency to this idea.

The rise of France under Louis XIV, accompanied as it was by the marked decline of the Spanish Hapsburgs, forced the Austrian branch to pay more attention to the politics of western Europe. The defeats inflicted by Austria upon the Turks in the later years of the seventeenth century lifted the threat which had impended over Vienna for more than a century and made possible a more active Austrian policy in the west. This must be directed to buttress in the meantime the failing strength of the Spanish branch and ultimately to acquire the whole of their territories, continental and colonial, for Austria. Their only hope of carrying out such an ambitious plan in the teeth of French opposition was to find efficient allies in western Europe. Just as France had used the Swedes and Turks against Austria in eastern Europe, so must Austria secure the help of the English and Dutch, threatened as they were even more directly by the aggressions of Louis XIV.

While this novel system of alliances had begun to take shape, so far as the Dutch and the Hapsburgs were concerned, even before 1688, it was not until the Revolution of that year that England joined the new system. Few of those concerned with the transformation can have foreseen how long it would last and, still less, how far-reaching its consequences would prove to be.

The three states concerned had entirely different political and social structures and diverse political traditions and interests. While the Maritime Powers were now the unquestioned leaders of European Protestantism, Austria was one of the best examples in Europe of the triumph of the Counter-Reformation; and its rulers, quite apart from their own deep convictions, were bound to support Roman Catholicism as one of the few remaining supports of their Imperial authority in the Empire.

It is true that the Dutch already depended to some extent upon trade within the Empire, which formed the main economic hinterland for Dutch seaports. Britain, too, was anxious to develop her trade with central Europe, especially in cloth, and Lord Chancellor Hardwicke, in the closing years of the 'old system', told the house of Lords that a commercial nation must maintain her political contacts with Austria, if only to defend her trade. Despite attempts at different times, no commercial treaty was actually concluded between Britain and Austria. Britain particularly resented Austrian restrictions upon the import of English cloth; but even during the Spanish Succession war she failed to secure any redress for British exporters of cloth. It was in vain that her diplomatists at Vienna pointed out that these merchants had influence in the house of Commons and especially on the granting of supplies out of which Austria's subsidies were paid.[1] Quite apart from Austrian customs barriers by the middle of the eighteenth century Silesian textile manufactures were certainly competing with British textiles in European markets.

Throughout the period when the alliance survived, economic interests therefore contributed little to hold it together and the ill-advised attempt to strengthen the bonds between the Maritime Powers and Austria by the Barrier treaty divided instead of, as was hoped at the time, bringing the allied powers more closely together. The contemporary Austrian attempt to develop Trieste as a Mediterranean port with British help likewise failed and Britain found at Leghorn a more convenient entrepôt for her Italian trade.

Nor was there any appreciable cultural contact. Hardly any Englishmen could read, let alone speak, German, even after the accession of the house of Hanover. Translations from English into German were as rare as those from German into English. Similarly in architecture, the baroque churches and rococo palaces of the Austrian dominions usually failed to win the respect of the few English tourists who included Austria in the Grand Tour.

Even at the high level of diplomatic contact, there were constant difficulties at the stiff-necked, precedent-ridden court of Vienna. The attempt to maintain relations by an exchange of ambassadors was soon abandoned, partly because of disputes over precedence with other ambassadors at the same court, but also because the Hapsburg emperors for long refused to grant the claims of William III and his successor to the royal title in formal correspondence with the Austrian chancellery. Henceforward agents of lower rank were appointed who were excluded by etiquette from much personal contact with the reigning emperors, and, later on, with Maria Theresa. When, exceptionally, a Sir Thomas Robinson

[1] *H.M.C. House of Lords Papers* VII (1921), xxv.

at Vienna managed to maintain closer contact with an allied power, he was at once accused by his employers of being 'a creature of the court of Vienna'. Similarly, when Baron Wasner did at London what Robinson did at Vienna, the court of Vienna treated him almost as though he had betrayed the interests of his sovereign.

At no time between 1689 and 1756 was there anything like the popular support for the Austrian alliance which was called into existence by the successes of Frederick the Great in the Seven Years war. The Austro-British alliance was never more than a marriage of political convenience. By tradition, upbringing, and outlook the rulers of Austria had no respect for the ecclesiastical and secular institutions of which Englishmen were so proud. British politicians, on the other hand, looked upon Austria merely as a convenient fulcrum for the restoration of a continental balance of power with the minimum of British exertions.

In the first war in which Britain and Austria co-operated—the war of the English Succession—the pattern was set. The main military burden of a land-war against France was to be shared by the Emperor and the Dutch. Britain would concentrate as far as possible upon the naval war with France, but would also help to support the continental efforts of her allies by paying subsidies, which could be used to supplement their armies by hiring foreign mercenaries. If this proved insufficient, as it did, then a few British regiments could be landed on the Continent and attached to the existing Allied armies in whatever theatre of the continental war they seemed to be most needed. Most often this turned out to be the Low Countries, but it might also be the Iberian peninsula, Italy or Germany.

One can hardly blame the Hapsburgs for disliking the limited support which experience soon showed was all they were likely to obtain from Britain. On the other hand they were sufficiently realists to appreciate that without such support they could not hope to secure their ambitions in western Europe, or, as time went on, even retain their possessions and position in the centre of the Continent. As Austria's prestige and power weakened under Charles VI, Britain not only raised her price but reserved to herself the right to intervene or not, as she judged her own interests required. This was most apparent during the war of the Polish Succession.

Every war in which Britain and Austria fought on the same side was ended by unilateral British action—at Ryswick (1697), Utrecht (1713), and Aix-la-Chapelle (1748). As Britain grew stronger and Austria weaker, Britain, by the threat of withholding her co-operation, deliberately coerced Austria into following the policy which best accorded with the supposed interests of Britain. This culminated in the war of the Austrian Succession, when Austria's position was particularly weak, when Britain more than once made terms on behalf of Austria almost as if Austria were a minor and Britain her guardian. It seemed to Maria Theresa that if British desertion had injured the legitimate interests of her predecessors in earlier wars, British dictation now added insult to injury. Maria Theresa was forced into the Diplomatic Revolution by the conviction that the decadence of the Dutch and the arrogance and unreliability of the British left her with no alternative.

It should be noted that the Anglo-Austrian alliance was not a stable and permanent factor in European diplomacy, even during the first half of the eighteenth century, which was certainly its heyday. Charles VI, who, as the Archduke Charles, had been the Whig candidate for the Spanish crown, never forgot nor forgave Britain's abandonment of his cause. His resentment was kept alive by the group of refugees from Spain and Italy, often referred to as the Spanish Council. For more than a decade after Britain's desertion of Austria by the treaty of Utrecht this group was very influential at Vienna. Under their influence Charles VI persisted in retaining the title of king of Spain, demanded effective British intervention in favour of the Catalans, who were now being made to pay for their support of the unsuccessful candidate for the Spanish throne, tried to retain Majorca, which was still garrisoned by Austrian troops, and demanded the support of the British fleet to carry on his war in the Mediterranean with the Bourbon king of Spain, whose claims Britain had recognized at Utrecht.

Neither Townshend nor Stanhope was prepared to encourage Charles VI in such flights of fantasy, although the return of the Whigs to power in England gave currency to rumours that George I was about to commence a new war against France. These rumours were propagated by self-interested Jacobites and found ready credence in France itself in the last months of Louis XIV's life. They encouraged Charles VI to think that he had more to expect from the British government than that government had any intention of granting to him. He was therefore the more disappointed with Townshend's firm rejection of any British participation in Austria's Mediterranean projects and his insistence that the renewal of the Austro-British alliance, secured by the treaty of Westminster in 1715, must be purely defensive in character and be based upon the Utrecht settlement which Charles VI was eager to overturn.

The attitude of Charles VI was the more distasteful to the British government because Austria's rival, Spain, made tempting offers of commercial advantages to Britain. No price was at first stipulated, and, until it became clear to British ministers that the price in fact was connivance at the restoration of Bourbon power in Italy, they were still less inclined to support Austria.

Another cause of alienation between Britain and Austria in the early years of George I's reign was the adjustment of the terms upon which the former Spanish Netherlands should be transferred, in accord with the treaty of Utrecht, to Austria. Here Britain had at first been inclined to take the side of the Emperor against the Dutch, partly at least because of commercial rivalry in the Netherlands. It was the outbreak of the Jacobite rising in 1715, and the military help readily supplied to Britain by the Dutch, when Austria maintained a position of reserve, that converted Britain to support of Dutch claims and forced Charles VI to accept the custody of the Netherlands upon terms which he considered both disadvantageous and dishonourable.

Louis XIV had sought to take advantage of Britain's desertion of Austria at Utrecht by effecting a reconciliation between the houses of Bourbon and Hapsburg. The knowledge that an alternative existed may well have contributed to the coolness between Vienna and London. Once the Regent Orleans assumed control of French foreign policy, he clearly showed his preference for an understanding with Britain. The conclusion of a Franco-British treaty of alliance in 1716, soon converted into the Triple Alliance by the reluctant accession of the Dutch, constituted a diplomatic revolution only less far-reaching than the better-known revolution of 1756. A Franco-British-Dutch accord, however personal and fragile it might be, drove Austria, already engaged in a quarrel with Spain and a war with the Turks, into the political wilderness.

Antagonism and isolation in Europe forced Austria back upon the policy associated with Schönborn—vice-chancellor of the Holy Roman Empire—of reviving her rights in Germany and seeking to strengthen the Imperial authority at the expense of the princes. And connected with this policy, which depended for success upon the Roman Catholic secular and ecclesiastical princes, was the support of Roman Catholicism within and without the Empire whenever and wherever it came into conflict with Protestantism. Directly and indirectly the Triple Alliance damaged Anglo-Austrian relations. Charles VI privately considered it almost as gross a betrayal of Austria by Britain as the treaty of Utrecht.

At this stage it is necessary to examine the nature and extent of Hanoverian influence upon the British attitude to Austria in the early years of George I's reign. It is usually assumed that George I was a stout Imperialist. He had indeed continued to support Austria in arms after the defection of Britain and his lifelong antipathy to the Tories in England was partly based on their behaviour in the closing years of Anne's reign. But George I was now one of the acknowledged leaders of German Protestantism and was bound to resist Hapsburg persecution and proselytism. Much more important, now that he had secured admission to the College of electors, he was dissatisfied with the conditions imposed upon him and blamed the Emperor for not exerting himself more vigorously to support Hanoverian claims.

Finally, the second Northern war brought Hanover to the verge of war with Charles VI, who was particularly indignant that the electors of Brandenburg and Hanover took a leading part in the war with complete disregard to the wishes and plans of their Imperial overlord. They tolerated, if they did not actually encourage, the presence of Russian troops in northern Germany. They declined to co-operate with the Emperor in restoring peace to the Empire. George I, by what can only be described as sharp practice, gained control of Bremen and Verden and then demanded formal investiture from the Emperor. When Charles VI demurred, he then added for good measure a long list of demands involving other privileges and territorial accessions for the new electorate.

George's actions as elector of Hanover therefore added dangerous combustible fuel to the already smouldering quarrels between Britain and Austria. While Britain and Austria were at times apparently reconciled in the next decade, the sources of dispute between the elector of Hanover and the Emperor were not adjusted until after the second treaty of Vienna of 1731. Indeed had

Charles VI not decided that a reconciliation with Britain was imperative in 1731, it seems unlikely that even then he would have yielded to the electoral demands of George II.

Charles VI was saved from a dangerous position of isolation by the aggression of Spain. Spanish troops landed first in Sardinia and then in Sicily and reduced the Austrian and Piedmontese garrisons in the islands. Austria joined the Triple Alliance and accepted Stanhope's ingenious scheme for peace in the Mediterranean. Savoy would exchange the island and kingship of Sicily for the less attractive territory and kingship of Sardinia. Austria would then add Sicily to Naples. The queen of Spain's claims to Parma and Tuscany, on the respective deaths of their present rulers, would be recognized by the Emperor and effectively guaranteed by the immediate introduction of neutral garrisons into both duchies.

No sooner had Charles VI accepted this sensible solution than he began to have doubts about his wisdom. The settlement had to some extent been forced upon him by Austrian inability to conduct simultaneous wars against the Turks and the Spaniards. Once he had ended the Turkish war, helped by British mediation, at the peace of Passarowitz, he was less inclined to compromise his quarrel with Spain. The Spanish Council at Vienna warned him that, once admitted to Parma, the Spanish Bourbons would never be content until they had extended their foothold in Italy and secured for themselves the domination of the peninsula formerly exercised by the Spanish Hapsburgs and now inherited and exercised by their Austrian cousins. Charles VI thought he stood to lose the one substantial gain his house had secured from the costly and unsatisfactory Spanish Succession war.

Austro-British divergence over the politics of Italy was intensified by British predilection for Piedmont, a state which traditionally exploited its geographical position and military resources to play the role of a balancing power in Italy between Hapsburgs and Bourbons. In her natural anxiety to win Piedmontese support against France, Britain was much readier than Austria to sacrifice Austrian territory as a reward for Piedmontese help. Also Britain felt that her naval control of the western Mediterranean was precarious and too narrowly based. British naval squadrons both in war and peace made some use of the Savoyard port of Villefranche; but it was not adequate for their needs. She would gladly have seen a really good port in the north-west of Italy, probably Genoa, in the hands of her protégé, the king of Savoy-Sardinia. Austria had other ideas about the future of Genoa, against which she herself had well-founded if somewhat antiquated claims.

More serious than either German or Italian conflicts of interest in bringing about the actual rupture of diplomatic relations between Britain and Austria in 1725 was a long-drawn-out dispute over the Netherlands. As has been mentioned earlier in this chapter Charles VI was dissatisfied with the terms of the Barrier treaty. He objected equally to the political and military control represented by the Dutch garrisons and to the economic vassalage to the Maritime Powers in which the terms of the treaty placed his territories in the Low Countries. If he could use these lands as a base for foreign and especially colonial trade—and this became even more important when his plans for Trieste collapsed—then it might be worth while being the nominal ruler of the Netherlands. Economic development would automatically increase the revenue to be drawn from them and this in turn would make the Emperor's contribution to the upkeep of Dutch garrisons less burdensome financially and less irksome politically.

When it became clear that Britain and France were either unable or unwilling to arrange a settlement acceptable both to Spain and to Charles VI, the Dutchman Ripperda came to Vienna as the agent of Philip V of Spain and his queen, Elizabeth Farnese. The Spanish sovereigns regarded the return of the infanta to Madrid and the reprobation of the bargain by which she was to marry Louis XV as adding insult to the numerous injuries they had already suffered at the hands of the Franco-British allies.[1] With the enthusiastic support of Charles VI's Spanish advisers, Ripperda negotiated a series of treaties known collectively to diplomatic historians as the first treaty of Vienna (1725). Inasmuch as this treaty was based—as it was in essentials—on the execution of the proposals originally made by Stanhope and included in the Quadruple Alliance of 1718, it ought to have been welcomed both by Britain and France. But it went considerably beyond this, since it included not merely a treaty of peace between Austria and Spain, but also a defensive alliance.

In addition Spain guaranteed the settlement of the Hapsburg succession, contained in a Pragmatic Sanction or Hapsburg house-law, which Charles VI had drawn up in substitution for an earlier

[1] See above, chapter 3, pp. 49–50.

Pragmatic Sanction promulgated by his father Leopold I. In default of male issue, the undivided succession was to pass, not in order of primogeniture to the daughters of his elder brother Joseph I, but to Maria Theresa, his eldest daughter, and, in default of legitimate heirs, to her younger sisters and their issue.

Another clause in the treaties secured for Spain the good offices of the Emperor, but not his active support if good offices failed, in persuading Britain to hand back Gibraltar to Spain. Much more objectionable was the clause by which Spain admitted the subjects of the Emperor to all trading privileges possessed by British subjects in Spain and her colonies. In particular the East India Company, recently founded at Ostend by Charles VI, was granted permission to trade with any part of the dominions of Spain, Spanish America only excepted.

Spain's guarantee of the Pragmatic Sanction infuriated France; the Emperor's attitude on Gibraltar and Spain's promises to the Ostend Company alarmed the British government and still more the British people. Townshend seems to have believed that the Emperor, triumphant against the Turks in eastern Europe, was now preparing to assert Hapsburg domination in the west. In particular, with the backing of Spanish fanaticism, the Emperor might revive in Germany a policy designed to re-establish the Imperial authority at the expense of the Protestant princes. This could recreate the conditions of the Thirty Years war. The policy which Charles VI had in fact pursued in previous years in Germany gave colour to what appears in retrospect to have been a groundless suspicion.

The known terms of the first treaty of Vienna were alarming enough; but, especially as they seemed to give the Emperor much the better of the bargain, it was widely believed that still more dangerous secret clauses had been included. Reports naturally varied, but there was a widespread belief that the Emperor had agreed to the marriage of his heiress under the Pragmatic Sanction, Maria Theresa, to the eldest son of Philip V and Elizabeth Farnese.

Townshend was impressed by the possibility that Don Carlos might recreate the Empire of Charles V and become the ruler both of the Hapsburg dominions and of the Spanish empire. Indeed it was conceivable that the early death of Louis XV without a direct heir might enable him to add to this already overwhelming territorial preponderance the title and resources of king of France. As Townshend saw, not only was the Protestant cause immediately in danger, but ultimately the liberties of Europe. The commercial interests of British merchants, though they could be useful in bringing Britain and Holland together, were in his view minor and subsidiary.

If William III had found it difficult to secure British and Dutch co-operation against the actual threat to the balance of power offered by Louis XIV in 1701, Townshend had much less chance of winning such support against a potential danger that was in fact unlikely to arise. Having concluded the League of Hanover, Townshend sought to win popular and especially parliamentary support for it by insisting that his league was the only way to save European Protestantism, defend Britain from the Jacobites and protect her trade both in Europe and overseas. When Shippen argued in the house of Commons that the league of Hanover would involve Britain in a war for defence of George I's electoral territories, Walpole retorted that it was much more likely that Charles VI's resentment at British opposition to his Ostend Company would lead him to reprisals against Hanover. Thanks largely to the prominence given to the threat to commerce, the government secured large majorities for its anti-Austrian policy enshrined in the league of Hanover.

The rupture of diplomatic relations lasted for not much more than a year. The last thing Walpole wanted was a general war on the Continent and this was equally true of the new controller of French foreign policy, Fleury. The much more bellicose Townshend was gradually edged out; Walpole and Fleury agreed that in his hands the league of Hanover had endangered rather than secured the peace of Europe. His alarm had been excessive and his diplomatic methods lacking in finesse. Public opinion moved in the same direction. Commercial hostility to the Ostend Company as a threat was submerged by a wave of hostility to Spain whose coastguards in the West Indies were now seizing British ships and ill-treating British sailors. At the same time Gibraltar, always a tender point with the eighteenth-century British public, was besieged by a Spanish army.

By this time it was clear that the Austro-Spanish alliance rested on a mutual misunderstanding. Charles VI had never intended that Maria Theresa should marry Don Carlos, unless the birth of a son should remove her from the direct line of succession. He had no serious intention of fighting against Britain for the benefit of the Spanish Bourbons. His reluctance actually to admit them to Italy was as great as ever.

Disillusionment with the Spanish alliance weakened the position of the Spanish Council at Vienna and was both cause and result of the reviving influence of Prince Eugene of Savoy and his associates. Eugene and Marlborough had been equal partners in the triumphs of the Spanish Succession war; and although Britain's desertion, and the failure of his mission to London to avert it, somewhat cooled his enthusiasm, he continued to be a firm advocate of the British alliance. Successive British diplomatic agents at Vienna depended on his advice and owed much to his wise counsel.

In view of its prominence in parliamentary debates, the first stage in the *rapprochement* of Britain and Austria was Charles VI's suspension of the Ostend Company for a period of years, while in Germany he abandoned or at least pursued much less openly and consistently the policy associated with Schönborn. But it was Spain and not Austria which was the first to renounce publicly its adhesion to the first treaty of Vienna. By doing so, at the treaty of Seville, Spain hoped to win British and French support for her claims in Italy, which continued to be much the most important cause of Austro-Spanish conflict. But Walpole had no intention of committing himself to such a unilateral policy, least of all when Britain's alliance with France, which had been the basis of her foreign policy since 1716, was becoming insecure.

The birth of a dauphin in 1729 removed the question of the succession in France from the forefront of European politics: a reconciliation between France and Spain seemed inevitable. This was a much more immediate threat to Britain than the distant dangers to the balance of power which had been foreseen by Townshend in 1727. A genuine reconciliation between France and Spain was only less dangerous to Britain than it was to Austria. Instead of trying to keep in diplomatic step with France as long as possible, Walpole preferred to reach agreement with the Hapsburgs. Even under Fleury, the most pacific of French foreign ministers, France would not accept the Pragmatic Sanction, which was directly opposed to the traditions and interests of France. Yet Walpole felt impelled to separate himself from France by guaranteeing the

Pragmatic Sanction. This bribe proved sufficient not only to restore the alliance between Britain and Austria by the second treaty of Vienna in 1731, but also to win for George II, as elector of Hanover, most of the advantages which Charles VI had refused to grant to his father in 1717.

In exchange for George II's guarantee of the Pragmatic Sanction, both as king and as elector, Charles VI abolished the Ostend Company and promised to admit Spanish garrisons to the imperial fiefs of Parma and Tuscany as a security for the eventual succession of Don Carlos. The second treaty of Vienna also included a clause by which both contracting parties mutually guaranteed their territorial possessions, which was soon to be a source of acrimonious dispute between the Anglo-Austrian allies. Any wars between Austria and the Turks were expressly excluded from this guarantee.

Britain having abandoned the policy of diplomatic co-operation with France by signing the second treaty of Vienna, France lost no time in concluding with Spain the first of the three Family Compacts between the Bourbon powers, which played so important a role in the diplomatic history of the eighteenth century. This amounted to an offensive alliance against Austria in the first instance, but also in the long run against Britain.

Unfortunately Charles VI by associating himself closely with Russia, in opposition to Stanislaus Leszczyński's attempts to recover the Polish crown, made it possible for France to claim that she was acting on the defensive. Stanislaus was now Louis XV's father-in-law; and this, in an age of dynastic diplomacy, gave France every right to support his candidature, quite apart from the long tradition of French intervention in the election of Polish kings. Had Fleury and Chauvelin, at once his coadjutor and rival in the direction of French foreign policy, concentrated their activities in Poland, there would have been no case for British intervention to help Austria in the war of the Polish Succession. But Fleury and Chauvelin agreed that there was no point in ruining France for the sake of the king's father-in-law. Consequently they made no serious attempt to resist the election of Augustus, elector of Saxony and son of the preceding king, as king of Poland and the expulsion of Stanislaus by Russian troops from his former kingdom.

Fleury deliberately used the perfunctory hostilities in Poland as a pretext for an all-out attack upon Austria in western Germany and in Italy. Here, and not in Poland, France might hope to win decisive victories and to acquire territory of strategic value. And these prospects were enhanced by the diplomatic skill with which Fleury secured the military support for France's campaigns in Italy of both Spain and Savoy-Sardinia, normally bitter rivals.

Faced with this powerful coalition, Charles VI turned confidently for support to Britain and appealed to the mutual guarantee of territories included in the second treaty of Vienna. George II, now that Hanover's claims and grievances had been adjusted with Charles VI, was ready, if not eager, to take part in the war. Walpole absolutely declined to give active support and pressed both Austria and France to accept the mediation of the Maritime Powers.

He defended this decision on two grounds, one legal and the other practical. Charles VI, by his intervention in Poland, had brought his troubles upon himself: the resulting war was not a defensive war on the part of Austria, and therefore the guarantees contained in the second treaty of Vienna were not operative. He argued also that the resolutely pacific attitude of the Dutch made effective British intervention in the war impossible in practice. There was this measure of truth in his second contention that no eighteenth-century British statesman, if he could possibly help it, was willing to go to war without the Dutch, since this would enable the Dutch as neutrals to profit by the war to extend their overseas trade. On the other hand by this time everybody who understood European politics knew that the Dutch had ceased to be the equals of Britain: if they still spoke of the Maritime Powers it was because they were convinced that the Dutch followed Britain's lead. Frederick the Great, in one of his most often quoted phrases, described the Dutch as a cockboat towed by the British man-o'-war.

Naturally Charles VI was not impressed by either Walpolean argument, and did not confine his activities at London to trying to convert Walpole to more reasonable views. Once again, as in the 1720's, he made contact with the Opposition and thus further embittered the relations of Britain and Austria. Walpole resented even more backstairs Austrian attempts to persuade George II to force him (Walpole) to choose between a change of policy and loss of office.

Apart from Russia, which could hardly exert much influence on campaigns in southern and western Europe, and a few German princes, who sent small contingents of troops to join Charles VI's armies, the Emperor was completely isolated. Prince Eugene did his best to hold the western frontier of the Empire against superior French attacks, but the Austrian armies in Italy were completely routed. Fortunately for the Emperor, the more moderate Fleury regained control of French foreign policy from the bellicose Chauvelin. Mutual dislike of Walpole helped to bring Charles VI and Fleury together. Pointedly refusing the proffered mediation of the Maritime Powers, they signed the third treaty of Vienna. This, in intention at least, was more than a peace treaty: it foreshadowed the Diplomatic Revolution of 1756, with this difference that the third treaty of Vienna made Austria for a year or two almost the satellite of France whereas the later Diplomatic Revolution soon enlisted France in support of Austrian ambitions.

Austria lost Naples and Sicily to Don Carlos, but gained Parma and, virtually, Tuscany, which was assigned to Francis Stephen of Lorraine, the bridegroom of Maria Theresa, in exchange for his ancestral duchy. Lorraine went to the ex-king of Poland; but on his death it was to be added to the dominions of the French crown. France, securing this extremely valuable bribe in advance, joined the long list of powers which had by now guaranteed the Pragmatic Sanction.

Partly to reward Russia for her quite ineffective support of Austria during the war, Charles VI involved himself in a Russo-Turkish war, in which his generals covered themselves with disgrace, and from which he had to be rescued by French mediation, naturally exercised in favour of the Turks, not of Austria.

Encouraged by success on the Continent, the Bourbon powers now turned against Britain overseas. Walpole's attempt to avoid war with Spain, by the treaty of the Pardo, misfired. When Charles VI died in 1740, Britain was already engaged in a naval and colonial war with Spain, and was that much less likely to honour her obligations (by the second treaty of Vienna) to support Maria Theresa in a continental war which would secure her succession to all the territories held by her father. Relations between the new ruler of Austria, who at first retained her father's principal advisers, and George II, still depending upon Walpole, were at first distinctly chilly. If France had given her adequate encouragement, she would probably have continued the policy of her father in his last years and depended upon France for support.

The quite unexpected attack launched by the young king of

Prussia upon Silesia forced France to choose between Austria and Prussia. The defeat of Austria at Mollwitz convinced French politicians as well as French soldiers that the time had come to settle accounts with the Hapsburgs. Fleury and Walpole were over-ruled and set aside. In England it was widely felt that Walpole had abandoned the traditional balance-of-power attitude to the Continent and the early failures of the war against Spain caused wide-spread and well-justified alarm that British interests were in jeopardy. Rather than lose office Walpole changed his policy. Not only did he now agree to fulfil the obligations he had undertaken in 1731 towards Austria: he was soon, albeit reluctantly, forced to go considerably beyond them.

George II was naturally pleased that his prime minister had accepted the policy he had advocated during the previous war; but, as soon as he found it involved practical dangers for his electorate, he hurriedly withdrew as elector of Hanover from the Austrian camp and made his peace for a time with France. Historians have tended to enlarge upon the disadvantages to Britain of the personal union with Hanover. Here we have perhaps the clearest example of the dangers to Hanover implicit in the accession of the elector to the throne of Great Britain.

The intransigence of France forced Maria Theresa to accept such help as she could get from Britain, Hanover, and the United Provinces; but, from the beginning of the war, she resented Britain's refusal to give her any help against Prussia, while insisting that she must yield territory to the robber-king as a condition of continued British help against France. British diplomatic pressure reinforced the military defeats inflicted on her by Prussia and France and forced her to yield Silesia. Carteret had sweetened the pill by offering to secure for her territorial compensation else-where; but his successors soon showed they had no serious intention of honouring their predecessor's promise.

Carlyle has described the Austrian Succession war as a huge and unintelligible English and foreign delirium. Fortunately there is no need to describe its course here. The longer it lasted the louder became the complaints of the British and Austrian allies against each other. Maria Theresa claimed with some justification that Britain never gave her adequate support in Germany. The British retorted that Maria Theresa threw upon them the main burden of the war in Italy and the Netherlands. Even after the war in Germany was ended by the treaty of Dresden, she concentrated upon attempts to recover her position in Italy and allowed Maurice de Saxe to overrun the Netherlands and attack the United Provinces.

When Maria Theresa denounced her British and Dutch pay-masters as stingy, they retorted that the troops Austria was bound to supply were never up to strength. To this Maria Theresa re-plied that the British generals sent to count them always arrived just after a battle in which they had suffered casualties; but there were dark suspicions at London that part of the money remitted to keep Austrian armies in being was actually being spent on re-building Maria Theresa's palace at Schönbrunn on the outskirts of Vienna.

These exchanges during the war, acrimonious and destructive of harmony as they were, were soon overshadowed by divergences, reflecting a basic conflict of interest between the Allies, over the making of peace. These were deliberately exploited by France, which in fact conducted parallel negotiations for peace with Austria and with Britain. Finally France preferred to accept the terms offered by Britain rather than those presented by Austria, largely because she was convinced that Austria, deserted by Britain, could not carry on the continental war unaided, whereas Britain, freed from the burden of supporting Austria in the war on the Con-tinent, might well continue the naval and colonial war, if indeed she did not succeed in mopping up the colonial empire of France. Once again, as at Utrecht, the way in which Britain had negotiated a separate peace caused almost as much irritation as the actual terms of the treaty.

During the war Carteret's hopes of using the Anglo-Austrian alliance as the basis of a great European coalition, which would once and for all end Bourbon domination of Europe, had proved chimerical. His influence gave way to that of the Pelhams and their ally, Lord Chancellor Hardwicke. Pelham wrote in 1745, in im-plied criticism of Carteret's policy, that 'engaging beyond our strength has been in my mind the great error of the last three years. It is better to avoid that evil now than persist in it to our ruin and that of our allies also; when I say allies I mean the Republic [United Provinces] only; for all the rest I look upon as burdens, not as friends engaged in the same interest and upon equal terms.'[1]

While this view of Anglo-Austrian relations was traditional and

[1] *H.M.C. Trevor MSS.*, p. 133.

not at all novel, it was given added force by a vital change in the
European balance of political and military power which emerged
clearly during the Austrian Succession war. The hopes entertained by Carteret, and some of his predecessors, that Austria
might recover sufficient control of the resources of the Empire to
enable her to act, without much support from the Maritime
Powers, as an effective counterweight to the house of Bourbon on
the Continent, were obviously not going to be realized. Much the
most important result of the war was to establish Prussia securely
as almost an equal power with Austria in Germany. Henceforth
for more than a century German politics were to be based upon
dualism and dominated by political, diplomatic, and, at times,
armed conflicts between these two military monarchies in the heart
of the Empire.

The dramatic rise of Prussia to greatness gave British ministers
what they had not hitherto had—a possible alternative to Austria
as Britain's 'continental sword'. Old Horatio Walpole made himself the standard-bearer of the new policy and preached, in season
and out, the advantages of alliance with Prussia. Pelham was so
impressed by the idea that he sent Harry Legge to Berlin at the
end of the war to sound Frederick. Hardwicke spoke for all his
colleagues when he pointed out that the war had conclusively
shown 'the lameness of the old system' without Prussia and the
necessity of adding Prussia to it.

This was the crux of the problem. British ministers saw no
difficulty in assuming that a genuine reconciliation between Austria
and Prussia on the terms arranged at Dresden in 1745 was practicable, and not merely desirable from the British point of view.
Frederick tried to undeceive them: he professed willingness to
take the place of Austria in Britain's system of alliances, but explained that he could not possibly join the old firm. Faced with a
clear choice between Austria and Prussia, the Pelhams were certainly right to stick to Austria, if only because the utter selfishness
and unreliability of Frederick as an ally had been demonstrated
over and over again during the war. The attempt had therefore to
be made to rebuild for the second time a purely political alliance
between Britain and Austria. Once again it was futile to think of
dynastic marriages, social contacts, community of intellectual ideas
or even of economic interests, to strengthen the political link once
it had been restored, still less to help in its restoration.

On the British side the leadership passed to Newcastle. Pelham, like his master Walpole, was fundamentally uninterested in foreign affairs, which he regarded merely as a distraction from much more interesting and important problems in domestic affairs. In actual fact his attitude did not differ much from that attributed in jest to one of his nineteenth-century successors—'how simple foreign affairs would be if it were not for these d—d foreigners!' Trade should be advanced and war avoided, not for the reasons which influenced Gladstone, but chiefly because war hampered trade and cost money, which had to be extracted from reluctant taxpayers or raised, with increasing difficulty as the war went on, from a closed group of London financiers, intent on making the maximum profit for themselves from the national emergency.

While Pelham's ideas on foreign policy, such as they were, may have been basically sounder in the existing situation, the fact that his brother the premier held such views undoubtedly contributed to Newcastle's failure as a foreign minister. Step by step he had to convince his brother, sometimes indeed by concealing from him the ultimate ends which he had in view, and drag Pelham reluctantly along a path he personally detested. That Newcastle managed this at all was largely due to the influence of Hardwicke, for whose opinion both brothers had the liveliest respect, and through whom they sometimes conducted their political arguments when they were not on speaking terms with each other.

Newcastle realized that the best route to Maria Theresa's heart lay through her purse and he persuaded his brother to treat her generously in settling up subsidy accounts at the end of the war. But when he proposed to pay subsidies to mercenary German princes in time of peace in order to strengthen the war-potential of the Anglo-Austrian alliance, Pelham's gorge rose. Indeed, had Pelham consented to make such unprecedented proposals in their original form to the house of Commons, his position might have been as badly shaken as was Walpole's by the Excise scheme. Newcastle found help in an unexpected quarter.

Sir Charles Hanbury Williams, man-about-town, writer of Society verse and political lampoons, and aspiring politician, had served as British minister to Saxony and Poland in the last years of the war. While abroad he had heard a lot of loose talk about the possibility of securing the election of the Archduke Joseph, the eldest son of Maria Theresa and the Emperor Francis I, as king of

the Romans. With the exception of the loss of Silesia, nothing had
annoyed Maria Theresa more than the election of the Wittelsbach
Emperor, Charles VII, in 1742. She had not rested until she had
hounded him from his own electorate and reduced him to the
position of an imperial vagabond. As soon as Charles VII died,
Maria Theresa had strained every nerve to secure the election of
her husband; and it was natural to assume that she would be
equally anxious to retain the Imperial Crown for her son. In
separate negotiations with Austria during the war France had
dangled this prospect before the Empress-queen. No sooner had
he been restored to the position of William III in the United
Provinces than William IV had mooted the idea in the hope of
strengthening the bonds between Austria and the Maritime Powers.

Hanbury Williams convinced Newcastle that this slightly shop-
soiled idea offered him the best means of re-establishing, on a basis
of cordiality and mutual confidence hitherto lacking, the alliance
of Britain and Austria. He also spelled out to Newcastle, in words
of one syllable, how this plan could be presented to Cabinet and
Parliament in such a way as to undermine the opposition to the
policy of concluding subsidy treaties upon which Newcastle had
already set his heart. All that was necessary was to convince the
opposition that such treaties were not a preparation for war, but
insurance policies, with very modest premiums payable, for the
preservation of peace.

Every self-respecting Englishman believed that France was
determined to renew the war at the earliest possible moment. The
death of the Emperor Charles VI had given her the opportunity in
1740 and had cost Britain many millions of pounds. By providing
in advance for the succession to Francis I another war of the Austrian succession could be avoided. In addition, to secure the Imperial Crown for the Hapsburgs for two lives might well be the
first step towards the reappearance of Germany as a Great Power
in the European balance. Though Germany was clearly superior
to France in population, natural resources and perhaps even in
commercial and industrial development, France had divided her
against herself. What was required now was the co-ordination and
direction of the resources of Germany by a dominant political
authority—and in the eighteenth century this could only be the
Emperor.

British hopes were reinforced by fears. Austria, unaided, could

no longer resist France with any hope of success. France already
had a strong party in Germany; if Britain did not belatedly follow
her example and try to organize her friends within the Empire,
France might well gain complete control of the resources of Germany with results equally disastrous to the balance of power and
the Protestant cause in Europe.

The election scheme was equally attractive to George II, though
for quite different reasons. During the Austrian Succession war,
Hanover had more than once been threatened with invasion. To
preserve the beloved electorate, George had had to accept from
France humiliating terms. Prussia had now clearly out-distanced
Hanover as the leading state of northern Germany; but British sub-
sidies to suitable German states might do something to strengthen
Hanoverian influence and interests in the Empire. George never
ceased to resent his position as the most junior of the electors:
this slur would be removed if he could take the lead in making an
Emperor. Finally he was not without hopes of making profits for
Hanover if he played his hand properly during the negotiations.
The Anglo-Austrian reconciliation of 1731, accompanied as it had
been by an Imperial grant of privileges and territories for the
elector of Hanover, was clearly in his mind as a precedent to be
followed.

The king and Newcastle seem to have rushed to adopt the king-
of-the-Romans scheme without examining either the legal or the
practical difficulties in the way of its realization. Since France had
mooted the scheme earlier, they may have thought she would not
now oppose it. Indeed had they set about the election project
differently, and consulted France in advance, they would certainly
have had a much better chance of carrying it through con-
stitutionally.

Equally basic was their failure to appreciate the attitude of
Maria Theresa. She can hardly have relished the idea of the
youngest elector in the Empire taking the lead in these matters and
posing as an emperor-maker. She knew by bitter experience the
self-interest and mercenariness of the German princes and was
determined not to repeat her father's costly and unsuccessful
attempts to secure their guarantees of his Pragmatic Sanction. She
could hardly veto the British attempt, but made it abundantly clear
from the very beginning that her own contributions to its accom-
plishment would be minimal, if not non-existent. And she realized

much more clearly than Newcastle the nature and extent of the constitutional difficulties which stood in the way of the election. Even if France abstained from opposition and remained neutral, success could not be guaranteed. Once France adopted a hostile attitude to the scheme, it became chimerical and ought to have been dropped by George II and Newcastle like a hot potato.

Maria Theresa's ambivalent attitude was bad enough. Much worse was the way in which her leading minister, Kaunitz, regarded the scheme. His experiences in Italy and the Austrian Netherlands had convinced him that the Anglo-Austrian alliance, even before its rupture at the end of the war, did not meet Austria's clamant needs. What Austria, faced by the hostility of the Turks in south-eastern Europe and the successful rivalry of Prussia in the Empire, really required was the diplomatic and military support of France. This was a much less revolutionary idea than was thought at one time: attempt after attempt had been made to realize it, occasionally from the Austrian but more often from the French side, for at least half a century.

By this time, the election negotiation had set Germany in uproar. France and Prussia, still nominally allied though on very cool terms with each other since 1745, were driven back into each other's arms. When Kaunitz tried to separate France from Prussia he found that Newcastle's clumsy attempts to secure Joseph's election had given France and Prussia a common interest in opposing it. The king-of-the-Romans scheme had welded together the Franco-Prussian alliance and for the time being made Kaunitz's great idea impossible of attainment. Naturally he thought even less of Newcastle's brainwave than did his Imperial mistress.

If the election negotiation occupied the front place in Anglo-Austrian negotiations between the wars, there were other older and hardly less divisive questions. Most important of these was probably the future of the Austrian Netherlands, where the course of the war should have convinced any doubters of the futility of the Barrier treaty as a defence for the United Provinces. Maria Theresa was not prepared to restore at her own expense the fortresses 'slighted' by the French invaders, nor did she intend to pay substantial sums towards the upkeep of Dutch garrisons which had contributed little to the defence of the Netherlands. Nor was she prepared any longer to tolerate restrictions imposed by the Barrier treaty upon the economic activities of her Netherlandish subjects in the interests of the Maritime Powers with their system of preferential tariffs. In attempting, as he persistently did, to press the Dutch point of view on these questions upon Maria Theresa, Newcastle did the Dutch no service and merely damaged the relations between Britain and Austria.

Maria Theresa felt that she had another grievance against Britain. She remembered how in the last war Britain had given her some support against France but none against Prussia. If she had to involve herself, again as the ally of Britain, in a new war, she was determined that this time Britain must previously commit herself to Austro-Russian hostility to Prussia. This was what underlay Kaunitz's persistent demands that Britain should accede to the fourth secret article of the so-called treaty of the Two Empresses, which had been signed by Maria Theresa and the Tsaritsa Elizabeth in 1746. While the two empresses professed every intention of observing the treaty of Dresden, by which Austria recognized Prussian rights to Silesia, the Russian Empress promised, if Frederick broke this treaty, to help Maria Theresa to recover Silesia and Glatz by force of arms. The British government for obvious reasons declined absolutely to have anything to do with such a risky and provocative undertaking. It acceded to the innocuous treaty but not to the secret article.

Foiled in this attempt, Kaunitz tried another way to involve Britain in Austrian hostility to Prussia. He pressed Newcastle to negotiate a subsidy treaty, not with pettifogging electors of Germany whom Newcastle was approaching with offers of subsidies in exchange for votes in favour of the archduke, but with Russia. This, he argued, was the only method which could be depended upon to produce two objects which George II and most of his ministers had much at heart—the keeping in awe of Prussia, now closely co-operating with France in the election negotiations, and the defence of Hanover from attack either by France or Prussia or both simultaneously.

Newcastle obligingly began to negotiate at the Russian court; but was soon brought up short by the magnitude of Russia's financial demands. Kaunitz believed that Newcastle's treaties with German electors were futile, if not positively dangerous, to Austria's position in Germany, because they provoked the enmity of France and Prussia and gave these powers a common cause of antagonism to Austria. Newcastle suspected that Kaunitz's real object in pressing upon him a treaty of subsidy with Russia was to embroil him with Prussia and force him to subserve Austrian vengeance. In any case neither Pelham nor Parliament would provide subsidies on the required scale in time of peace.

What kept the Anglo-Austrian alliance alive in the early 'fifties was Prussia's refusal to make an alliance with Britain, and France's refusal to accept Kaunitz's propositions. What finally brought it to an end was the imminence of a war beyond Europe between France and Britain. In such a war the odds were in favour of Britain, in spite of the financial reforms of Machault and the plans of Maurepas, partly carried out by Rouillé and Machault in the 'fifties, for the expansion of the French navy; but it was widely believed on the Continent, as well as in Britain, that France would revenge herself upon George II by occupying Hanover and holding it to ransom. Pitt, now in Opposition, could look on such an eventuality with complacence: the king's ministers could not.

Newcastle believed that former treaties between Britain and Austria, notably the second treaty of Vienna of 1731, gave him a legal claim to Austrian armed assistance in such a continental war. Kaunitz demurred, partly on the ground that Austria's guarantee of George II's territories did not extend beyond Europe, partly on the argument that it was far from clear that in the war between France and Britain in the colonies Britain was on the defensive. There was, he pointed out, an almost exact parallel between Charles VI's position in 1733, at the outbreak of the Polish Succession war, and George II's situation in 1755. Britain had then made clear her lack of interest in Polish affairs and had refused to recognize the *casus foederis* contained in the second treaty of Vienna. Kaunitz now made clear Austria's complete disinterest in the colonial squabbles between Britain and France and hinted that even when the war spread to Europe Austria would follow the precedent set by Britain in the Polish Succession war and refuse to recognize it as being a defensive war for Britain.

When Newcastle argued that, irrespective of legal obligation, Maria Theresa was morally bound to come to the help of Britain —the power whose help had enabled her to establish herself securely in the Austrian dominions and recover the Imperial Crown—Kaunitz replied that it seemed to him that Britain had merely pursued a self-interested policy and that it was almost as much the fault of Britain as of France that Maria Theresa had lost

Silesia. Kaunitz was even less influenced by what Newcastle hoped might be the clinching argument—the services he had personally rendered to the house of Austria and the likelihood that if Austria did not help him to carry on the war his successors would adopt a different line of policy. In spite of the failure of his mission to Versailles, Kaunitz was still convinced that the British alliance could never be more than a pale second-best.

While he waited for a suitable moment to make a new approach to Louis XV, he was not averse to putting the screws on Newcastle. At the beginning of previous wars in which Britain and Austria had fought as allies, Austria had been the power much more immediately concerned in the issues which made war inevitable. Now at long last the roles were reversed and Kaunitz exploited the strength of his bargaining position to the utmost.

By supporting the extravagant claims of the Dutch against Austria, Newcastle, he said, had reduced Austria's inclination to defend the Netherlands almost to vanishing point. Since the Maritime Powers attached so much importance to this territory they must themselves take effective measures to defend it, with only a minimum of support from Austria, who was not only less interested but logistically ill-placed to take the leading part in its defence. Moreover a powerful army in the Netherlands would inhibit French designs upon Hanover. If Britain had not enough troops of her own to spare for this purpose, she could always hire German mercenaries. In addition, Britain must take up again with urgency the old negotiation for a subsidy treaty with Russia. This was the way to immobilize Prussia, and the cost of a subsidy to Russia, even at the exorbitant rates quoted by Bestuzhev, was a mere bagatelle compared with the cost of a war in Germany.

Newcastle did his best to comply. He hurriedly arranged subsidy treaties with Hesse-Cassel and Russia and forced them through the house of Commons. He tried, though without success, to stir up the Dutch to take part in their own defence. He comforted himself with the belief that Spain, under the pacific Ferdinand VI, was on his side. But he simply could not take upon Britain the main, indeed almost the sole, defence of the Netherlands. Whether Kaunitz really thought Newcastle could do this, or was merely demanding the impossible, in order to be able to blame Britain for the breakdown of the old alliance between them, is not clear.

Whatever his intentions, the result was the same. Although some of its members hoped that Austria would change her mind, the British Cabinet decided meantime to abandon the Continent. The Anglo-Austrian alliance came to an end in 1755 and all attempts to revive it failed until the outbreak of the French Revolution changed the basis of the European system of states. Immediately Kaunitz realized that Britain was not going to accept his terms, he decided not to try to defend the Netherlands, but to use them as a bait to bring France into alliance with Austria.

This would probably have failed but for Newcastle's simultaneous approaches to Prussia, culminating in the convention of Westminster (January 1756).[1] Kaunitz's terms were stiff, but France, losing Prussia, felt that she must accept them. Accordingly when Robert Keith, on Newcastle's instructions, informed the Empress-queen that Britain had neutralized Germany by agreement with Prussia, he received her ironical congratulations. The insolence shown towards the Empress by the two electors, who had made this agreement for the Empire without even a pretence of consultation with the head of the Empire, was resented at Vienna almost as much as the exclusion of the Austrian Netherlands from the area to be neutralized. Britain had not merely deserted Austria: she was deliberately encouraging France to attack the Netherlands instead of threatening Hanover. Newcastle retorted that what he had done he had been forced to do unwillingly by Maria Theresa's desertion of Britain on the first occasion upon which Britain required Austria's help. Keith stayed on at Vienna through the summer of 1756, shunned by the ministers and neglected at the court.

When Frederick marched into Saxony, thus breaking the convention of Westminster, it was hoped that Britain would repudiate the connexion. Clearly Prussia was no longer in a position to guarantee Hanover, and Kaunitz made genuine efforts to persuade France not to attack the electorate. It is true that he was not moved by any concern for British interests, but wished France to concentrate all her available resources against his arch-enemy, Prussia. In spite of this he sought to represent his activities as designed to help his former ally; and many people in Britain, who still preferred the Austrian to the Prussian alliance, were inclined to believe him. Even when France persisted in invading western Ger-

[1] See below, chapter 6, pp. 154–6.

many, they were reluctant to do anything that would make more difficult the restoration at the end of the war of the Anglo-Austrian alliance. But tension inevitably increased between two powers who were now fighting on opposite sides in Germany, and Keith left Vienna in July 1757, without taking leave of the Empress-queen. Diplomatic relations were not restored until the arrival of Lord Stormont in November 1763.

Newcastle's hankering, even during the Seven Years war, for the old alliance with Austria contributed to the celebrated quarrel between Bute and Frederick the Great and left Britain in complete isolation when the war ended. Though some Englishmen preferred such a situation on principle and others believed that it might be advantageous in the existing political situation of Europe, most were still convinced that the undying hostility of the Bourbon courts could only be effectively countered by alliance with a strong continental power.

Politicians in the earlier years of George III's reign were however divided amongst themselves as to which continental power offered maximum advantage and the minimum of dangerous involvement in continental affairs. Since Russia was still rarely considered a power which could exert much influence in western Europe, the practical choice lay between Austria and Prussia. Frederick's resentment in fact made the latter quite impracticable, as was demonstrated once and for all by the failure of Pitt's overtures during his ministry in 1766-8.

Henceforth Austria was the almost automatic choice of any Briton who saw the necessity or desirability of a continental ally. This had already been demonstrated as soon as the Seven Years war came to an end. Lord Stormont was hurriedly despatched to Vienna with the rank of ambassador. He remained there for nine years and was succeeded by another conscientious and personally popular minister, Sir Robert Murray Keith. The fundamental reason why neither could make any real progress was the continued alliance between Austria and France. Though the Franco-Austrian alliance had completely failed to achieve the objectives Kaunitz had had in view when he concluded it, he still believed that it served the interests of Austria much more satisfactorily than the British alliance had ever done—or could do.

Only when tension between Austria and France became acute was there any improvement in the relations between Austria and

Britain. And even on those occasions some British ministers, and George III himself, were beginning to wonder whether the approach should be made to France rather than to Austria. This was notably the case at the time of the first Partition of Poland, when Austrian desertion of France and concurrence with Russia and Prussia nearly broke off the Franco-Austrian alliance. At such times what had been, on both sides, a cold-blooded and unsatisfactory political expedient was often represented in Britain as a glamorous and glorious league which had made possible her rise to greatness in Europe and her now almost unquestioned domination beyond Europe.

The accession of Joseph II as Emperor in 1765 and the distrust of France which he had inherited from his father, Francis I, seemed at first to increase the prospects of an Anglo-Austrian alliance. While his father had been a political nonentity at the Hapsburg court, Joseph was determined to make his influence felt. Archdeacon Coxe, whose *House of Austria* (originally published in 1807) is still of value for the study of British foreign policy, spent the winter of 1777–8 at Vienna and testified from personal acquaintance with Joseph II to the anti-Bourbon sentiments of the young Emperor and the severe sarcasms which he uttered in private societies against the French.[1] His visit to Paris in 1777 had proved a comparative failure and he returned to Vienna even less of a Francophil than when he set out.

By this time Britain was engaged in war with her American colonies and in no condition to give effective support to a power which was becoming more and more bound up in east European interests. Yet Austria's attitude during the American war was in marked contrast to that of her French ally. The Cabinet of Vienna professed openly its distaste for rebels and refused to receive the agents of the revolting colonies in a diplomatic capacity. They also prohibited all commerce between the Americans and the Austrian Netherlands. Joseph told Murray Keith that the cause on which England was engaged was the cause of all sovereigns.[2] It may be doubted whether this was more than diplomatic courtesy.

Joseph had set his sights on the alliance of Russia which was obviously readier and in a much better position than Britain to support him in the aggressive plans on the Continent which he had most at heart. The death of his mother enabled him to conclude in

<hr />

[1] Op. cit. (ed. 1853) III. 456n.   [2] Ibid. III. 472.

1780–1 his celebrated alliance with the Tsaritsa, the foundations of which had been laid at personal interviews between the eastern autocrats. He valued the new alliance all the more because he had displaced Frederick the Great from the position he had held since 1764 as Russia's principal ally and counsellor. Had this alliance been concluded a few years earlier it might well have promoted more cordial relations between Britain and Austria, but in the 'eighties Russia, as the effective power behind the Armed Neutrality, could no longer be considered as Britain's safe friend.

Indeed the Austro-Russian Alliance was based on mutual help in areas which would tend to reduce Russian activity in the Baltic, where alone British support of the Austro-Russian allies was likely to be either enthusiastic or effective. Both Austria and Russia therefore turned towards France in the 'eighties, particularly since Joseph II's determination to abrogate the Barrier treaties, revive the prosperity of the Austrian Netherlands, and recover from the Dutch certain border provinces of which his ancestors had been unjustly deprived, was certain to be opposed by Britain. Joseph paid a second, and more successful, visit to France and declined an invitation from George III to extend his tour across the English Channel.

The basic cause of the ineffectiveness of British foreign policy in the first thirty years of the reign of George III was therefore the isolation of Great Britain and the inability of successive British foreign ministers to establish a stable system. Up to the disasters of the American war of Independence many British politicians, like Lord Salisbury more than a century later, thought isolation a lesser evil than close engagement in continental politics with the recurring risk of involvement in wars between continental powers in which Britain had little direct interest.

The formation of a continental coalition against Britain during the American war destroyed such facile optimism. Yet, in the first years of his ministry the younger Pitt showed reluctance to reverse the foreign policy of his predecessors and conclude a binding alliance with a continental power. It is not clear at this stage whether he personally preferred the understanding with Prussia, which had made possible his father's triumphs in the Seven Years war, to the revival of the older alliance with Austria, the inadequacy of which his father had denounced before and during the Austrian Succession war. That Britain emerged from isolation in the late 'eighties as the ally of Prussia rather than of Austria seems to have been due to the chapter of accidents, not to a deliberate preference on the part of the British prime minister.

The Triple Alliance of Britain, Prussia, and the United Provinces (1788), although it exerted a great influence upon European politics for two or three years, rested on a misunderstanding.[1] The Hapsburg Emperor, Leopold II, had no difficulty in driving a wedge between Britain and Prussia. This made possible the revival of the Anglo-Austrian alliance, based on the defence of the Low Countries against French aggression.

The influence of the Austrian chancellor, Kaunitz, who had engineered the Diplomatic Revolution and continued to prefer a French to a British alliance, lessened as Leopold II became his own foreign minister, though it was not until 1794, under Leopold's son, Francis II, that he was formally superseded by Thugut. The new foreign minister was regarded at Vienna as a determined advocate of continuing the war against France in alliance with like-minded powers, above all Britain. In practice he proved a disappointment to Pitt, partly because his influence at Vienna was never dominant and other ministers frequently thwarted him, but mainly because he preferred in his negotiations with Britain and other interested powers to drive the best possible bargain for Austria rather than to make concessions to his allies which would consolidate the opposition to France.

It may be suggested that in any case the attitudes of Britain and Austria were so different and their interests so divergent that even a less rigid and more conciliatory minister than Thugut might have failed to create the atmosphere of mutual tolerance and goodwill among the Allies necessary for the successful prosecution of the war against France in the 1790's. There was the further difficulty that the Austrian military machine and the resources of the Austrian state, even with the best will in the world, were incapable of achieving the results expected by Pitt.

In the spring of 1793 all this lay in the future. Not only was the recovery of the Austrian alliance, which most Britons had vainly desired since the end of the Seven Years war, a triumph for Pitt; but, better still from the British point of view, Prussia seemed to be ready to co-operate with Austria in resisting the French republicans who were already threatening the whole established order in

---

[1] Details in chapter 6, pp. 172-4.

Europe. The favourable conditions for British intervention in a continental war, which had made possible Marlborough's victories at the beginning of the century, had at last been restored. Instead of fighting side by side with Austria against France and Prussia, as in the Austrian Succession war, or with Prussia against France and Austria, as in the Seven Years war, there seemed a reasonable prospect of organizing something very like a national German opposition to France under the Emperor, as in the Spanish Succession war.

Pitt was ready to act as paymaster to any prince who would contribute an army to fight against France on the Continent. Large subsidies each year were paid to the king of Prussia and lesser German princes; but for reasons which are somewhat mysterious, he declined, both at the time of the First and at that of the Second Coalition, to subsidize Austria. He insisted that the Austrian government must raise the sums it needed for military purposes by loans on the London money market and accept responsibility for repaying and servicing these loans. Since Austria's credit was low, Pitt was rather reluctantly forced to give a British government guarantee both of capital and interest: otherwise the loans could not have been raised at all.

Neither loan secured the objects which Pitt had in view. In 1794–5, when the Austrian armies suffered one reverse after another, the Imperial government did not even make use of the instalments of the loan which had been remitted to Hamburg to provide the Emperor with the sinews of war. In the case of the second loan, before the details had been adjusted, Austria had already withdrawn from the war by the preliminaries of Leoben (1796); and she repudiated the action of her diplomatic agent at London in signing the convention of 1797 which had been intended to settle the questions still in dispute between the two governments. One of the considerations which annoyed the British government was the risk that the proceeds of a loan intended to make effective Austrian resistance to France might eventually be used to pay off part of a war contribution imposed by the victorious French upon an unsuccessful Austrian ally. So strained were Anglo-Austrian relations after the treaty of Campo Formio (1797) that the British foreign minister thought of recalling the minister plenipotentiary from Vienna or even of breaking off diplomatic relations with Vienna altogether in 1798.

When Austria re-entered the war her Italian armies were speedily routed by Napoleon at Marengo (14 June 1800). Six days later Austria accepted the financial and other stipulations of the loan convention of 1797 which had been much whittled down by three years of obstinate negotiation by Thugut. She also undertook not to make a separate peace with France before the end of February 1801. In spite of Thugut's signature the Austrian armies remained inactive both in Italy and in Germany until the crushing defeat of the Austrians at Hohenlinden and the French threat to Vienna caused the resignation of Thugut and the withdrawal of Austria from the war by the treaty of Lunéville (February 1801). The second loan had done even less than the first to animate Austria and enable her to wage a successful war against France.

Finally when Austria agreed to join the Third Coalition in 1805, Pitt gave her the subsidies he had earlier refused and the British government continued to service the Imperial loans, which were not finally liquidated by a token payment from the Emperor to the British government until 1824.[1] Austrian co-operation in 1805 hastened the dispersal of the Napoleonic army at Boulogne but neither in 1805 nor in 1809, though now lavishly subsidized by Britain, did Austria prove capable of defending herself against Napoleon. When Metternich took over control of Austrian foreign policy in 1809 he had at first to accept the role of a French satellite state.

Britain now found in Russia and a reformed Prussia the 'continental dagger' without which the overthrow of Napoleon would have been impracticable. Up to 1809 Austria had certainly been the most persistent, but also the most frequently defeated of the continental opponents of revolutionary and Napoleonic France. Metternich in 1809 had reversed the policy pursued by his predecessors and had even advised his master to accept Napoleon as his son-in-law. Then in 1813 when Russia and Prussia had at long last shown themselves capable of resisting Napoleon, and Wellington had driven the French armies out of Spain, Metternich adopted what he called the role of 'armed mediator'. In other words he sought to impose upon France and her opponents a compromise peace which would safeguard the vital interests of Austria. The violence of Napoleon's reaction to what he regarded as Austrian

[1] The preceding paragraphs are based on K. F. Helleiner, *The Imperial Loans* (Clarendon Press, Oxford, 1965).

insolence forced Metternich almost willy-nilly into the Allied camp. It says much for his diplomatic ability that he was able to play the part he did at the final congress of Vienna and that British statesmen in the first half of the nineteenth century continued to regard the support of the Hapsburg Empire as a major British interest on the European continent.

A. *Primary Sources*

Österreichische Staatsverträge: England, ed. A. F. Pribram (2 vols., Innsbruck, 1907, and Vienna, 1913)
Turkey its History and Progress, ed. Sir George Larpent (2 vols., 1854) [vol. I, Appendix, pp. 406–97, documents Carteret's approaches to Maria Theresa]

B. *Secondary Authorities*

Braubach, M., *Prinz Eugen* (5 vols., Munich, 1963–5)
Coxe, W., *History of the House of Austria* (3rd ed., 1847–53, in 3 vols.)
Dollot, R., 'La Garnison de la Barrière dans les Pays-Bas autrichiens, 1715–82' in *RHD* 17 (1904), 421–37
Gachard, L.-P., *Histoire de la Belgique au commencement du XVIII* *siècle* (Brussels, 1880)
Gehling, T., *Ein europäischer Diplomat am Kaiserhof zu Wien* [St. Saphorin, 1718–1727] (Bonn, 1964)
Gibbs, G. C., 'Great Britain and the Alliance of Hanover' in *EHR* 73 (1958), 404–30
Helleiner, K. F., 'Ein unbekanntes Kapitel aus der anglo-österreichische Finanzgeschichte' in *MIOG* 71 (1963), 395–407
— *The Imperial Loans* (Oxford, 1965)
Hertz, G. B., 'England and the Ostend Company' in *EHR* 22 (1907), 255–79
Horn, D. B., *Sir Charles Hanbury Williams and European Diplomacy* (1930), chapter 8
Kospach, H., 'Englische Stimmen über Österreich und Prinz Eugen' in *MIOG* 73 (1965), 39–62
Mayer, F. M., 'Zur Geschichte der Österreichische Handelspolitik unter Kaiser Karl VI' in *MIOG* 18 (1897), 129–45 [deals with attempts to develop Trieste and Fiume]
Naumann, M., *Österreich, England und das Reich 1719–32* (Berlin, 1936)
Oehler, H., *Prinz Eugen im Urteil Europas* (Munich, 1944) [English views pp. 289–346]
Otruba, G., 'Die Bedeutung englischer Subsidien und Antizipationen für die Finanzen Österreichs 1701 bis 1748' in *Vierteljahrschrift für Sozial- und Wirtschaftsgeschichte* 51 (1964), 192–234
Steuer, G., 'Englands österreichpolitik um den Jahren 1730–35' [Bonn dissertation (unpublished)]

CHAPTER 6

Great Britain and Prussia

EVEN after the Revolution of 1688 had brought Britain more closely into the European state-system as the ally of the Emperor and the Dutch, relations between Britain and Brandenburg-Prussia remained distant and unimportant. Both states were Protestant and both took the side of Austria against France in the wars fought in the reigns of William III and Anne; but missions of compliment were as frequent as diplomatic missions with real business to transact at Berlin and there were long gaps in representation. It was really the accession of the house of Hanover to the throne of Great Britain that brought Britain and Prussia into regular diplomatic contact and it is probably in this area of British foreign policy that the personal influence of George I and George II was most clearly and effectively directed.

Hanover and Prussia were already in 1714 close allies in the politics of the Empire with a common interest in wringing concessions from the Emperor in exchange for their support. Brandenburg had backed the dynastic policy of Ernest Augustus, directed towards the reunion of the Guelf duchies of Lüneburg and Celle and the creation of a ninth electorate of Hanover for his enlarged dominions. In exchange the Hanover dukes had been partisans of the elevation of the Hohenzollerns to the dignity of kings in Prussia. Both states took an active part against France in the Spanish Succession war and continued to support the Imperial cause after British desertion. Each had received a modest reward which it privately regarded as inadequate. Continued co-operation in the politics of the Empire seemed the most promising route to convincing the Emperor that they deserved better than they had so far received. But in other respects Hanover and Brandenburg-Prussia were rivals, if not enemies, as was made clear in the course of the second Northern war.

The conversion to Roman Catholicism of the elector of Saxony, hitherto the unquestioned head of German Protestantism, added competition for the leadership of the *corpus evangelicorum* to other causes of friction between them. It is true that this was partially masked by the active policy of persecution and proselytism concurrently pursued by Charles VI, under the influence of the Imperial vice-chancellor, Schönborn, against the Protestants of central Europe in the years following upon the Utrecht settlement. Close co-operation in the confessional politics of the Empire seemed to be almost a necessary condition for the continued existence of German Protestantism.

At first Hanover and Prussia continued to co-operate as closely in the secular politics of the Northern war as they did to their mutual advantage in German confessional politics. By judiciously blackmailing Sweden's enemies, Hanover secured from Denmark the occupation of Bremen and Verden, immediately to the north of Hanover and long coveted by the Guelf dukes. By following a similar policy, Frederick William I of Prussia gained control of the port of Stettin and part of the adjoining duchy of Pomerania, though, unlike George I, he had to take an active part, along with the Russians and Saxons, in expelling the Swedes. Britain had little, if any, interest in these territorial squabbles and no inclination to take part in the Northern war.

Even under the Tory government of Anne's last years, Britain had shown her determination to protect her Baltic trade from attack by the belligerents. A joint British and Dutch squadron had escorted a merchant fleet to Baltic ports, and then convoyed them home, laden with the tar, hemp, timber, and other naval stores without which Britain could not hope to keep her fleets in being. As the war went on, and especially after the return of Charles XII to the scene of the struggle in 1714, exercise of their maritime rights both by Sweden and Russia became more and more stringent. Charles XII in 1714 absolutely prohibited, by what would later have been called a paper blockade, trade with the former Swedish ports in the eastern Baltic which were now controlled by Russia.

George I had the bright idea that a British fleet in the Baltic, ostensibly protecting British commerce, could be used to cut off communications between Sweden and Pomerania. This would facilitate the conquest of Pomerania by his allies and could be represented to them as Hanover's contribution to the common, and particularly to the Hanoverian-Prussian, cause. Though British fleets continued for some years to be sent to the Baltic, George found it more and more difficult to get his allies to accept his point of view, while Charles XII's indignation led him to engage with the Jacobites. Soon George quarrelled openly with Peter the Great over the Russian occupation of Mecklenburg and the threatened consolidation of Russian influence in the duchy through the marriage of the duke to one of Peter the Great's nieces.

While Britain on the whole had a tradition of friendship, based on community of ecclesiastical and economic interests, with Sweden, she had no such tradition towards Russia and feared that Russian ascendency in the Baltic would be disadvantageous, if not disastrous, to her commerce there. Without naval stores from the Baltic there could be no British navy: without a navy Britain could neither defend herself from France nor make her influence felt in Europe and overseas. There was a much greater measure of agreement between the interests of Britain and Hanover in respect to Russia than there could ever be with regard to Sweden.

The stand taken by George as king and as elector against his *quondam* ally, Russia, forced Frederick William to choose between George, who had persistently evaded his obligations as an ally, and Peter, who had contributed much more than Frederick William himself to the conquest of Pomerania. Frederick William, however, was more moved by fear than by gratitude: he had no conception of the dangers which the rise of Russia would bring to Germany, but was afraid that, if he joined Hanover in opposition to Russian penetration of Germany, Peter might seize East Prussia, the territory from which he drew the title of king and thereby enjoyed the *mystique* of royalty. Other personal factors, especially his jealousy of the sudden rise of George I to European prominence, if not dominance, influenced his decision in favour of Peter.

For two or three years Britain-Hanover and Prussia were on opposite sides; but Peter failed either to conquer Sweden or to coerce her to make peace on his terms. Co-operation, though not cordiality, was restored between George and Frederick William when Britain secured Sweden's formal recognition of Prussia's claim to part of Pomerania with the valuable port of Stettin.

The Emperor showed clearly his resentment of the parts played by Hanover and Prussia, in complete disregard of his own policy and wishes, in the Northern war. He refused to recognize their legal claims to the territories they had annexed. The courts of the Empire decided against Hanover and Prussia in lawsuits between either of them and other members of the Empire. Already Frederick William's determination to press his claims to Jülich and Berg, as soon as the Neuburg line of electors Palatine died out, endangered his relations with the Emperor, who had good reasons for supporting the rival claimant. Schönborn was allowed, if not encouraged, to press on with his policy of giving countenance and aid to Roman Catholic princes and to make things unpleasant for the Protestants—unless they saw the light and became converts, as did the electoral prince of Saxony, to Roman Catholicism. George and Frederick William in self-defence against the Emperor signed the treaty of Charlottenburg in 1723. Britain had her own reasons for opposition to the Hapsburgs, notably the Ostend Company, and Townshend readily promised to support Prussian claims to Jülich and Berg. When the hostility between Britain and Austria became still more overt, Prussia had at first no hesitation in aligning herself with Britain and her ally France in the league of Hanover. But soon Frederick William came under the influence of the Austrian general Seckendorff, while his own chief minister, Grumbkow, became the paid adherent of Austria.

The proposal for a double marriage between the houses of Hohenzollern and Hanover, originally intended to perpetuate and consolidate the political understanding between them, became a source of resentment and division. Frederick William had a pronounced antipathy towards his cousin, George II, who warmly reciprocated it. Frederick William had been jealous of the successes of George I: he hated George II, not entirely without reason, but with a personal malignity, bordering on mania, for which no adequate political explanation can be offered.

Deserting Britain once and for all in 1726, Frederick William signed in 1728 with the Emperor a perpetual treaty of defensive alliance which included a mutual guarantee of each other's territories. Frederick William also guaranteed the Pragmatic Sanction and promised to vote for Maria Theresa's husband as Emperor: in exchange Charles VI undertook to support, when the time came, Prussian claims to Berg and Ravenstein. Walpole, having got rid of Townshend, made a last effort to recover Prussia as an ally for Britain by reviving the double marriage proposals; but the envoy he sent to Berlin, Sir Charles Hotham, bungled badly and helped to bring to a head the quarrels within the Prussian royal family which had been simmering for some years. The Prussian crown prince narrowly escaped with his life and his sister and *confidante*,

Wilhelmina, was married off to a distant cousin whom she secretly despised.

Even after Walpole had made his peace with the Emperor by the second treaty of Vienna, and Britain and Prussia were once again on the same side in European politics, there was no real improvement in the relations between the two courts. Frederick William accused George II of stirring up his family against him. He would have been even angrier had he known that George II continued to dole out to the Prussian crown prince small sums of money. This ran counter to his hopes of keeping his son docile and politically harmless by keeping him chronically short of ready money. He claimed also that George had destroyed the will of George I, under which the queen of Prussia would have received a substantial legacy. The two kings had contradictory claims to the duchy of East Friesland on the death of the reigning duke and were already looking around for support. But what caused most feeling was Frederick William's resentment of George's special position as the Emperor's delegate in Mecklenburg, which dated back to Peter the Great's occupation of the duchy, and his determination either to destroy or share it.

Charles VI, by accident or design, made things worse by showing unmistakably that he attached much greater importance to the British-Hanoverian alliance than to the Prussian, even after Britain had let him down in the Polish Succession war and Prussia had punctiliously fulfilled her obligations. Nor did the Tsaritsa Anne help matters when she showed her contempt for Prussia by repudiating the agreement she had made to secure the Polish throne for a Portuguese prince and substituting the young elector of Saxony, whose exclusion from his father's kingdom had been the main reason for Prussian concurrence with the Portuguese plans of Russia and Austria. At the very time when she spurned Prussia, she took a long step towards reconciliation with George II by signing a commercial treaty with Britain in 1734, which safeguarded British trading interests in the Baltic and was to form the indispensable basis for political co-operation between Britain and Russia.

Respected by Austria and Russia in the 'thirties, Britain had no occasion for a Prussian alliance. Prussia sank lower and lower until the Emperor secretly repudiated the promises which had persuaded Frederick William to join with Austria in 1728. Even then, though he is reputed to have said of his son the crown prince, 'there goes one who will avenge me', he made no serious attempt to alter course. As long as he lived Britain and Prussia remained estranged from each other.

The accession of Frederick II opened a new era in the story of the political and cultural relations between Britain and Prussia in the eighteenth century. Such contact as had hitherto existed had been at diplomatic levels and dominated by Hanoverian interests. So far as purely British interests were concerned if there was very little to bring Britain and Prussia together, there was even less to separate them. Once personal antipathies and quarrels between the sovereigns were removed or at least mollified by Frederick William's death, there was little to stop a reconciliation, but even less upon which to base political co-operation, let alone social and cultural contacts. Frederick made his position clear at the beginning of his reign when he pointedly inquired of the British diplomatic agent at Berlin what was the attitude of his government to Prussian claims on (1) Jülich and Berg, (2) East Friesland, and (3) Mecklenburg. If the British ministers were not prepared to give up support of Hanoverian territorial claims in favour of Prussia they could not expect to make progress at Berlin.

The outbreak of the Austrian Succession war, and Prussia's astonishing victory over Austria at Mollwitz, while Britain was failing to make much progress in her colonial war with Spain, altered the balance in favour of Prussia. So long as he remained in office, Walpole's principal aim in foreign policy was to prevent further extension of the colonial war with Spain, upon which he had engaged with notorious reluctance. Terrified that Austria, already weakened by loss of prestige and territory in the Polish Succession war, would disappear altogether from the political map of Europe, he sought to damp down the threatened conflicts in central Europe. Austria must yield to the moderate demands of the young king of Prussia and secure his help against her other enemies, now organizing themselves under the leadership of France.

When Carteret took over control of foreign affairs and the conduct of the war in 1742, his attitude towards Prussia was not very different. Helped by Maria Theresa's gradual consolidation of her position in Germany and Hungary, he however gave an offensive twist to the purely defensive war strategy of his predecessor. He and Lord Stair, the commander of the Pragmatic army in Germany, had visions of repeating once again the military successes of

Marlborough and Eugene in a frontal attack upon France, in which the troops of Austria and Prussia would combine with the subsidiary troops paid for by the Maritime Powers. Carteret, mainly by undertaking to guarantee Frederick's conquests from Austria, was able to take the first step—the signature of a defensive alliance at Westminster (November 1742) between Britain and Prussia.

Frederick signed the treaty with reluctance and made it abundantly clear that he objected strongly to Carteret's ultimate aims. The more clearly Carteret's offensive strategy was revealed, the worse the relations of Britain and Prussia became, especially when Carteret, for reasons which are still not entirely clear, gave up the attempt to reconcile Maria Theresa and Charles VII, the Wittelsbach Emperor, who was now the client of Prussia. He thus left Frederick, if he wished to remain in possession of Silesia, no alternative but to re-enter the German war as the ally of France.

Carteret naturally resented Frederick's action, which transformed the war from an offensive against the house of Bourbon, conducted mainly on the borders of France, into a German struggle which threatened further territorial loss to Austria. Frederick made things worse by explaining that, in his view, Hanover had never been included in the treaty of Westminster, and that, anyhow, Britain was engaged in an offensive war to which the stipulations of this defensive treaty were inapplicable.

George II had never been enthusiastic about the alliance with Prussia. The death of the duke of East Friesland in 1744 brought to a head the long-simmering quarrel over the succession in this duchy. The young king of Prussia was playing a much more successful and decisive part in the politics of Europe than George himself. Even in the German war, the glory of Dettingen paled in comparison with the Prussian victories at Mollwitz and Chotusitz; and Frederick II rubbed salt in George II's wound by repeatedly pointing out that the military superiority of his army made it easy for him to occupy Hanover at will.

With the support of Carteret, George II threw over the policy of trying to reconcile Austria and Prussia. By the treaty of Warsaw (January 1745) signed by Britain, Austria, Saxony, and the Dutch, Britain promised to contribute large subsidies towards an Austro-Saxon campaign, intended to deprive Prussia of Silesia. Before the treaty had actually been signed Carteret had been forced out of office. His bid to retain the confidence of the king cost him the support of his colleagues in the ministry and their majority in the house of Commons.

The Pelhams succeeded to the control of British foreign policy, reluctantly vacated by Carteret at the behest of his ministerial colleagues. The doubts they already had about his change of policy deepened when it became clear that the reconquest of Silesia would be a much more difficult, expensive, and long-drawn-out task than the enthusiastic and optimistic Carteret had expected. When Frederick won a victory at Hohenfriedberg over the Austro-Saxon army which was invading Silesia, the Pelhams signed with Prussia the secret convention of Hanover (August 1745). Prussia undertook to make peace with Austria on the basis of the *status quo ante bellum*. Britain promised to use her influence with Austria to get her to accept peace on this condition. If she were successful, she would secure the insertion, in the final treaty of peace, of a guarantee for Silesia to Prussia, while Prussia would give the Brandenburg vote for Maria Theresa's husband at the forthcoming election of an Emperor to succeed Charles VII.

When the Austrians and Saxons persisted in continuing their Silesian campaign, Frederick again defeated them at Soor and forced Saxony out of the war by invading the electorate and occupying Dresden. Maria Theresa reluctantly made peace on the terms foreshadowed by the convention of Hanover. Once actual war between Austria and Prussia had been concluded, the Pelhams were as eager as Carteret had been in 1742 to arrange a defensive alliance between Britain and Prussia. For this purpose Villiers, who had negotiated the treaty of Dresden and might therefore be expected to be *persona gratissima* at the Prussian court, was sent to Berlin. His mission proved a fiasco. Nothing corresponding even to the treaty of Westminster of 1742, unsatisfactory as it had soon proved to both parties, was signed.

Frederick, as always, was deeply suspicious of Hanoverian influence over British foreign policy; a new cause for Prussian alienation from Britain had emerged during the war. Britain was making more and more stringent use of her belligerent rights to interfere with neutral trade. Since Prussia had no treaty with Britain which could be applied to in mitigation of these rights, she suffered the maximum of interference and secured the minimum of compensation. British ministers replied blandly to Frederick's protests that they had no power, under the British constitution, to interfere with the decisions of the Admiralty courts which settled all such questions of seizure and contraband.

Frederick was much better informed about the oddities of the British constitution than most continental rulers; but he really could not swallow such an improbable story. If the British government would not pay compensation to his subjects, he would simply stop making payment to British subjects of the capital and interest which he had obliged himself to pay in respect of a loan, originally made by them to the Emperor Charles VI, and secured upon the revenues of Silesia. He would thus have in his own hands ample funds to compensate his own subjects once their claims had been examined and adjusted by his own civil servants.

In spite of the emergence of this ticklish problem, the near-collapse of the Dutch forced the Pelhams in the closing months of the war to make a new approach to Frederick. Their agent, Henry Legge, proved no more successful than Villiers—and for much the same reasons. Frederick would join with Britain, but only if she completely abandoned Austria. Newcastle was the last man to take such a leap in the dark. By temperament, inclination and policy he clung firmly to the old system. Pelham was much more open to conviction on the advantages of the Prussian alliance, but contented himself with obstructing his brother's policy, especially if it involved spending money abroad. Once peace had been concluded at Aix-la-Chapelle, all the initiatives came from Newcastle.

That Newcastle had given up any idea of improving British relations with Prussia is proved by the instructions he gave to the next British envoy to the court of Berlin, Sir Charles Hanbury Williams, in 1750. These reduced Williams to the role of an accredited spy while he was at Berlin, and also ordered him shortly to leave Berlin for Warsaw, where he was to do his best to thwart the schemes of Frederick, while still remaining accredited to the Prussian court. Few diplomatists could have carried out successfully two such missions concurrently. Williams soon made things worse than they need have been by openly showing his contempt and distaste for Frederician Prussia, if not also for its philosopher-king. He would 'rather be a monkey in the island of Borneo than a subject of his Prussian majesty', he remarked with much more point than tact.

When he returned from an official visit to Dresden, the Prussian foreign ministers who had at first treated him, by his own account, with a 'distinguished shyness', declined to discuss business with him at all. Frederick then asked the British government to recall their agent. Newcastle had no option but to comply. It was obviously futile to retain at Berlin a diplomatist who exacerbated instead of trying to improve relations between the two courts.

The end of the war left Frederick, at least for the time being, in secure possession of Silesia. After he had secured the guarantee of Silesia by all the parties to the treaty of Aix-la-Chapelle and had compensated his subjects for their war losses, out of the funds withheld by him from payment of the Silesian loan, he had nothing to hope for from Britain. He was already contemplating further conquests and was well aware that France was both more ready and more able than Britain to offer him support in such aggressive plans. He could therefore display his antipathy to his uncle and his contempt for Hanover with impunity. Indeed the worse his relations with Britain and Hanover, the closer would be his alliance with France. These general considerations were confirmed and reinforced by the emergence of specific questions, which contributed to the existing tension and soon transformed it into acute hostility on both sides.

For one thing, Frederick believed that Britain was supporting Russia in an aggressive Baltic policy directed against Sweden, with which Prussia was in alliance. Britain's accession to the celebrated treaty of the Two Empresses in 1750 and the beginning of negotiations for a Russo-British treaty of subsidy 'to keep Prussia in awe' confirmed him in this unfounded belief. He became even angrier when Britain attempted to rush through the election of the Archduke Joseph as king of the Romans.[1] Frederick stirred up France to oppose the favourite plan of Newcastle and George II to secure the peace of Europe, and then acted as the principal agent of France in defeating it.

By this time the British attitude to Prussia was no longer dominated by Hanoverian grievances, although these continued to play a part in determining the relations of Britain and Prussia up to the death of George II. Britain now had her own reasons for disliking and actively opposing Frederick. Prussian action during the last war had destroyed the effectiveness of the legendary old system of alliances. Frederick's decision to adhere after the war to the French alliance, which he had treated so cavalierly during the war, was bitterly resented at London. His attempts to establish, especially

---

[1] See above, chapter 5, pp. 129–32.

at Emden, overseas trading companies in competition with British merchants aroused almost as much indignation in London as Charles VI's Ostend Company had done a generation earlier. His refusal to honour his obligation to repay the Silesian loan was naturally denounced by British financiers.

Frederick's repeated demands for compensation for Prussian ships detained or confiscated by the British Admiralty court during the war caused indignation in British government circles, especially when he argued that this was not only contrary to international law but to undertakings given by Carteret as secretary of state to the Prussian minister at London. Newcastle took more seriously than he need have done Frederick's flamboyant posing as the latter-day champion of Jacobitism and his employment of Jacobite exiles not only in the Prussian army but at least on one important diplomatic mission.

But alike on the British as on the Prussian side, it was the ill-fated king-of-the-Romans election which produced most heat and did most damage to Anglo-Prussian relations at this time. The reserved attitude of Austria towards it made Britain its protagonist, while Prussia, as the ally of France as well as in her own right, took the lead in opposition.

From 1750 to 1754 the state of the election served as a barometer which accurately measured the pressures exerted within the empire by Anglo-Prussian competition and conflict. Britain won votes by giving subsidies and trying to win concessions from Maria Theresa for German princes who supported the scheme. Prussia threatened that anyone who acted with Britain was a traitor to the Empire and might expect the displeasure of France, if not an invasion of her dominions by Prussian troops. The longer Newcastle and George II persisted the greater their loss of face when they should finally accept the inevitable. One reason why Newcastle speeded up the negotiation of a subsidy treaty with Russia was the need to bolster up the British party in the Empire which threatened to disintegrate under the impact of Prussian military might.

But even before the signature of this Russo-British treaty, the desertion of Austria led Newcastle to reconsider the uses to which it could be put. A strong European coalition against France being out of the question after June 1755, Newcastle and his colleague in the southern department, Holdernesse, began to wonder whether British interests on the Continent, and particularly the security of Hanover, could not be attained in another way. Instead of undertaking to contribute men and money for a continental war when both were desperately needed for the impending struggle with France in the colonies and upon the oceans, it would be much more satisfactory to reach an agreement with Prussia for the neutralization of Germany. Recent memories of the Austrian Succession war convinced Newcastle how expensive and ineffective such a war policy had been, even when Britain had been aided by Austria and the Dutch.

Frederick's attitude to British overtures shows at one and the same time the strength and the weakness which characterized his diplomacy—its flexibility and its impetuosity. Again, as at the beginning of the Austrian Succession war, he was being courted by the two Great Powers who were competing with each other for pre-eminence in Europe and world-wide empire. Surely with a foot in both camps he could gain something for Prussia?

But there was a difference between Frederick's outlook in 1740 and in 1755. In 1740 his diplomatic sky was clear of clouds and he was eager to demonstrate to the powers who had treated Prussia with contempt that under new management the Prussian army was a force to be reckoned with. In 1755 he knew well that he was surrounded by enemies eager to demolish the upstart power of Prussia and that his only ally, France, had neither the will nor the ability to protect him from his enemies. He had treated France badly and France had repaid him in his own coin during the previous war. Much better therefore not to run the risk of disaster.

As soon as he was convinced that British influence at St. Petersburg was strong enough to prevent a Russian attack upon Prussia, he closed with Britain and signed the convention of Westminster (January 1756). Hanbury Williams's subsidy treaty[1] had not merely fulfilled its original purpose of keeping Prussia in awe: it had secured an explicit Prussian promise to co-operate with Britain in preserving the peace of the Empire. That two electors, without even the formality of consulting the Emperor, should take upon themselves to settle the fate of Germany was not the least of Maria Theresa's reasons for resenting their actions.

Frederick was pleased to contribute to the growing coolness between Austria and Britain; and this may partly explain why he

[1] See below, chapter 8, p. 211.

insisted upon excluding the Austrian Netherlands from the territory to be protected by the convention of Westminster. He had however a still more substantial reason. It was never his intention in reaching agreement with Britain to abandon his alliance with France. If France should resent his attempt to prohibit her military intervention in Germany, he could reply that he had left open to French attack the Netherlands, where the successes of Saxe, which had forced the Maritime Powers to make peace, had been won in the last war, whereas her costly military campaigns in Germany had failed to produce any decisive results.

The convention of Westminster, like many another treaty hailed at the time as a diplomatic triumph, failed completely to produce the results confidently anticipated by its signatories. Frederick discovered to his dismay that British influence at Petersburg was on a very shaky basis once Britain had separated herself from Austria. Even more serious was the open indignation of Louis XV over the convention of Westminster, his refusal to continue his alliance with Prussia and his signature of a defensive alliance with Frederick's arch-enemy, the Empress-queen (May 1756). Frederick's attempt to secure Prussia from the dangers of war in Germany had cost him his only ally and encouraged his enemies to attack him, with or without the concurrence of France.

George II and Newcastle soon saw that they had miscalculated almost as badly as Frederick. The Tsaritsa made it abundantly clear that the troops she had promised by her treaty of subsidy with Britain might be used to attack but never to defend Prussia and soon repudiated any obligations to Britain under the treaty. The reconciliation of Austria and France, the immediate result of the convention of Westminster, removed the last lingering hope of British politicians that they might yet secure Austrian help in a continental war. Worse still, without the formality of consulting them until it was too late, Frederick marched into Saxony and thus transformed the threat of continental war into a disastrous reality.

Although Holdernesse in June 1756 had sent to Berlin a rough draft of a Prusso-British defensive treaty, designed as a counterblast to the first treaty of Versailles between France and Austria, the extremity of the common danger failed to bring Britain and Prussia together. Indeed Frederick's attack upon Saxony not only ran counter to his convention of Westminster: it made it quite impossible for him to carry out the obligations he had undertaken towards Britain a few months earlier. So far from helping to defend Hanover, he could only hope to hold out against Austria and Russia if Britain was able to organize successful resistance against France in western Germany and thus defend the Rhenish territories of Prussia as well as Hanover.

Holdernesse complained that even if Frederick were victorious in Saxony it would be of little use to Britain against France: if he were defeated, Britain would be ruined as well as Prussia. Frederick retorted that 'it was his misfortune to have allied himself with England in her decadence and to have been used as no ally of England ever was'. He particularly resented the eagerness of the Hanoverian ministers to escape becoming involved in the Prussian offensive war by arranging for the neutrality of the electorate on much the same terms as in 1741. The dissatisfaction of George II's British ministers, and the stringent conditions attached by the French ministers to what was originally a proposal by their Austrian ally, caused the failure of this negotiation.

The duke of Cumberland at the head of a mainly Hanoverian army failed disastrously to protect the electorate in the campaign of 1757 and had to conclude the convention of Klosterseven for the disbandment of his army at the dictation of France. Hanover had already been largely occupied by the French; and the Rhenish provinces of Prussia, and even Magdeburg, lay open to occupation. Frederick attributed the impending ruin of Prussia to his having, by the convention of Westminster, agreed to join in defending Hanover from foreign attack. Holdernesse insisted that Frederick's invasion of Saxony had undone the work of the Westminster convention and was solely responsible for their common danger.

Both Britain and Prussia also objected that they had not received the support which they were entitled to expect from the other. Holdernesse rather unreasonably complained that Frederick had taken no part in the defence of Hanover in the campaign of 1757. Frederick retorted that Britain had not sent British-born troops to take part in the German war and, on one pretext or another, had evaded her promise to send a fleet into the Baltic to help to defend Prussia from Russian and Swedish attack. War brought out the fundamental weakness of the convention of Westminster—still the only formal tie between Britain and Prussia. Britain had intended to secure Prussian co-operation against France, whereas Prussia believed the convention would commit Britain to help her against Austria.

This impasse was solved by the coming into power of the Pitt–Newcastle ministry in June 1757. Pitt's first act was to bribe George II to repudiate the convention of Klosterseven by agreeing to take the Hanoverian troops into British pay. Frederick's great victories over France and Austria at Rossbach and Leuthen not only encouraged George II to risk the fortunes of war for the beloved electorate, but produced an outburst of popular feeling in England in favour of Prussia, for which there was no precedent in the much longer story of the Anglo-Austrian alliance.

This measure of popular support strengthened Pitt's hands in dealing with obstruction in the Closet, the Cabinet, and the house of Commons: equally it strengthened his hands in negotiating with Frederick the terms of a treaty of alliance. Even now it proved impossible to conclude such a treaty with detailed provisions for military and diplomatic co-operation against the Franco-Austrian coalition. All that could be secured was a mutual undertaking not to negotiate for peace without the consent of the other party to the alliance. Pitt readily accepted Frederick's estimate that Prussia needed an annual subsidy of £250,000 to carry on the war. These two stipulations were included in the Anglo-Prussian subsidy convention of April 1758, which saved Prussia from ruin and enabled Britain to defeat her rival France, and become for nearly two centuries the leading colonial power.

For the next few years this subsidy convention was automatically renewed annually, but Britain's obligations were not limited to providing a subsidy to Prussia. She had to organize, under a general lent by Frederick, his brother-in-law Ferdinand of Brunswick, an army for the defence of western Germany. As the war continued Britain had not only to raise the number of Hanoverians, Hessians, and Brunswickers hired directly from their sovereigns, but also to increase the size of British-born contingents required to bring this army up to the strength necessary to defeat French attacks. Although Pitt had gained notoriety and popularity by attacking such British participation in continental campaigns during the preceding war, he had no hesitation in adopting it now that he himself was in charge of operations and co-operating harmoniously and on the whole successfully with the first general of the age. Whether or not Prussia could ultimately escape the fate foreshadowed for her by the Franco-Austrian coalition, Canada in the meantime could be won for Britain by active participation in this German war.

Britain and Prussia, quite unexpectedly and without any real desire on either side for an alliance between them, found themselves engaged in a war against the rest of Europe. Even now, as the neutrality negotiations over Hanover had demonstrated, they did not have a common enemy. Though he had to fight also against the French, Russians, Swedes, the Imperial army of the circles, and the troops of many German princes who supported Austria, Frederick's arch-enemy was Austria. Britain at the beginning of the war had no quarrel with any power except France. In the early years of the war Frederick made desperate attempts, through his sister Wilhelmina and other intermediaries, to induce France to extricate him from the dangerous situation in which his own impetuosity had landed him, while many people in Britain believed that the alliance of France and Austria was unnatural and would not last. Britain therefore should exert her utmost efforts against France and abstain from any action which would commit her to Prussian hostility towards Austria.

The really surprising thing is not that the Prusso-British alliance lasted as long as it did, and in the main achieved the objects desired by both contracting parties, but that it survived at all. This is particularly true once the war had ceased to be a war of survival both for Britain and for Prussia.

Pitt soon organized a militia for home defence, while his celebrated western squadron combined first-line defence of the home countries with support of his offensive strategy in North America and the West Indies. His decisive naval victories soon freed British fleets for colonial conquests and the complete destruction of French, and massive interception of neutral, overseas trade. When Spain, alarmed by British successes, intervened to support France, her fleets and commerce were swept from the seas and some of her most lucrative colonies added to Pitt's earlier conquests from France.

It is true that Frederick was still winning victories on the Continent more often than he was being defeated; but each victory seemed to bring him nearer to exhaustion and final disaster. Once Britain was assured of victory over the Bourbon powers beyond Europe, even Frederick's friends, Pitt himself amongst them, began to urge him to escape irretrievable disaster by making concessions to his enemies sufficient to secure a speedy peace on the Continent. These suggestions, however cautiously phrased and proffered, further alarmed Frederick, who already had good cause to doubt the solidity of his alliance with Britain.

The division in Britain between the advocates of purely naval and colonial warfare against the Bourbons, and those who believed that to be successful overseas Britain must have a 'continental sword', had disappeared during the crisis of 1756. Soon it reappeared. And once Britain was assured of naval and colonial victory, many Britons openly declared their belief that there was no longer anything to be gained for Britain by continued participation, on a steadily increasing scale, in the German war.

This attitude was put with cogency in an influential pamphlet written by Israel Mauduit *On the Causes of the German War* and published in 1760. The duke of Bedford, previously the rival of Newcastle in the secretariat of state and now leader of a splinter-group of Whigs, expressed similar views in the house of Lords. The young king and his favourite, Bute, at once associated themselves with these views by referring, in the first king's speech of George III's reign, to the bloody and expensive war being waged on the Continent by Britain. When they forced Pitt, the only British politician Frederick trusted, out of office in October 1761, the stage was all set for a rupture between Britain and Prussia.

Bute had set his heart on a separate peace with France, which would end British participation in the German war while leaving her free to subsidize Frederick against Russia and Austria, if he determined to continue the struggle. He recognized that the successive subsidy conventions between Britain and Prussia bound his hands, but ascertained that Frederick would not object to a separate peace between Britain and France, which secured the continuance of his subsidy and the restoration of the Prussian lands in western Germany which were occupied by France. Spanish intervention in the naval war (January 1762), with the consequent need to provide troops for the defence of Portugal, increased Britain's financial burdens and *pro tanto* Bute's eagerness to reduce the cost of the war in Germany to the British Exchequer.

Newcastle, who remained in office after the fall of Pitt, thought the moment opportune to restore the old alliance with Austria. He sent an obscurely worded offer to negotiate about Silesia, which reached Kaunitz in a garbled form, and was at once leaked by that astute statesman to Prussia. It reached Frederick as a convincing story that the British government was ready to work its passage back to alliance with Austria by betraying its present ally. Bute, in ignorance of Newcastle's effort at personal diplomacy, told Frederick bluntly he had better make peace with Austria on the best terms obtainable, which Frederick interpreted as meaning with the loss of at least part of Silesia.

It was the death of the Tsaritsa Elizabeth (January 1762) which enabled Frederick to escape from increasingly galling dependence on Britain. Her successor, Peter III, was an ardent Prussophil, who promptly transferred his armies from the Austrian to the Prussian side, and restored East Prussia to Frederick. Before long Frederick and his new protégé were planning to extend the Continental war by attacking Denmark. When Bute, as a condition of continuing payment of subsidies to Frederick for 1762, inquired what were Frederick's plans and resources for carrying on the war, Frederick declined to reveal them to a power which he had reason to consider capable of betraying them to his enemies. He was confirmed in his refusal by a mistaken or malicious report from the Russian ambassador at London of a conversation with Bute, in which Bute was represented as urging Russia to join with Britain in exercising pressure upon Prussia to make substantial concessions to her enemies and thus bring the Continental war to a speedy end.

It was not Bute who refused to continue the payment of Frederick's subsidy, but Frederick who declined to accept the conditions Bute sought to impose. In the mistaken belief that Bute's treatment of him was contrary to British public opinion, Frederick vainly tried to drive Bute from office by conducting a press campaign against him. British historians have been too ready to give credence to Frederick's spiteful and unjustifiable assertions, though it is curious and perhaps significant that Prussia, in her turn, should claim that Perfidious Albion had once again deserted her faithful continental ally. In fact, Frederick, by negotiating separately with Russia, and planning to extend the Continental war and transform it into a war of revenge against Austria, was as much to blame as Bute and Newcastle, who were sufficiently informed about his offensive plans to resent them. Even the leading Prussophil, Pitt, in attacking the separate peace between Britain and France concentrated not upon the desertion of Prussia but on the inadequacy of Britain's colonial gains.

Had the Prusso-British alliance survived the strains of peace-making, the European centre of gravity would not have moved so decisively as it did in the next generation towards eastern Europe. Catherine II might well have been attracted into its orbit, whereas, after the quarrel between Frederick and Bute and the conclusion of the Russo-Prussian alliance of 1764, Prussia repeatedly thwarted British attempts to secure inclusion in the northern system of alliances. The Goths and Vandals of eastern Europe, as David Hume saw them, were clearly in the ascendant over the civilized and enlightened western powers, divided as they now were by the triumphs of Britain and the determination of France to avenge them at the earliest possible moment.

Frederick's attempts to appeal to British public opinion during his actual quarrel with Bute prove that originally his hostility was personal to the minister and the policy Frederick thought he represented. Soon he extended his antipathies to the whole British nation; and his outspokenness and vindictiveness made recon-ciliation impossible long after Bute's disappearance from political life. Even when Pitt returned to office in 1766 hopes of improve-ment in the relations between Britain and Prussia were short-lived. Andrew Mitchell, Frederick's constant companion during the Seven Years war, remained at Berlin until his death in 1771 but effective political contacts had long ceased.

When France joined in the war of American Independence and Prussian armies once again fought the Austrians in the war of the Bavarian Succession, a situation apparently similar to that which had brought about the co-operation of Prussia with Britain in the Seven Years war recurred. Frederick did his best to prevent Britain from recruiting mercenaries in Germany for service in America, but was careful not to adopt openly the American side of the war. In his quarrel with Joseph II over the Bavarian Succession, Frederick appealed for support to the other princes of Germany, not least to Hanover: all were equally threatened by the Emperor's land-hunger. French caution, and in particular her refusal to recognize Joseph's attempt to add to his German lands as being within the terms of the Franco-Austrian alliance, ended any possibility that the Bavarian Succession war would bring about renewed co-operation between Britain and Prussia. In getting his way, Frederick owed much more to France than he did to Britain and Hanover.

It was not until Prussia lost the alliance of Russia in 1780 that there was a real chance of improvement in the relations of Britain and Prussia. Prussia was now as isolated in the east as Britain was in the west; and by this time Europe was clearly a single political system. Two isolated powers in the same system of states tend to gravitate together. Although the Austro-Russian alliance was directed primarily against Turkey it was potentially as dangerous to Prussia as that of France and Austria seemed to be to British interests in the Netherlands and Italy. In retrospect it can be clearly established that neither the Austro-Russian nor the Franco-Austrian alliance was securely based and likely to endure; but Frederick II and George III could not foretell the future course of European diplomacy.

There were however other forces at work. Frederick, hoping against hope to retain his alliance with Russia, associated himself with the Armed Neutrality of 1780, which had been organized by Catherine II to set effective limits to the exercise of British maritime rights during the American war. Still more important Frederick, who had been ostracized by France since 1756, now saw some chance of recovering the alliance of France which he had wantonly abandoned in 1756. The Austro-Russian alliance was inevitably directed against France's ally, Turkey. Joseph II's aggressions in Germany forced France to resume her Westphalian role in German politics, which had been in eclipse since the Diplomatic Revolution. As the price of restoration to favour at Versailles, Frederick would have been willing to give—or at least to promise—a modest measure of support for France's ally Turkey and to take up again with enthusiasm his old role of France's principal agent in the Empire.

The crisis came when Joseph II determined to get rid of the Netherlands in exchange for something more useful to Austria. Charles Theodore, who now combined the Palatine and Bavarian electorates, was very ready to hand over Bavaria to Austria in exchange for the Austrian Netherlands with the coveted title of king. Britain at once protested that this scheme was prohibited by the terms of the Barrier treaty of 1715. Frederick argued that it was equally contrary to the fundamental constitution of the Holy Roman Empire and invoked the aid of France as the principal guarantor of that constitution. At the same time he succeeded in doing what he had failed to do in the preceding crisis of the Bavarian Succession War—a league of German princes was organized to resist the barefaced attempt of Joseph II to exploit his headship of the Empire in order to secure Austrian territorial preponderance in Germany.

So real did the danger seem to the German princes that it brought to an end the last remnant of 'confessional politics'. The elector of Mainz, arch-chancellor of the Empire and acknowledged leader of the Roman Catholic princes, joined with the leading Protestant electors in the *Fürstenbund*. France had no objection to the exchange and would gladly have seen the last remnants of the Barrier obliterated from the public law of Europe, but shared the fears of her German clients that Austria might again become a danger to German dualism and the peace of Europe. Her support was essential to Frederick's success; but hardly less vital was the much more whole-hearted assistance he received from George III both as king and as elector.

At the height of the crisis the British and Prussian envoys at the Russian courts co-operated in representing to Catherine II the dangers of the exchange scheme and the British foreign secretary, Carmarthen, made overtures for joint action by Britain and Prussia to limit, if they could not obliterate, French influence over the United Provinces. The final show-down was deferred by Frederick's prompt rejection of this suggestion, while French persuasion induced Joseph to abandon his territorial claims against the Dutch and not to press his attempt to reopen the Scheldt to the detriment of Dutch commerce and the advantage of his Netherlandish subjects.

Failure to convert a *rapprochement* into an alliance at this time must not be attributed wholly to Frederick. The view was generally held in the British Foreign Office that, in spite of all that had happened since 1756, Austria was the natural and perpetual ally of Britain and that an alliance with Prussia was desirable only when Austria was irrevocably united with France.

Sir Robert Murray Keith was so sure of this that he was furious when he belatedly heard that Carmarthen, without a word of warning to his subordinate at Vienna, had been engaged in negotiating an alliance with Prussia.

Even after Frederick's death in 1786 had removed the greatest obstacle to real co-operation between Britain and Prussia, the signature of the Triple Alliance between Britain, Prussia, and the Dutch was therefore by no means a foregone conclusion. While it was favoured by influential people in both countries, it was opposed by others, and came about in the end more by accident than by design. The French party, headed by Prince Henry, Frederick's brother, at Berlin, was at least as powerful as the Austrophils in the British Foreign Office. Frederick's successor was his nephew Frederick William II. The new king had been regarded by his uncle as a ne'er-do-well and his reign proved that he was a political nonentity. But he depended at first largely on the advice of Hertzberg, the foreign minister whom he had inherited from his uncle. It is probably true to say that Hertzberg and the British diplomatic agent at Berlin, Joseph Ewart, were almost the only men who deliberately worked to re-establish a close political connexion, on what they hoped would be a permanent basis, between Britain and Prussia.

Hertzberg shared Frederick's alarm at the Austro-Russian alliance of 1781, and, even before Frederick's death, had worked out various plans for countering its malign influence. He reckoned that French support was unlikely, since France was the ally of Austria and was also showing a disposition to reconcile herself to Russia and make profit from, instead of opposing, Russian advances in the area of the Black Sea. Therefore if he could persuade Britain to take a more active interest in east European politics, he was prepared to give her some support in the west and particularly in the Low Countries, where British influence had been virtually replaced by that of France.

The only obstacle to complete French domination of the United Provinces lay in the existence and powers of the stadholderate. The 'patriot' party, France's traditional allies, therefore sought to undermine its political and military prerogatives. The Orange party rallied to the support of William V, but, though it retained a precarious control of the States-General, the 'patriots' dominated the provincial Estates of Holland, much the most wealthy of the provinces and, traditionally the leader of them all in times of crisis.

While France was in close touch with the 'patriots' and had recently done them good service by protecting them from the demands of Joseph II, British contacts with the Orange party had been broken off during the war of American Independence and had not been fully restored after the peace of 1784. It was generally assumed that France would intervene with alacrity when the crisis developed, whereas Britain's action would be dilatory, if indeed she ventured to interfere at all. The Hohenzollerns also had ancient links with the house of Orange, reinforced by territorial acquisitions which made them the neighbours of the United Provinces. Frederick II's foreign policy had merely strengthened Dutch convictions that the Hohenzollerns would be uncomfortable, if not positively dangerous, neighbours.

If Britain should ultimately nerve herself to active intervention in Dutch politics, she could only hope to defeat France by securing in advance a lien on Prussian troops. The science of logistics made it abundantly clear that France, aided by the volunteer Dutch army of 'patriots', could occupy the United Provinces and expel the stadholder before a single British soldier could be landed in Zealand. While Frederick would never have sent his troops across the Dutch frontier without previously driving a hard bargain with Britain, his successor took the risk of engaging in war with France without the least assurance of British help. Family pride and personal resentment at insults offered to his sister, Wilhelmina, the wife of William V, by the Estates of Holland, carried the day at Berlin. When the Estates haughtily refused to yield to Prussian demands for restoration of the constitutional *status quo*, accompanied by humble apologies to Wilhelmina, Prussian troops marched into the United Provinces and were greeted as deliverers by the hard-pressed Orange party. To the consternation of the 'patriots' and the astonishment of European diplomatists, France made no move to support the republican party against the Prussian invaders. Frederick William had run the risk of war with France, perhaps even of a renewal of a general European war not unlike the Seven Years war.

France's loss of nerve transformed the situation not only in the Low Countries but also in Europe. Pitt, if less Austrophil than Carmarthen, was even more determined to avoid being entangled in a European war except for what he regarded as the vital interests of Britain. He would never have made an alliance with Prussia to overthrow French control of the Low Countries by waging war against her. Once Prussia by unilateral action had achieved, without a war, the restoration of the stadholderate to its legitimate position in the United Provinces, he was prepared to join with

Prussia in guaranteeing and defending the restored stadholderate in the possession of its rights under the established constitution of the United Provinces. This was the essential clause of a secret agreement signed by Britain and Prussia in October 1787. There were many influential people, both at London and Berlin, who felt no need for a closer or more extensive agreement between Britain and Prussia. They included Finck von Finckenstein, one of Frederick William II's two foreign ministers, and a strong party at court, headed by Prince Henry of Prussia, the king's uncle and would-be mentor. At London the decision rested with Pitt, who had qualms about committing Britain to support the fantastic schemes of Frederick William's other foreign minister, Hertzberg, for territorial rearrangements in eastern Europe designed solely for the advantage of Prussia. Finally in August 1788 Britain and Prussia concluded a general defensive alliance at Berlin, providing for mutual aid if either power were attacked and including a specific guarantee of the Dutch settlement of the previous year. As well as a force of at least 20,000 auxiliaries or the equivalent in hard cash, Pitt promised naval support to Prussia, which his father had refused to Frederick the Great in the Seven Years war, and undertook not to employ the auxiliary troops to be furnished by Prussia beyond Europe or in the defence of Gibraltar. It proved impossible to conclude a definite bargain in regard to eastern Europe owing to the divergent attitudes and interests of the two powers. This basic weakness in the alliance was temporarily concealed by a clause by which the two courts undertook to act in intimate and substantial concord in the war between the two Imperial courts and the Ottoman Porte.

The treaty, the provisions of which have been outlined in the preceding paragraph, was the first formal treaty of defensive alliance between Britain and Prussia since 1742. It seemed that in Frederick's grave had been buried the enmity which had so long divided Britain and Prussia. Yet this treaty of Berlin proved from the very beginning as insecure, as it was a transient, basis for Prusso-British diplomatic co-operation. Even in regard to the Dutch crisis, which had brought them together, their interests diverged. The divergence was more marked in eastern Europe where Hertzberg soon discovered that Pitt would be a reluctant and inefficient ally, if indeed he could be regarded as an ally at all. Hertzberg was eager to make territorial acquisitions for Prussia and his rivals at Berlin were ready, as he was not, to launch the Prussian army once more against Austria. Pitt favoured the *status quo* and was more interested in east European commerce[1] than in supporting Hertzberg's elaborate diplomatic combinations: the last thing he wanted was a war between Austria and Prussia. Carmarthen was soon informing Hertzberg that his exchange schemes indicated that Prussia wanted aggrandizement, not security, and could only be effected by offensive means which Britain, intent on restoring the general tranquillity, could neither support nor countenance.

This survey of the diplomatic relations between Britain and Prussia in the reign of Frederick the Great indicates how little they were affected by any real contact between the two peoples. Few Prussians visited England and those British subjects who included Prussia in their German itineraries rarely stayed long at Berlin. In the later years of the reign they were mostly military men who had secured, often with difficulty, permission to attend the manoeuvres of Frederick's army. Though they usually returned home full of admiration for Prussian drill and Frederician strategy and advocated the adoption of both in the backward British army, they made no direct contribution to a better political understanding between the two countries.

Even at the close of Frederick's reign few Englishmen spoke German, though it should be remembered that the 'political nation' in Germany, as in most other European countries, themselves preferred to use French. Only a handful of British scholars were competent to read the works of their Prussian compeers, with the result that the works of the Göttingen school of historians, for example, made little impact on England. Similarly English writers on politics would have profited from closer acquaintance with the works of German cameralists.

Contact at all levels of learning and journalism was maintained mainly by translation of key works, or rather of such books, often of ephemeral interest, as were likely to attract the attention of a sufficient number of British readers. Since Frederick himself was practically the only Prussian in a position to exert much influence

---

[1] Anglo-Prussian commercial negotiations in the Triple Alliance period are so closely connected with the proposed transfer of British trade from Russia to Poland that they are treated below in chapter 8, where the political aspects of the Ochakov crisis are also treated at some length.

upon the foreign policy of his country, translation of English and Scottish authors into German contributed nothing to his understanding of the British way of life. So far as he read the works of the British enlightenment at all he made use of French translations. As he grew older he lost touch with the new generation, though it is surprising that he never seems to have heard of Adam Smith.

Frederick's grasp of British politics, though less shaky than that of any other European sovereign of his day, was never more than superficial. He depended too much on Bolingbroke, who was in some respects out of date and in other respects a political prophet rather than a political anatomist. Personal association with distinguished Jacobite exiles was a hindrance rather than a help. Although some of his ministers at London, certainly Knyphausen, tried to guide him to a sounder and better informed appreciation of British politics and the British constitution, Frederick suffered all his life from the disease of superiority and infallibility. In this as in other respects he proved incapable of learning from subordinates. If he did not find in their dispatches from London what he expected to find, he accused them of stupidity or even treachery.

When we consider the difficulties in the way of British understanding of Frederick and his system of government, it is on the whole surprising that his personal motives and achievements, the basis of his power and his outlook on foreign policy were all so justly appreciated in his own lifetime. English readers were presented both with the Prussian and with the Austrian case during the three Silesian wars. Some writers swallowed Prussian propaganda uncritically, while others, who usually were dyed-in-the-wool partisans of Austria, believed that nothing good could come out of Prussia. Dr. Schlenke has argued that it is not true to say that the Prussian alliance first became popular when it was concluded.[1] In support of this view he adduced evidence that the elder Horace Walpole, Lord Chesterfield, and even Pelham at times favoured an Anglo-Prussian alliance during the war of the Austrian Succession. But this evidence is insufficient to prove that an alliance with Prussia would have been 'popular' during this war. However this may be there is no evidence known to me to suggest that Newcastle concluded the convention of Westminster because he thought that alliance with Prussia would be popular in Britain. His aim was simply to avoid the expense and manifold

---

[1] *England und das friderizianische Preussen 1740–1763*, p. 337.

disadvantages of a continental war: he had no thought of fighting side by side with Prussia against Austria.

If Whitefield spoke for many Methodists and Dissenters when he hailed Frederick the Great as a Protestant hero during the Seven Years war, writers better informed about German and European politics denounced his invasion of Silesia earlier in his reign and his attack upon Saxony in 1756 as calculated to bring about an overwhelming Roman Catholic confederacy: his policy would merely involve the other Protestant powers in his own inevitable ruin. Except in the early years of George I's reign and for a year or two at the opening of the Seven Years war the confessional argument had little influence in bringing Britain and Prussia together. Frederick himself did not disdain to use it on occasion and British secretaries of state often threw it into their dispatches as a makeweight, but Frederick's character and outlook were too well known in British political circles for much weight to be attached to it. The disappearance of Jacobitism finally ended its political role so far as Britain was concerned.

The secretaries of state attached rather more importance to another old shibboleth which often appeared in their letters to Berlin, 'the liberties of Europe'. This was sometimes countered by the odd argument that, in seeking freedom from oppression by the Emperor, the Germans needed the help of France. More often, Frederick's behaviour was resented on the ground that only by rallying to the support of the Emperor and making the nominal unity of the Empire a reality, could Britain secure from Austria the measure of help which she required to end French domination of Europe.

By publishing his *Antimachiavel*, and then behaving as he did, Frederick gave his enemies openings which they were not slow to use. On the other hand, and especially during the war of the Austrian Succession, the parliamentary Opposition in Britain repeatedly attacked the government for not securing an effective alliance with Prussia, though they must have been well aware that this could only be obtained, if at all, by sacrificing more vital British interests. Chesterfield, who began as an enthusiastic admirer of Frederick's enlightenment, and who continued to take a keen interest in the legal reforms of the Prussian chancellor, Samuel von Cocceji, soon despaired of winning Prussia without enraging and losing Austria and Russia.

If British politicians and journalists were quick to grasp the salient fact that a new Great Power had emerged in the course of the Austrian Succession war, they were slow to appreciate its effect upon European politics. Newcastle, in particular, failed to understand that Britain had ceased to be a balancing power and had become a protagonist in European politics and that the position of balancing power, formerly held by Britain between Austria and the Bourbons, had now been inherited by Prussia.

After 1740 admiration for the Prussian army and its discipline was general in Britain. In 1756 the Guards performed in St. James's Park 'for the first time the manual exercise of the Prussians'. The Royal Scots, as the first regiment of foot, followed this example a month later amid a great concourse of spectators. Some militia regiments followed in the steps of the regulars. Some Prussian influence is traceable in military uniforms and Dr. Schlenke conjectures that respect for the Prussian army may have helped to undermine the traditional English suspicion of a standing army.[1]

Englishmen were less unanimous over Frederick's economic policies. His example was quoted in arguments about the Jew naturalization bill of 1753: to acquire for one's state, as Frederick did throughout his reign, industrious subjects with specialized skills was clearly in accordance with the dominant mercantilist philosophy. But there was also a feeling of economic rivalry, especially due to Frederick's development of textile industries in Silesia and elsewhere. British journalists gleefully reported that a shower of rain had so shrunk the new uniforms, made from Prussian cloth, of a Russian regiment during a review by the Empress, that the whole effect had been spoiled. Prussian journalists adopted the story with one alteration—the uniforms had been made from English cloth. There was a less well-founded fear that Prussia as a rising maritime power was a menace to British commercial supremacy, culminating in near-hysteria over the Emden company, and overt hostility to Prussia during Frederick's ill-treatment of Danzig after the first Partition of Poland.

Less controversial were Frederick's cultural policies and achievements. British visitors admired his palaces at Berlin and Potsdam, though they had little chance of appreciating his literary works at their true worth. His legal reforms continued to attract favourable

[1] Op cit., pp. 278–88.

notice: an English translation of his (or rather Cocceji's) law code was published at Edinburgh in 1761. There was even a suggestion that English lawyers might be sent to Prussia to learn their business, though what Blackstone would have thought of this does not appear in the record. Soon after his death there appeared a competent life of the Prussian king by Gillies and an English edition of his works, most of them posthumously published at Berlin. His outspoken remarks about British sovereigns and politicians in his history of his own time, now first published, cannot have improved relations between Britain and Prussia, while his attributions of motives for the actions of British statesmen show how defective was his grasp of British politics.

The alliance of Britain and Prussia, concluded in 1788, is one of the best remembered diplomatic compacts of the eighteenth century, but its actual influence on events was much less than it seemed to contemporaries. Neither from the British nor from the Prussian point of view can it be regarded as a success. That it played the part it did for two or three years was due not to its inherent strength but to the temporary eclipse of France. During these years the British government tried to use the Prussian alliance to support against Austria and Russia France's former clients in eastern and northern Europe.

Without instructions from London, Hugh Elliot, British diplomatic agent at Copenhagen, showed correct anticipation of his government's wishes and was able to prevent Russia's Baltic ally, Denmark, from pressing home an invasion of Sweden. Prussia gave valuable help by threatening an attack upon Holstein, already the Achilles heel of Denmark. The Poles seized upon the chance to throw off the Russian yoke and to undertake an extensive programme of internal reforms which might have transformed their country into a progressive and viable state. While British opinion sympathized with the Polish reformers, Prussia promised them active support in order to embarrass Russia, threatened by Gustavus III of Sweden and already at war with the Turks. Similarly Hertzberg, as a pupil of Frederick the Great, was anxious to support the Turks in order to facilitate his ambitious plans for the reorganization of central Europe to the advantage of Prussia. Though Pitt refused at first to be dragged into Hertzberg's schemes he came to be impressed by the commercial and other arguments for supporting both Poland and the Turks against Russia and thus involved Britain in the Ochakov crisis.[1] By signing early in 1790 formal alliances with Poland and Turkey Prussia undertook onerous obligations towards both, which went far beyond what Pitt was prepared to accept.

In western Europe Prussia did her best to embarrass Austria by encouraging the Belgian opponents of Joseph II and at times showed some inclination to help them to establish an independent Belgian state. This, Pitt at once pointed out, would be contrary to British interests, which were best served by maintaining Belgium, nominally under Austrian rule, as a Dutch-British satellite. This would protect, equally against France and against Austria, one of the few regions on the European continent in which Britain took a direct interest. Beyond Europe the most important effect of the Prusso-British alliance was to strengthen Britain's position against Spain in the Nootka Sound crisis; but even here the French decision not to support Spain was certainly more influential than Prussia's diplomatic support of Britain.

Earlier in 1790 Joseph II had died and his brother and successor, Leopold II, undertook to withdraw from the war against the Porte and to conclude peace on the basis of the *status quo*. So far as the Netherlands were concerned, Prussia was now to join with the Maritime Powers in guaranteeing the provinces to Austria and their provincial liberties and constitutions to their inhabitants. Regarded at the time as a success for the Triple Alliance, the terms of the convention of Reichenbach hastened its collapse. Whereas the Maritime Powers were entirely satisfied with the Reichenbach terms, Prussia had failed to gain anything for herself; and there was no longer the remotest prospect of securing British support for a Prussian attack upon Austria designed to transfer from Austria to Prussia the territorial gains which Austria had made in the first Partition of Poland. It may also be argued that the convention of Reichenbach encouraged Pitt to believe that similar tactics to those which seemed to have succeeded against Austria would be equally successful against Russia, weakened as she was by the imminent withdrawal of Austria from the Turkish war and threatened by Prussian support of the Poles.

The complete collapse of the half-hearted attempt to force Russia to make peace with the Turks on terms dictated to her by the Triple Alliance (April 1791) marks the end of the Triple

[1] See below, chapter 8, pp. 223-31.

Alliance as an effective force in European politics. It had never rested on firm support either at London or at Berlin and even the politicians who had brought it about now ceased to believe in it. Hertzberg, by negotiating privately with Russia before the Ochakov ultimatum had been launched, contributed to its failure. Ewart, the British diplomatic agent at Berlin, and perhaps the principal architect of the alliance on the British side, had to suffer the sneers both of Fox and Burke for his pains. When, after the collapse of opposition to Russia, he returned at Pitt's behest to his post at Berlin to undo all that he had done in previous years, he had to admit that 'England was actually more disliked in this country than any other court, Austria not excepted.'[1]

As long as Britain remained at peace with revolutionary France her relations with Prussia were as cool as her attitude towards Austria. Since British war aims included the renunciation by France of the territorial conquests she had already made and her promise to abstain in future from interference in the internal affairs of other states, both Prussia and Austria welcomed British support in the war they were already waging against the French Revolution. But by this time Prussia was already much more interested in the second Partition of Poland than in opposing France in the Netherlands. When the British government declined Frederick William's demands for an exorbitant British subsidy and a guarantee of his Polish territories, he ordered his armies in the west to remain inactive. Lord Malmesbury was sent on a special mission to the king of Prussia and by offering a subsidy of £2,000,000 for the campaign of 1794, one-fifth of it payable by the Dutch, and other financial advantages, he secured Frederick William's promise to provide over 60,000 men for service against France. Frederick William used the money for other purposes and his army in the west was even less active in 1794 than it had been in the previous year. When Pitt stopped payment of the promised subsidy during the campaign, Frederick William threatened to withdraw his army from the west altogether unless the arrears were immediately paid to him. By the treaty of Basel (1795) Prussia made peace with France on humiliating terms which permitted France to occupy Prussian provinces on the west bank of the Rhine and denied to her former allies the right of passage over all the Prussian territories. The defection of Prussia carried with it that of the lesser north

[1] Quoted in R. Lodge, *Great Britain and Prussia*, p. 205.

German states and split the Holy Roman Empire. The Imperial circles of Saxony, Westphalia, Franconia, and part of those of the Rhine were no longer at war with France.

What Frederick William II had reluctantly accepted on the plea of financial and military necessity, became the fixed policy of Frederick William III, who succeeded his father in 1797. Both were mainly influenced by Haugwitz, who was able to play off Britain and France against each other for a decade. In this contest for Prussia's favours, France had the great advantage that all she required from Prussia was neutrality while Britain needed Prussian intervention in the war against France. As early as 1796 Pitt made Frederick William II an offer of Belgium or equivalent gains in Germany, but Haugwitz had already accepted a French promise to secure for Prussia eventually the bishopric of Münster in exchange for continued Prussian neutrality. When the Tsar Paul joined with Britain against France in 1798, Pitt hoped that Russian influence at Berlin would be strong enough to secure Prussian co-operation in the Second Coalition and in particular the junction of Prussian and Russian troops for a projected invasion of the United Provinces designed to restore the stadholder. Frederick William III lacked the courage of his convictions. Haugwitz preferred to continue his policy of wavering neutrality, which was the more attractive since France was now pursuing a policy of mediatization and secularization in the Empire, which opened up for Prussia the prospect of tempting territorial gains.

The opening campaign of the Third Coalition in 1805 found Prussia as undecided as ever. Frederick William III, momentarily annoyed by French violation of Prussian territory in Anspach, allowed Russian troops to enter his territories. He even had delusions that Prussia by her armed mediation could impose peace upon the belligerents and acquire more territory as a reward for her services to European peace. As soon as the French evacuated Hanover in order to concentrate their forces against Austria, Frederick William occupied the electorate and stipulated for Prussia's acquisition of this territory as the *sine qua non* for Prussia's joining the Third Coalition. Indignant as Pitt was at the treachery and presumption of Prussia, he sought to satisfy elsewhere the land-hunger of the Prussian king; but Napoleon was only too delighted to purchase the continued neutrality of Prussia by promising Hanover to Frederick William. For a brief space

Britain and Prussia were technically at war. Then Napoleon, having demolished the Austrian armies, turned against Prussia, crushed her at Jena, and issued from Berlin a decree declaring a paper blockade of the British Isles. Even now Britain was ready to subsidize any power which would really fight against France—even the state which had been France's jackal for a whole decade—but before this could be arranged the Russian defeat at Friedland forced Prussia to make peace with France.

Not until after the expedition of Napoleon to Moscow, when the Russian and Prussian armies were fighting Napoleon in Germany did Britain and Prussia really co-operate against France and even then the conclusion of the subsidy treaties was followed rapidly by the acceptance both by Russia and Prussia of an armistice. It required all Castlereagh's skill and determination to bring together the three great military powers of the Continent along with Britain in an alliance against Napoleon by the treaty of Chaumont (1814). Once he had succeeded in this and provided his allies with subsidies adequate to their military needs, the overthrow of Napoleon was inevitable. Blücher's co-operation with Wellington to win the last battle of the war did something to obscure and atone for the sorry story of Anglo-Prussian relations in the previous twenty-five years.

A. *Primary Sources*

Mauduit, I., *Considerations on the Present German War* (1760)
Memoirs and Papers of Sir Andrew Mitchell, ed. A. Bisset (2 vols., 1850)
Memoirs of Horatio, Lord Walpole, ed. W. Coxe (2 vols., 1802) [Old
    Horace was the most prominent and persistent advocate of alliance
    with Prussia]
Politische Correspondenz Friedrichs des Grossen, ed. R. Koser and others
    (46 vols., Berlin, 1879–1939)

B. *Secondary Authorities*

Browning, O., 'Hugh Elliot in Berlin' in *TRHS* New Series, 4 (1889),
    85–101
— 'Hugh Elliot at Berlin' in *RHD* 2 (1888), 225–73
Chance, J. F., 'The Treaty of Charlottenburg' in *EHR* 27 (1912), 52–77
Charteris, E., *The Duke of Cumberland and the Seven Years War* (1925)
Dorn, W. L., 'Frederick the Great and Lord Bute' in *JMH* 1 (1929),
    529–60

Elliot, D. C., 'The Grenville Mission to Berlin, 1799' in *HLQ* 18 (1954–5), 129–46

Horn, D. B., *Sir Charles Hanbury Williams and European Diplomacy* (1930), chapter 4

Lodge, Sir R., *Great Britain and Prussia in the Eighteenth Century* (Oxford, 1923)

— 'The Mission of Henry Legge to Berlin' in *TRHS* 4th series, 14 (1931), 1–38

Oncken, W., 'Sir Charles Hotham und Friedrich Wilhelm I im Jahre 1730' in *FBPG* VII. 377–407, VIII. 487–522 and IX. 23–53

Portzek, H., *Friedrich der Grosse und Hannover in ihren gegenseitig Urteil* (Hildesheim, 1958)

Rose, J. H., 'Frederick the Great and England, 1756–63' in *EHR* 29 (1914), 79–93 and 257–75

Satow, Sir E., *The Silesian Loan and Frederick the Great* (Oxford, 1915)

Schlenke, M., *England und das friderizianische Preussen 1740–63* (Freiburg–Munich, 1963)

Spencer, F., 'The Anglo-Prussian breach of 1762' in *History* 41 (1956), 100–12

Wittichen, F. K., *Preussen und England in der europäischen Politik 1785–88* (Heidelberger Abhandlungen zur . . . Geschichte, 1902)

CHAPTER 7

Great Britain and the Lesser States of Germany

A ROUGH and ready indication of the intensity of British interest in Germany is afforded by the number of missions which the British Crown found it worth-while to accredit to the separate principalities. If a regular succession of diplomatic agents was maintained at a German court throughout the eighteenth century, then it may be concluded that the British government believed that this court had an essential part to play in the British field of foreign policy. Only two German states answer up to this test—Austria and Prussia—and for this reason they have already been treated in separate chapters of this book. Austria, from 1688, and Prussia, at least after 1714, were regarded as European powers and, as such, actual or potential allies against Britain's natural enemy, France.

If the criterion of continuous British representation by accredited diplomatic agents is applied to the other German courts, then there is not one which passes the test. Britain's closest connexion was at first with Hanover, owing mainly to adventitious dynastic reasons. Once the house of Hanover had been transferred from Herrenhausen to London, the need to maintain diplomatic missions to Hanover disappeared.

At first there was bitter rivalry between George I's German and British courtiers at St. James as well as between the Hanoverian ministers and their English counterparts. Lady Cowper's diary gives a vivid picture of the backbiting and jostling for position and the mutual distaste of English and Germans for each other which preoccupied the male and female courtiers in the early days of the first Hanoverian king. Untravelled German nobles a generation later assumed that under a German-speaking king the whole English court would have conversed with their master and with each other in fluent German. In fact English soon became the court language and, apart from some use of French in diplomacy and in the law courts, it continued to be the official language.

The only minister who learned to speak German was Carteret and, so far as the mass of George I's and George II's subjects were concerned, these reigns saw no appreciable increase of interest in

German language or literature. Only in music, where linguistic barriers had no meaning, was there a noticeable increase of German influence in England in the reigns of the first two Georges. After the early days of George I few of his German subjects visited London. Fewer still of his English subjects found much to interest them in the electorate. English visitors to Hanover were either official visitors to George I's court there, such as the secretary of state who usually accompanied him and his successor on their periodic visits to Hanover, or else took in Hanover on their way to somewhere else.

Nor was there much literary or scholarly contact between the kingdom and the electorate. In historical writing for example the historical schools of Edinburgh and Göttingen developed independently of each other. In spite of certain similarities in their approach, Hume and Robertson owed nothing to the work of contemporary German historians. Their works, translated into German, may have had some effect on the Göttingen historians of the later eighteenth century.

Not until eighteenth-century Classicism was in retreat in both countries before the Romantic revival of the closing years of the century did literary and scholarly contacts become closer. It was at this time that Göttingen came to take the place held a century earlier by Leyden, and Canning wrote of

> Sweet! sweet Matilda Pottingen!
> Thou wast the daughter of my tu-
> -tor, Law Professor at the U-
> -niversity of Gottingen . . .

Before cultural contact between Britain and Hanover became at all close, the political influence of Hanover upon British policy had ceased to be even a plausible pretext for Opposition attacks upon a Hanoverian king. George III, although he never set foot in his electorate, took an interest in its welfare and showed some appreciation of its potential value in the sphere of British foreign policy. Whatever may have been the case under the first two Georges, the electorate under George III lost more than it gained by political attachment to Great Britain.

In 1801 Hanover was occupied by Prussia and in 1803 by France. The capitulation of the Hanoverian army to France at Suhlingen repeated, in essentials, the melancholy story of the duke of

Cumberland's signature of the convention of Klosterseven in the opening stages of the Seven Years war. After being used as a bait to secure Prussian inaction by Napoleon, Hanover was offered, in whole or in part by Britain to gain Prussian co-operation with Austria and Russia against Napoleon. Then after the eclipse of Prussia at Jena, Hanover was included in the French satellite kingdom of Westphalia. Yet British prestige and exertions were partly responsible for the compensation for Hanover's sufferings during the Napoleonic wars which she secured at the Vienna congress. Increased in territory and raised to the rank of a kingdom, Hanover remained united in a personal union with Britain until 1837.

While no British diplomatic agents were accredited to the Hanoverian court after the accession of George I, during the whole of the eighteenth century, a regular succession of Hanoverian diplomatists resided at London in the capacity of minister. Anyone who compared the range of the Hanoverian diplomatic service (as set out in the second volume of the *Repertorium der diplomatischen Vertreter aller Länder*) on the accession of George I and at the death of George II would conclude that there had been a process of attrition. In 1714 Hanoverian legations covered central Europe and extended as far as France, Sweden, Russia, and Venice. In 1760 separate Hanoverian missions were in existence only at Ratisbon, Copenhagen, and The Hague, although electoral 'agents' were also maintained at a few places, especially Augsburg and Hamburg, within the Empire. This contrast is largely illusory. Owing to the Seven Years war diplomatic relations in 1760 were broken off between Hanover and several of the states with which she had formerly exchanged diplomatic missions, including the Emperor and several German princes.

Regular diplomatic contacts with France had really ceased in 1737 and until the end of the Napoleonic wars there were only two or three short-lived special missions. With the Emperor, on the other hand, diplomatic relations were restored in 1763 and continued unbroken for the rest of the eighteenth century. If the Swedish mission had been closed down in 1739, regular diplomatic contacts continued between Hanover and Denmark until 1776. The post at Venice, which had long been without an object, came to an end in 1750; and that at Geneva in 1766. If relations with Prussia were somewhat irregular George I and George II could count on George II's sister, Frederick William I's queen, to

look after their interests at Berlin. Subsequently the two governments often preferred to negotiate directly with each other by
exchanging views and memoranda without using diplomatic agents
as intermediaries. At other times the dukes of Brunswick discharged informally some of the duties which normally would have
fallen to formally accredited agents at Berlin and Hanover.
Ferdinand of Brunswick rendered notable services of this kind
during the Seven Years war. Not until the *Fürstenbund* was regular
Hanoverian diplomatic representation instituted or restored at
Berlin. Indeed the 'eighties and 'nineties saw a remarkable revival
of Hanoverian diplomatic activity which continued even after the
overrunning of Hanover in the Napoleonic wars. For the first time
since the early years of George I Hanover maintained a series of
diplomatic agents at the Russian court from 1801 to 1808, while
she also began to be represented regularly at several German courts
including Saxony, Bavaria, and Anspach-Bayreuth.

For us the most interesting question is how far the reduction in
Hanoverian diplomatic representation in the middle years of the
eighteenth century contributed to the expansion of the network of
British diplomatic missions which certainly occurred about this
time. It is hard to resist the conclusion that the end of regular
Hanoverian missions to Paris (1737), Stockholm (1739), Venice
(1751), and Copenhagen (1776) was connected with the presence
at each of these courts of British diplomatic agents capable of
representing, without cost to the elector, the interests of Hanover.
Indeed one may well be surprised that dual representation of the
king-elector survived as long as it did at these courts. On the other
hand it continued to the end of the century at Vienna, The Hague,
Ratisbon, Brussels, and was even introduced to certain courts
where Britain had long been represented and Hanover had not,
especially St. Petersburg, Dresden, and other German courts.

Russia is an interesting special case. Though Hanover ceased to
be represented at the Tsar's court in 1719 this was not due to lack
of Hanoverian interest, but at first to the rupture of diplomatic
relations and subsequently to the conviction of the Hanoverian
ministers that the most effective method of securing aid from
Russia against the menace of Prussia under Frederick II lay in
procuring British subsidies to set the Russian military machine in
motion. To avoid giving umbrage to Prussia the Hanoverian government preferred to remain as far as possible in the background,

while it pushed Britain into, and pressed her to continue, the subsidy negotiations with Russia. It is the opinion of Professor Mediger that the Hanoverian government, by making use of Britain in this and other ways, in large measure secured these objects in the decade preceding the Diplomatic Revolution.

As one would expect, relations between British and Hanoverian ministers, where both were resident at the same court, varied from covert hostility to close co-operation. British diplomatic agents were normally instructed to report on all points of business which concerned Hanover to the electoral government. Many of them corresponded directly with Hanover, especially in the 'forties and 'fifties. Guy Dickens and Hanbury Williams spent a good deal of their time trying to collect at Berlin and Dresden debts due to George II as elector. Hyndford, in a secret correspondence with the head of the German Chancellary in London, gave George II information about the springs of Russian and Austrian policy which he did not include in his official despatches.[1] So long as George I and George II reigned it was widely believed that efficient and successful advancement of the king's electoral interests was the high road to success in the British diplomatic service. Especially under George II Hanoverian policy was remarkably active and independent, and often directed in a way diametrically opposite to the wishes of George II's British ministers.

Under George III this was no longer the case and in the last years of Frederick II's reign Hanover, which under George II had helped to keep Britain and Prussia apart, now became a bridge between them. Britain and Hanover had a common interest in the 'eighties in resisting the designs of Joseph II in the Empire, and both rallied to the Prussian side in the *Fürstenbund* crisis since Prussia was clearly the only power in Germany capable of effective resistance to Austria. If the belief that British diplomacy expanded in central Europe to fill a void caused by the attrition of the Hanoverian diplomatic service cannot be maintained, other factors certainly led to an increase in the number of British missions to German courts.

One of these was the desire to strengthen the position of our ally

---

[1] W. Mediger, *Moskaus Weg nach Europa*, pp. 425–35. I owe much of the information contained in the preceding paragraphs to a private letter from Professor Mediger, who generously communicated to me the results of his researches in the Hanoverian archives.

Austria in the Empire and to thwart French designs to break up the Empire into political units, none of them strong enough to offer effectual resistance to French domination of central Europe. A long list of such missions could be compiled from the middle years of the century. Obviously, as long as Britain was the ally of France, as she was from 1716 to 1731, little could be done along these lines. British missions to the lesser German courts in this period were more likely to be intended to support than to counteract French policy. The breach with France after 1731 led to a reversal of British policy in Germany and to increased British interest in German politics. From 1731 until the end of the Austro-British alliance Britain made sincere but quite ineffective attempts to buttress the position of the emperors in Germany and build up a German national opposition to France. Any British politician, who was convinced during these years by the balance-of-power argument, had to take an interest in German politics.

Only in the special case of Hamburg, Bremen, and the Baltic ports, especially Lübeck and Danzig, was there much sign of the influence of commercial interests upon British policy. Adherents of the 'blue water' school of British politics were, however, sometimes reminded by their opponents that if they neglected to oppose France at the lesser courts of Germany then French political domination of central Europe would inevitably damage Britain's commercial interests in this important region.

The link of common Protestantism also had some bearing upon British diplomatic contacts with certain German princes in the early years of the eighteenth century. In general it ran counter to the prevailing political tendency, since Roman Catholic persecution and proselytism was usually supported by the Imperial authority, which, for political reasons, Britain normally wished to strengthen. After the death of George I the British government virtually ceased to protest to the Emperor and Roman Catholic princes of Germany against persecution of their Protestant subjects. Such protests had merely provoked counter-protests against Britain's treatment of her own Roman Catholic minority, as it did when discriminatory taxation had been imposed upon them in 1722. Thereafter the British government usually offered Protestant refugees from Germany privileges in England, such as easier naturalization, or else aided them to migrate to the American colonies. In the second half of the eighteenth century religious fanaticism declined and mutual tolerance seems to have been achieved in some areas. We even hear of the British envoys at Munich making use of the Scots Roman Catholic monks in Bavaria to help with the clerical work of the legation.

Not all British missions to German courts were the result of British interest in German politics, economics, and religious controversies. The threat of a general European war, and still more its actual outbreak, heightened British interest. After the early years of the eighteenth century, Germany became the only area from which Britain found it possible to hire the mercenary troops with which she preferred to wage campaigns. Many special missions to German princes were actuated by the desire to secure troops for the defence of Britain or the carrying on of war in America.

War with France always increased British interest in Germany for another reason. To secure intelligence of French naval and military strength, spies had to be posted near the frontiers and arrangements made to procure from inside France reliable and early news of the likely movements of French troops and ships. While the Netherlands and Switzerland had certain advantages over Germany and were also extensively used, no secretary of state in time of war could do without intelligence from western Germany. Once the British alliance had been transferred from Austria to Prussia, and Britain was taking a larger part in German campaigns than she had done in the Austrian Succession war, it became even more important to collect information from the west German courts, which were in closer contact with France and more dependent upon her than ever before.

After the peace of Paris (1763) Britain recoiled from participation in German politics even more decisively than she normally did at the end of a war; but the diplomatic contacts which had been established in the previous generation were not broken off. Even the Saxon legation, which had been established partly owing to the personal union of Saxony and Poland, was maintained after the separation of the electorate and the kingdom on the death of Augustus II of Poland and III of Saxony in 1763. The Bavarian legation was also retained, but its functions were combined with those of the resident to the Imperial Diet at Ratisbon. The decline of British political interest in the lesser German courts, after the combination of France and the Emperor in 1756 and the celebrated quarrel between Frederick the Great and Bute in 1762 made her political role nugatory, was seen clearly in the way in which successive heads of these missions were allowed to discharge their duties by deputy or even to treat their posts as complete sinecures.

Revival of British interest, on the new basis of co-operation with Prussia and such lesser German princes as could be induced to join Prussia and Britain against the Emperor, in the Bavarian Succession and Exchange crises of 1779 and 1785–6, was temporary and not very influential. Not until the outbreak of the French Revolutionary war and the threat to British interests in the Low Countries, did Britain take up again the role she had played in the middle years of the century as the instigator of German hostility to France and the paymaster of German mercenary armies.

This attempt to discuss in general terms the relationships between Britain and the lesser states of Germany must now descend to particulars. Leaving out of account, for reasons which have already been stated, Austria, Prussia, and Hanover, we may consider first the courts of the other electors. Three of them were ecclesiastical princes, the archbishops of Mainz, Trier, and Cologne. The other three were secular potentates, the elector Palatine and the elector of Bavaria, both of them Wittelsbachs and Roman Catholics, and the elector of Saxony, who had been since 1697 also Roman Catholic, although ruler of a Lutheran state and anxious for political reasons to retain his predecessors' leadership of the German Protestants.

It is unnecessary for our purposes to make any distinctions between the electors of Mainz, Trier, and Cologne. All three normally acted in Imperial politics with the Emperor, unless intimidated or bribed by France. As long as they were under Austrian influence and Britain was the ally of Austria, British representation at the three courts was usually judged otiose. Once France had asserted control over them by threats of force or bribes, British representation would be futile. Only George Stepney (1695–7), Thomas Villiers (1743)[1] and Onslow Burrish (1745–58) were entrusted with a political role at the courts of the ecclesiastical electors.

Onslow Burrish was originally accredited in 1745 to all three in the hope of persuading them to give their support to the newly elected Emperor, Francis Stephen of Lorraine. Equally futile were his attempts in the 1750's to win their assistance for the election of

[1] See below, p. 194.

Francis Stephen's eldest son, the Archduke Joseph, as king of the Romans. Burrish did however prove useful in procuring intelligence about French preparations for the Seven Years war. His successor, George Cressener, who already had long years of experience as a spy, took over these functions in 1755 and continued to send intelligence to his government until the French army of occupation expelled him from Cologne in 1759. Operating from Maestricht for the remainder of the war he returned to Cologne in 1763 and died there in 1781.

Whereas Burrish had consistently supported the interests of Austria in the Rhineland, and Cressener had at first been employed in attempts to restore good relations with Austria at the end of the Seven Years war, the basis of Cressener's position at Bonn soon came to be the alienation between Austria and the elector of Cologne. When Cressener applied to anyone the epithet 'a good German' he implied that the person in question was an opponent of Austrian influence and pretensions. The harsh treatment of the Rhineland by French troops during the Seven Years war weakened French influence over all three ecclesiastical electors and made them anxious to maintain their neutrality more effectively in any subsequent war in western Germany; but it also made them anxious for French subsidies on the plea that such subsidies should be regarded as compensation for the damage they had suffered under French occupation during the Seven Years war. One of the few political functions of Cressener and his successor, Heathcote, was to observe and as far as they could, without holding out any hope of a British subsidy, oppose French negotiations for subsidy treaties with the three ecclesiastical electors.

After as before he entered the ranks of the diplomatists Cressener's vital role was that of intelligencer. He had reliable and sometimes even influential correspondents at nearly all the princely courts of western Germany. He kept a close eye on developments in the Austrian Netherlands and remained in unofficial contact with the bishopric of Liège, partly through his annual visits to Spa. He sent on to London reports he received from Dr. Baylies, one of Frederick the Great's physicians, about the health of the Prussian king. He was in contact with that rising star in the Prussian political firmament, Hertzberg. Above all he remained in touch with a particularly well-informed correspondent at Paris, whose identity he was careful to conceal from the British government. It was an indirect recognition of the value attached to Cressener's intelligence that a successor to him at Bonn was promptly appointed and given instructions to report to London all intelligence he could obtain, whether it was connected with the business of the court at which he resided or not.

Apart from his activity as an intelligencer, Cressener entertained British visitors to Bonn from royal dukes downwards, and helped German emigrants to reach the American colonies. Much to his regret his attempts to develop British trade with the Rhenish electorates proved futile. Not one British merchant was in business at Cologne, although one German merchant house at Frankfurt imported some goods directly from England. British trade with the Rhineland continued to be indirect, conducted mainly through Holland and Hamburg.

The outbreak of the war of American Independence extended Cressener's responsibilities. He helped to repatriate, in conjunction with Consul Udney at Leghorn, British sailors from the Mediterranean. More important he was concerned in raising mercenary troops from Hesse and Anspach for service in America and in arranging for their transport to the sea coast in spite of obstruction from the electors of Mainz and Trier and, at times, of Prussia.

Had Britain not been at war when Cressener died, still accredited to the three ecclesiastical electors, it seems unlikely that the British government would have appointed a successor to the Bonn legation. The man they did appoint, Ralph Heathcote, was singularly ill chosen. He was quite incapable of continuing Cressener's intelligence work and had practically no business to transact at Bonn. But like his predecessor he soon became a personal friend of the elector and the French envoy spread scandalous stories about his wife's intimacy with the elector. He evaded successfully his government's instructions to remove to Hesse-Cassel, to which court he had been also accredited in 1784. The outbreak of the French Revolutionary wars gave Heathcote opportunities which he made no attempt to seize. Fleeing from Bonn with the electoral court to escape the advance of French armies he followed the elector from place to place in Germany until his death in 1801.[1]

[1] The preceding paragraphs are based on two works by Dr. Albert Schulte, which were kindly brought to my notice by Professor Max Braubach of Bonn: Schulte's doctoral dissertation at Bonn, examined on 22 December 1954, on Cressener; and his article in *Annalen des historischen Vereins für den Niederrhein* 165 (1963), 153–227, on Heathcote.

From start to finish Heathcote's career was utterly futile and it is not surprising that he was the last British diplomatic agent to reside at Bonn.

Similar considerations applied to the two lay Wittelsbach electors. The Lower Palatinate on the Rhine, ruled by the elector Palatine, was dangerously exposed to French aggression. Almost as exposed was the Upper Palatinate which was contiguous to Bavaria and ruled by the elector. On the extinction of the Bavarian line all those territories came under the rule of the elector Palatine. Apart from two eccentric political missions, one (intended but not carried out) to Bavaria in 1704, with the forlorn hope of detaching Bavaria from France, the other in 1719–20 to the elector Palatine, with the equally forlorn hope of securing some relaxation of his persecution of his Protestant subjects, there was virtually no sign of British interest in either electorate until Onslow Burrish's arrival in the Rhineland in 1745. It was vainly hoped that the Bavarian elector, Maximilian Joseph, who had succeeded Charles Albert and made peace with Austria, would give vigorous support to the association of the circles in conjunction with the three ecclesiastical electors.

A few years later, however, Burrish managed to conclude a subsidy treaty with the Bavarian elector by which the elector promised to vote for the Archduke Joseph as king of the Romans. This treaty was also defended in the British Parliament on the ground that it completed the transfer of Bavaria from the French to the British side and would therefore make it more difficult for France to stir up troubles in the Empire which might involve Britain in an unpopular continental war. The Diplomatic Revolution of 1756 destroyed the *raison d'être* of British diplomatic representation at Munich and the post, after the end of the Seven Years war, was conjoined with that of minister to the Diet of the Empire at Ratisbon.[1] The holders of the combined post sometimes resided at Ratisbon but more often at Munich.

Not until the union of Bavaria and the Palatinate did Britain think it worth while to arrange for regular diplomatic representation at the court of the electors Palatine. Apart from cultural contacts and geographical propinquity, the electors in the first half of the century were bound to France by the need to secure support for their claims to transmit to their successors their share of the

[1] See below, p. 198.

Cleve inheritance, to which the Hohenzollerns also asserted their pretensions. Once Frederick the Great had abandoned the Prussian claims, the elector Palatine acted as the stooge of France and Prussia in the politics of the Empire and in particular opposed the election of the Archduke Joseph as king of the Romans in the 'fifties.

When their divergent attitudes to the question of the Bavarian succession drove a wedge between France and Austria in 1778, George III, both as king and as elector, stood forward as an opponent of Joseph II's attempt to misuse the Imperial authority to gain advantages for Austria. At last a British minister was formally accredited to the elector Palatine in 1778 and continued to reside at his court at Munich, Mannheim, or Düsseldorf.

When Joseph had to give up his claims in 1779 to large parts of Bavaria, he again tried to gain most of it in another way by arranging with the elector to exchange it for the Austrian Netherlands with the title of king. Since this scheme was contrary both to the letter and spirit of the Barrier treaty of 1715 between Great Britain, the United Provinces, and Austria, George III had good reason for intervening to thwart Joseph's plans. He joined with Prussia and Saxony to organize the *Fürstenbund*, which included many Roman Catholic as well as Protestant princes. Once again Joseph retired defeated, the union of Bavaria and the Palatinate was not disturbed and the rights of succession of the dukes of Zweibrücken (Deux Ponts) to the disputed territories were formally recognized.

There can be no doubt that in the eighteenth century Britain was more interested in Saxony than in any other German state of the second rank, except Hanover. Memories of the place of Saxony in the history of the Reformation survived the conversion of the elector, Augustus II, in 1697 and of his son and heir in 1712 to Roman Catholicism. Although these conversions inevitably weakened the ties between Britain, Hanover, and Saxony, they did not at once destroy them. George I and Augustus II had both won reputations as soldiers while serving in the Imperial armies. The worse George I's relations with the Emperor and Frederick William I of Prussia—and they were often very bad in the 1720's—the more reason he had to seek the friendship of Saxony. It was also widely believed that Augustus II's success in becoming king of Poland would add to the political weight of Saxony in European politics, while the title of king, albeit of an inferior elective monarchy, gave the electors for most of the eighteenth century the *mystique* and some of the attendant advantages of royalty.

The geographical situation of Saxony within Germany freed it from the oppressive neighbourhood and overwhelming political influence of France. A British diplomatist at the court of Dresden might therefore hope to play a more active and influential part than at Cologne or Munich. Unlike Bavaria, which transferred its allegiance from Austria to France at the opening of the Spanish Succession war, Saxony took the Austrian side in the wars both of the English and Spanish Succession. Most of the British missions to Saxony and Poland alike during the last years of the seventeenth and the first years of the eighteenth century were concerned with the problems of co-operation in these wars.

In the second decade of the eighteenth century British interest was mainly concentrated on Poland's situation in the fluctuating episodes of the Great Northern war. But Britain also showed acute concern over the conversion of the electoral prince of Saxony to Roman Catholicism in 1712 and the oppression of Protestants in Poland. When British relations with Russia were at their worst, a former British minister to the Tsar, who had been expelled from Russia, was established as resident to Danzig and operated there as a spy from 1719 to 1725. The infiltration of the English factory at Danzig by Scottish Jacobites also gave the British government some concern in the 'twenties. Danzig, though legally subject to the Polish republic and geographically surrounded by Polish territory which served as its economic hinterland, was in practice almost an independent state.

The international crisis caused by Townshend's violent reaction to the Austro-Spanish alliance of 1725 made the rival leagues of Vienna and Hanover competitors for Saxon support, insignificant as it was likely to be in practice. Since Augustus II owed the Polish crown to Russia and was already the ally of Charles VI, he joined the league of Vienna and vigorously supported Prussia in her quarrels with Hanover. Sir Luke Schaub had to be sent specially to Dresden to patch up peace between the electors of Saxony and Hanover in 1730.

Although Britain took no part in the actual election of Augustus III of Saxony to succeed his father as king of Poland in 1733, she could not avoid taking some interest in the Polish aspects of the war of the Polish Succession. Walpole's alliance with Austria by the second treaty of Vienna (1731) made it desirable for Britain to have someone at Dresden or Warsaw in a position to report promptly the intrigues of France and if possible help to defeat them. This became still more essential with the manifest decline of Austrian power and influence within the Empire and the consequent British fear that Austria would herself become a satellite of France.

Saxony joined the league of Nymphenburg, organized by France against Maria Theresa, in the hope of securing territory in Germany which would make easier communication between Saxony and Poland. As the electress of Saxony was a daughter of Charles VI's elder brother, Joseph I, she could hardly be expected to accept without protest the substitution in the succession to the Hapsburg lands of the daughter of Charles VI in preference to the elder line represented by herself and her sister, the electress of Bavaria. Saxony proved an incapable ally and, jealous of Prussian triumphs, went over to the Austrian side in the Second Silesian war (1744–5).

George II and Carteret promised to subsidize the Saxon army, which would help Maria Theresa to recover Silesia from Prussia. The fall of Carteret gave the Pelhams control of British foreign policy. The defeats suffered by their Austrian and Saxon allies and the difficulties they experienced in raising money to carry on a large-scale German war soon convinced the Pelhams that Carteret's policy was impracticable. Aided by a Prussian military occupation of Saxony, they coerced Austria and Saxony to make peace at Dresden on Christmas day 1745.

Austria and Saxony blamed each other: both blamed Britain for the collapse of their schemes. French influence at Dresden recovered rapidly and in April 1746 Saxony signed a treaty of neutrality and subsidy with France. As in so many other instances France was prepared to pay handsomely for mere inaction, whereas Britain consistently demanded active participation in war in exchange for less generous subsidies. Saxony's return to the French alliance seemed to be consolidated by the marriage of one of Augustus III's daughters to the French dauphin; but the Saxon prime minister, Brühl, continued to balance himself dextrously on the tight-rope between France and the Austro-Russian allies.

When Newcastle finally lost the support of the elector of

Cologne for the election of the Archduke Joseph as king of the Romans, he turned again to Saxony. In exchange for British subsidies the elector of Saxony in 1751 promised to give his vote for the archduke and to hold a corps of troops in readiness to serve the Maritime Powers. This enabled Newcastle to continue the election negotiations, which must otherwise have foundered; but it was soon apparent that Brühl had merely changed his paymaster, while he pursued the old policy of balance between the contending leagues.

There was no real increase of British influence at Dresden, though Brühl vainly tried at this time to secure active British support for the continuance of the Saxo-Polish union on the death of Augustus III and II. The British envoy at Dresden posed as the king-maker of Poland, but failed to entangle his government any further in the confused and to them unimportant politics of eastern Europe. The weakening of Britain's alliance with Austria and the revival of her colonial quarrels with France ended the brief period in which Britain pursued an active and independent policy of her own at the Saxon court. Although Britain continued to be represented at Dresden during the Seven Years war and even took some interest in the Polish succession she now acted merely as the supporter of Prussia during the war and of Russia after the peace of Hubertusburg.

With the election of Stanislaus Poniatowski as king of Poland in 1764 and the consequent rupture of the personal union between Saxony and Poland which had subsisted from 1697, British interest in Saxony markedly declined. After 1764 the elector lost any claim to be treated as a European power. Though he retained hopes of restoring the link between Saxony and Poland, and this was in fact provided for by the reformed Polish constitution of 1791, it never became effective. Deprived of the support of Russia, which had made possible the prominence of the two Augustuses in the politics of Europe, Saxony had perforce to abandon their ambitious policies. Even with Russian aid, seventy years' experience had shown that Saxon-Polish resources were inadequate for the role of a European power. The long-continued attempt to maintain this status had several times brought Saxony to the verge of irretrievable disaster, if not annihilation. Even when apparently successful it had done nothing to strengthen the electorate, still less to benefit her people.

From 1764 Britain continued her diplomatic representation both at Dresden and at Warsaw, but abandoned the attempt, which had never been very satisfactory, to entrust both posts to a single agent. The envoys extraordinary who followed each other in regular succession were allowed to absent themselves from their posts for long periods. When one of them died or was promoted to a more important post, the government showed no undue haste in despatching his successor to Dresden. The separate Hanoverian missions, which had been sent to Dresden in the 'thirties and 'forties, virtually disappeared after 1748.

The routine of diplomacy between Britain and Saxony came to be discharged, quite adequately, by the British envoys' private secretaries, who were appointed as chargés d'affaires when their masters were absent from Dresden on some specious excuse or another. Apart from some exchange of views when Joseph II set Germany in uproar over his claims to the Bavarian succession, and rather more active co-operation in opposition to his attempt to exchange Bavaria for the Austrian Netherlands, there was little British or Hanoverian business to transact in Saxony. According to a well-informed contemporary the Dresden legation at this time was 'a pleasant and respectable situation, and the expenses [were] not unequal to the pay'.[1]

While something like regular diplomatic representation had come to be established in the course of the eighteenth century with some, but by no means all the German electors, this practice did not extend to members of the College of princes nor to the free towns. The most important of the inferior German princes to Britain were the dukes of Brunswick and the landgraves of Hesse-Cassel.

The former occasionally supplied troops in exchange for a subsidy, especially during the continental campaigns of the Seven Years war; but their importance lay in their relationship to Prussia. Brunswick brides frequently married Hohenzollern princes, including Frederick the Great and his brother Prince Henry. Although in neither of these cases was the marriage a great success, the practice continued with happier results. Brunswick princes frequently served as officers in the Prussian army, the most famous being Ferdinand, victor over the French at Minden. With the reigning house of Hanover in Britain, the dukes of Brunswick were linked by a common ancestry derived ultimately from medieval

[1] *Auckland Journal* I. 37.

emperors, by common Protestantism and by the proximity of their German territories, equally exposed to French occupation when their rulers were involved in a continental war against France, provoked by British insular interests.

The usefulness of Brunswick as a channel of communication was best illustrated by the negotiations leading to the Diplomatic Revolution of 1756; but this was only one of several occasions when the Brunswick dukes helped to arrange a reconciliation between Britain and Prussia. At least once, in 1729-31, they played some part in averting war between George II and Frederick William I.

British contacts with the landgraves of Hesse-Cassel were mostly occasioned by military necessity. Whenever war threatened and even more so when it had actually broken out, British missions were to be found appealing to the landgrave for the use of his troops. Hessians were used in every war from 1689 to 1789. Failure to secure Swiss mercenaries and Danish refusals after 1714 to provide troops in exchange for a British subsidy enhanced the value of Hesse as a source of mercenary soldiers.

Apart from this specialized function, Hesse was of some significance to Britain owing to the election of a prince of Hesse as king of Sweden in 1720. In practice the king of Sweden retained so little authority that he was powerless to direct the foreign policy of Sweden. More important for a short time later in the century was the attempt of Hesse-Cassel to mediate at Hanau between Charles VII, the Bavarian Emperor, and Maria Theresa. For reasons which are still not entirely clear, Carteret, who had begun by warmly supporting the Hanau negotiation, abruptly dropped it.

Few of the other inferior princes of Germany received more than two or three British missions in the whole of the eighteenth century. Most of these were entrusted to Thomas Villiers, Onslow Burrish, and William Faucitt. Villiers was sent by Carteret in 1743 on a series of missions in the hope of strengthening the position of Maria Theresa in the Empire. He received creditive letters for Bamberg, Anspach, Bayreuth, Hesse-Darmstadt, Saxe-Gotha, Württemberg, and Würzburg as well as to the three ecclesiastical electors and the landgrave of Hesse-Cassel. Onslow Burrish travelled extensively in Germany between 1745 and 1758, scattering a trail of creditive letters behind him but achieving very little. Faucitt, during the war of American Independence, had a roving commission in Germany which led him to visit, usually with a view to hiring troops, Anhalt-Zerbst, Anspach, Wolfenbüttel, Waldeck, and Württemberg, as well as the principal supplier of troops to the British government, the landgrave of Hesse.

The only free cities with which Britain maintained regular diplomatic representation were the Hanse towns of Hamburg, Bremen, and Lübeck. Residents were separately accredited to each city, and after 1763 were styled also 'minister plenipotentiary' to the circle of Lower Saxony. Useful in time of war or disturbance for naval or military intelligence, particularly from the Baltic, their duties in peace were largely consular.

Of the three Hanse ports Hamburg, originally a minor member of the Hanseatic league and dependent politically on Lübeck, was much the most important in the eighteenth century. While most of the Hanse cities declined economically and entirely lost their former political importance, Hamburg prospered. This was largely owing to the establishment by the Merchant Adventurers of London of a factory there in 1567, from which they sold England's staple—cloth—to the countries of northern and central Europe. Soon the English traders were joined by Netherlanders and refugee Jews from the Iberian kingdoms.

Though not technically a free port, duties were low and facilities so extensive that the practical difference was slight. The aristocratic Senate which governed the town never tried to become a political or even a naval power: it wisely remained consistently neutral in politics. While the rest of Germany was being ravaged by domestic wars and foreign invasions, Hamburg actually profited by these disturbances. As in the case of Leghorn its prosperity led to attempts to emulate it; but neither the electors of Hanover with their port across the Elbe at Harburg nor the kings of Denmark at the neighbouring free port of Altona made much headway.

When Parliament deprived the company of Merchant Adventurers of its monopoly in 1689, this merely enabled independent English merchants and their factors to settle at Hamburg and share in its prosperity. Both Austria and Prussia sought to prohibit, in favour of their own textile manufactures, the importation of English cloth in the eighteenth century, but the German demand for it continued at a high level. Hamburg never attempted to trade directly either with the East or the West Indies, but it became a recognized market for colonial produce, such as cottons and calicoes from India, tobacco from the mainland American colonies and sugar from the West Indies. Although Hamburg merchants showed a disposition to take shares in the Scottish Darien scheme and to support the Ostend East India Company, nothing came of these proposals. Periodic French competition, especially in sugar, proved more serious but was usually defeated by the outbreak of successive wars when British fleets cut off French supplies and forced the Hamburg refiners and distributors to fall back on British products. Hamburg was also a main distribution centre for British hardware and fish, especially herrings. The records of the British legation are full of references to stinking fish, which unscrupulous British traders were alleged to have unloaded on unwary foreigners, or even on native Hamburgers who ought to have known better. Even coal and beer were included in the list of British exports to Hamburg.

Hamburg itself produced nothing suitable for export to Britain, but British imports from Germany and even countries to the east were largely channelled through the port. The Hamburg merchants and their agents bought on a large scale at the leading German fairs various textiles, especially linens, although the quantity of these diminished in the eighteenth century with the rise of the Scottish and Irish linen industries, luxury goods such as Meissen and other porcelain made in Germany, and even timber from Prussia and furs from Russia.

It added to the value of Hamburg in British eyes that exports and imports were carried in British ships manned by British sailors. Hamburg served a dismembered and divided Germany as a passive outlet and inlet valve. It developed rapidly during the eighteenth century and consolidated its position as a centre for banking, insurance, and other international financial dealings.[1] When Amsterdam fell under French control in 1795, Hamburg became even more important than before. Just as the French conquest of Tuscany was followed by the evacuation of the British factory at Leghorn, so Napoleon, when he occupied Hamburg in 1803, ordered the expulsion of the English colony and the severance of the trading link which had been the basis of Hamburg's prosperity for two centuries.[2]

[1] See M. S. Anderson, *Europe in the Eighteenth Century*, p. 72.
[2] See the long historical account of British trade with Hamburg in P.R.O. S.P. 82/100.

The political functions of the Hamburg mission were at their height during the Great Northern war. British agents at the port were sometimes commissioned to treat with the duke and administrator of Holstein-Gottorp, while one or two British diplomatists who were not accredited to the Senate, notably John Robinson, found Hamburg a convenient centre to transact business with other princes to whom they were accredited.[1] Again during the Seven Years war it was found a convenient place of refuge for one or two British agents who owing to war operations had to retire from their normal posts in Germany. When Queen Caroline Matilda of Denmark was separated from her children the British diplomatic representative at Hamburg was entrusted with the task of keeping her regularly informed about their health.[2] The outbreak of the French Revolutionary wars and the loss of contact with the Low Countries increased the value of Hamburg as a source of intelligence and a means of communication with Britain's continental allies. It was partly for this reason that Napoleon ordered its occupation by French troops in 1803.

Apart from the regular succession of British diplomatists resident at Hamburg, though accredited also to Lübeck and Bremen, there are very few instances of diplomatic representation to individual free towns in the Empire. Cressener's creditive letter to the city of Cologne in 1755 was unique. It was intended to give him some protection in discharging his duties as a master-spy for the British government. The appointment of one or two residents to Danzig, in addition to the normal succession of consuls, has been mentioned earlier in this chapter.

Apart from these missions to individual German princes, lay and clerical, the British government maintained an intermittent succession of diplomatic agents accredited to the Imperial Diet at Ratisbon which included them all. This dated back to the days when the Diet had been a political body capable of taking effective decisions in matters of domestic and foreign policy. William III thought that under changed conditions there was not enough for a British minister to do at Ratisbon and left the post vacant during the latter part of his reign. The fact that he left the secretary appointed by James II undisturbed at Ratisbon until he dispensed with the post altogether is a further indication of its lack of importance in his eyes. The accession of George I gave it new

---

[1] See below, chapter 9, p. 243.   [2] See below, chapter 9, p. 263.

significance as a means of supporting Hanoverian interests in the Empire, and, after 1716, of co-operating with France. Charles VI seized the opportunity of the expulsion of his minister from England during the quarrel over the league of Vienna to exclude the British minister from Ratisbon in 1727. Thereafter until the end of the Seven Years war Britain was virtually unrepresented at the Imperial Diet.

As the political functions of the Diet dwindled to zero, and it became in effect a congress of diplomatic agents of independent states, ceremonial became more important than ever at Ratisbon. Difficulties of this kind were used to prevent the reception of Philip Stanhope in 1763, and his successor, William Gordon, was warned by a more experienced friend that 'your post at R[atisbon] is full of ceremony. You cannot spit out of the window without offending the head or paraphernalia of an *Excellence*. You are all so, that ceremonial there is looked on as essential and subject to contests.'[1] Now that France and Austria were allies there was even less for a British minister to do at Ratisbon than in the first half of the century. Gordon's successors were all accredited to the electors of Bavaria and, after the union of Bavaria with the Palatinate, to the electors Palatine. After presenting their credentials to the Diet, they normally resided at the Wittelsbach court. Further confirmation of the decline of the political importance of the Empire in British eyes is afforded by the failure of Thomas Walpole, who had received credentials to the Diet on his appointment to Munich in 1784, even to put in a formal appearance at Ratisbon.

In 1689 the Emperor had still retained some shreds of authority in the Holy Roman Empire and it remained a shibboleth of British foreign policy until the middle of the eighteenth century that perhaps the best method of tilting the European balance against France would be to aid the Emperor to recover sufficient of his lost control over the Empire to make Germany an effective counter-balance to France. Such hopes, already chimerical, completely vanished with the Diplomatic Revolution. George Cressener in the interval between the signing of the preliminaries in 1762 and the conclusion of a definitive peace in 1763 was sent to influence the German princes towards neutrality in the Austro-Prussian war and to persuade the Circles to withdraw their contingents from the Imperial army. The conclusion of the peace of Hubertusburg a

---

[1] *H.M.C. Report XII, App. 9*, 339 (Aitken MSS.).

week after Cressener's arrival at Ratisbon deprived this mission of its object. In any case it was probably intended merely as a gesture towards Prussia. Cressener was however succeeded immediately by Philip Stanhope. So far as British ministers to the Diet from Stanhope to Walpole[1] had any political function, it was to co-operate with other interested parties in thwarting the aggressive territorial designs of Joseph II. This was manifest chiefly in the crises connected with the Bavarian Succession and Exchange questions.

After Germany became involved in the wars of the French Revolution, Britain reverted to her earlier role of fomenting German resistance to French domination of central Europe. Pitt's repeated failures against revolutionary and Napoleonic France between 1793 and 1805 resulted in sweeping away the network of British diplomatic posts in Germany. The Continental System was designed to complete the ruin of British influence by cutting off her trade with Germany and other continental states. German refusal to be starved of British imports to suit the convenience and add to the prosperity of France was one of the factors which led to the final overthrow of Napoleon and the restoration of British political and economic contact with the lesser states of Germany.

List's *System of Political Economy* did more than Napoleon in the long run to destroy the economic bases of British power. As long as German liberalism, with its dependence on British political thought and practice, continued to influence German politics—and it was at its strongest in some of the lesser courts—Britain remained influential. Indeed she now had a common interest with the lesser courts which she had not had in the eighteenth century, while the dynastic links forged by the early Hanoverians survived the separation of Hanover from Britain. Increasing Prussian domination of Germany, and Bismarck's monopoly of political power, extension of the sphere of the state, and introduction of general tariffs in Prussia struck the final blow. The German economy no longer depended upon British exports and imports, and the second *Reich* developed a political philosophy, an imperialist outlook and diplomatic techniques which made otiose

[1] Walpole, who left Ratisbon in 1796, was in effect the last British minister to the Diet. Though Paget and Drake both received a credential letter to the Diet neither presented it (*British Diplomatic Representatives 1789-1852* (Camden Soc., 1934)).

Britain's eighteenth-century role as protector of the north German Protestant princes, and ultimately substituted the Protestant but Hohenzollern *Reich* in the place formerly held by France as Britain's natural enemy.

A. *Primary Source*

Rosenfeld, Sybil (ed.), *Letter Book of Sir George Etherege* (1928)

B. *Secondary Authorities*

Becker, R., *Der Dresdener Friede und die Politik Brühls* (Leipzig, 1902)

Braubach, M., 'Kurtrier und die Seemächte während des spanischen Erbfolgekrieges' in *HJ* 57 (1937), 385–419

Brauer, G., *Die hannoversch–englischen Subsidienverträge 1702–48* (Aachen, 1962)

Drögereit, R., *Das Testament König Georgs I und die Frage der Personal Union zwischen England und Hannover* (Neidersächsisches Jahrbuch für Landesgeschichte XIV (1937) [summarized in *Research and Progress*, vol. 5, no. 2, pp. 83–87]

Fauchier-Magnan, A., *Les petites cours d'Allemagne au XVIIIe siècle* (Paris, 1947)

Horn, D. B., 'Saxony in the War of the Austrian Succession' in *EHR* 44 (1929), 33–47

Kielmansegge, F. von, *Diary of a Journey to England* [1761–62] (1902)

Lingelbach, W. E., 'The Merchant Adventurers at Hamburg' in *AHR* 9 (1903–4), 265–87

Mare, Margaret L., and Quarrell, W. H. (edd.), *Lichtenberg's Visits to England* (Oxford, 1938)

Matheson, P. E. (ed.), *German Visitors to England 1770–95* (Oxford, 1930)

Portzek, H., *Friedrich der Grosse und Hannover in ihren gegenseitig Urteil* (Hildesheim, 1958)

Pottle, F. A. (ed.), *Boswell on the Grand Tour* (1953)

Schmidt, H. D., 'The Hessian Mercenaries: the career of a political cliché' in *History* 48 (1958), 207–12

Schulte, A., Ein englischer Gesandter am Rhein [Cressener] (Bonn dissertation, 1954, unpublished)

— 'Ralph Heathcote, der letzte englische Gesandte bei Kurköln' in *Annalen des historischen Vereins für der Niederrhein* 165 (1963), 153–227

Ward, Sir A. W., *Great Britain and Hanover* (Oxford, 1899)

CHAPTER 8

Great Britain, Russia, and Poland

RICHARD CHANCELLOR'S visit to Russia in the mid-sixteenth century set the keynote of Anglo-Russian relations for the next two hundred years. A mutually advantageous exchange of commodities with, on the English side, some contribution of personnel to the autocracy and westernizing policies of the Tsars, was the basis of the relationship. Trade prospered under Elizabeth and James I, but then declined until the execution of Charles I virtually destroyed English influence in Russia. What the English lost the Dutch gained: Cromwell and Charles II were alike in one thing—their attempts to restore English trade with Russia totally failed, though a mere trickle of commerce continued through Archangel.

It was the Great Northern war which first gave English politicians a glimpse of the potential value of a political alliance with Russia. Peter the Great's visit to England in 1698 naturally attracted attention to his country and, after his defeat at Narva by Charles XII of Sweden, Peter accepted English offers to mediate a peace between Sweden and Russia. At first William III and his successors would have liked to involve Sweden in their quarrel with France and this was plainly impossible as long as Sweden and Russia were at war with each other. In the end British mediation proved ineffective and Peter's great victory at Poltava in 1709 opened up to the English ministers the unwelcome prospect of Russian domination in the Baltic. It seemed that Russia might even take the place which Sweden had held as a member of the Empire since the Westphalian settlement.

The Tory leaders in the last years of Anne's reign were well aware of these dangers, but, as long as war with France continued, could do nothing to avert them. The completion of the Utrecht settlement ended British inactivity in the Northern war and the personal policy of George I, as elector of Hanover, largely determined the form and direction taken by that activity. Even before his accession to the throne of Great Britain, George I had been closely associated with the anti-Swedish coalition led by Peter: since 1712 his troops were in occupation of Verden, one of Charles

XII's German duchies, upon which the Hanover dukes had long cast covetous eyes. Charles XII's contacts with Jacobite exiles after 1714 may also have contributed to George's preference for the Russian alliance. Townshend's failure to restore cordiality to Britain's old system of alliances with Austria and the Dutch, and the possibility of a reopening of the quarrel with Louis XIV, no doubt raised the value of an understanding with what was now clearly the strongest power in north-eastern Europe.

More important in the eyes of British ministers, was the prospect of a commercial treaty which the Tsar held out to them as a reward for political co-operation in the Baltic. Since the Revolution of 1688 there had been some revival of British trade with Russia. About 1696 an English merchant at Hamburg, Charles Goodfellow, had been sent on what appears at first sight a singularly unpromising mission to sell Hudson Bay Company furs at Archangel. Other merchants in Russia were pushing the sale of Virginian tobacco. It is significant that the first diplomatic agent to be accredited to Russia since 1688 was the merchant Goodfellow and that his creditive letter expressly stated that his appointment had been made in the interests of commerce and particularly of the tobacco trade. Soon Goodfellow was reinforced by a regular diplomatist, Charles Whitworth, who also devoted much of his time to promoting the sale of tobacco. So deeply was the British government concerned that when an unfortunate incident occurred in London over the arrest for debt of the Russian ambassador, A. A. Matveev, Whitworth was specially commissioned and sent to Russia to present their formal apologies and to exhibit to Peter the text of an act of Parliament, which had been passed to remedy the defective provision under English common law for the diplomatic immunity of foreign agents in London.

Peter's conquest of the Swedish provinces in the eastern Baltic and his removal of the seat of government from Moscow to St. Petersburg did not merely alter the political relationship between Russia and Britain. They led also to the transformation of the pattern of Anglo-Russian commerce and to its remarkable development in the eighteenth century. Trade with the eastern Baltic was still seasonal; but it was much less risky than when it had perforce been conducted along the Arctic convoy route to Archangel. Russia now virtually controlled the supply of naval stores, pitch, tar, hemp, and timber, which were essential to the British merchant navy in peace. British diplomatists had urged their government to prevent Russian occupation of Esthonia and Livonia since this would 'lay our nation and Navy at his [Peter the Great's] discretion'.[1] Meantime attempts were being made to find and develop alternative sources of supply, especially in the American colonies, by the Board of Trade and Plantations; but it was a long time before these produced much result.

Until well on in the century it was generally agreed that American supplies were inferior in quality to the products of the Baltic: they were certainly quite inadequate to keep the British mercantile marine on the seas in peace-time, let alone fit out the royal navy when war threatened. There is a good deal to be said for the view recently expressed by several Soviet historians that without Russian naval stores Britain would soon have dropped out of the ranks of the Great Powers and might never have founded the first British empire. So obvious to English contemporaries was the need for obtaining supplies that there was general agreement that, no matter how much bullion was lost to the country in purchasing naval stores from Russia, the Muscovy trade must be maintained. Here was an obvious case for the application of the mercantilist maxim, as stated by Adam Smith, that national defence was more important than opulence.

Naval stores became still more important with the extension of the area of conflict which was characteristic of Britain's eighteenth-century wars. The Spanish Succession war, apart from abortive plans for an expedition to the St. Lawrence, was confined to Europe. The American war of Independence was fought on the oceans of the world and on the land of three continents. Catherine II had some reason for thinking she could blackmail Britain into accepting the principles she had espoused and proclaimed in the Armed Neutrality of 1780.

Another stable feature of Anglo-Russian trade was that Russia's role was passive and Britain's active. It was carried on almost exclusively by seasonal fleets of merchant vessels, which sailed from England in the spring and returned with the coveted exports from Russia in the autumn. This not only added to its economic profitability: it provided yet another mercantilist argument in its favour. It trained in peace the merchant seamen who could be impressed for the royal navy in war.

---

[1] Quoted by M. S. Anderson, *Britain's Discovery of Russia*, p. 68.

The Russians were naturally less satisfied with the arrangement, especially as Peter I and some of his successors were keenly interested in organizing and developing the naval power of Russia. In the second half of the century Russian negotiators demanded reciprocity in trade treaties with Britain—concessions granted by Russia to British merchants in Russia should be equally available for Russian merchants in Britain. Though such a clause was included in the trade treaty of 1766, it did not produce any immediate change in the pattern of Russo-British trade. Russia continued to depend upon British merchants and ship-captains to export her principal commodities and, as late as the Napoleonic wars, this made it difficult for her to break off relations with Britain.

If Britain needed Russian exports, Russia would find it difficult to sell them elsewhere to equal advantage, if indeed she could dispose of most of them at all. Britain by the middle of the century had the lion's share of Baltic trade and was crowding out the Dutch who were unable or unwilling to give long-term credit to their Russian suppliers. There was little direct trade with France and, apart from luxuries for the nobles, France exported little that Russia wanted. Such trade as there was, notably in French colonial produce, was conducted largely through the Dutch and north German ports, especially Hamburg. The modernization of the Russian army increased the Russian demand for English cloth for uniforms. Britain with her existing contacts and resources was also particularly well placed to act as Russia's supplier of colonial produce. Even to practising mercantilists, trade between Britain and Russia seemed to be that rare exception—a trade between two countries which was of benefit to both.

These developments still lay in the future and did nothing to abate the sudden flare-up of hostility to Russia which now occurred both in Britain and Hanover. Peter planned to invade the Swedish mainland in 1716, and, when this enterprise miscarried, he withdrew the bulk of his forces to the duchy of Mecklenburg. The duke was engaged in chronic disputes with the Estates, which seemed to offer the neighbouring elector of Hanover a chance to get a footing in the duchy. George I as a good German not only resented the presence of foreign troops in the Empire in close proximity to his electorate: he saw in Russian occupation a barrier to his personal ambitions. Already suspicious of Peter's plans, and encouraged by his Hanoverian ministers, he appealed to the Emperor for support, and tried to seduce Prussia and Denmark from the Russian alliance.

Stanhope, now clearly the leader of George I's English ministers, shared Hanoverian distrust of the Tsar. With some help from partisans of Sweden, his propaganda whipped up British opinion. The Tsar was depicted as a treacherous autocrat with boundless ambitions, which could be realized only at the expense of his neighbours. By hobnobbing with the Jacobites, Peter increased to something like a frenzy the antagonism of all true Whigs to Russia, though they could not entirely overlook the fact that Peter's opponent Charles XII was much more closely in touch with the Jacobites and probably in a better position to support them effectively. Though Peter soon gave up any idea of using the Jacobites, his temporary association with them was remembered in England. Dependence upon Russia for naval stores proved a bitter pill for British statesmen to swallow and partisans of Sweden urged them to join with the Swedes in limiting Russian conquests and nipping in the bud her naval power, before it grew to still more dangerous heights in the ruin of Sweden.

Political and economic reasons for Russophobia were confirmed in a manner characteristic of the age by ecclesiastical considerations. Sweden's history proved that she was the most consistent and effective champion of Protestantism on the Continent, whereas Russia, by occupying Mecklenburg and threatening the territories of the Protestants of northern Germany, showed herself to be a danger to the Protestant cause. If Sweden were diminished in power and prestige, the Protestant interest could be maintained only by an extension of Prussian and Hanoverian influence in the Empire, where the Catholics, under the patronage of the Emperor, were already caballing for the ruin of the Protestant princes.

While much of this anti-Russian feeling was artificially stimulated, there was a substratum of genuine feeling which survived the end of the diplomatic crisis in 1721. The main role in settling the problems raised for Britain by the Northern war was at first taken by Stanhope. The death of Charles XII and the bankruptcy of his policy ended autocracy in Sweden and enabled those who had opposed him to change the Swedish constitution and gain control of Swedish foreign policy. The beginning of the 'Age of Liberty' and Sweden's decision not to make peace immediately with Russia, but, under British mediation, to settle first her quarrels with

Russia's former partners in the war, provoked more bad feeling between Britain and Russia. The closer British cooperation with Sweden, the worse the relations between Britain–Hanover and Russia.

Stanhope was able to negotiate in rapid succession peace treaties between Sweden and Hanover, Sweden and Prussia, and Sweden and Denmark. In each case Sweden had to pay dearly for peace by territorial and other concessions; and it was an implied part of the bargain that Britain would give Sweden effective help to continue war against Russia until a peace favourable to Sweden could be made with her arch-enemy. By this time Peter was again in touch with the Jacobites and boasted that his naval power was little, if at all, inferior to that of Britain. Point was given to his boasts by the inability of British naval squadrons, sent almost annually to the Baltic, either to bring the Russians to battle or to defend Sweden from Russian attacks. Even when Denmark withdrew from the war and Britain could count on Danish neutrality, if not some support, British naval operations in the Baltic did little to affect the course of the war and nothing to coerce Russia to make peace with Sweden. Indeed they so irritated Peter that he determined to impose his own terms upon Sweden and to punish Britain by entirely excluding her from the negotiation of the treaty of Nystad.

The signature of this treaty by Sweden and Russia was therefore a diplomatic defeat for Britain. The British government had induced Sweden to surrender territory to Russia's *quondam* allies, but had completely failed to set limits to Russian territorial and other gains at Sweden's expense. Russia was confirmed in her occupation of former Swedish provinces in the eastern Baltic. This was not only a blow to British prestige, but an actual threat to the very foundations of British naval power, upon which all else depended. And under the pacific 'caps', disenchanted as they were with the help they had received from Britain, there was no prospect of Sweden again challenging Russian domination of the Baltic. As elector of Hanover, George I had made profit from the war by securing actual occupation of Bremen and Verden, with some control over the administration of Mecklenburg as the Emperor's delegate. Even in Germany, however, after the treaty of Nystad Peter was in a position to support the claims of the duke of Holstein to the duchy of Schleswig which might well threaten Hanover's new possessions, while his special position in Mecklenburg infuriated the king of Prussia.

For a decade the treaty of Nystad set the stage for Anglo-Hanoverian-Russian relations. Indeed the rupture of diplomatic relations between the two countries which had begun in 1719 was not ended until 1728 and then only by the appointment of a consul-general. Not until 1731 were normal diplomatic relations re-established. In the intervening years Russia, rebuffed by the Regent Orleans, had concluded an alliance with Austria and British hostility to Austria, particularly during the crisis of the league of Hanover, reinforced the older causes of British and Hanoverian resentment and fear of Russia. This was intensified when Prussia after deserting the western powers joined in 1728 with the eastern powers of Russia and Austria in what may be justly described as the prototype of the neo-Holy alliances and Three Emperors' leagues which were to play such an important part in the diplomatic history of nine-teenth-century Europe.

The close union of Regency France and Hanoverian England at this time offers a faint parallel to the partial co-operation in the nineteenth century of the relatively liberal western powers against the eastern autocrats. English pamphleteers in the 1720's were quick to point out that Peter the Great's system of government was more autocratic and much more brutal than that of Louis XIV himself. The unlimited authority of the reigning Tsar made Russia more dangerous to English interests, if not to English liberties. Not until the great Ochakov crisis at the end of the century were Anglo-Russian relations so tense as they became in the 'twenties.

In conjunction with France, attempts were made by the secretaries of state to isolate Russia. Sufficient support was given to the Swedish 'caps' to prevent Sweden from becoming merely a Russian satellite. Prussian and Danish suspicions of Russia, now clearly the mistress of the Baltic, were fostered and as far as possible utilized. British technical experts, especially shipwrights, were urged to return home in the belief that this would be sufficient to cripple the naval power of Russia, or at least prevent further development. Britain even took a leaf from her French ally's book and tried to stir up the Turks to attack Russia in the south in order to distract her and hamper her activities in the Baltic.

The death of Peter, and the aristocratic reaction against his government and policies under the weak rule of the women and children who in turn succeeded him on the throne, took some of the bitterness out of the cold war which Britain had waged against him in the closing years of his reign. The British government counted on the Russian nobility, who depended for their prosperity on exporting the produce of their estates to Britain, to resist autocracy in Russia, influence the nominal ruler in favour of Britain, and veto the aggressive foreign policy which Peter had pursued. Though a British naval squadron was sent to the Baltic in 1727 to resist the pressure exerted by Peter's widow, Catherine I, upon Sweden and Denmark by supporting the territorial claims of the duke of Holstein, it came to be realized that Britain's fears of Russia had been exaggerated, if not unfounded. Experience in the 1720's showed that Peter I and his successors were not using their newly established ascendancy in the Baltic to damage British trading interests there. Peter's moderation bore fruit after his death in the commercial treaty of 1734 which sealed the reconciliation of Britain and Russia.

On the death of George I in 1727, his son George II was securely established as elector in Bremen and Verden, and as king on the throne of Great Britain. But as long as Townshend remained in office he continued to oppose any reconciliation with Austria. In his view it was essential to detach Russia from Austria and it was Townshend who took the first step towards negotiating a commercial treaty with Russia which was partly designed to secure this object. Before Townshend's dispatch had been sent off, Walpole took over responsibility for the direction of foreign policy and patched up in 1731 Townshend's quarrel with Austria. Consequently Walpole was no longer much influenced by Townshend's main reason for desiring closer contact with Russia, but it was now clearly in the interests of Austria to improve relations between her two major allies, Britain and Russia. As long as Walpole remained on good terms with France, and, even after the second treaty of Vienna, not particularly friendly towards Austria, Britain's political relationship with Russia remained distant and not very important.

It was Britain's reaction to the pursuit in the Baltic of an independent French policy, designed to secure control both of Denmark and Sweden, that in the end provided the immediate impulse to the Anglo-Russian treaty of commerce of 1734. Russia was prepared to co-operate with Britain in opposing the intrigues and aggression of France, but she demanded a guarantee of the Russian territories recently conquered from Sweden which the British government could not give, if only because it would have bitterly offended the Swedes. Even more alarming to the British government was the risk that Russia, failing to get a firm undertaking of British support, might go over to the French side and in conjunction with the Scandinavian powers, always dangerously liable to be influenced by France, exclude Britain altogether from the Baltic. Worse still, the surrender to Sweden of the territories of Bremen and Verden which George I had won in the Great Northern war, might provide at the expense of George II the basis for a Russo-Swedish reconciliation, mediated by France and supported by her subsidies and prestige. It was fear of France, and particularly of her superior political influence in Baltic politics, that forced Britain to abandon the hostility she had shown to Russia in the 1720's and to seek Russian support against France and her Baltic satellites. Both Austria and Russia tried to drive Britain into a close political alliance with them which was the last thing Walpole wanted. He escaped from the dilemma, which was a recurring one in the course of Anglo-Russian relations in the eighteenth century, by concluding the commercial treaty 'which included a declaration of friendship and was itself evidence of it'.[1]

This treaty gave Britain what was coming to be called most-favoured-nation privileges in Russia. A special tariff reduction on imports of British cloth to Russia led to a marked increase in the use of British woollens and prevented the competitive Silesian woollen industry from gaining a foothold in Russia. Russia also allowed British merchants to trade overland with Persia—a much coveted privilege of which little advantage could in fact be taken, even after the alteration of the Navigation Laws by the British Parliament made such trade legal in 1741. While Russia secured on paper the privilege of most-favoured nation in Britain, Russian merchants made no use of it; and the other rights given to British traders in Russia were not reciprocated even on paper. The Navigation Acts, for example, remained fully in force so far as Russia was concerned. Although 'the treaty itself was a masterful British commercial triumph',[2] the Russian negotiators were content with their gains—the prospect of political co-operation with Britain and the continuance of a favourable balance of trade which gave the Russian state a substantial subsidy in ready money every year. According to

---

[1] N. C. Hunt, 'The Russia Company and the Government, 1730–42' in *Oxford Slavonic Papers* 7 (1957), 52.

[2] D. K. Reading, *The Anglo-Russian Commercial Treaty of 1734*, p. 301.

the Russia Company's figures for 1729 it imported about £300,000 of goods from Russia and exported no more than £75,000.[1]

Walpole had at first no intention of completing by a political understanding the economic agreement of 1734, though he remained throughout the Polish Succession war benevolently neutral towards Russia and Austria and even tried, as his predecessors had done earlier, to mediate between Russia, Austria, and Turkey when these powers became engaged in a war over the Eastern Question. France finally mediated at Belgrade a settlement of the Eastern war with great advantage to herself. Continued decline of British trade with Turkey made easier British political alignment with Russia, while British non-intervention in the war of the Polish Succession and consequent alienation of the Emperor left Walpole to face in isolation the increasingly overt hostility of Spain and France. The fall of the Swedish 'caps', followed by a Franco-Swedish subsidy treaty, presaged a new Northern war. Walpole's overtures for a political alliance with Russia in 1738 led eventually to the defensive alliance of 1742.

Walpole had fallen and it was Carteret who hailed the treaty as a necessary step towards humbling France in Europe. Once Britain had engaged in a major war against the Bourbon courts, Russia became potentially a valuable member of an anti-Bourbon coalition. Carteret hoped that the treaty would put paid to Franco-Swedish aggression in the Baltic. Properly used, it might even undo the damage wrought by the treaty of Nystad to Britain's position in the Baltic. In fact it was almost destitute of immediate consequences. The Tsaritsa Elizabeth defeated the Swedes without help from Britain; but she was at first too insecure on the Russian throne and herself so impelled in different directions by tradition, sympathies, and personal predilections, that she took no effective diplomatic or military initiative until the closing years of the Austrian Succession war.

At first hostile to Maria Theresa, who had backed her rival for the Russian throne, Elizabeth became, under the influence of her chancellor, Alexis Bestuzhev, the firm ally of Austria by the treaty of the Two Empresses in 1746. It was partly Austrian influence at St. Petersburg that contributed to a second and more important defensive treaty between Britain and Russia, supple-

[1] N. C. Hunt, op. cit., 36. I have used Dr. Hunt's researches in the preceding paragraphs.

mented by a subsidy convention which arranged for a march across Europe by the Russian mercenaries to take part in the struggle against France in western Europe. Though these troops arrived too late to fight, it is possible that their march had some influence upon the French decision to make peace on very moderate terms. Although British ministers had had a practical demonstration of the expense and delay of securing actual help from Russia, they were ready to try the expedient again a few years later. Impending war with France forced them to consider means of defending Hanover, should it be attacked by France or her ally Prussia. The best method of securing this object seemed to be to arrange for transport by sea of a much larger Russian force which could be landed at some point of the Baltic coast to make a direct attack upon Prussia. It was hoped that this would forestall Prussian attack on Hanover or at the worst compel Prussia to recall her invading army for her own defence. Not only would Hanover be saved, but French domination of Germany would be averted. Kaunitz, for reasons of his own, persistently pressed Newcastle to conclude a subsidy treaty with Russia.

British overtures for such a treaty agreed well with Russia's and Austria's plans to reduce to insignificance the dangerous power of a state which had become, under Frederick the Great, the deadly rival of both courts. Newcastle's bright idea that the Russian treaty could be used to keep the peace in Germany, not, as Russia intended, to start a war there, roused the Tsaritsa to fury and put her chancellor, Alexis Bestuzhev, in an impossible situation. Even before the reconciliation of Austria and France in May 1756 a Franco-Russian *rapprochement* began. The subsidy convention with Britain was promptly repudiated in the early months of 1756. After a ding-dong battle at St. Petersburg, in which the heir to the throne, the grand duke Peter, and his wife, the future Catherine II, played leading roles, Russia aligned herself with Austria and France by acceding in January 1757 to the first treaty of Versailles between France and Austria.

Though Russian troops played a more and more prominent part as the Seven Years war went on, and Russia inflicted upon Britain's ally, Frederick the Great, his worst defeats, diplomatic relations between Britain and Russia were not broken off during the war. The need for naval stores which only Russia could supply and continued Russian dependence upon her best customer proved stronger than the political forces which naturally tended to drive them apart when they were engaged on opposite sides in a bitter and protracted war. Britain firmly refused to send a fleet into the Baltic, as her ally Frederick continually demanded, largely because this would have infuriated Russia. It must however be added that Pitt knew of more profitable uses to which the British navy could be, and was, put; and it would have been difficult and dangerous to intervene when Russia and Sweden were on the same side. Russia, on her part, put no obstacles in the way of Britain securing from the Baltic the naval stores which she required to wage war at sea and in the colonies.

Also, it was during the war that there appeared in Britain the first traces of an idea which was to become prominent after it had ended. Having lost the Austrian alliance, Britain should try to replace it by a so-called Northern System strong enough to face, with some prospect of success, the Bourbon–Hapsburg alliance of southern Europe. The first requirement was to add Russia to Pitt's alliance with Prussia: the known difficulties which were preventing effective co-operation between Russia and France, even during the war, encouraged a belief that this, though difficult, was not quite impracticable.

The death of the Tsaritsa Elizabeth, the implacable enemy of Frederick, in 1762 brought to the throne of the Tsars Peter III, the admirer and disciple of Frederick, and his Anglophil wife, Catherine. Since there was no Prussian diplomatic agent at the Russian court, the British minister there, Robert Keith, acted as an intermediary. But it soon became clear that the war-weary British politicians would not countenance the aggressive plans of the new Tsar against Denmark, whereas Frederick had no option but to appear to join heartily in them. The deposition and subsequent murder of Tsar Peter consequently eased Russo-British tensions and seemed to offer a real chance of Russo-Prussian-British alliance, had it not been for the ill-timed quarrel between Frederick and Bute. Frederick secured for himself an alliance with Russia in 1764 and spent much of his time until 1780 in making quite sure that Britain was not admitted to it.

Certainly the end of the Seven Years war relaxed tension between Britain and Russia. Catherine II had a much wider grasp of European politics than any of her predecessors since Peter the Great. Unlike them she had also a genuine interest in the European enlightenment and a desire to introduce some of its tenets into the actual government of Russia. Personally Anglophil, she read—in French or German translations—the works of British scholars, philosophers, and economists. She particularly admired the historical works of Hume and Robertson and allowed a few Russian students to attend the Scottish universities. She personally translated, from French or German versions, some of Shakespeare's plays into Russian and encouraged English professional actors to perform *Othello* and other popular English plays at St. Petersburg in the early 1770's. A considerable number of other English classics by Swift, Fielding, Robertson, Blackstone, and Dr. Johnson appeared in Russian dress during the reign of Catherine II. Under such an enlightened sovereign—and Catherine paid much attention to her image abroad—the old British idea of Muscovy as a barbarous non-European state ruled by an oriental despot of more than customary brutality was modified, though by no means entirely erased.

More important in leading to improved diplomatic relations between the two countries was the recognition on both sides that they shared certain political interests in the post-war world. As long as Panin's influence counted with the Tsaritsa, she was more interested in the Baltic than in the Black Sea. France had induced Sweden to join in the Seven Years war, yet Sweden had gained no advantage. In spite of this, French influence was still dominant at Stockholm and at first Catherine and Panin saw in it the main obstacle to the attainment of their ambitious schemes. They sought co-operation from Britain in undermining the ascendancy of the Swedish 'hats', patronized by France, at Stockholm, and George III shared for a time the expense of bribing Swedish party leaders and senators.

Catherine also angled for British financial and other support to confirm the position established by Russia during the war in Poland, when it had been occupied by Russian troops. She made it clear also that she would expect active British support if she were attacked in the south by France's ally, Turkey. As Catherine's ambitions were diverted from the pursuit of Panin's not very profitable concentration on the Baltic and Poland towards the almost unlimited field of expansion offered by the southern Steppes, the so-called Turkish clause became the most important single factor in negotiations for a political alliance between Britain and Russia.

Once again the British government took a much more active and continuous interest in the commercial than in the political negotiations between the two countries. The commercial treaty of 1734 expired at the beginning of the Seven Years war, but this does not seem to have had any effect on the exchange of commodities. In 1762, according to figures in *H.M.C. Lothian MSS.*, p. 234, British merchants took out of Russia nearly two million roubles'[1] worth of exports out of a total of about three and a half million. Russian merchants exported nearly 400,000, the Dutch nearly 250,000 and the French only 73,000 roubles in value, the rest being divided between the north German ports, Hamburg, Lübeck, Rostock, &c. Russia imported just under three million roubles' worth, giving her an over-all favourable trade balance of half a million roubles. Of these Russian merchants imported just under 800,000, British merchants 650,000 roubles in value. Britain's nearest competitors were the Dutch with nearly 350,000 roubles, Hamburg and Danzig with over 250,000 and over 200,000 respectively. Direct French imports were only valued at 46,000 roubles; but, as with Russian exports, most French trade was conducted by Dutch shipping.

The most reliable 'break-down' of British imports from, and exports to, Russia relates to 1763.[2] Its main features appear in the table on page 215.

For purposes of comparison the figures given by Sir Charles Whitworth in his *State of Trade*, based on unreal and out-of-date custom-house values, may be added. He calculated that in 1762 Britain took from Russia goods to the value of £627,451 and exported £61,509 to Russia. With the end of the war there was a normal jump in 1763 both for exports and imports. British imports from Russia rose to £801,279 and her exports to Russia to £78,901.

Careful analysis of these figures may be left to the economic historians with all their professional skills but some conclusions may safely be drawn even by an amateur. Trade between Britain and Russia had greatly increased since the beginning of the century. British ships had largely ousted the Dutch, and Britain was now by far Russia's best customer. While the volume and value of British imports from Russia rose from £124,220 on an average in the years 1700, 1701, and 1702, to £1,110,093 on an average in the years 1770, 1771, and 1772, the value of British

---

[1] The rouble may be reckoned to be worth about 4*s*. at this time.
[2] *Buckinghamshire Despatches*, ed. Collyer (Camden Society) I, pp. 255–6.

exports increased only from £76,784 to £145,125.[1] To a mercantilist the most striking change in the pattern of Russo-British trade was not so much that both exports and imports had increased; but that, in consequence of the comparatively slight rise in exports to Russia, an adverse trade balance of £47,436 had increased to the monstrous total of £964,968.

British Imports from Russia			British Exports to Russia		
Hemp	1,089,484	roubles	Cloth	236,540	roubles
Iron[2]	530,238	,,	Shalloons	100,610	,,
Flax	415,265	,,	Sugar	100,600	,,
Hides	372,300	,,	Indigo	89,795	,,
Sailcloth, &c.	318,918	,,	Tin	61,354	,,
Linen	155,925	,,	Stuffs	53,120	,,
Isinglass			Beaverskins	40,637	,,
(gelatine)	125,015	,,	Logwood	36,360	,,
Saltpetre	110,847	,,	Hardware	35,120	,,
Drillings	104,520	,,	Buxton ale	18,907	,,
Bristles	59,135	,,	Lead	18,620	,,
Tallow	48,190	,,			
	3,329,837	,,		791,663	,,
Miscellaneous			Miscellaneous		
items (each			items (each		
under 30,000			under 15,000		
roubles)	135,163	,,	roubles)	118,337	,,
Total	3,465,000	,,	Total	910,000	,,

The government drew the conclusion that since Britain could not do without the great bulk of its imports from Russia, every effort should be made to export more to Russia. Successive British envoys to Russia from Sir Charles Hanbury Williams in 1755 received instructions to seek the renewal of the commercial treaty of 1734 but it was not until 1766 that George Macartney managed to carry out these instructions. Even then concessions had to be made to the Russian point of view, which not only reduced the value of the new commercial treaty at the time, in the opinion of the British government, but laid a basis for acrimonious disputes between the two governments during the war of American Independence.

[1] Chalmers, *Estimate of the Comparative Strength of Britain* (1782), p. 72. These figures are ultimately derived from Whitworth's *State of Trade*.

[2] To improve their seaworthiness when loaded with bulky cargoes of naval stores, ships were often ballasted with bar-iron which the captains sometimes carried without charging freight on it.

In the meantime success in commercial negotiation with Russia might well lead, as it had done in the 'thirties, to a defensive alliance between Britain and Russia. Catherine's success in transferring most of her Baltic fleet to the Mediterranean and its defeat of the Turks at the naval battle of Chesmé in July 1770 made the more impression in Britain, because without help of various kinds from Britain it could never have been accomplished. Previous naval successes achieved by Russia had been mostly in defence of her own coasts. Now it appeared that it might be easier and cheaper to arrange for a Russian squadron to operate in the seas off western Europe than it had proved to secure the help of a Russian army on western battlefields. That Russian successes had been won at the expense of France's ally, Turkey, and that French opposition to a Russian fleet in the Mediterranean had been overcome by British threats were additional reasons for British satisfaction. Russian gratitude to Britain could surely be counted upon to help on the languishing negotiation for a political alliance.

The first Russo-Turkish war of Catherine's reign, which had markedly improved relations between Britain and Russia, had been a by-product of her persistent intervention in Poland. Her objects were to maintain Poland's anarchic constitution and to protect religious minorities in order to stabilize and perpetuate the ascendancy in Poland which Russia had gained during the Seven Years war. By rousing the patriotism and fanaticism of the Polish nobles, who monopolized political power in the kingdom of Poland to the exclusion alike of king and people, she found herself engaged in fighting a guerrilla war against the Polish Opposition and at the same time a regular war against their Turkish allies in the Danubian provinces, while the new king of Sweden, Gustavus III, was planning mischief in the Baltic with the secret support of France. To escape from this awkward and exposed position, she agreed to the first Partition of Poland with Prussia and Austria.

Neither the British government nor the British people cared much about Poland. They felt about the Poles much as Neville Chamberlain felt about another people of eastern Europe, the Czechs, in the 1930's. Even if they had been interested the geographical situation of Poland would have been sufficient to prevent any effective intervention. The British fleet, as Horace Walpole pointed out, could not hope to sail to Warsaw. Fervid Protestants regarded Poland as a bigoted and persecuting Roman Catholic country, while advocates of the enlightenment denounced its government as a medieval anachronism in modern Europe. Poland lacked ethnographic frontiers to the east, if not also in Prussia and Galicia: if the benevolent despots took such territory from her the lot of the great majority would be markedly improved.

If there was general agreement, helped by vigorous Polish propaganda in Britain, that the Partition was undoubtedly a crime, there was also a widespread belief that it might also turn out to be a blunder from the standpoint of the partitioning powers—or of some of them. Such was the attitude of Edmund Burke, as expressed in the *Annual Register* and elsewhere. What the partitioning powers had taken from Poland was merely a breakfast for them. 'Where,' he inquired meaningly, 'would they dine?' Chatham, the self-styled apostle of the cause of liberty, did not believe that this cause was affected by the fall of Poland, and avowed to Shelburne that he was 'quite a Russ'. It is significant that he gave as his reason for supporting Russia that her defeat of the Turks 'will pull down the house of Bourbon in [their] fall'. Even without a political alliance between Britain and Russia, Catherine was working in the interests of Britain. That to oppose Catherine in Poland, Britain must first ally herself with France was for most Englishmen a sufficient reason for not attempting to do so.

The furthest the British government ever went towards an official condemnation of the first Partition was to inform Russia that a guarantee of Russian conquests from Poland could never compose part of a treaty between Russia and Britain. Suffolk, secretary of state for the northern department, attributed the Partition to the over-great influence of Frederick at St. Petersburg and thought it possible that once she had extricated herself from her immediate difficulties Catherine would throw off Frederick's yoke.[1] The Tsaritsa might be caught on the rebound and he would do nothing to make more difficult the reunion of Britain and Russia. So long as Russia did not expect Britain to co-operate actively in eastern Europe, there was virtually no limit to what she could do there. Indeed the more vigorous her policy and the more damaging it proved to the prestige and interests of France in eastern Europe, the more presentable Russia appeared as an ally to many Britons, such as Chatham.

[1] See for the preceding paragraphs D. B. Horn, *British Public Opinion and the First Partition of Poland, passim.*

In spite of these favourable circumstances, the long-drawn-out negotiations for a political alliance outlived the 'sixties and continued intermittently well into the 'seventies. Catherine's alliance with Frederick secured her immediate needs, and to force him to admit Britain would not merely alienate him but also weaken instead of strengthening it. In fact the British government, believing that time was on their side, offered Catherine so little that from her point of view the risks of concluding the treaty were far greater than any possible advantage to Russia. Britain absolutely refused to help her either against Sweden or Turkey, nor would she do anything to support Russia's position in Poland.

The approach of the war of American Independence galvanized the almost defunct political negotiation into life. Once again, as in 1739 and 1755, Britain turned to Russia for help in the confident belief that Russia was her natural ally. This time the proposal was that Russia should provide 20,000 troops which would be sent to fight the colonists in America. If Russia desired a subsidy this would be readily paid. If not, Britain would meet all out-of-pocket expenses incurred by the Tsaritsa. This was a pretty tall order and the precedents were not encouraging. The Russian Empress could hardly be expected to supply the troops free of charge, but if she accepted even a disguised form of subsidy, she felt she would be lowering herself to the level of a mercenary German prince. In any case the active Russian army was not large when compared to the forces kept on foot by Prussia and Austria: Catherine might well have need for all her available regiments much nearer home.

Rebuffed in 1775, Britain tried a new approach in 1779. Stormont promised British assistance to Russia in the event of a war with Turkey in exchange for active Russian support of Britain in the war now going on against a European coalition. Under pressure of war Britain gave up the refusal she had maintained hitherto to become the ally of Russia against the Turks. When even this proved unacceptable to Russia—and after all she was being invited to take part in a war already in progress, in exchange for favours to come in a war which had not yet broken out—Stormont tried again. This time he offered an immediate cession of Minorca, which would admit Russia to the Mediterranean and give her a base of operations either against the Bourbon courts, who held the western Mediterranean, or against the Turks, who were still dominant in the Levant. Stormont's intention was undoubtedly to embroil Russia in the war of American Independence; but at the Russian court the offer of Minorca was considered rather as a bonus to be secured by Russia, should she succeed in negotiating a peace that Britain could accept without dishonour.

The protracted Russo-British negotiation over Minorca thus rested on a misunderstanding by each government of the other's intentions and was foredoomed to failure. Indeed as understood by Stormont, it ran counter to Catherine's policy and Russia's clear interests. The weaker Britain's military and naval position, the less likely Catherine was to accept involvement in a war in order to pull Britain's chestnuts out of the fire. She remained personally friendly to Britain. She expressed and really felt satisfaction at such successes as Malmesbury was able to report to her. The last thing she wanted to see was the complete defeat of Britain by her continental enemies and her relegation to the second league of European powers. But Vergennes was as anxious as Catherine to avoid continental war and this gave them something in common.

When Catherine organized the Armed Neutrality of 1780 and thus put herself at the head of the neutral powers Vergennes humoured her, whereas Britain treated Russian opposition to the exercise of Britain's maritime rights as an unfriendly act. Having consolidated her leadership of the neutrals—and these included not merely the Scandinavians and the Dutch but also Austria and Prussia—and drawn nearer to France and Spain by the Armed Neutrality, Catherine in 1781 saw herself as the arbiter of Europe and was eager to mediate a general peace which would enshrine the principles of the neutral league. Such a peace would never be accepted by Britain except after total defeat in the maritime war.

On the Russian side, Russia could not have accepted Harris's offers even had she been so disposed, since this would clearly infringe her impartiality as a mediator and cause France to reject her offers of mediation. Britain made it clear that when she invoked Russian mediation she meant Russian 'good offices' in favour of Britain, reinforced by an implied threat that if Britain's enemies did not accept Russia's suggestions then Russia would enter the war on Britain's side. Russia's repeated refusal of such help and her patronage of the league of neutrals struck a blow at British ideas of Russia as a natural ally from which they never fully recovered.

The Armed Neutrality may be regarded as a landmark in the

economic almost as much as in the political relations of Britain and Russia. It was based not only on Catherine's personal vanity and political ambition; but also on growing resentment in Russia of Britain's stranglehold on Russia's foreign trade. France and Russia had a common interest in making use of neutral Dutch ships to bring colonial produce to Russia and take away naval stores needed by France and Spain to carry on their naval war against Britain. Once Britain had forced the Dutch out of neutrality, their place was filled by some ports of northern Germany. The opportunity was also taken to expand the merchant navy of Russia. Although there was a decline after 1783, between 1775 and 1787 the number of Russian ships engaged in foreign trade rose from 17 to 141. The threat to Britain's position is more clearly represented by the fact that in this period of twelve years British ships engaged in Russian trade trebled, whereas the number of ships of other nations, including Russian ships, increased sevenfold.[1]

Throughout the war British diplomacy in Russia showed the defects which in general characterized it in the eighteenth century —lack of realism and grasp of the other man's point of view. Successive secretaries of state put forward one unrealistic proposal after another—the offer of Minorca was followed by suggestions that Russia should attack Majorca in 1780 or try to establish a colony in South America at a time when Catherine was straining every nerve to secure the Crimea. Even Harris, whose capacity and opportunities for such an exercise were much greater than those of an insular secretary of state at home, never tried to put himself in the place of one of Catherine's ministers and appreciate the situation from the opposite side of the diplomatic round-table.

It is a minor criticism that the old idea that anything could be obtained from Russia by judicious bribes, which had proved fallacious a generation earlier, was still generally accepted at London as a self-evident axiom. Personally Harris fell into the error frequently made by his predecessors in Russia—he associated himself so closely with one of the contenders for control of Russian foreign policy (Potemkin) that he alienated the other (Panin), without securing any guarantee that his favourite minister would effectu-

---

[1] Isabel de Madariaga, *Britain, Russia and the Armed Neutrality of 1780*, p. 443. These Russian figures apparently take no account of the tonnage of ships involved.

ally serve the interests of Britain at the Russian court. Harris's attitude may have helped to secure the victory of Potemkin, but it soon became clear that Britain would gain nothing by the eclipse of Panin.

What in the end saved Britain from accepting at Russian dictation the principles of the Armed Neutrality was total Russian involvement in the Crimea. When negotiations for renewal of the commercial treaty of 1766 began in 1785, Catherine insisted on modifications, which the British negotiators unhesitatingly rejected, to take account not only of the Armed Neutrality, but of the changing character of Russian foreign trade. Russian persistence in attempting to secure economic emancipation from Britain was one of the factors which brought about the Ochakov crisis of 1791.

During the war what was virtually a new factor emerged in Anglo-Russian relations. It is true that in previous crises governments had made treaties with Russia, which had been violently attacked by the parliamentary Opposition, usually on the ground that they were ruinously expensive and could in any case serve no useful purpose. But during the American war Fox went much further than any of his predecessors. His persistent denigration of North not only played into the hands of Catherine: it led her to expect that the fall of North's government and the coming into power of the Whigs would lead to peace, perhaps even to a peace which would include a renunciation by Britain of her belligerent rights at sea. Fox's acts and speeches had little effect upon Anglo-Russian relations at the time; but, by attempting to forge a link between his own party and the Russian empress, he brought concrete questions of foreign policy openly into the party arena and induced an inclination amongst his opponents to take a different line. Here too may be seen a connexion between the American war of Independence and Pitt's attitude to Russia in 1791.

While British attitudes to Russia underwent fundamental changes in the 1780's, Russia's approach to Britain remained basically unaltered. Russia, as in previous decades, continued to resent British assumptions of diplomatic leadership, superior political and cultural status, and economic superiority. The American war had made Russia for a time an arbiter over the belligerents and proved her capable of taking over the advantageous diplomatic position, held by Britain in the first half of the century, of the supreme balancing power of Europe. The Armed Neutrality and her refusal to renew the commercial treaty of 1766 with Britain demonstrated her economic emancipation. Catherine's deliberate policy had done much to level the score; but the traditional attitude of resentment at British airs of superiority lingered on. More important in spite of a *rapprochement* with France, begun during the war and continued after it, 'Britain remained the pivot of Russian policy in the west'.[1]

That Russia ceased to be the ally of Prussia and allied herself closely with Austria in 1781 might have been expected to reduce the tension between Britain and Russia, which had undoubtedly developed during the American war. Frederick the Great's vindictiveness was notorious and apparently unassuaged by time, whereas most politically minded Englishmen still thought nostalgically of the 'old alliance' between Britain and Austria. In fact, believing that he could count on Russian support for his German projects, Joseph II set Germany in uproar and forced Prussia and Hanover to join forces to oppose him.

Worse still, when the Turks, alarmed by the close alliance between their two traditional enemies, and particularly resenting Russian activities in the Balkans and the Caucasus, declared war on Russia in 1787, Catherine II rightly held the influence of the British ambassador at Constantinople to be partly responsible for this decision. When Pitt firmly refused to give Russia the facilities, readily offered by his predecessors in 1769, to send part of her Baltic fleet to attack the Turks in the Levant, while he allowed British merchantmen to carry contraband for Turkish armies, the Tsaritsa was furious. So angry was she that she claimed that the Triple Alliance of 1788 between Britain, Prussia, and the Dutch, which had arisen out of incidents in western Europe, was directed against her. Pitt had no such intention when he negotiated the treaty of alliance; but, by associating Britain with Prussia, he ended the isolation which had proved damaging to Prussian interests in eastern Europe, and therefore enabled Prussia to take up a much firmer line against both Austria and Russia. Catherine reacted by openly supporting Fox and his friends in their opposition to Pitt's measures. Friends of the government then accused the Opposition of treason.

Even in the Baltic, where Britain and Russia had found it easier

[1] Isabel de Madariaga, op. cit. (upon which the preceding paragraphs are based), p. 458.

to work together than anywhere else in the middle years of the century, Pitt tried to reach in 1789 an agreement with France against Russian expansion. When France refused, he joined in 1790 with Prussia to pursue what had formerly been the French policy of subsidizing Sweden to wage war upon Russia. In these circumstances it was natural that British naval mobilization to enforce her claims against Spain to Nootka Sound led to rumours that the British fleet was really intended for service in the Baltic. Catherine had some reason to suspect that Pitt was about to revert to the policy of Stanhope in the years immediately after the accession of George I.

More important, so far as the British government was concerned, was a growing interest in Poland, which indeed occupied a central position in the plans of Britain's Prussian ally. Hertzberg's elaborate and artificial exchange projects had no admirers or supporters in Britain, but Joseph Ewart, the British diplomatic representative at Berlin and the most outspoken enemy of Russia, was winning some converts in London. The anti-Russian lobby, which was now being formed, saw in Poland an alternative to Russia as the chief supplier of naval stores, timber, grain, and other commodities which Britain needed from the Baltic countries. With a little help from Prussia, Poland could supply sufficient quantities of naval stores, timber, hides, grain, and flax to meet British needs. Poland and the neighbouring countries offered an expanding market for British manufactured goods and colonial produce which could be readily and economically distributed by river transport. Iron was the only commodity exported by Russia that Poland and Prussia could not supply.

This idea was not entirely new, but it gained strength when Russia refused to renew her commercial treaty with Britain and made instead a similar treaty with France. The British consul at Memel, James Durno, seems to have been the originator of such schemes, but others in more influential positions soon took them up. Russia had always disliked the privileges her weakness had forced her to grant to British traders, and the deterioration of political relations between the two countries was likely to be followed by further reduction, or even total abolition, of these privileges. Already there were complaints that Russian favouritism of French trade was putting British merchants in Russia in the position of the least-favoured nation.

Obviously the British government, before finally committing itself to a fundamental alteration in its trade channels with eastern Europe, must have some guarantee of mutual co-operation between Prussia, her political ally in the Triple Alliance, and Poland, the economic partner she wished to favour in the east. For years, indeed long before the first Partition, the relations of Prussia and Poland had been bad. Poland resented the leading part taken by Frederick the Great in this discreditable transaction. Frederick's cold war against Danzig and his success in using territories gained in the First Partition to undermine its former prosperity kept Polish resentment alive. The essential basis for developing British trade with Poland was the negotiation of a settlement acceptable to both Prussia and Poland of the thorny problem of Danzig.

Realizing that they must have Prussian support if Poland was to survive as an independent state the Poles were prepared to surrender Danzig and the Vistula fortress of Thorn to Prussia if they could recover Galicia, which Austria had taken as her share in the first Partition. Pitt was not prepared to support Poland in a demand for Galicia—least of all when he was trying to persuade his Prussian ally to give up her plans for territorial acquisitions in central Europe. He told the Polish agent Oginski in London that Poland must give up Danzig and Thorn in exchange for Prussia's agreement to reduce the customs barriers she had erected to check Poland's Vistula trade. What seemed an obvious solution at London had little chance of acceptance either at Berlin or Warsaw.[1]

Ewart cared little about trade, but pointed out that these economic projects could be realized only if Poland remained independent of Russia. Hence Pitt's government, which had hitherto shown a marked reluctance to back up Prussia in eastern Europe, was given a direct incentive to do so. Ewart secured adroitly what he really wanted—a continuance, if not a consolidation of the Anglo-Prussian alliance. From Poland came the suggestion that a port on her Baltic coast-line might be sold or mortgaged to Britain in order to guarantee British access to Polish exports and provide a market where British exports could be conveniently stored and displayed for sale.

An alternative and in some respects better route for the inter-

[1] This and the preceding paragraph are based on J. Ehrman, *British Government and Commercial Negotiations with Europe 1783–93*, chapter 5.

change of commodities on a large scale between Britain and Poland would be down the Polish rivers to the Black Sea. Russian advance to its northern coast and increasing pressure from other powers had compelled the Turks, who had hitherto treated it as a *mare clausum*, to open it to the navigation of other powers. So far Austria and France had been more active than Britain in this sphere; but this was merely another reason why Britain too should stake her claims and secure a share in a new and promising outlet for her international trade.

Here again it was Russia which stood in the way. Catherine's policy of expansion in this area, and her increasingly effective control of the Cossacks and Tartars who lived in it, enabled her to interfere with what might come to be in time a Polish life-line to western Europe. Even before the Turkish declaration of war, Russia was hampering Poland's trade by way of the Dniester to the Black Sea. During the war her troops took Ochakov, a Turkish fortress which Pitt's advisers believed would enable Russia, if she retained it at the peace, to control the navigation both of the Bug and the Dniester. It would thus be within Russia's power not merely to hamper or even stop Poland's trade with Britain via the Black Sea, but to allow France what she denied to Britain—free access to plentiful supplies of naval stores both in Poland and in the Ukraine.

Merely by shifting the balance of trade from the Baltic, where Britain had laboriously established commercial superiority, to the Black Sea, where France enjoyed the political and economic advantages of her ancient alliance with the Turks and the natural advantage of a comparatively short, inland-sea passage to Marseilles and Toulon, Russia could do irretrievable harm to British trade and national security. Plans to develop British trade with Poland were not so much the product of economic imperialism as of a growing conviction that Russia's attitude to Britain and her persistent flirtation with France was a threat not merely to the British economy, but to the continued existence of Britain as a Great Power.

How widely such views were held in Britain is difficult to determine: in view of the actual course of the Ochakov crisis the opinion may be hazarded that they were deeply rather than widely held. In the case of many pamphleteers and newspaper correspondents resentment at Catherine's habit of making 'one conquest only a step to the acquisition of another'[1] was balanced by the conviction that Russia was still a natural ally of Britain and that any increase of Russian power would in the long run be detrimental to the house of Bourbon. Sir John Dalrymple, a well-known historian in his own day, refurbished the Chathamite ideas of the 'sixties with the novel addition that Russia would be an invaluable ally not only against the Bourbons but against the growing naval power of the United States of America. Jeremy Bentham even argued that the Armed Neutrality of 1780 was 'a measure of self-defence, of equality, of peace'[2] and that British resentment was quite unjustified. Some of those who argued on the other side were foreigners interested in stirring up British opinion against their enemy, Russia.

Not for the only time in his career Pitt drifted along until he found himself in an exceedingly awkward position. In March 1791 Frederick William II asked whether the British government would join with him in presenting an ultimatum to Russia and, if necessary, in naval and military measures intended to force Russia to make peace with the Turks on the basis of the *status quo ante bellum*. Although Frederick William II had already proved himself a political weathercock, and there were powerful forces at Berlin opposed to any definitive breach with Russia—let alone a frontal attack upon Russia—Pitt could hardly avoid giving a straight answer to a direct question.

After two meetings of the Cabinet and with the express approval of the king, a message was despatched to St. Petersburg via Berlin to require from Catherine II a statement of her readiness to make peace with the Turks without the further cession of Turkish territory. Pitt followed up this decisive though secret step, which he could surely have avoided, by publicly handing to the Commons a royal message proposing further augmentation of the navy. This was undoubtedly intended to reinforce British diplomacy at Berlin and St. Petersburg. Yet the Cabinet was split over the ultimatum and Pitt himself was clearly in two minds, as was shown when he proposed almost at once to postpone the presentation of the ultimatum.

The basic criticism of Pitt's handling of the crisis is that he him-

---

[1] Sir John Sinclair, quoted by M. S. Anderson, *Britain's Discovery of Russia*, p. 151.

[2] Quoted ibid., p. 153.

self brought it to a head by the quite unnecessarily explicit answer his government gave to Frederick William without first making some attempt to discover (1) how firm the ground was at Berlin and (2) how much support he was likely to obtain in Parliament and the country for what was, after all, a sudden and complete reversal of the policy pursued by successive British governments towards Russia for two generations. His action is the more inexplicable since he must have had in his mind memories of the difficulties which his government had experienced in the previous year, when Britain and Prussia had tried, not too successfully, to extract an undertaking from Austria similar to the one now to be presented to Russia in the form of an ultimatum. And the prospect of dictating to Russia terms of peace after she had waged a successful war—never very bright—were obviously still further diminished by Russia's conclusion of her war with Sweden by the treaty of Verela (August 1790).

It is a minor but still serious criticism of the Cabinet's decision that while some attempt was made to find out about the prospects of naval warfare in the Baltic—mainly by asking a Dutch admiral, who had served there, a number of rather obvious questions to most of which he returned discouraging answers—Pitt plunged into the crisis without concerting any plan for combined operations with Prussia. The idea of British naval intervention in the Black Sea was an afterthought. More curious still was the government's failure adequately to inform itself about the actual situation of affairs on the Black Sea and its coasts in order to convince the country that the restoration of Ochakov to the Turks was indeed a British interest of such moment as to justify a war against Russia.

The duke of Leeds as foreign secretary had been the principal advocate in the Cabinet of the change of policy towards Russia: his resignation inevitably followed its collapse when Pitt withdrew his support and sent a special envoy to St. Petersburg on what was meant to be a face-saving mission but merely increased Pitt's embarrassment. Catherine naturally resisted the envoy's blandishments as firmly as she had resisted previous British threats, and Russia made peace with Turkey in January 1792 on her own terms. Pitt's failure over Ochakov not merely impaired Britain's relations with Russia, but destroyed the Triple Alliance, by which he had hoped to give the law to Europe and complete the restoration of Britain to her leading position amongst the Great Powers.

The real puzzle of the Ochakov incident is not why Pitt speedily dropped a new and untried line of policy, but why he ever adopted it. Half the Cabinet, headed by the home secretary, Lord Grenville, either opposed it openly or regarded it with deep suspicion. For reasons which are still debated, Pitt failed to present and refused to allow others to present to the houses of Parliament the arguments which had influenced him in adopting what proved to be an unpopular policy. Members who had strongly supported him, including some politicians but a much larger number of independents, turned against him in the debates or refrained from voting. Even newspapers which had earlier expressed suspicions and fear of Russian aggrandizement turned against the government when they realized that Pitt's policy was leading his country into war. If only because they believed that peace promoted and war harmed trade, most Britons were always reluctant to go to war except for practical and immediate interests. Even the balance-of-power argument, so beloved of pamphleteers in the early days of the struggle against France, had been depreciated by constant use and abuse. When Pitt's supporters tried to use it, it turned in their hands. And the arguments in favour of making a stand in eastern Europe against Russia which have been presented, with an historian's hindsight, earlier in this chapter were never put fairly and squarely to the British public any more than to the houses of Parliament. In particular no effective rejoinder was made to the powerful argument that Ochakov was not an object of sufficient importance to justify a war against Russia.

Although public opinion would in any case have declared against fighting Russia for the sake of Ochakov, interested parties helped to direct it. Count Vorontsov, the recently appointed Russian ambassador to London, used his personal influence upon some of Pitt's supporters, encouraged the Opposition in Parliament, and supplied them with arguments against the government. He was also active in propaganda through the printing press. Fox, who had long ago established his reputation at St. Petersburg as a useful Russian agent, excelled himself during the crisis and even dispatched one of his followers, Robert Adair, on what can fairly be described as a diplomatic mission from His Majesty's Opposition to Catherine II.

Merchants interested in the Baltic trade naturally objected to the prospect of a war which would make continuance of that trade difficult if not entirely impracticable. Indeed how could Britain take part in a war against Russia, no matter how justifiable, except with her fleet? Russia had merely to cut off the supply of naval stores to Britain and no British government could do her any harm. Others appealed to historical precedents dating back to the reign of Peter the Great—none of the British naval squadrons then dispatched to the Baltic had achieved more than a tactical and temporary success. Russia had become a much stronger naval power in the intervening years.

War with Russia would be followed immediately by the infiltration of neutral, and especially American, ships into the Baltic trade at the expense of the London and Hull merchants and shipmasters. Russia would not merely proclaim once again the principles of the Armed Neutrality; she had the power to damage British commercial interests. Towns such as Norwich, Manchester, and Leeds which shared in exports of cloth to Russia were naturally opposed to war with one of their best customers.[1]

Evangelicals and Methodists joined in protest against fighting for Mohammedan Turks against Christian Russians: the confessional argument reappeared in a rather different form.[2] In the reign of George I English churchmen had resented the political activity of Peter the Great in Germany because it was undermining incidentally the prestige and power of the Protestant princes of the Empire. At the time of the Seven Years war, Russia had sometimes been viewed as a collaborator with the Roman Catholic powers who were seeking to overwhelm Frederick the Great, the Protestant hero, and the continental ally without whose help Canada could not be won. Later on Catherine the Great's determined championship of the Polish dissidents, who included many Protestants in West Prussia, won support from Protestant churchmen and helped to damp down British protests at the immorality of the first Partition.

By the end of the eighteenth century Russia had clearly displaced Austria as the arch-enemy of the Turks and Russia therefore inherited some measure of the Christian enthusiasm which

[1] This account of the Ochakov crisis leans heavily on M. S. Anderson's *Britain's Discovery of Russia*, chapter 6.

[2] It was stated with his usual impetuosity by James Boswell (Letter to Temple, 6 April 1791, ed. Tinker): 'What a horrible rumour of war is this! To join the Turks!—It *must* not be . . . I am hesitating whether I should not write one of my characteristical pamphlets upon this crisis.'

had manifested itself in the seventeenth century, when Austria won victories over the Turk in defence of central Europe. This feeling was nourished by the appearance of a Russian fleet in the Mediterranean and the first stirrings of Balkan nationalism. The Orlovs might reasonably aspire to the role of Don John of Austria two centuries earlier. Nor was Christian enthusiasm neutralized to any extent by the Turcophil attitudes which came to exert powerful influence upon nineteenth-century Britain. These were not entirely unknown at the time of the Ochakov incident, but seem to have exerted little, if any, effect upon its course. Turcophilism was a result rather than a cause of hostility between Britain and Russia. The really surprising thing is that the idea of Christian solidarity with Russia survived as long as it did to influence such early nineteenth-century radicals as Cobbett and Somerville, and even Gladstone himself, in the great eastern crisis of the 1870's.

If his own story is to be believed, Pitt gave up the attempt to set limits to Russian conquests, not because he changed his mind, but simply because to persevere with it would have led to the defeat of his government. As Walpole had done on the outbreak of war with Spain in 1739, he changed his policy in order to cling to office. After all he had already abandoned his Irish proposals of 1785 for similar reasons. He was destined to do much the same thing later in his ministry, especially when he failed to press home his sincerely held ideas on parliamentary reform and Catholic emancipation. By then he had come to feel that such minor matters must yield to the overwhelming national interest which demanded his own continuance in the office of prime minister.

The elements of drama, if not melodrama—personal, party, and international—involved in the Ochakov crisis have helped to give it an outstanding position in any account of the relations of Britain and Russia in the eighteenth century. It destroyed Joseph Ewart, the British diplomatist whose ideas on foreign policy Pitt had been induced to adopt. He died at Bath aged thirty-two in 1792, the victim, as it was sometimes believed, of a Russian poisoner. The foreign minister Carmarthen, though technically he resigned office, was in effect dismissed by Pitt and resented being thrown overboard. Fox had played for high stakes: if he had failed to take Pitt's place, he had certainly forced the prime minister to accept his policy. The indecision of the British government is in marked contrast to the firm attitude of the Tsaritsa. Internationally, the final rupture of the Triple Alliance and the inevitable revulsion in Britain against a policy of involvement in eastern Europe left Britain once again in a position of isolation. Her partner Prussia resumed her associations with Austria and Russia and the three eastern powers completed the destruction of Poland. It is perhaps not too fanciful to suggest that had Britain supported Pitt in 1791 a great war in eastern Europe would have broken out; and the French Revolution, without the intervention of foreign powers, might have pursued an entirely different course.

Yet the Ochakov crisis, dramatic as it undoubtedly was and a portent for the future, was short-lived. Before the end of the year negotiations for the revival of the commercial treaty of 1766 which had lapsed in 1787 were beginning at St. Petersburg. Russia denounced her commercial treaty with France and in 1793 the Anglo-Russian trade agreement of 1766 was renewed with little change of substance. In her anxiety to win the political support of Britain against the Revolution Catherine II had abandoned her assault upon the privileged position of British merchants in Russia and her attempts to secure effective, and not merely nominal reciprocity from the British government in favour of her own subjects and their commerce.

In the long run Russian leadership in effecting the second and third Partitions of Poland had much greater influence on Anglo-Russian relations in the nineteenth century. In 1772–5 most British writers had blamed the Partition on Frederick the Great rather than on Catherine the Great, who was often represented as the dupe of the Prussian king. The Ochakov crisis, if it did nothing else, opened the eyes of many Britons to Russia's predominant position in eastern Europe and it was no longer possible to lay the blame on anybody but Catherine II for what was happening in Poland. Also the Ochakov crisis had directed British attention to Poland; and resentment at Russia's triumph, combined with a genuine development of liberal ideas in Britain, swelled the trickle of criticism of the first Partition into a raging torrent. No doubt 'freedom shrieked when Kosciuszko fell', but the fact that he was fighting against the Russians contributed at least as much to his popularity in Britain.

It was widely realized that the Poland of 1791 was not the Poland of 1772. The Polish constitution of 1791 had, as it deserved, a very good press. Burke spoke not only for the Whigs but for the political nation when he extolled its virtues. The Polish reformers, it was widely believed, were seeking to transform Poland into a kind of continental Britain, endowed with the blessings of constitutional monarchy, religious toleration, and an independent judiciary. The Palmerstonian ideas that British institutions could, and should, be exported, and that they might serve at least as a makeweight in preserving a balance of power, strengthened the violence of the anti-Russian reaction. From this time dates the nexus between radicalism at home and hostility to tsarism in foreign policy.

Any possibility that hostility to Russia would induce active intervention by the British government in Poland was removed by the outbreak of war with France in 1793. As always in the eighteenth century, in spite of the recent outbursts of Russophobia, the British government looked to Russia for help—always in vain —when embroiled in war with its near neighbour and rival. Once again a commercial agreement was signed with Russia in 1793 and a formal treaty of defensive alliance in 1795; but Catherine the Great, apart from sending some war-ships to join in a blockade of the Dutch coast, remained inactive until her death. The offer of Corsica suggested by George III proved no more attractive than that of Minorca in the American war. Catherine's son, Paul I, did take part in the war against France for a few months in 1798–9, but then reverted to Catherine the Great's policy by organizing a new Armed Neutrality against Britain. Paul's son and successor, Alexander I, followed at first a policy as oscillatory as that of his father; but the self-evident domination exerted by Napoleon in western and central Europe finally forced him, aided by British sea-power and subsidies, to take the lead in defeating the emperor of the French.

Such being the diplomatic relations between the two states during the long French war, the dominant British attitude to Russia fluctuated as violently as Russian foreign policy. When it was hoped to secure Russian help or to keep Russia active in opposition to France, use was made of the old argument that she was Britain's natural ally. When Russia proved so lacking in appreciation of her own interests as to withdraw from the struggle —still more when she actually allied herself with France—there was a natural revulsion in British opinion.

In fact new causes of mutual suspicion and hostility were coming to the fore as Britain and Russia began to transform themselves from European Great Powers into World Powers. Friction was most acute in the Near East, where Napoleonic activity forced Britain for the first time to take a political interest and to adopt a definite policy. The rapid changes in Napoleonic diplomacy and war in this area led to corresponding fluctuations in Russo-British relationships, varying from close alliance to actual hostility. As early as 1791 Pitt's henchman, Henry Dundas, had been influenced by considerations of the security of British power in India in his opposition to Russia.[1]

When Russia under Paul I joined in the war against the French Revolution he put his mother's ally, Fox, in the awkward position of having to choose between Russia and the French Revolution. Fox and nearly all his friends rejected Russia, some on the ground that she was now an aggressive imperialist power, others because they thought her powerless to act effectively in western Europe where British interests were still concentrated. Though this attitude was by no means stable, and the changing course of the war affected the attitude of Foxite Whigs as much as that of other Englishmen, henceforth they were usually to be found along with the radicals in the anti-Russian camp. The seeds of ideological conflict between British constitutionalism and liberalism and Russian autocracy and imperialism, sown by pamphleteers in the reign of Peter the Great, had now produced an abundant harvest.

Closer contacts forced upon Britain and Russia by war conditions harmed rather than helped mutual understanding. When, at the end of the war, Castlereagh engaged on the task of peace-making at Vienna, he devoted almost as much time and attention to checking the over-great power of his Russian ally as he did to establishing a Europe in which France would find it difficult to resume the Napoleonic role of dictator. Similar ideas bulked large in the political furniture of most of his nineteenth-century successors.

A. *Primary Sources*

Despatches and Correspondence of John, second earl of Buckinghamshire, ed.
    A. d'A. Collyer (2 vols., Camden Society, 1900–2) [covers the years
    of Buckinghamshire's mission 1762–5]
Hanway, Jonas, *Historical Account of the British Trade over the Caspian
    Sea* (1753)

[1] National Library of Scotland MS. 3944.

Historical Manuscripts Commission Lothian MSS. (1905) [chiefly papers relating to Buckinghamshire's mission 1762–5]

Lind, John, *Letters concerning the present state of Poland* (1773)

Sbornik Imperatorskago Russkago Istoriceskago Obscestva (148 vols., St. Petersburg, 1867–1916) [prints in English the correspondence of British diplomatists accredited to the Russian court 1714–19, 1727–62, and 1764–78]

Whitworth, Charles, Lord, *Account of Russia . . . 1710* (Strawberry Hill, 1758)

B. *Secondary Authorities*

Anderson, M. S., *Britain's Discovery of Russia 1553–1815* (1958)

— 'Great Britain and the Russian Fleet 1769–70' in *SEER* 31 (1952), 148–63

— 'Great Britain and the Russo-Turkish War of 1768–1774' in *EHR* 59 (1954), 39–58

Chance, J. F., 'George I and Peter the Great after the Peace of Nystad' in *EHR* 26 (1911), 278–309

Clapham, J. H., 'The Project for an Anglo-Polish Treaty (1782–1792)' in *Baltic Countries* 1 (1935), 33–35

Collyer, A. d'A., 'Notes on the diplomatic correspondence between England and Russia [1700–50]' in *TRHS* New Series 14 (1900), 143–73

Gerhard, D., *England und der Aufstieg Russlands* (Munich and Berlin, 1933)

Golder, F. A., 'Catherine II and the American Revolution' in *AHR* 21 (1915–16), 92–96

Horn, D. B., *Sir Charles Hanbury Williams and European Diplomacy* (1930), chapters 7, 9, 10–14

— *British Public Opinion and the First Partition of Poland* (Edinburgh, 1945)

Hunt, N. C., 'The Russia Company and the Government 1730–42' in *OSP* 7 (1957), 27–65

Jacob, Ilse, *Beziehungen Englands zu Russland und zur Türkei 1718–27* (Basel, 1945)

Kaplan, H. K., *The First Partition of Poland* [based in part on reports of British diplomatic agents] (New York, 1962)

Konopczynski, W., 'England and the First Partition of Poland' in *JCEA* 8 (1948–9), 1–23

Lodge, Sir R., Five articles on diplomatic relations of Britain and Russia from 1739 to 1749 in *EHR* 43 (1928), 354–75, 540–71; *EHR* 45 (1930), 579–611, and *EHR* 46 (1931), 48–76 and 389–422

Madariaga, I. de, *Britain, Russia and the Armed Neutrality of 1780* (1962)

Mediger, W., *Moskaus Weg nach Europa* (Brunswick, 1952)

Michael, W., *Englands Stellung zur ersten Teilung Polens* (Hamburg and Leipsig, 1890)

Nikiforow, I. N., *Russische-Englische Beziehungen unter Peter I* (Weimar, 1954)

Piechowiak, A. B., 'The Anglo–Russian Expedition to Holland in 1799' in *SEER* 41 (1962–3), 182–95

Price, J. M., 'The Tobacco Adventure to Russia' in *Transactions of the American Philosophical Society*, New Series 51, Part I (Philadelphia, 1961)

Przezdziecki, R., *Diplomatic Ventures and Adventures* (1953) [in spite of its title offers a workmanlike account of Anglo-Polish diplomatic relations]

Putnam, P., *Seven Britons in Imperial Russia 1698–1812* (Princeton, 1952)

Reading, D. K., *The Anglo-Russian Commercial Treaty of 1734* (Yale U.P., New Haven, 1938)

Reddaway, W. F., 'Macartney in Russia' in *CHJ* 3 (1929–31), 260–94

Rich, E. E., 'Russia and the Colonial Fur Trade' in *EcHR* 2nd series, 7 (1954–5), 307–28

Ruffman, K.-H., 'Die diplomatische Vertretung Grossbritanniens am Zarenhof im 18 Jahrhundert' in *JGO* 2 (1954), 405–21

— 'England und der russische Zaren und Kaisertitel' in *JGO* 3 (1955), 217–24

— 'Das englische Interesse am russischen Thronwechsel im Jahre 1730' in *JGO* 5 (1957), 257–70

Shprygova, M. N., 'The American War of Independence as treated by N. I. Novikov's Moscow Gazette' in *Soviet Studies in History* 1 (1962–3), 51–62

Struve, G., 'Un chapitre oublié des rapports Russo-Polonais' in *RHD* 61 (1947), 199–214 [deals with Simon Vorontsov's residence at London 1785–1806]

Wittram, R., *Peter I, Czar und Kaiser* (Göttingen, 1964) [essential for the diplomacy of the Northern war]

CHAPTER 9

Great Britain and Scandinavia

In the seventeenth century Sweden had clearly outdistanced Denmark, become mistress of the Baltic, and one of the European Great Powers. In the periodical struggles between the two Scandinavian powers, the Swedes had repeatedly defeated the Danes, retaining several provinces which had once been part of Denmark or of Norway. They had also conquered Finland in the Middle Ages and firmly established themselves during the seventeenth century in Ingria, Esthonia, Carelia, and Livonia, provinces which completely excluded Russia from the Baltic Sea. On the southern shores of the Baltic they controlled the important ports of Stralsund, Stettin, and Wismar, and held extensive territories in the interior, notably the secularized lands of Bremen and Verden, which gave them command of the Elbe and the Weser.

Though the king of Denmark contrived to retain possession of the kingdom of Norway, control of the Sound dues,[1] and the guardianship over admission to the Baltic, Sweden had become vital to English commercial interests. Her conquests gave her control of Baltic naval stores, without which the English merchant and royal navies could not remain operative. Only less vital to England than naval stores were the rapidly increasing imports of Swedish iron in the second half of the seventeenth century. From the kingdom of Denmark the most valued import consisted of timber from the Norwegian forests. From the English point of view, economic interests gave Sweden a clear priority over Denmark when there was a clash between the two Scandinavian powers.

These considerations were reinforced by the much more extensive and successful diplomatic and military activities of the Vasa kings during the seventeenth century not only in Baltic affairs, but as a balancing power in the general politics of Europe. Whereas Christian IV of Denmark had utterly failed to protect German Protestantism in the 1620's, Gustavus Adolphus had taken over the leadership of the anti-Hapsburg forces and his successors had

[1] Details in C. E. Hill, *The Danish Sound Dues and the Command of the Baltic,* passim.

established themselves securely in Germany. Long after religion had ceased to exert influence upon Swedish foreign policy, many Britons remembered with gratitude the services Sweden had rendered to the Protestant cause.

Denmark was likewise a Protestant state, but endowed with inferior resources. It lacked both the military reputation and political prestige of the Swedes. In English eyes its political role was almost limited to providing a potential check to the overvaulting ambitions of the Vasa kings; and some Englishmen, influenced by a basic coincidence of English and Swedish religious and economic interests, were reluctant to use Denmark even for this purpose. In Scotland this feeling was even more widespread, owing to the links between Scotland and Sweden, forged by the service of Scots volunteers in the Swedish armies and the consequent links between the nobles of both countries. The Scots were also prominent in developing trade between Sweden and Britain and many Scots middle-class families transferred themselves to Sweden without breaking the links which bound them to their kinsmen in Scotland.

At the beginning of the eighteenth century both Scandinavian kingdoms were autocracies. Whereas Charles XII's abuse of his power produced a reaction which killed absolutism in Sweden, Danish kings continued to rule absolutely well into the nineteenth century. They were all, in varying degrees and ways, influenced by the enlightenment. Some were genuinely anxious to improve the condition of their subjects and with the aid of intelligent and hard-working ministers carried through important domestic reforms. Others were more concerned to engage upon a spirited foreign policy and increase their territories. 'The Age of Liberty', which began in Sweden with the death of Charles XII in 1718, appreciably strengthened the position of the Danish monarchy both directly and indirectly. A weak government in Sweden was less of a threat to Denmark than a strong autocrat had been. Also the Swedish peasants who supported the claims of the Danish crown prince to the Swedish throne in 1743 hoped that he would clip the wings of the Swedish nobility as his ancestors had already reduced the privilege and power of their opposite numbers in Denmark. Indirectly, many Danes attributed to the selfish rule of the Swedish nobles the disasters which Sweden had to suffer in the next half-century and preferred to support the relatively enlightened autocracy of their own kings. As the Danish kings in the eighteenth century were, on the whole, careful to look after the interests of Norway and ceased to treat it merely as a vassal state, their autocracy was well regarded in both Twin-Kingdoms, Norway no less than Denmark.

Even in the years before the Revolution of 1688, there had been some doubt in England about the political reliability of Sweden owing to her close diplomatic relations with France. The role of Gustavus Adolphus in the Thirty Years war had been based on French subsidies, and his victories had been consolidated and exploited by the diplomacy of Richelieu and Mazarin. If Sweden had joined momentarily with England and the United Provinces in the Triple Alliance of 1668, she had for most of Louis XIV's reign been a client of France. Denmark however, after 1680, came to be more closely linked to France than was Sweden at this time. This was unimportant to Cromwell and Charles II, themselves allies of France; but, as soon as the Revolution of 1688 had recognized England to be the permanent enemy of France, a new era began in Anglo-Swedish and Anglo-Danish relations.

This long-term change was somewhat masked at the time by the attitudes of both Sweden and Denmark to the Revolution. Sweden readily agreed to provide 6,000 troops from Swedish garrisons in Germany to assist in the defence of the United Provinces should Louis XIV attack them while William was establishing himself in England. Yet the Swedes viewed William III's success with some dubiety. The close alliance of England and the United Provinces, and the possibility of an actual Anglo-Dutch union, were alike contrary to Swedish interests. The Dutch were their most dangerous rivals in Baltic trade and the Revolution would certainly make it more difficult for Sweden to play off the English against the Dutch. Also the union of the Maritime Powers with the Emperor was believed at Stockholm to affect the European balance adversely and to reduce the weight which could be exercised by Sweden as a balancing power.

Denmark, closely bound to France by a subsidy treaty (1682), made no secret of her disapproval of the deposition of James II. Quite apart from the dominant influence of France at Copenhagen, Denmark disliked, as much as Sweden, and for the same reasons, the close contacts between the Maritime Powers, which they considered to be the most important result of the Revolution in international politics. The primary object of Danish foreign policy at this time was to secure the parts of Schleswig which belonged to the house of Holstein-Gottorp.[1] Though Christian V occupied these in 1684 he was forced to give them up by the congress of Altona (1687-9).

Though William III appreciated the reserve with which the northern courts regarded his success in England, he hoped to secure their co-operation against France. This was most likely to take the form of the hiring of troops in exchange for a British subsidy. There was also a possibility that the northern Crowns might agree to cut off the supply of naval stores and timber to France, while Denmark might deny to her the use of Norwegian harbours, from which to conduct a *guerre de course* against the merchant vessels of the Maritime Powers.

Even if none of these aims could be achieved, the mere neutrality of Sweden and Denmark represented important gains for William III. If Louis XIV succeeded in his persistent endeavours to reconcile the two northern courts and persuade them to enter the war on his side, the allies of William III would have been attacked from the rear and the entry to the Baltic would have been closed to the shipping of the Maritime Powers, with disastrous results upon their war effort. Even if the worst did not happen, Sweden and Denmark might combine to impose peace upon France's enemies or threaten war upon them if they persisted in a policy prejudicial to Scandinavian interests.

In fact, so acute was Swedish-Danish rivalry and suspicion, such a combination was unlikely in spite of their common interests as Baltic trading states. William III realized that success in winning the support of either power would almost certainly drive the other into the French camp. In particular to secure Swedish aid on terms which would certainly make Denmark his open enemy, extend the scope of the war against France to the Baltic, and compel him to divert forces, subsidies, and supplies from the main theatre of the war, would be bad strategy and therefore bad policy. This must be borne in mind in considering the failure of William III's approaches to both courts. Apparent failure with both was more profitable than success in securing active support from either, on terms which would have made the other an active enemy.

Charles XI had little inclination to take part in a war in which

---

[1] See below, pp. 241-2.

Swedish interests were minimal.[1] He had a personal aversion to engaging in such a war and imposing unnecessary sacrifices upon his subjects. He was also afraid that discontented nobles might exploit a war to recover some of their former power, while peace was essential to his plans for extensive military reorganization. Diplomatically he grasped the basic fact that an aggressive Swedish policy would provoke a coalition of Sweden's neighbours in active opposition. As long as Sweden remained neutral, while her Dutch and British commercial rivals were harassed by enemy privateers and subjected to the delays and difficulties of a system of convoys, Swedish trade would benefit, as in fact it did during the war of Anne's reign, as well as in William III's war. As long as neither side gained a decisive advantage over the other, Charles XI preferred to remain on good terms with both, partly in the hope that Sweden might play the role of mediator in a peace of compromise. This would raise her prestige and might be expected also to secure for the mediating power more material if minor advantages.

The position of Christian V of Denmark at this time was much less favourable than that of Charles XI. Once the English and Dutch had gained the upper hand against the French fleet, an Anglo-Dutch squadron might appear off Copenhagen, and no help from France could be anticipated. Denmark was too weak to follow an independent line of foreign policy, although she did join with Sweden in defence of neutral rights against belligerent interference with their trade. Apart from this, she gradually drifted into a half-hearted alliance with the Maritime Powers which was signed late in 1696. Christian V undertook to ban trade with France and close his ports to French war-ships and privateers in exchange for a subsidy which was supposed to compensate him for his losses, actual and potential, during the war. Even before the treaty had been ratified, he was negotiating for subsidies from France on the same pretext. It was clear that William III could only have won active Danish support by promises which would have extended the scope of the war to the Baltic.

Neither Sweden nor Denmark was prepared to stop trading with France to suit the convenience of William III. Apart from the outcries from their own merchants, this would have produced reprisals from France and have ended Charles XI's hopes of being

[1] See, for an admirable assessment of Charles XI and his policies, Michael Roberts 'Charles XI' in *History* 50 (1965), 160–92.

accepted by both sides as a mediator. When Christian V, too late to have any effect upon the course of the war, did give the required promise, France threatened retaliation and cut off the subsidies she had been paying to Denmark.

William III's fears of what the Scandinavian powers might do to his detriment proved as exaggerated as his hopes. Though Sweden and Denmark signed treaties of armed neutrality, which seemed to foreshadow the exclusion of the merchant navies of the Maritime Powers from the Baltic, their co-operation was not whole-hearted. William III had to abandon the extreme assertion of belligerent rights against neutral trade and even pay compensation to Swedish and Danish traders; but at a modest price he prevented the extension of Danish-Swedish co-operation over a wider field and contributed to keep apart the two Scandinavian powers. Louis XIV's hopes of creating a third force in the Baltic, headed by Sweden, and supported by Denmark and some of the northern German principalities, proved to be as chimerical as William III's own hopes of adding Sweden to his allies. France could not offer either to Sweden or to Denmark the minimum of protection and support for their ambitions which would have given them a real incentive to join with her. In spite of his failure to understand the secret ambitions of the Scandinavian courts, William III 'exploited the limited resources at his disposal with skill, and the maintenance of friendly relations with both Sweden and Denmark . . . was no mean achievement'.[1]

The treaty of Ryswick, which ended in 1697 the war between France and the Anglo-Dutch-Imperial coalition, might have been expected to reduce to their former political unimportance the relations of Great Britain with the northern courts, especially as William III now engaged on a determined effort to reach a settlement of outstanding problems with Louis XIV. But, contrary to the wishes both of William III and Louis XIV, Sweden's enemies saw in the accession of Charles XII, at the age of fourteen, to the Swedish throne, an opportunity to achieve their ambitions.

In the sixteenth century Christian III of Denmark had carved out of the Elbe duchies of Schleswig and Holstein appanages for

---

[1] The account given in the text of William III's Scandinavian policies is based on the unpublished London Ph.D. thesis by S. P. Oakley, 'William III and the Northern crowns during the Nine Years War 1689–97'. The quotation comes from Volume I, p. 334.

his younger brothers, while retaining other parts in his own possession. Within a century the non-royal fiefs had been reunited in
the hands of the dukes of Holstein-Gottorp, who naturally turned
to Sweden for assistance in maintaining their position in the
duchies against the determined encroachments of their royal
cousins, the kings of Denmark. Christian V had already made
abortive attempts to gain complete control of the duchies.

What altered the position now in favour of Denmark was that
Peter the Great was ready to support Denmark's claims. The Tsar
claimed that he had been insulted on a visit to Riga and used
this as a pretext for attacking Sweden. But there were more
serious causes of the Russo-Swedish war. Peter realized that he
must break through the Swedish barrier between Russia and the
Baltic. Support of Danish claims gave him a colourable pretext for
war against Charles XII, who, partly because of his rivalry with
Denmark, backed the claims of his brother-in-law, the duke of
Holstein-Gottorp, in the Elbe duchies. Frederick IV, who succeeded his father, Christian V, in 1699, was a young and ambitious
prince, anxious to undo the treaty of Altona and secure complete
control of Holstein. In 1699 he concluded treaties directed against
Sweden and the duke of Holstein-Gottorp, with Russia and her
protégé, Augustus I of Poland. Augustus began the Great Northern
war by attacking the Swedes in Livonia, while Frederick IV of
Denmark invaded Holstein. The Maritime Powers intervened
promptly with their fleets and swept the Danes off the sea. The
Swedes crossed the Sound and Frederick IV, coerced by this
threat, signed the treaty of Travendal (1700), by which he withdrew from the anti-Swedish coalition. The young king of Sweden
then set out to defend Livonia from the Saxons and the Russians.
The war thus begun raged for twenty-one years and ended with
the complete transformation of the political and economic balance
of power in the Baltic.

  Although bound by treaty to support Sweden and her Gottorp
ally against Danish attack, William III had no such obligation
against Russia. Even before the opening of the Spanish Succession
war he was urging Charles XII to make peace on moderate terms.
Once war between the Maritime Powers and France was seen to
be inevitable, he redoubled his efforts in the hope of securing
active Swedish aid. Charles XII in 1703 actually promised to provide 10,000 Swedish troops once he had settled accounts with the

Poles and Russians. But after defeating the Russians at Narva and making himself master of Poland, Charles XII, instead of sending a Swedish force to operate with the Allies, as the English war-leaders vainly hoped, seemed to them to threaten the Emperor, England's chief ally against France. So explosive was the situation that Marlborough himself had to be dispatched on a special mission to Altranstädt in 1706. Marlborough's assurances were sufficient to postpone the execution of Charles XII's threats and to secure his provisional neutrality in the southern war.

Once committed to a full-scale invasion of Russia in 1707, Charles XII obviously could take no part either for or against Britain in the Spanish Succession war. His epoch-making defeat at Poltava by Peter the Great revived the Danish-Saxon-Russian league of 1698–1700. But in 1709 the western powers, which had protected Sweden in 1700, were locked in battle with each other. The most the Maritime Powers could do for Sweden was to offer to guarantee an arrangement originally proposed by Sweden's enemies, for the neutralization of Germany. The diplomatists of the Maritime Powers pointed out to Charles XII that this would prevent Sweden's enemies from attacking his German provinces; but if Sweden's German lands were to be protected in this way, Sweden must obviously undertake not to use them as a base for attacks on Peter and his allies. Charles XII, who had by now taken refuge in the Ottoman empire, absolutely rejected the well-meant attempts to fetter his freedom of action against his enemies. When Queen Anne offered her mediation Charles XII retorted that she was bound by previous treaties to take part in the war against the Danes and the Saxons.

In the earlier stages of the Northern war the difficulties which had occurred between England and Sweden in the Nine Years war over commerce in the Baltic had again impaired good relations between the two countries. With Peter's establishment in Sweden's east Baltic provinces in 1710, the Swedes first restricted, and then prohibited, trade with this area, which was vital to the Maritime Powers. They also fitted out privateers to prey upon merchantmen which attempted to run the blockade. By this time Charles XII's refusal to compromise had caused the complete breakdown of the neutrality negotiations for his German lands. Russians, Danes, and Saxons overran Pomerania and the Elbe duchies and set themselves to destroy the few pockets of Swedish resistance

(1712–13). By 1713 Peter the Great had made a definitive treaty of peace with the Turks, which left him free to concentrate all his strength against Charles XII.

The Tory government in Britain were not blind to the significance of these events. Sweden was regarded as a Protestant ally with which Britain had long-established and mutually advantageous commercial links. British politicians were readier to take advantage of, rather than to seek to overthrow, Swedish mastery of the Baltic. Russia was a barbarous power whose aggressive policy was a threat to north-German Protestantism; and it was proving difficult to establish and maintain normal diplomatic relations, let alone negotiate a commercial treaty, with her. Though Queen Anne had formally congratulated Peter the Great on his victory at Poltava, she continued to assure Charles XII of her friendship.

So long as Britain was at war with France active support of Sweden was impossible. Once the treaty of Utrecht had been signed Britain was completely isolated in Europe. Remonstrances directed to Sweden's enemies were ignored and threats laughed at. Even the Dutch declined to co-operate in making good their common commercial grievances against belligerent interference with Baltic trade. A tiny British naval squadron intended to convoy merchantmen through the Baltic was not even allowed to pass through the Sound and suffered numerous indignities at Gothenburg.

The accession of George I opened a new era in the story of British relations with the Scandinavian Crowns. The dukes of Brunswick-Lüneburg had supported Sweden against Denmark in the crises settled by the treaties of Altona and Travendal.[1] George I himself, after Poltava, had at first refused to join the new Danish-Polish-Russian league against Charles XII, but later he made a treaty of alliance with Russia and financed a Danish attack upon Swedish lands within the Empire. He pleaded as justification for this change of policy the danger of Swedish attacks upon his own dominions and the intransigence of Charles XII, which was allowing the Russians to establish themselves in northern Germany.

When the Danes occupied Bremen in 1712, George showed his hand by occupying the neighbouring province of Verden, which

[1] See above, pp. 239, 242.

lay between Hanover and Bremen. His aim was now to get the Danes out of Bremen and extract from his former ally and his new friends formal agreement to his adding both Bremen and Verden to his ancestral territories. For some years these Hanoverian ambitions bulked much more largely in British foreign policy than the commercial interests of Britain, with which however they could be combined up to a point, and the traditional but rather vague political and confessional British sympathies with Sweden.

Charles XII at last returned to Germany at the end of 1714 and hoped to drive the Prussians out of Pomerania from the Swedish base at Stralsund. At the same time he tightened up the Swedish blockade of the former Swedish provinces in the eastern Baltic, which were now controlled by the Russians. On the plea of instituting an effective system of Baltic convoys, George I secured the dispatch to the Baltic of a Dutch naval squadron, sufficient, when added to a British fleet, to overawe the Swedish or Danish fleets and give effective protection to British and Dutch trade. At the same time he assured the king of Prussia that the British squadron would prevent the Swedes from reinforcing Charles XII in Pomerania and would co-operate with Prussia in reducing Stralsund. The British admiral, Sir John Norris, concentrated on commerce protection and gave the Prussians no help. The attitude of the Dutch made any other course impracticable: there would have been loud protests had the Dutch succeeded in convoying home the much-valued quota of naval stores, while their British rivals failed to get their share owing to the diversion of British war-ships to other tasks.

In 1716, after Swedish resistance in Pomerania had been crushed, Frederick IV concerted plans with Peter the Great for an invasion of Sweden itself. The British government believed that Charles XII had supported the Jacobite rebellion and that his campaign in Norway against the Danes, if successful, might be the first step to another invasion of Scotland. Norris was sent back to the Baltic in 1716, at first with instructions to demand satisfaction from Charles XII. When this was refused, he was authorized to join his forces with the Danish fleet, to aid the allies in their projected invasion of Scania, and to take reprisals against Swedish interference with British trade. Before these orders could be fully executed Peter the Great decided to abandon his plans and transferred most of his troops to Mecklenburg.

This was a blow to George I, who was anxious to consolidate his own influence in a neighbouring duchy which had long been torn asunder by quarrels between the duke and the Estates. He also, as a patriotic German, hated the growth of foreign influence in the Empire and had a clearer vision of the potential danger of Russia to western Europe than most of his contemporaries. He told Peter the Great bluntly that the landing of Russian troops in Mecklenburg would make him Peter's enemy for life, collected troops on the Mecklenburg frontier and concluded an alliance with France.

Thus George I, primarily for Hanoverian reasons, had become the open enemy of both Charles XII and Peter the Great, while his Hanoverian ambitions to acquire Bremen and Verden could only be realized at the expense both of Charles XII and Frederick IV. Finally his unsuccessful attempt in 1715 to make use of the presence of a British fleet in the Baltic to fulfil his Hanoverian obligations to Prussia had antagonized Frederick William. While some of his enemies were concerting measures with the Jacobites, others were stirring up opposition within England to the new king's Hanoverian foreign policy.

The Whig schism of 1717 left Stanhope and Sunderland in an exposed position in Parliament, from which they escaped by publishing intercepted dispatches between Charles XII's agents and the Jacobites. Gyllenborg, Charles XII's diplomatic agent in London, was put under arrest; and Goertz, his man of confidence, while on a business trip to the United Provinces, was imprisoned, at the request of George I, by the Estates of Gelderland. Charles XII retaliated by imprisoning Jackson, the British diplomatic agent at Stockholm, and diplomatic relations between the two countries were broken off. Even with the revelation of this Swedish plot, Stanhope and Sunderland found it very difficult to obtain parliamentary supplies for a war against the Swedes. They dispatched a powerful fleet under Byng with orders to prevent the Swedes emerging from the Baltic and to blockade the coast of Sweden. They wooed Denmark as a potential ally with tempting offers, which the Danes could not accept without offending their Russian and Prussian allies.

Fortunately for George I, his French ally persuaded Peter the Great to promise to withdraw his forces from Mecklenburg, where, indeed, with the abandonment of plans to invade the Swedish mainland, they no longer had much pretext for remaining.

And it was French mediation which arranged for the exchange of Gyllenborg and Jackson and the resumption of diplomatic contact between Britain and Sweden. Nevertheless yet another British fleet sailed to the Baltic in 1718, when there were fears of a Russo-Swedish reconciliation and support by both countries for a fresh Jacobite invasion of Britain. This time Norris was instructed not merely to join with the Danes in offensive action against the Swedes but equally against the Russian fleet, supposed to be operating in the Baltic under the personal command of Peter the Great. Had it been possible to obtain from Parliament the sub-sidies demanded by Frederick IV a defensive alliance between Britain and Denmark would have been concluded at this time.

It was the death of Charles XII that enabled George I to escape from the dangerous position into which he had blundered in his single-minded pursuit of the interests of his electorate. Sweden ceased to be a great power, and the autocracy of her kings crumbled. Charles's younger sister, Ulrica Eleanora, wife of Frederick of Hesse-Cassel, was elected as his successor; but the Swedish nobility imposed conditions which left the monarchy powerless and themselves the supreme authority at Stockholm. The first task of the new government was to make the peace which a more reasonable monarch than Charles XII would have made years earlier.

The break-up of the anti-Swedish coalition, and the contra-dictory aims and ambitions of its members, gave the Swedes some freedom of manœuvre. If they preferred to retain their German lands, they must abandon to Peter the Great the territories he had conquered from them in the eastern Baltic. If they were willing to sacrifice Sweden's position as a strong power in northern Ger-many, then they might be able to recover some of the eastern Baltic lands now occupied by Peter the Great. The Swedes realized that peace could only be made with Russia on terms which transferred to Russia Sweden's ascendancy in the Baltic. Peace with George I and his allies would, they hoped, protect Sweden from Russian attacks in the meantime and might make it possible to continue or renew the struggle with Russia under more favour-able conditions.

This last calculation proved decisive at Stockholm, although the new government continued to negotiate with Russia as well as with Britain and Hanover. Norris returned to the Baltic in 1719, this time to defend Sweden against threats of Russian combined operations upon her coasts, and Carteret was sent to Stockholm to strike a bargain with Sweden. George, as elector, was to receive Bremen and Verden in return for a cash payment. The old alliance between Britain and Sweden was formally renewed and Sweden undertook to give most-favoured-nation treatment to British commerce.

George then succeeded in arranging terms of peace between his Swedish protégé and his Prussian and Danish allies. Sweden yielded to Prussia Stettin and the surrounding district in Pomerania. Partly owing to the attitude of France, which was anxious that Sweden should retain territories in the Empire, the Swedes retained the rest of Pomerania, including Stralsund. Frederick IV was so indignant that he reopened the war against Sweden and gained successes both on land and sea. But the young duke of Holstein-Gottorp, supported by the Emperor and Peter the Great, was claiming restitution of his ancestral rights in Schleswig-Holstein. To secure French and British guarantees of the whole of Schleswig, though not of Holstein, parts of which he had to return to the duke of Holstein-Gottorp, Frederick IV abandoned finally his hopes of keeping the Pomeranian territory he had conquered during the war.

In exchange he obtained a cash payment and a formal renunciation by Sweden of her exemption, under previous international treaties, from payment of tolls by her vessels on passing through the Sound or the Belts. Henceforth Swedish ships would pay dues at the same rate as the most-favoured nations which included both the English and the Dutch. When, after the treaty of Nystad, Peter the Great claimed that his Baltic provinces, formerly Swedish, were still entitled to exemption from Sound dues, the Danes could reply that before the surrender of these provinces to Russia, their legitimate ruler had formally renounced any such privilege. Thus the settlement of the Sound dues in 1720–1 remained essentially unchanged and caused little international tension until the end of the eighteenth century.[1]

By 1720 it was clear to the Swedes that they had backed the wrong horse. The British fleet hesitated to advance into the Baltic

[1] Not until they became linked with the problem of transit dues on goods passing overland from Hamburg and other North Sea ports to the Baltic did international tension again become acute. See C. E. Hill, op. cit., chapters 8 and 9.

as long as Denmark was still a potential enemy engaged actively in a war against Britain's ally, Sweden. Even when it did, the men-o'-war found it impossible to bring the Russian squadrons to battle. Nor could they prevent Russian galleys from raiding Swedish coasts and islands. Carteret's promise of protection had proved almost worthless and there was obviously even less chance of effective British aid in further resistance to Russian domination of the Baltic.

Sweden made peace with Russia by the treaty of Nystad (1721) on terms which surrendered to Peter the Great nearly all the territories which he had conquered in the course of the war. The bulk of Finland remained Swedish as did a fragment of her Pomeranian lands; but that she retained any part of the coast-line of the southern Baltic was due more to France than to Britain. And Peter the Great had been strong enough to exclude completely the intervention of the western powers in the settlement of his quarrel with Sweden. He retained in his hand a weapon which he could use either against Sweden or against the western powers. He could put forward the duke of Holstein-Gottorp, son of Charles XII's elder sister, either as a pretender to the Swedish throne or as claimant to Schleswig, which the western powers had guaranteed to Denmark as the price of peace between the two Scandinavian crowns.

The treaty of Nystad was followed in 1724 by the treaty of Stockholm between Russia and the Swedes. The contracting parties were to try to secure the restoration of the duke of Holstein-Gottorp to his territories in Schleswig-Holstein by peaceful means. If the Danes refused to comply, Russia and Sweden would appeal to the Emperor Charles VI and invite him to impose a settlement by the Imperial authority. Since George I and the Emperor Charles VI were now on the worst of terms, this infuriated George. He would have liked to make an alliance with the Danes, directly threatened by the Russo-Swedish alliance, but dared not separate himself from France, which insisted that both Britain and Denmark would gain more by compromising their quarrels with Russia, preferably under French mediation, than by pushing them to extremities as George I was anxious to do. The French government continually pressed Britain to reach a settlement with Russia, but George I's terms were so unrealistic that no progress could be made.

Ulrica Eleanora's husband had been elected king of Sweden in

1720 on terms which made him the vassal of the nobles. His government was weak and unpopular and he himself completely disillusioned. Rumours spread that he was about to abdicate and that the Swedes, under Russian influence, would elect as his successor Frederick of Holstein-Gottorp. Townshend had visions of a Russo-Swedish fleet emerging from the Baltic, cruising in the North Sea and perhaps even attacking the defenceless coasts of England. The death of Peter the Great and the belief that his widow and successor, Catherine I, might have her hands full at home somewhat reduced these apprehensions.

The quarrel between France and Spain over the return to Spain of the infanta, who had been betrothed to Louis XV, and the Austro-Spanish alliance of 1725, concluded at Vienna, produced the rival league of Hanover. For two years there was a very real danger of a European war and the leagues of Vienna and Hanover set about winning recruits. Newcastle became secretary of state for the southern province during the crisis and attached the greatest importance to securing Sweden as a member of the league of Hanover. Denmark's support should also be secured, but he shared the firm preference of his predecessors for Sweden as an ally. He believed that Sweden's army was still powerful enough to keep the peace of the north and that the Tsaritsa, deprived of Swedish support, would have to compromise her predecessor's quarrel with George I.

Not for the last time Newcastle proved to be a poor prophet. Catherine mobilized her forces, joined the league of Vienna and threatened to use force to restore Frederick of Holstein-Gottorp, now her son-in-law, to his ancestral lands. For two years Britain and France, on the one hand, and Russia on the other, struggled for mastery at Stockholm. Both sides distributed bribes with a lavish hand, while British squadrons in the Baltic tried to counteract Russian threats of force. Finally in March 1727, and mainly owing to the policy of Count Arvid Horn, the Swedish chancellor and party leader, Sweden adhered to the league of Hanover.

Denmark, directly threatened by Catherine's support of Holstein-Gottorp claims to Schleswig, would gladly have joined the league of Hanover, but was not invited. It was felt that the inclusion of Denmark would make it difficult, if not impossible, for Sweden to become a member. Once Sweden was safely enrolled, Britain and France concluded a military convention for the defence of Denmark (April 1727). In accordance with its terms Norris was again dispatched to the Baltic, and France paid subsidies to Denmark for Danish troops, which were to join with Hanoverian and other forces in defending the Elbe duchies against Austria and Russia. The death of Catherine, her successor Peter II's lack of interest in the Holstein-Gottorp claims, and the Emperor's decision to suspend the Ostend Company, soon made these arrangements unnecessary.

As tension eased with Russia, the Swedish alliance became less important to Britain. Soon divergent interpretations of the terms of the treaty of 1727 caused disputes between the contracting powers. Britain withheld payment of part of the promised subsidies. The Swedes rejected proposals for a commercial treaty, laid new restrictions on British trade, and in 1731 founded a Swedish East India Company, which inevitably competed with the English one. When France and Britain parted company in the early 1730's most Swedes took the side of France and supported the French candidate, Stanislaus Leszczyński, for the Polish throne. Horn was strong enough to preserve an attitude of official neutrality in the Polish Succession war; but his position at Stockholm was weakening.

The Swedish Senate showed a clear preference for concluding a treaty of subsidy with France rather than with Britain. The main reason for this was anti-Russian feeling and the conviction that French support was essential if Sweden was ever to recover her Baltic ascendancy, whereas by now Britain had made her peace with Russia. The British government even approved Horn's counterstroke to the Francophils at Stockholm—the renewal of the Russo-Swedish pact of 1724, which had been so objectionable to Britain when first concluded. Horn and his allies lost control in 1738, and their triumphant rivals, the 'hats', proposed a league with France and Denmark to attack Russia, while she was engaged in war with the Turks. They got no encouragement from Fleury and Christian VI, though after France had made peace between Russia and the Porte, they managed to conclude a defensive alliance with the Turks.

The disputed succession in Russia, which followed the death of the Tsaritsa Anne in 1740, seemed to the Swedes too good a chance to lose. They gave support to the French intrigues which enabled Peter the Great's daughter, Elizabeth, to ascend her father's throne in 1741; but they also, in spite of the combined efforts of the Russian and British diplomatic agents at Stockholm, declared war against Russia. As soon as she became Tsaritsa, Elizabeth turned upon the Swedes. A short campaign proved, even to the 'hats' themselves, their military incompetence: they sued for peace to their former protégée.

Meantime the death of the queen without issue in 1741 raised the question of the Swedish succession. The legitimate heir was undoubtedly the grandson of the late queen's elder sister, Charles Peter Ulrich of Holstein-Gottorp, who had become duke of Holstein on the death of his father in 1739; but the Tsaritsa decided that he should succeed her on the Russian throne. If the Swedes would elect, as successor to their present king, Frederick of Hesse-Cassel, Adolphus Frederick, cousin and heir presumptive of Charles Peter Ulrich,[1] she would restore most of Finland to Sweden. Adolphus Frederick's chief rival for the Swedish succession was Prince Frederick of Denmark, who had the support of the Swedish peasant order. When George II saw the futility of supporting the claims of the present king's brother, William of Hesse-Cassel, he rallied, but reluctantly and half-heartedly, to the support of the Russian candidate. In the hope of retaining Danish friendship, George II kept this change of attitude as quiet as possible; but it could not be concealed for long.

British relations with Denmark, since the end of the international crisis of 1725–7, had been concerned mainly with questions of trade. Frederick IV's attempt to set up a branch of the Danish East India Company at Altona, a port near Hamburg, which he wished to develop as a competitor for trade with Hamburg's hinterland, was bitterly opposed by Britain and other countries which already had East India companies. A trade war followed between Hamburg and the Danes, in which Britain consistently supported Hamburg, which none the less had in the end to submit to Denmark in 1736.

Hanover and Denmark had both profited by the Great Northern war and had a common interest in retaining their gains. Frederick IV consistently backed George II in his disputes with the Emperor Charles VI and with Frederick William of Prussia. His death brought Christian VI to the throne (1730) and the ending of

---

[1] See Sir R. Lodge, 'The Treaty of Åbo and the Swedish Succession' (*EHR* 43 (1928), 555) for the Holstein-Gottorp family tree.

Russian support for the duke of Holstein-Gottorp's claims against Denmark weakened the ties between Britain and Denmark. By guaranteeing the Pragmatic Sanction in 1732, Christian VI secured Austrian and Russian recognition of his rights to the whole of Schleswig. More important, Walpole's *rapprochement* with Austria ended the co-operation—never very close—between Britain and France at the northern courts.

The breach between the two western powers helped Austria and Russia, close allies since 1727, to gain ascendancy at Copenhagen in 1732. The effect of a treaty concluded in 1734 by Denmark with Austria and Russia was to secure their abandonment of support for the duke of Holstein-Gottorp's claims. Danish troops fought under Prince Eugene in his Rhine campaign during the Polish Succession war. At the same time Denmark signed a treaty with Sweden designed to preserve the neutrality of both in the existing war but also with a hint of future co-operation against Russian domination of the Baltic. Denmark followed this up by signing a treaty of subsidy with Britain (1734) which also contained a clause binding the contracting parties to remain neutral in the Polish Succession war.

This treaty proved the prelude to a revival of French influence at Copenhagen. Britain had now abandoned her policy of opposition to Russia and was seeking to detach Sweden finally from dependence on France. The more she wooed Sweden the less she had to offer to Denmark, which found Louis XV a much readier and less exigent paymaster than George II. Danish attempts to safeguard her infant industries by prohibiting import of British manufactured goods, and still more by seducing British technologists from their allegiance, contributed to destroy the short-lived cordiality of Anglo-Danish relations. None the less, and partly because of the triumph of France in Sweden, the Danish government in 1739 renewed its treaty of 1734 with Britain and at first supplied the stipulated number of troops for service in Germany during the Austrian Succession war. It was not until George II tried to save his electorate by arranging a treaty with France for its neutrality, that Christian VI followed his example.

In 1742 Christian VI signed a formal treaty with Louis XV, by which he promised to remain neutral in exchange for an annual subsidy and a French guarantee of Schleswig to Denmark. By playing off Britain and France against each other, Christian VI had made a good bargain for himself and his country without promising anything which would give Britain and Russia a legitimate grievance against Denmark. Louis XV had paid a substantial price, but had laid the solid foundations of French predominance at Copenhagen for two decades.

One reason for Christian VI's decision to remain neutral and not supply troops to either side in the German war was his determination to press the claims of his son, Frederick, to the Swedish succession. This contributed to his preference for alliance with France rather than with Britain, since it was vital for Frederick to gain the support of the Francophil 'hats' at Stockholm. Though in appearance offensive, Christian VI's policy was basically defensive in intention.

The house of Holstein-Gottorp was Denmark's arch-enemy. Christian simply could not afford to see one of its princes on the throne of the Tsars and another wearing the Swedish crown. When the Swedes by the treaty of Åbo with Russia accepted Adolphus Frederick as successor to their king, Frederick of Hesse-Cassel, and ceded a strip of Finland to Russia, Christian hesitated no longer. He projected an attack upon the Swedes in Scania and openly showed his sympathy with the Swedish peasants, who had risen against the nobles and were willing to accept his son as their king.

It was generally believed at Stockholm that the election of Prince Frederick of Denmark as successor to the crown would carry with it Danish support for continuing the war against Russia and perhaps even a chance to recover the lost parts of Finland, while many members of the other orders were in favour of the avowed intention of the peasant leaders to reform the Swedish constitution by a reduction of the power of the nobles. This could be readily effected by restoring to the monarchy some of the prerogatives of which the nobles had deprived it in 1719–20.

The armed conflict between the two Scandinavian kingdoms and the prospect of their eventual union were as alarming to Britain as to Russia. Britain urged Christian VI to abandon the projected invasion of Scania and to renounce his son's candidature for the Swedish succession; but it was Russia which exerted the decisive influence in the crisis. The Tsaritsa Elizabeth warned the Danes that she would employ whatever force was necessary to support the Swedish government and actually disembarked 12,000

Russian troops to defend Stockholm. Christian VI had no option but to accept Adolphus Frederick as successor to the Swedish crown. The peasant revolt had collapsed the day before the Riksdag adopted Adolphus Frederick as heir. The Tsaritsa was careful to remove Christian's main grievance by renewing the guarantees given by her predecessor in 1734 of Danish rights in the Elbe duchies against the pretensions of the house of Gottorp.

George II had hoped to arrange the marriage of Adolphus Frederick to one of his daughters, but was once again thwarted by Frederick of Prussia, who secured the coveted prize for his sister, Louisa Ulrica. Their majesties of Britain and Prussia argued that the marriage they respectively favoured would strengthen Sweden and consolidate the peace of the north. George II found partial compensation for the failure of his Swedish matrimonial plan in the marriage of his daughter, Louisa, with Prince Frederick of Denmark. Frederick of Prussia's victory at Stockholm was a sign of reviving French influence there, once the need for Russian protection against the Danes had passed.

Although the Russo-Swedish defensive alliance was renewed in 1745, even the crown prince, who owed his own position to the Tsaritsa, soon showed that he was under the influence of Swedish national hostility to Russia, or at least found it politic to swim with the prevailing current at Stockholm. The Tsaritsa Elizabeth promptly transferred her favour to Denmark and engaged in threats and demonstrations against the ungrateful Swedes. The only result of her tactics was to weaken the position of her partisans in Sweden and to enable their opponents, the 'hats', to pose as champions of Swedish independence. Russia's suggestion, made with British approval, that Sweden should accede to the so-called treaty of the Two Empresses of 1746 was unhesitatingly rejected at Stockholm.

Instead the 'hats', once again dominant in Sweden, renewed the convention they had originally made with France in 1738, concluded a defensive alliance with France's German client, Frederick the Great, and began a negotiation with the Porte for combined action against their common enemy, Russia. Adolphus Frederick and his Prussian consort joined with the 'hats' to proscribe the few remaining friends of Russia and Britain at Stockholm. The British diplomatic agent, Guy Dickens, was insulted and had to be re-recalled in 1748.

The decline and fall of British influence at Stockholm during the Austrian Succession war did not lead to any marked improvement in relations with the Danish Crown. Negotiations for the marriage of a Danish princess to the duke of Cumberland, which would have strengthened the dynastic link between the two courts, broke down. All efforts to secure the use of Danish troops for use either on the Continent or in Britain during the Jacobite rebellion failed. Denmark was already being paid more by France for doing nothing, than Britain was willing to pay her for taking an active part in the war. This continued to be the case after the accession in 1746 of Frederick V and his English wife.

French influence even increased in the new reign with the prospect that France could obtain a formal renunciation by Adolphus Frederick of his claims to Schleswig and Holstein, which would strengthen the Danish hold over the duchies. This promise was fulfilled when the treaties between Denmark, Sweden, and France were renewed in 1750. To consolidate the improving relations between the Scandinavian courts under French auspices a marriage was arranged between the Swedish heir apparent, Gustavus, and one of Frederick V's daughters, Sophia Magdalena: it was in an attempt to counteract this project that the ill-omened marriage of an English princess to Frederick V's heir was first proposed. The death of Queen Louisa in 1751 proved a more immediate blow to English influence at Copenhagen, although Frederick V promptly remarried a Brunswick princess, closely related to the house of Hanover.

For some years after the end of the Austrian Succession war there was an acute northern crisis, which threatened to disrupt the fragile peace of Aix-la-Chapelle and cause a renewal of general European war. France and her supporters claimed that Russia's Baltic ambitions and her threats against Sweden endangered the peace of the north. Russia and her friends retorted that French predominance at Stockholm and her open encouragement of Swedish hopes of revenge were a manifest threat to the security of Russia and to her enjoyment of the Baltic position assured to her by existing treaties. While Britain and Austria sympathized to some extent with Russia's attitude, they were both more concerned to prevent the renewal of war than to give Russia encouragement. Since the French government was equally pacific, the northern crisis petered out in 1751.

Even then there was no improvement in the relations of Britain with either Sweden or Denmark. The Swedes accused George II of trying to secure support for the duke of Cumberland as successor to the Swedish throne and executed an unfortunate Scotsman, Blackwell, whom they accused, without much, if any justification, of being a British secret agent. When, on the outbreak of the continental Seven Years war, Britain and Prussia found themselves much to their surprise on the same side, a British agent, Robert Campbell, was dispatched to Stockholm to sound the ground and, if possible, to prevent Sweden from joining in the attack upon Prussia which followed upon Frederick the Great's invasion of Saxony.

Campbell's mission proved abortive. After the suppression of a royalist conspiracy in 1756 the Prussian queen and her husband were powerless; and the dominant 'hats' had already decided to take the proffered subsidies from France and join the anti-Prussian coalition. Campbell had to be recalled without being received officially as minister resident at Stockholm. His successor, Sir John Goodricke, was not even allowed to enter Sweden, but tried to conduct his business from Copenhagen during the Seven Years war. Not until after the end of the war did he succeed in establishing himself at Stockholm.

While Britain's relations with Denmark were not so tense as with Sweden in the 'fifties and early 'sixties, Denmark remained firmly within the French orbit. British proposals to hire Danish troops for use in Ireland were rejected in 1755 because this would be contrary to Danish neutrality. Since it would free British troops to operate elsewhere against France, such a treaty was contrary to existing Danish obligations to France. Between 1746 and 1756 Denmark had concluded a series of commercial treaties with Mediterranean states which proved advantageous to her. As in previous wars Sweden and Denmark joined in defence of their trade in 1756. They undertook to exclude all belligerent war-ships and privateers from the Baltic and to join their fleets to protect neutral trade in non-contraband goods. Britain continued to exercise what she regarded as her legitimate belligerent rights until the danger of a league of neutrals induced her government to promise some relaxation in her treatment of Danish trade.

On the other hand Denmark still regarded Hanover as 'a kind of bulwark to Denmark on the side of Germany',[1] and was sus-

---

[1] *British Diplomatic Instructions 1689–1789*, III (1926) (Denmark), ed. J. F. Chance, p. xxx.

picious of French and Prussian designs to occupy the electorate. Frederick V joined with Austria in 1756 to try to arrange for its neutrality, but on conditions which were not acceptable to Britain. In the following year he signed with France a treaty for the security of Bremen and Verden and sought in this way to fulfil his obligations to guarantee these provinces to Hanover. It was a Danish negotiator who arranged the convention of Klosterseven and Frederick V was ready to guarantee the execution of its provisions.

When the Russians joined the Swedes in their attacks on Prussian Pomerania, Danish uneasiness was countered by French willingness to pay the cost of an army for the defence of Holstein and to negotiate with the Grand-duke Peter the surrender of his claims in Holstein in exchange for other territories. With Peter's refusal to compromise relations between Denmark and Russia rapidly deteriorated in spite of Russo-Swedish-Danish common interest in the protection of neutral trade in the Baltic. When Peter in 1762 became Tsar and joined with Frederick the Great to assert his claims as duke of Holstein-Gottorp against Denmark, the Danish government appealed to Britain which had, jointly with France, guaranteed Denmark's position in Schleswig in 1720. George III, reasonably enough in view of Danish dependence on France in the preceding years, declined to intervene in favour of the Danish Crown. With equal firmness he declined to countenance the schemes of Peter III and Frederick the Great.

Louis XV chose this moment to renounce the predominance he had so long exercised at Copenhagen. French subsidies stopped and the Franco-Danish convention was allowed to expire in 1764. The manifest disinterest of France in Danish affairs contributed to the marriage of Christian VII, who succeeded his father in 1766, to Caroline Matilda, daughter of Frederick, prince of Wales, a few months after his accession. But once again the negotiation for a British subsidy languished and the predominant influence at Copenhagen soon passed not to Britain but to Russia.

This was the result of Catherine II's handling of the Holstein-Gottorp claims of her deposed and deceased husband, Peter III. She at once put an end to the incipient war waged by Peter III, with the connivance of Frederick the Great, against Denmark; and in 1767 she negotiated a settlement which satisfied both sides and firmly established Russian influence at Copenhagen. Catherine promised that as soon as Peter III's son, the Grand-duke Paul, came of age, he would exchange the ducal portions of Holstein which were still in his possession and abandon all claims to Schleswig in exchange for the duchy of Oldenburg and a cash payment. The bargain was executed in 1773. On the Danish side the elder Bernstorff was the architect of the agreement of 1767, which committed Denmark to side with Russia against her former protector, France, and in particular to uphold the cause of the noble order in Sweden against the attempts of the royalists to overthrow the Swedish constitution. In Bernstorff's view Denmark had a vested interest in the continuance of the 'age of liberty' in Sweden.

The total failure of Swedish arms in the Seven Years war and the inability of Swedish politicians to secure any advantages from the peace negotiations at the end of the war had discredited the 'hats'. A powerful reaction against French control of Swedish foreign policy set in. Russia's friends reappeared openly at Stockholm, and, after Prussia became the ally of Russia in 1764, the queen of Sweden and her courtiers usually co-operated with them. The overthrow of French influence would be of direct advantage to Britain as the arch-enemy of France and might also prove advantageous to British trading interests in the Baltic. But large sums of money were required to win support, consolidate the opposition to the 'hats', and stimulate their zeal. George III somewhat reluctantly agreed to make, out of his civil list, a substantial contribution to 'cap' party funds.

The changed position in Sweden encouraged those British politicians who saw in a Northern System of alliances Britain's best hope of escaping from isolation. Co-operation with Russia and Prussia in Sweden might be followed by the firm establishment of a triple alliance against France. Although the younger 'caps' had the upper hand in the Diet of 1765–6, the 'hats' retained many important offices. France was ready to give subsidies to Sweden, whereas Britain absolutely declined to make subsidy treaties with any foreign power in time of peace. The most that could be done was to sign a treaty of friendship (1766) which ended French subsidies and allowed the Swedes to claim compensation in some form or other from Britain. If British traditions barred subsidies in time of peace, a loan would be acceptable. A treaty of commerce between Britain and Sweden was concluded in the same year, but had little effect upon the declining commerce between the two countries.

In the later 'sixties there was a revival of the court party in Sweden under Prince Gustavus, who was determined to assert royal authority over the contending parties. In 1771, on succeeding his father, he won the firm support of France. The queen had by now ceased to be a Prussian stooge and was closely linked with the projects of her ambitious son. The strongest argument in favour of the court party was that 'hats' and 'caps' by internecine strife had subordinated Swedish interests to the wishes of their foreign paymasters, had destroyed Sweden's reputation abroad and had repeatedly brought the country to the verge of civil war. While the 'hats' were securely in control of the order of nobles, the younger 'caps' advocated the abolition of noble privileges and were firmly established as dominant in the less influential orders of burghers peasants, and clergy. After vainly urging both parties to put the interests of the Swedish nation before those of a faction and offering his services as mediator between them, Gustavus III carried through in August 1772 his celebrated *coup d'état*.

The British attitude to this revolution was not much affected by theoretical considerations of liberty or despotism. Since the young king of Sweden was unmistakably the protégé of France, any increase in his power must be resisted. To the Russians and their Danish satellite the restoration of anything approaching absolute monarchy in Sweden was a direct and immediate danger. They had undertaken by their treaty of alliance to resist any alteration of the constitution of 1720, which had ensured the powerlessness of Sweden to reverse the decisions of the Great Northern war.

Bernstorff, the Danish minister who had struck the bargain with Russia over Schleswig-Holstein, was dismissed in 1770. Christian VII was insane and his wife, Caroline Matilda, daughter of Frederick, prince of Wales, became infatuated with the adventurer Struensee, and supported his dictatorship. Struensee's declared policy of non-intervention in Swedish politics seemed likely to end the tripartite co-operation of Russia, Britain, and Denmark at Stockholm, which had been the basis of the partial successes of the younger 'caps'.

About this time, too, the British government, weary of Russian charges of British parsimony in contributing to the expenses of

keeping up a party at Stockholm, and feeling also that its contributions to the common cause had not brought appreciably
nearer the Russo-British alliance at which they aimed, decided to
stop financing the younger 'caps'. Yet when news of the *coup d'état*
reached Suffolk, secretary of state for the northern province, he
was at first disposed to join with Catherine II, in demanding the
restoration of the 1720 Swedish constitution. Soon Suffolk saw
that this line of policy might well lead to a general European war
over issues with which the British government was only indirectly
concerned. He told Russia that though Britain would have joined
with her to prevent the overthrow of the 1720 constitution, this
did not mean that she was committed to intervention in order to
restore it, once it had been overthrown by the Swedes.

From this position he soon advanced. Russia was told that if she
took action against Sweden, Britain would give her no support, but
would remain neutral. Suffolk sought in this way to discourage
Catherine from warlike demonstrations against the new régime
in Sweden. At the same time his brother secretary, Rochford,
repeatedly warned France that any French naval armaments, either
in the Mediterranean, where they would be designed to help the
Turks in their war against Russia, or in the Baltic to strengthen
Sweden against the allied Russians and Danes, would be followed
immediately by British naval intervention on a scale sufficient to
counteract French mobilization. It was essential for the success of
British policy that these threats to France should not become
known to the Russian government, since they would counteract
Suffolk's refusal of support and encourage the war party at St.
Petersburg.

Britain and France were at one in their determination not to be
dragged into a great European war by their respective friends
amongst the Baltic powers; and Frederick the Great was at least
as eager to keep Prussia at peace. Unfortunately old quarrels and
present suspicions of each other made it impossible for the three
powers to co-operate effectively. In the end the best that Rochford
could do was to promise the French government that if it intervened promptly with a naval force in the Baltic, British counter-
action would be delayed until the French fleet had done its business
and was on its way back to Brest.

In the end Catherine decided against intervention early in 1773.
It is difficult to tell how far this decision was due to British denial

of support and the consequent fear that Russian transports ferrying troops for an invasion of Sweden would be exposed to continued attacks by French frigates. She may even have suspected (wrongly) that, in spite of superficial appearances of Franco-British brinksmanship, the British government would connive at such French action. In the months following Gustavus III's *coup d'état* British public opinion had shown itself in favour of his reforms, while the government was impressed by his assurances that he had no designs upon the security of his neighbours. Britain had ceased during the northern crisis of 1772–3 to be a mere echo of the voice of Russia at Stockholm.[1]

The outbreak of the war of American Independence led to British protests against the use of Swedish ports, especially Marstrand, by American privateers. When France joined in the war Britain seized Swedish merchantmen on suspicion of their trading with the enemy. Gustavus III adopted the system of armed convoys and joined the Armed Neutrality under the leadership of his former enemy, Catherine II of Russia. As soon as the American war ended, Gustavus vainly tried to secure Russian connivance in a Swedish attack upon Denmark. The Danes retaliated by giving support to Gustavus III's opponents in the Diet of 1786, which had to be prematurely dissolved. Claiming that he was a democrat himself, Gustavus sought to counter the underhand opposition of the nobles by granting new rights to the other estates in 1789.

When war between Russia and Turkey was renewed in 1787, Gustavus launched in the following year a single-handed attack upon Russia from Swedish Finland. But his officers mutinied and the Danes, as auxiliaries of Russia, invaded Sweden while the bulk of Gustavus's army was occupied in Finland. France, preoccupied with the early stages of Revolution, could no longer be counted upon to extricate Gustavus from his perilous situation. What saved him was the prompt intervention of the Triple Alliance of Britain, the United Provinces, and Prussia. The British diplomatic agent at Copenhagen, Hugh Elliot, by the threat of force secured the withdrawal of the Danish troops and the neutrality of Denmark in the Russo-Swedish war.

Britain's relations with Denmark in the 'seventies and 'eighties had followed a somewhat chequered course. After the downfall

---

[1] See Michael Roberts, 'Great Britain and the Swedish Revolution 1772–73' in *Historical Journal* 7 (1964), 1–46.

of Struensee in 1772, the British diplomatic agent at Copenhagen, Robert Murray Keith, had laid the foundations of a successful career in the British diplomatic service by rescuing the queen, Caroline Matilda, from a compromising position. Some of her enemies were soon professing their desire for a British alliance, but George III would have nothing to do with the persecutors of his sister. Although French interest and influence in Denmark began to revive with the success of her Swedish policy, Russian supremacy at Copenhagen was not seriously threatened in the 'seventies.

The outbreak of the American war of Independence and the critical position of Britain, consequent upon French intervention in the war, caused Britain to appeal for Danish naval assistance and to revive once again the traditional idea of a league of northern powers against France. The prospect of such a league was less favourable than ever. Gustavus III was firmly wedded to France and Swedish convoys successfully defied British attempts to seize neutral shipping. So far as Denmark was concerned the best Britain could do was to postpone Danish co-operation with the Swedes by negotiating at Copenhagen for an extension of Danish treaty rights under the Anglo-Danish commercial treaty of 1670. When Catherine II decided to organize the Armed Neutrality, using as a basis proposals originally put forward by Denmark, Danish accession was inevitable.

Even after the Crown Prince Frederick of Denmark came of age in 1784 and carried through a palace revolution, Hugh Elliot, the British diplomatic agent at Copenhagen, had to report sorrowfully to his government that 'to enjoy a menial and temporary security under the haughty protection of Russia' remained 'the ultimate view of Danish politics'.[1] In spite of the failure of previous dynastic marriages to make any effective contribution to British influence in Danish politics, Elliot pinned his hopes on Frederick's marriage to an English princess; but his coercion of the Danes in 1788[2] destroyed any chance of such a marriage. In 1790 Frederick married a Hessian princess.

Gustavus III's sudden attack upon Russia in 1788 forced Denmark, under existing treaties, to give support to Russia. Britain and Prussia, now united in the Triple Alliance, urged her to

[1] Quoted by J. F. Chance, op. cit., III, xl.
[2] See below, p. 264.

observe neutrality; but the Danes gave Russia naval support and, from their base in Norway, invaded the Swedish mainland. Without instructions from his government, Elliot warned the commanders of the Danish army that perseverance in this project would bring in, on the Swedish side, a British fleet and a Prussian army. Frederick desisted and Gustavus III was saved.

Elliot was successful in forcing Denmark into neutrality; but his vehemence indisposed Frederick and his success inevitably won for Britain the enmity of the dominant Russian party at Copenhagen. Though the Danes had undertaken to remain neutral, the Danish dockyards refitted fifteen Russian men-o'-war, and the Danish fleet gave them a convoy to join the main Russian Baltic fleet. Again, when Pitt attempted to set limits to Russian conquests from the Turks in the Ochakov crisis of 1791, the Danes firmly supported Catherine II, although they would gladly have acted as mediators between Britain and Russia.

While the Danes continued to rely on Russian protection, the decline of France in the early stages of the Revolution deprived Gustavus III of his principal supporter. The course of the French Revolution and his championship of the cause of absolute monarchy brought about a sudden reversal of Swedish policy. Helped by British and Prussian threats against Denmark and by subsidies from the Triple Alliance, Gustavus escaped from the precarious situation into which his own folly had led him. Indeed, after concluding with Russia the peace of Verela in 1790, he strengthened his hold over Sweden, since Russia tacitly abandoned earlier treaties which had given her rights of interference in Swedish domestic affairs. Though he continued to offer his alliance to the British government on terms which they regarded as extortionate, he soon struck a bargain with Russia, based on co-operation against the French Revolution and a common objection to British naval intervention in the Baltic.

Gustavus III was assassinated in March 1792 as a result of a conspiracy of malcontent nobles. Under a weak regent and torn by faction, Sweden continued to be dominated by the influence of Russia for the rest of the eighteenth century, although the attempt to marry the young king, Gustavus IV Adolphus, to a granddaughter of Catherine II broke down at the last moment owing to Gustavus's refusal to allow to the Orthodox Church the privileges demanded on behalf of the bride. At first irritated, like his predecessors in previous Franco-British wars, by British exercise of belligerent naval rights, he joined with Russia in a new Armed Neutrality. Britain retaliated by sending a fleet to bombard Copenhagen and the death of Tsar Paul (1801) ended the Armed Neutrality.

Gustavus IV by this time had convinced himself that the French Revolution, incarnate in Napoleon, was the work of the Devil. In 1804 he placed Stralsund at the disposal of the British government in exchange for a modest subsidy. In 1805 he joined Britain and Russia in what he believed was a crusade against France. When Tsar Alexander made his famous compact with Napoleon at Tilsit, Gustavus continued the unequal struggle, in alliance with Britain, against France, Russia and Denmark. Although a British fleet again bombarded Copenhagen and took possession of the entire Danish fleet in 1807, Gustavus IV soon quarrelled with his only ally. In any case British sea-power could do nothing to check a massive Russian invasion of Swedish Finland.

Deposed by a *coup d'état* in 1809, Gustavus IV was succeeded by his uncle, Charles XIII, but the politicians now in control attempted vainly to play off Napoleon against Alexander and had to accept Russia's terms—the surrender of Finland and the Åland islands to Russia—in the same year. Sweden joined in the Continental System organized by Napoleon against Britain, and accepted as successor to Charles XIII, one of Napoleon's marshals, Bernadotte. She even issued a paper declaration of war against Britain in 1811. When Napoleon remained dissatisfied and occupied Swedish Pomerania, Bernadotte entered into alliance with Britain and also with Russia, now completely estranged from France. Denmark, on the other hand, continued her policy, due more perhaps to geography than to choice, as a satellite of France.

Bernadotte believed that the long-term interest of Sweden required the surrender of Finland to Russia, provided he could obtain as compensation Norway, which had been ruled for some centuries by Denmark. Britain and Russia were ready to accept these terms, and the Norwegians, who had suffered severely by Denmark's enforcement of the Continental System, were anxious to throw off Danish rule. Before the Allied Powers met in congress at Vienna to settle the disposal of the Napoleonic empire in 1814, Bernadotte had used force to compel the Danes to surrender their rights in Norway and then made terms with the Norwegian rebels, who had elected a Danish prince as their king, which ensured the union of Norway with Sweden. Not only had Bernadotte chosen the right side, but his sense of timing was admirable. By finally abandoning Finland and Pomerania, Sweden had become a purely Scandinavian power and had divested herself of territories which had continually involved her in quarrels with Russia and led her to attempt to play a role far beyond her resources in German politics.

Denmark had remained faithful to Napoleon, more by necessity than by choice perhaps, until it was too late to win the favour of the Coalition, already pre-empted by her Swedish rival. She paid heavily for this by the loss of Norway. Such compensation as she obtained at the congress of Vienna merely increased her involvement in German politics, which was to lead to the war between Denmark and the two great German powers in the 1860's and the loss of the Elbe duchies, the retention of which had been the basic aim of Danish foreign policy in the eighteenth century.

So far as Britain was concerned, the two Scandinavian powers, taken together or separately—and owing to their insuperable rivalry it usually had to be separately—were much less important in 1815 than they had been at the beginning of the eighteenth century. Common Protestantism had ceased to count in foreign policy. With the great upsurge of British trade with non-European areas which marked the second half of the eighteenth century and continued in the nineteenth, British interest in the Baltic markedly declined. Although as late as the Napoleonic wars supplies of hemp and masts from the Baltic had still been an important consideration to Britain, naval stores in sufficient quality and quantity could now be obtained elsewhere. Soon iron and steel replaced the wooden walls of old England and the new iron-clads were driven not by sails but by steam. The gap between the resources of the great industrial powers, with their massive war potential, and the lesser and mainly under-developed states of Europe became wider and more significant than it had been in the eighteenth century.

The days of subsidy treaties, when the help of 6,000 Danes or Swedes could perhaps exert a decisive influence upon a campaign between Great Powers, had gone never to return. After 1815 the British fleet could take on all comers and did not need the assistance of a Swedish or Danish squadron. Such interest as Sweden retained for Britain was chiefly as a potential ally against Russia, notably during the Crimean war.

Unlike Sweden, Denmark relied for a time upon the support of Britain and Russia against German threats to the Elbe duchies, but the outcome of the Schleswig-Holstein crisis in the 1860's revealed the futility of this policy. Henceforth both Scandinavian powers moved slowly and erratically in the direction of total neutrality in war and non-alignment in peace in Great-Power politics.

In the eighteenth century Sweden and Denmark had tried to retain their position and if possible to add to their possessions by jumping rapidly from an alliance with one Great Power into alliance with another. France and Russia by turns, sometimes Britain, occasionally even Austria, had possessed the principal interest at one or other of the Scandinavian courts. Great dexterity had been required to make each jump at the right moment. It was important also to keep open, if at all possible, a reverse jump, should the new alliance prove unrewarding.

All this adds to the interest and amusement of the study of the relations between the Scandinavian powers and their principal backers in the eighteenth century; but neither Sweden nor Denmark found the exercise particularly profitable. They have benefited by the more recent policy of avoiding, as far as possible, involvement in Great-Power politics.

A. *Primary Sources*

British Diplomatic Instructions 1689–1789, vols. 1, 3, 5, ed. J. F. Chance for the Camden Series (1922–8)

H.M.C. Polwarth MSS., vols. 1–5 (1911–61)

Molesworth, Robert, Viscount, *An Account of Denmark as it was in the year 1692* (1694)

Robinson, Rev. John, *An Account of Sweden* (London, 1694) with Ragnhild Hatton's commentary in *BIHR* 28 (1955), 128–55

B. *Secondary Authorities*

Åström, S.-E., *From Stockholm to St. Petersburg* [1660–1721] (Helsinki, 1962)

— *From Cloth to Iron* (Helsingfors, 1963–5)

Berg, J., and Lagercrantz, B., *Scots in Sweden* (Edinburgh, 1962)

Cambridge Modern History, vol. VI (1909), articles by R. N. Bain, pp. 758–84, and W. F. Reddaway, pp. 735–57

Chance, J. F., Articles on Anglo-Swedish relations, 1689–1727, especially in *EHR* 16 (1900), 676–711, *EHR* 17 (1901), 50–75 and *EHR* 39 (1924), 571–87

Lane, Margery, 'England and Denmark, 1689–97' in *TRHS* 3rd series, 5 (1911), 157–91

Lodge, Sir R., 'The Treaty of Åbo and the Swedish Succession' in *EHR* 43 (1928), 540–71

Milne, June, 'The Diplomacy of Dr John Robinson at the Court of Charles XII' in *TRHS* 4th series, 30 (1948), 75–93

Murray, J. J., 'Robert Jackson's Mission to Sweden' in *JMH* 21 (1949), 1–16

— 'Sweden and the Jacobites in 1716' in *HLQ* 8 (1944–5), 259–76

New Cambridge Modern History, vol. VII (1957) article by Ragnhild Hatton on 'Scandinavia and the Baltic', pp. 339–64

Nordmann, C. J., *La Crise du Nord au Début du XVIIIe siècle* (Paris, 1962)

Oakley, S. P., 'William III and the Northern Crowns during the Nine Years War 1689–97' [unpublished Ph.D. thesis, University of London]

— *The Story of Sweden* (1966), pp. 111–83

Roberts, M., 'Great Britain and the Swedish Revolution 1772–73' in *H. Journal* 7 (1964), 1–46

Ryan, A. N., Various articles, especially 'Trade with the Enemy . . . during the Napoleonic War' in *TRHS* 5th series, 12 (1962), 123–40

Svenska Utrikes Politikens Historia (various authors), vols. 2–3 cover 1697–1844 (Stockholm, 1952–7)

Torntoft, P., 'William III and Denmark-Norway, 1697–1702' in *EHR* 81 (1966), 1–25

Tunberg, S. (and others), *Histoire de l'Administration des Affaires Étrangères de Suède* (Uppsala, 1940)

Unger, W. S., 'Trade through the Sound in the 17th and 18th Centuries' in *EcHR* 2nd series, 2 (1959–60), 206–21

Addendum

Hautala, K., *European and American·Tar in the English Market during the Eighteenth and Early Nineteenth Centuries* (Helsinki, 1963)

CHAPTER 10

Great Britain, Spain, Portugal, and the Barbary States

SPAIN had been regarded by Elizabethan and Protestant Englishmen as their national and natural enemy. Philip II, although he was sometimes in fact on bad terms with the Pope, was universally regarded as the eldest son of the Papacy and the chief secular instrument of its ecclesiastical policy. Combined with the apparently imminent threat of a restoration, by force or guile, of the papal supremacy in England and the introduction of the Inquisition and *autos da fé*, was the fear of Spanish domination. If Elizabeth's reign came to be regarded as glorious by her contemporaries, it was largely because she stood forth as the champion of Protestantism and the traditional constitution against the insidious infiltration of Spanish and papal influences as well as against the armed assault of the Spanish Armada later in her reign.

Elizabeth left behind her to the seventeenth century not only a legacy of hatred of Spain, but some ideas as to how it could best be politically expressed. From time to time she had formed alliances and tried to co-operate in wars against Spain with two other west European powers which were also threatened by Spanish predominance—France and the Netherlands. In fact the criticism has often been made both of Cromwellian and of Restoration foreign policy that it followed the patterns set by Elizabeth after the European situation had changed so fundamentally that Elizabeth herself would have violently disapproved of what her successors were doing. Even in Elizabeth's reign, and with all her clear-sightedness and diplomatic skill, backed by the technical *expertise* of such ministers as Burghley and Walsingham, she had not been very successful in organizing a triple alliance of England, France, and the United Provinces against Spain.

As the seventeenth century went on two things became clear—at least in retrospect. France succeeded in undermining the political ascendancy of the Hapsburgs and at the treaty of the Pyrenees in 1659 she took the place of Spain as the dominant European power. Henceforth the balance-of-power argument required

English support of Spain, as a declining but still influential state, against the threatened predominance of its more powerful and now much more aggressive rival. This led to a revulsion in the dominant English opinion about Spain, which was forcibly expressed by the diarist Pepys, when he wrote that the English 'do naturally hate the French and love the Spaniards'. That Charles II and James II ignored this trend was one of the reasons why the latter received so little support from his subjects in his hour of need.

Hardly less striking than the rise of France was the simultaneous development of the political and economic forces of the United Provinces, and especially Holland, much the wealthiest and most influential of the seven Sovereign states which had finally secured their independence from Spain in 1648. What in Elizabeth's reign had been a satellite power, wavering in its allegiance between England and France and constantly threatened by Spanish reconquest, had become a Great Power in its own right. By the middle of the seventeenth century the Dutch, at least economically, overshadowed both their sixteenth-century protectors. The anti-Dutch policy of the Commonwealth and of the restored Stuarts was more in accord with mercantile if not public opinion than was their continued dependence on France.

Elizabethan hostility to Spain had partly resulted from, and partly caused, the piratical expeditions of her subjects to Spanish America. The very fact that the Papacy had excluded England from a whole continent was a reason for such attacks; and some leaders of such expeditions hoped that in despoiling the Spaniards they were laying up treasure in heaven as well as on earth. Other merchants who were already trading successfully in Europe with 'Old Spain', and were liable to suffer from Spanish retaliation for the misdeeds of their countrymen in America, much preferred to gain by private bargains some share in the profits derived by Spain from the New World. This conflict of English mercantile interests was partly obscured by Spanish fanaticism, which led to continual complaints from 'Old Spain' traders of religious persecution and proselytism, exercised by Spanish secular and ecclesiastical authorities against English subjects resident in Spain.

Elizabeth had been the somewhat ineffective ally of the Portuguese Pretender, Don Antonio, who had in 1580 attempted unsuccessfully to prevent Philip II from extending his power over the whole Iberian peninsula. Her action was in accordance with still older English traditions, dating back to John of Gaunt and the medieval Hundred Years war against France. The union, not merely of the Iberian peninsula, but of the Spanish and Portuguese overseas empires, obviously increased the threat to English independence in the 1580's, if it also extended the area of anti-Spanish piratical activity. When Portuguese nationalism reasserted itself in 1640 it was however France, not England, which gave it active support and exerted pressure on Spain to recognize the independence of Portugal.

Cromwell, as the ally of France, took some interest in this question. He concluded the treaty of 1654 which placed English merchants in a more favoured position to carry on Anglo-Portuguese trade than the Portuguese themselves. Maximum customs duties which could only be increased with the consent of the English merchants' representatives were fixed by this treaty. A judge conservator was to watch over their legal rights and they were even admitted to some trade with the Portuguese colonies. This treaty, and not the more celebrated Methuen treaties of 1703, was the foundation of English commercial ascendancy in Portugal during the eighteenth century. The marriage of Charles II to Catherine of Braganza, a princess of the royal house of Portugal, and the economically advantageous bargain of which it formed a part, were usually regarded as a sign that the restored Stuarts were still following the Elizabethan policy of using Portugal as a check to the over-great power of Spain.

Indeed for more than a century after 1654 the maintenance of Portuguese independence and the integrity of Portugal's colonies remained a cardinal factor in British foreign policy. British naval squadrons cruised when required off the Portuguese coast and gave some protection to her overseas colonies and trade. British armies landed several times in Portugal to protect her from Spanish attacks, actual or threatened. In spite of its long duration the Anglo-Portuguese alliance was neither a lifelong love-match nor a marriage of true minds: it functioned solely as a marriage of convenience.[1] If it rested on the complementary character of the Portuguese and British economies and proved advantageous to both countries, it never developed from its strategic and economic

[1] C. R. Boxer, 'Vicissitudes of the Anglo-Portuguese Alliance 1670–1700' in *Universidade de Lisboa Revista da Faculdade de Letras*, IIIᵉ série, No. 2, pp. 15–34 (Lisbon, 1958).

bases to become an *entente cordiale*. Hardly any cultural influences can be attributed to it either on Britain or on Portugal, unless one believes that port is more likely than claret to induce gout. The less direct contact there was between the British and the Portuguese the better the alliance worked. British and Portuguese generals and admirals never co-operated successfully and there were constant complaints about Portuguese treatment of Protestant traders resident in Portugal. British merchants never ceased to covet the privilege of direct trade with Brazil, which the Portuguese were determined not to grant. On the Portuguese side what was most resented was the calm British assumption of superiority and the well-founded suspicion that Portugal was regarded at London as a British pawn in the cold and hot war Britain was alternately waging against the Bourbon courts. Not until the third quarter of the eighteenth century did Pombal place the Anglo-Portuguese alliance upon a more equal basis; but his success inevitably reduced the value attached at London by diplomatists and merchants to the connexion with Portugal.

Even more important in the story of Anglo-Spanish relations than Charles II's marriage was his commercial treaty of 1667 with Spain, which placed English trade with 'Old Spain' on a secure footing for a generation and which was constantly appealed to in the eighteenth century as an ideal to be once again attained. By this time the Spanish woollen industry was in decline and large quantities of best-quality woollens were regularly imported from England. The heavy cloths, in which some English manufacturers specialized, were particularly suitable for making habits for the monks and nuns, whose excessive numbers were a constant cause of complaint to Spanish economists. In view of English preoccupation with developing her fisheries, not only around the British islands but also on the Newfoundland cod-banks, contemporaries approved greatly of another main item in the English export-trade to Spain—salt fish. This could be kept indefinitely and used as a substitute for meat on fast-days. Spain also took smaller quantities of metals, especially tin and lead, other textiles, especially stockings, and tobacco.

What commodities had Spain to offer in exchange? Most highly regarded was wool of fine quality, grown on the Castilian mountains and exported mainly from Bilbao and San Sebastian. From the south-eastern provinces, especially Andalusia, came olive oil and soap, which were partly used to clean wool before it was made into cloth. Equally important for English woollen manufacturers were the various dye-stuffs, most of them produced in the Spanish colonies and exported by English merchants from Cadiz.

Even supplemented by exports of iron from the Biscay ports and some wine, nuts, and fruit, the balance of trade was heavily in England's favour, especially when the extent to which England was now exporting goods through Spain to the Spanish colonies is taken into account. A large proportion of England's staple exports found its way through Seville and Cadiz to Spanish America, especially woollen cloth and salted fish. Hence another reason why trade with Spain was so highly regarded in the seventeenth and eighteenth centuries—it was the main, indeed, with the exception of the sister Iberian kingdom of Portugal, the only, source of bullion to which England had access. Export of bullion was naturally prohibited by Spanish laws, but English merchants found it possible to evade this prohibition; and the commercial treaty of 1667 was valued partly because it made evasion easier and less dangerous.

In the dominant mercantilist philosophy bullion imports had a special place. For one thing it was realized that without bullion other trades which contemporaries regarded as essential could not be carried on. Without Spanish bullion exports, the East India Company would have had to go out of business and the Muscovy Company could not have imported from the Baltic in the eighteenth century the naval stores necessary to maintain British maritime supremacy. If the bullion imported from Spain was not required for such unbalanced but nationally advantageous trades, it would be stored at home as a contribution to national defence in time of emergency or might be used as capital for the development of commerce and industry.

One more reason for what may seem the excessive importance attached by English contemporaries to trade with Spain must be mentioned. Spain's part in the trade was passive, England's active. It was conducted mainly by English merchants in English ships; and the Navigation Acts were designed to perpetuate this happy state of affairs. In time of war the merchant ships which traded with Spain could still on occasion be used in war. Even after this ceased to be practicable, the seamen who fished off the Newfoundland banks and the mariners who manned the ships which traded with Spanish ports formed an invaluable reservoir of skilled man-power, which impressment made readily available for the royal navy.

So far Anglo-Spanish trade has been considered from the English point of view. While Spanish writers on trade naturally objected to the bullion drain, which was its most important advantage to England, they usually preferred to lose bullion to England than to her rivals, France and the Dutch, who were less willing than England to take Spanish exports in part-payment of the manufactured goods they wished to supply to Spanish America. Horatio Walpole asserted that there was current in Spain at the beginning of the eighteenth century a proverbial saying 'peace with England and war with all the world besides', which, he believed, showed the value attached in Spain to commerce with England. It seems clear on the other hand that, when war broke off commercial contacts between Spain and England in the seven-teenth century, it was the English merchants who suffered much more heavily than the Spaniards.

The commercial treaty of 1667 was the outcome of a political *rapprochement*. It benefited English carrying trade to Spain by allowing exports of English colonial goods from North America or the East Indies to be imported into Spain as though they were the native products of the home country. It exempted English imports of fish from certain taxes on consumption within Spain properly payable by the consumers of the fish. In regard to customs duties there was no general favoured-nation clause; but in practice English merchants seem to have been able to make individual bargains with Spanish customs-house officers which they found satisfactory.

The treaty recognized the need for English consulates at the ports chiefly frequented by English merchants. It also made provision for the appointment of a *Juez Conservador*, a Spanish national, who was entrusted with the defence of the rights of English merchants in Spain. His functions covered not only financial exactions, but also complaints against molestation by ecclesiastical authorities. The institution of this office, and the speedy and cheap justice it afforded to English merchants, are perhaps the most interesting, if not the most important features of the treaty.

Unfortunately English traders were not content with the indirect access they were afforded to Spanish America. Some of them believed that enormous profits could be made if English ships were allowed to export from Africa the slave-labour, and from England the manufactured goods, essential to the Spanish plantations. Bullion would be received in part-exchange without the irksome need to bribe or circumvent Spanish customs-house officials. Political pressure was at times exerted upon the last Hapsburg king of Spain, Charles II, to try to secure his compliance; and in the eighteenth century these demands came to be linked with the belief that there was a great continent in the southern Pacific which had only to be discovered to provide rich rewards for English merchants. Louis XIV's intervention, after the accession of his grandson Philip V to the Spanish throne, to secure for French traders some of the advantages granted by Charles II of Spain to English and Dutch merchants, provided one of the causes for English intervention in the Spanish Succession war. That such fears were not unfounded was shown during the war of the Spanish Succession when the French, on the pretext of geographical discovery, carried through a series of voyages to the Pacific coast of South America and even to China and beyond.

English Protestant merchants gave up business in 1702, few of them returned at the end of the war and although the English factories continued to exist they were manned largely by Roman Catholic Irishmen and Jacobites. This factor naturally increased the rivalry between the old-established trading houses, which after the war resumed participation in Spain's colonial trade via Cadiz, and the merchants who hoped to make their fortunes by direct trade with the colonies. The Utrecht settlement granted to the English South Sea Company the privilege of supplying Spanish America with slaves subject to payment each year of a substantial duty to the king of Spain. It added, as a makeweight, permission to send one ship a year laden with English exports directly to Spanish America, thus by-passing Cadiz, now the headquarters of the English houses trading mainly to Old Spain, but also indirectly with Spanish America. This conflict of interest remained as long as the South Sea Company continued to trade, and at times had a significant influence on British foreign policy.

The Asiento trade soon proved as great a disappointment as the failure to discover a southern continent was to its adherents. The amount of trade was small, and bullion proved almost impossible to obtain in the Spanish colonies. Tropical fruits &c. had to be taken in exchange for British exports so that the South Sea Company came into competition with the West India lobby as well as with traders to Old Spain. The chronic political conflicts between Britain and Bourbon Spain in the eighteenth century fostered Spanish resentment against British exercise of what seemed on paper valuable economic privileges, but proved in fact to be singularly restricted, even in peace-time. Complaints of illicit trade and of smuggling by the company's factors on the Spanish American coasts were met on the English side by howls of protest over the arbitrary seizure by Spanish officials of innocent British merchantmen and their brutal treatment of captive British sailors. It was the Depredations crisis which more than anything else produced war between Spain and Britain in 1739—the so-called 'war of Jenkins's ear'.

If Charles II's attitude towards Spain had been somewhat ambivalent, William III after the Revolution of 1688 made England as well as Holland the ally of Spain. On one occasion when he had to leave England to take part in a campaign on the Continent, he had advised his wife in any difficult question of foreign policy to take the advice of the Spanish ambassador at London. On the other side, Spain's economic decline and military weakness forced her to depend on the Maritime Powers for the defence of the Spanish Netherlands against France in the closing years of the seventeenth century.

Although William III was a great diplomatist, he certainly over-reached himself in concluding the second of his Partition treaties with France. As a man of international mind, he did not appreciate the strength of Castilian resentment against foreign powers, which sought to partition their empire and reduce the ancient kingdom of Castile to insignificance. His signature of the second Partition treaty convinced the Castilians that the only chance of avoiding partition was to throw themselves into the arms of France. They had preserved their national independence for two centuries while ruled by a branch of the house of Hapsburg and they believed they could still remain an independent state under the rule of a branch of the house of Bourbon. The end of the war of the English Succession by the treaty of Ryswick had already impaired William III's relations with the Austrian Hapsburgs. By signing the second Partition treaty he separated the Maritime

Powers from Austria and destroyed the alliance which alone had
enabled them to resist Louis XIV during the war. Finally he had
acted against the dominant trend of opinion both in England and
in the United Provinces. Both countries were weary of war against
France which had proved ruinously expensive and far from
glorious. Doubts were openly expressed about the soundness of the
old-fashioned idea of a European balance of power. In any case
even if a Bourbon instead of a Hapsburg ruled in Spain, he would
depend on the advice of Spanish ministers and the support of the
grandees, who could be counted upon to put Spanish interests
before Bourbon solidarity. Only a clear and unmistakable threat
to their immediate interests would convince Dutch merchants,
English squires, and Whig traders that it was necessary once again
to challenge Louis XIV.

After some hesitation, Louis XIV obliged. He made, or was
believed to have made, the remark that there was now no frontier
between France and Spain. He sent French troops into the Spanish
Netherlands to slight the Barrier fortresses and expel their Dutch
garrisons. The Dutch might have accepted the absence of a
frontier between France and Spain; but even the republicans, who
were traditionally the friends of France, could not accept the
virtual expansion of France across the Spanish Netherlands and
the establishment of direct territorial contact between France and
their own country. Even after nearly a century of increasingly close
and friendly contact between France and the Dutch Regent party,
when the French republic in 1792 followed the example of
Louis XIV, war followed.

Louis's activities in the Netherlands alarmed Tory squires and
English merchants almost as much as the Dutch 'patriots'. They
opened up to France control of ports on the other side of the
English channel. Louis might well reopen the Scheldt to commerce
in peace-time and revive Antwerp as a rival to London. In war, the
Netherlands ports were not only a base for French invasions of the
British Isles, but traditionally pirate-nests which could damage, if
not entirely cut off, English trade through the Channel and pursue
with disastrous effects a *guerre de course* on the oceans of the
world. It was regarded as significant of his intentions that Louis
XIV was already influencing the new king of Spain to withdraw
some of the commercial privileges granted by his predecessor to
English and Dutch merchants and in particular to transfer the

slave-trade to a French company. Even trade with Old Spain was subjected to extra duties and hampered in various ways.

What finally clinched matters, so far as England was concerned, was Louis XIV's recognition of James, the Old Pretender, as the legitimate sovereign of Great Britain. This was generally regarded not only as a breach of the treaty of Ryswick, but as an insult to the English nation, which had solemnly by the Act of Settlement reaffirmed the exclusion of James from the succession. Louis XIV, by revoking the edict of Nantes, had taken the place formerly held by Philip II as the eldest son of the Papacy. Strengthened by *de facto* control of the Spanish Netherlands, he now stood forth as the great patron of the Jacobites. The Protestant succession was not merely an end in itself but the essential condition of national security, religious liberty, and commercial prosperity. A new war against France, of which William had almost despaired, was bequeathed by him as a valuable legacy to Marlborough.

The expulsion of Philip V from the throne of Spain, upon which he had now been established, was no part of the original aims of the Grand Alliance of the Maritime Powers and Austria which was formed to fight France in 1701. Its inclusion in British war-aims resulted partly from British interest in Portugal. At first Portugal, which had been neutral in William III's French war, had been inclined to join the French side in the new war and it was regarded as a great diplomatic victory over France when the two Methuens were able to conclude a defensive alliance with the king of Portugal in 1703. This treaty operated a diplomatic revolution at Lisbon since for the whole of the eighteenth century the kings of Portugal looked to London rather than to Paris. The political agreements of 16 May 1703, largely negotiated by John Methuen, though signed during his absence from Lisbon by his son, Paul, led naturally to a commercial treaty which John Methuen signed on 27 December 1703. In spite of attempts to minimize its effects, this third treaty, usually known as *the* Methuen treaty, had almost as great an effect upon the economic contacts of the two countries as the earlier ones upon their political relationship during the eighteenth century.[1]

England's export trade to Portugal in 1703 was not very different in character from her trade with Spain, except that Portugal had even less than Spain to offer in exchange. There was however a

[1] I have learned much from M. E. Turner, 'Anglo-Portuguese Relations and the War of the Spanish Succession' (unpublished Oxford D.Phil. thesis, 1952).

rapid development of gold, and, to a less extent, of diamond, mining in Brazil in the first half of the eighteenth century. The greater the prosperity of Brazil, the larger the demand both in Brazil and Portugal for English manufactured goods. The historian Rapin dedicated the sixth volume of his *History of England* (London, 1728) to the gentlemen of the English Factory at Lisbon 'the largest and noblest Factory in the World'. English exports to Portugal, according to the official figures, doubled between 1700 and 1740, rose to a peak in the late 'fifties and then declined markedly in the 'sixties. The great bulk of these exports consisted of woollen cloth, especially 'bays', but there were also appreciable and fairly steady exports of grain. Four-fifths by value of Portuguese exports to Britain consisted of wine, the remainder including modest quantities of fruit, oil, cork, and salt. The balance of trade in favour of Britain, already considerable in 1700, had reached over a million pounds sterling by the late 'fifties. Large quantities of bullion were therefore remitted to England by the Falmouth–Lisbon packet-boats and in other ways.

Spain and Portugal have been described as almost the only European countries where there was an expanding market for British manufactures in the first half of the eighteenth century. Cloth imports to the rest of Europe were declining, as were imports of manufactured goods to Britain from the partially industrialized countries of north-western Europe. The exceptional demand for English manufactures in Spain and Portugal was largely for export to their respective colonies, since the Iberian countries were insufficiently industrialized to supply the needs of their colonies from the products of their own manufactures. Not until industrial development got under way in the Iberian countries about the middle of the eighteenth century did British exports to them lose their upward thrust.[1]

Portugal's decision in 1703 to transfer her political dependence from France to Britain was largely inspired by economic motives. The continuance of alliance with France would expose her trade and colonies to the tender mercies of English sailors and might cost her the bullion which alone kept her economy from disaster. Alliance with Britain, it was hoped, would afford maritime protection both to the mother country and her colonies, while in times of

---

[1] The preceding paragraphs are based on H. E. S. Fisher, 'Anglo-Portuguese Trade 1700–1770' in *Econ. Hist. Rev.* 16 (1963), 219–33.

scarcity convoys of provisions from Ireland and grain from England would reduce the recurrent risk of famine on a large scale. Whereas France and Portugal were engaged in a tariff war, in which Portugal was trying to exclude French luxury goods and France sought to prohibit the entry of Brazilian sugar and tobacco into France, a bargain beneficial to both sides could be struck with Britain. Portugal had already given up ideas of industrial development and during William III's French wars Portuguese wines made headway on the London market. Since there was no hope of selling their wines to France, the Portuguese nobles, who were financing the growing vineyards of Portugal, had perforce to turn to London if there was to be any substantial development of the export wine-trade. The breach between Britain and Spain had increased the importance of Portugal in the eyes of British merchants since the Portuguese market offered an alternative outlet and could also be used as an indirect means of exporting to Spain after direct trade had ceased.

The actual provisions of the Methuen treaty may be briefly stated.[1] Portugal would for ever admit English woollen manu-factures under the conditions which had existed prior to recent prohibitions. England would admit for ever Portuguese wines on payment of duties which were not to exceed two-thirds of the duties imposed from time to time on French wines. Since Portu-guese wines in 1703 were paying only half the duties levied in England on French wines, the Methuen treaty allowed an im-mediate increase in these duties. This clause was deliberately drafted to avoid any apparent limitation of parliamentary control of taxation. Had the Methuen treaty tried to freeze existing duties, an act of Parliament would have been required to give effect to the clause, and opposition would certainly have been aroused.

During the Spanish Succession war English exports to Portugal rose rapidly without any comparable increase in Portuguese ex-ports to England, although this is obviously due in part to equip-ment and supplies needed for the English expeditionary force for the defence of Portugal. Before the signature of the Methuen treaty, port, strictly so-called, was already a fashionable upper-class drink in England and the rate of duty levied on its import seems to have had little effect upon consumption. It was the cheaper

---

[1] English translation of the essential articles is given by A. D. Francis, 'John Methuen and the Anglo-Portuguese Treaties' in *Historical Journal* 3 (1960), 121.

Portuguese wines, grown on the Douro and exported mainly from Oporto, which really came to benefit after 1715 from the Methuen treaty.[1]

Godolphin asserted in 1712 that English trade with Portugal during the war had proved twice as profitable as trade with Spain in peace-time.[2] The British consul at Lisbon was popularly believed to have made a fortune during the war since he was paid out of a levy on British ships entering the harbour at Lisbon. In 1713 the English merchants trading to Portugal were active in opposing the commercial clauses of the treaty of Utrecht which were contrary to their interests. A vested interest had been created, which for the rest of the eighteenth century affected British foreign policy not only towards the Iberian countries, but also towards France. The imports of Portuguese wines, once Bolingbroke had failed to buttress by a commercial treaty his political *entente* with France, rose substantially and remained at a high level.

The significance of the Methuen treaty was essentially long-term. Much more important at the time was the preceding political agreement. Lisbon proved an essential base for the royal navy in the early part of the Spanish Succession war. Without the full use of its harbour and dockyards the British government would have found it very difficult to carry on the war in the western Mediterranean and support the Allied land campaigns in Italy as well as in Spain. Even after the conquest of Gibraltar in 1704 and Port Mahon in 1708, it was much used. Once the decision had been taken to support the claims of the Archduke Charles to the Spanish crown, largely to satisfy Portuguese ideas for their security, Portugal came to be used as a military as well as a naval base against Spain. Britain recognized her obligation to support her oldest ally against the Bourbons by land as well as by sea, but the Portuguese contribution to her own defence proved so disappointing that the main area of British operations in the peninsula soon moved to Barcelona and Valencia, which seemed to offer better prospects of a successful allied advance upon Madrid. Some British troops were however retained in Portugal and British subsidies were paid to the king until 1711.

Indeed the difficulties and expense of keeping an effective army in existence in the Iberian peninsula, capable of conducting

[1] M. E. Turner, op. cit., *passim*.
[2] Jean O. Maclachlan, *Trade and Peace with Old Spain*, p. 19.

operations against the Bourbon king of Spain, influenced the fall
of Harley from office in 1708 and the disastrous end of Stanhope's
military career at Brihuega in 1710. The Whigs foolishly committed
themselves to the slogan 'No peace without Spain' at the very time
when it was becoming clear that British resources were inadequate
to carry on two major campaigns on the Continent with any hope
of success in either. Once the British were established in Gibraltar
and Port Mahon, the Portuguese alliance lost much of its value in
their eyes. The Portuguese, on the other hand, claimed that
Britain was reaping the benefits of the Methuen treaty without
providing the forces required to protect Portugal from Bourbon
resentment. There was even a feeling in some quarters at Lisbon
that British predominance in the western Mediterranean, and the
commercial and colonial advantages Britain gained by the Utrecht
settlement made her a danger to both Portugal and Spain. Britain
unilaterally repudiated the promises she had made in 1703 to
secure for Portugal certain border fortresses from Spain and
argued that a British guarantee of the peace treaty between Spain
and Portugal was the best barrier which Portugal could have
against the aggression of a Bourbon king of Spain. In the end
Bolingbroke, in negotiating peace with France, improved Portugal's position in Brazil by excluding France from any right to
navigate the Amazon; and, after his fall, Portugal was glad to
accept George I's guarantee of the terms of the peace concluded at
Utrecht in 1713 between herself and Spain.

The Utrecht settlement also included a commercial treaty
between Britain and Spain. This contained a most-favoured-
nation clause in respect of customs duties and in some other
respects renewed the commercial treaty of 1667, although the
Juez Conservador no longer exercised his protective functions. At
first there were bitter complaints about Spanish treatment of
British trade both with Old and New Spain until Alberoni gained
ascendancy over Philip V and his queen, Elizabeth Farnese. The
basis of his ascendancy was his plan for the restoration of Spanish
influence in Italy, from which country Spain had been deliberately
excluded by the Utrecht settlement.

This might be secured in more than one way. Elizabeth Farnese
herself had claims to succeed eventually to the duchies both of
Parma and Tuscany or at least to transmit the succession to her
sons, Don Carlos and Don Philip, who would presumably be

excluded from succeeding to the Spanish crown by the prior claims of their half-brothers Don Luis and Don Ferdinand. But there is no doubt that Alberoni also encouraged the Spanish sovereigns in their more immediate plans for Italy. Spain and the Emperor Charles VI were still at war. Charles VI claimed to be the legitimate king of Spain and Philip V had not abandoned his pretensions to his predecessor's Italian territories, which had included the duchy of Milan and the kingdom of the Two Sicilies.

Alberoni's plans required the revival of Spain's naval power, which could be conveniently exercised in conquering from Charles VI the island of Sardinia and from the duke of Savoy the island of Sicily. The reconquest of Majorca from Austria by a purely Spanish force encouraged Alberoni in these plans. Neither Austria nor Savoy could hope to defend Sardinia and Sicily without the help of the British naval squadrons which had been established, as a result of the Spanish Succession war, in the western Mediterranean. Alberoni thought it worth while to buy British support, or at least neutrality, by redressing the commercial grievances of her merchants in Spain and Spanish America. Much to his astonishment George Bubb, the British minister at Madrid, was able to sign a new commercial treaty on 14 December 1715, which not merely recapitulated the paper concessions of 1713 which had since been ignored in practice, but restored the office of *Juez Conservador*. In another commercial treaty signed in 1716 Alberoni also made concessions in regard to trade with Spanish America. Bubb realized what Alberoni wanted in exchange; but Stanhope, secretary of state for the southern department, declined even to consider making a political alliance with Spain.

Whatever the economic advantages to be obtained from Spain, there can be no doubt that Stanhope's decision was politically sound. It would have been a *volte-face*, very difficult to justify, for the Whig party, which had staked everything on driving Philip of Anjou from the throne of Spain, to become his ally against their former protégé, the Archduke Charles, now by the death of his elder brother, Charles VI, Holy Roman Emperor. Stanhope had already renewed England's alliance with Austria by the treaty of Westminster, and he now tried to combine this with an alliance with France based on the dynastic interests of the houses of Hanover and Orleans, but also in accordance with the dominant trend of English, if not of French, opinion.

Since the Regent Orleans and Philip V were openly competing with each other for the succession to the boy king of France, Louis XV, a political alliance with Philip V would have been contrary to the spirit if not to the letter of the Triple Alliance of 1717. To satisfy the Spanish sovereigns it would also have had to be directed against the Utrecht settlement, which Stanhope and his colleagues, in spite of their criticisms of a Tory peace at the time when it was signed, had now accepted as the basis of the new Europe.

While aligning himself firmly with France and favouring the Emperor rather than Spain in Italy and the Mediterranean, Stanhope believed he could effect a compromise which would satisfy all three. Charles VI would resign his impracticable claims to the Spanish crown and receive a guarantee of his possessions in Italy and the Netherlands. He would be allowed to exchange Sardinia, which he did not value, for Sicily by mutual exchange with the duke of Savoy, now titular king of Sardinia; but he must grant to Don Carlos the reversion of the Italian duchies of Parma and Piacenza. On French insistence he agreed to add Tuscany to Don Carlos's eventual share. These terms were reluctantly accepted in principle by Austria, when she joined the Triple Alliance powers in the Quadruple Alliance of 1718.

Meantime Stanhope went in person to Madrid to press upon Alberoni acceptance of this compromise. Failing to get the help to which he considered himself entitled either from France or Britain, Philip V had sent a Spanish armada to conquer Sardinia from Savoy and Sicily from the Emperor. England was undoubtedly bound by the treaty of Westminster to defend Sicily. Admiral Byng, acting under instructions from Stanhope, destroyed the Spanish fleet off the coast of Sicily at Cape Passaro. Orleans then coerced Philip V and Elizabeth Farnese by a military demonstration in their northern provinces to dismiss Alberoni, upon whom Orleans and Stanhope rather unjustly placed responsibility for Spanish aggression. The invading French army occupied the naval bases where the Spanish fleet had been built and destroyed the dockyards—a service which Stanhope greatly appreciated as a contribution to British naval ascendancy in the western Mediterranean.

Philip V then accepted the stipulations of the Quadruple Alliance and in a natural revulsion of feeling the Regent Orleans and Stanhope vied with each other to gratify him. On his mission to Madrid before the outbreak of war in the Mediterranean, Stanhope had offered, as a bribe to persuade Spain to accept a compromise which obviously favoured the Emperor, the restoration of Gibraltar to Spain. Though this proposition was not included in the terms of the peace settlement the Regent pressed Stanhope and George I to hand over the fortress. Stanhope and his colleagues, who did not attach much importance to the Rock and were anxious to consolidate the settlement of the Mediterranean crisis, were willing to do this in exchange for a reasonable equivalent, say Hispaniola or Florida. This solution was unhesitatingly rejected by Philip V; and George I, after Stanhope's death in 1721, agreed to its surrender without any equivalent, at an indefinite time in the future and always subject to the prior approval of the British Parliament.

Whether the Cabinet realized it or not, the conditions they attached to the offer of Gibraltar meant that it would not be surrendered until Spain had in fact reconquered the fortress by force. For the rest of the eighteenth century, and on occasions even later, the Rock proved a stumbling block to the restoration and maintenance of good relations between the two countries. Charles III in the second half of the eighteenth century was even more anxious than Philip V to recover it. What had been tolerable when Spanish nationalism was latent, if not defunct, became intolerable with the revival of Spanish prestige in international politics and the growth of a genuine nationalism within Spain. There was also in the eighteenth century a religious element in Spanish resentment— a deep-seated feeling that Spanish territory was being desecrated by the rule of heretics. This is best seen in the anger of many Spaniards when Britain allowed Jews to settle, and even to have a synagogue, in Gibraltar. For similar reasons there was a good deal of friction over the British administration of Minorca.

The revival of Spanish prestige depended upon the firm assertion of Castilian hegemony within the Peninsula and the supression by the Bourbon kings of the remains of local privilege and independence in the other Spanish kingdoms and provinces. After the peace Philip V's treatment of the Catalans, who had been the most effective supporters of the Archduke Charles, was exploited by the Opposition and contributed to bad feeling between Spain and Britain.

Perhaps even more than British occupation of Gibraltar and

Minorca, Philip V resented the transfer to Britain of the naval supremacy formerly held by Spain in the western Mediterranean. Indeed British naval supremacy was both cause and result of the possession of the two naval bases by Britain. Philip V and Elizabeth Farnese had in view as the ultimate end of the revival of Spanish naval power, after the reconquest of Sicily and Sardinia, the destruction of British sea-power in the Mediterranean.

Britain's natural allies against Spain in the western Mediterranean were the Barbary states of Morocco, Algiers, Tunis, and Tripoli. While Morocco was technically an independent empire with ports on the Atlantic as well as on the Mediterranean, the others were still reckoned as dependencies of the Ottoman empire with its headquarters at Constantinople. In practice they all had to be treated as sovereign states. Consular representation, reinforced by occasional naval missions, was maintained throughout the eighteenth century by the British government at all four capitals. Though the days when the Barbary corsairs had dominated the Mediterranean and even threatened to ravage the coasts of England—thus providing Charles I with an excuse for levying ship-money—were long past, the North African states still had a considerable nuisance value. Well on in the eighteenth century church collections were still being made in Britain to ransom prisoners taken into slavery by Barbary pirates.

If the Barbary pirates took occasionally a British ship, they were much more troublesome to lesser naval powers with much larger merchant navies operating in the Mediterranean. The Scandinavians, Italians, even the Dutch, suffered much more heavily and had not the means of retaliation possessed by Britain. Also the Barbary pirates, rivals and enemies of Spain for centuries, were not ill-disposed to a new Mediterranean power, which based its position on the overthrow of Spanish naval domination of the Mediterranean and showed willingness to make common cause with the Barbary states against their common enemy. British consuls in North Africa lost no opportunity of keeping alive hostility between the Bourbon courts and the Barbaresques and when, in the 1760's and later, there were clear signs of *rapprochement* between the old enemies, the British government and its local agents were much perturbed. Vergennes summed up the characteristic role of the Barbary states in eighteenth-century Mediterranean politics when he remarked that while 'Algiers and Morocco are flies, more annoying than dangerous, England is the master against whom we must always be prepared'.

Apart from their role of crippling the Mediterranean commerce of Britain's rivals, the Barbary states supplied Gibraltar and Minorca with food. Once Spain, under pretext of quarantine regulation, had effectually cut off trade whether overland or by sea with Gibraltar, it was Morocco and the other Barbary states which supplied cattle, wheat, vegetables, and fruit to the garrison. Only during the reign of Ferdinand VI was the ban effectually relaxed by Spain. When the emperor of Morocco cut off supplies, either in the course of one of the periodic quarrels with Britain or in order to extort larger profits, the garrison suffered real hardship. Although Gibraltar was able to hold out in the famous siege of 1779–82 without help from Moroccan supplies, the experience showed how expensive and difficult it was to arrange an alternative. Even in the Revolutionary and Napoleonic wars Gibraltar had to be supplied largely from the Barbary ports.

If Gibraltar depended on Morocco, Minorca needed wheat from Algiers, except in the rare years of good harvest when enough grain was produced on the island. So hostile was Algiers to France that there was a prospect of active intervention by the Dey in the Spanish Succession war on the side of Britain. After Spain seized the North African port of Oran in 1732, and succeeded in retaining it until 1791–2, Algiers vainly tried to secure British naval co-operation in recovering it during the war of the Austrian Succession. Earlier the emperor of Morocco had made similar proposals to Britain during the Spanish Succession war, combined with an offer of Ceuta as a bribe—a proposal which was revived during the Nootka Sound crisis at the end of the century. More attractive to Britain was the offer from Tunis in the 'fifties of the island of Tabarka, which would have been a useful counterweight to growing French control of Corsica, but this too was not followed up by the British government.

One cause of friction during the century between Britain and the Barbary states was the occasional seizure of British ships. Morocco was the chief offender, since the length of its coastline, and the fact that the emperor usually resided in the interior, made gunboat diplomacy less effective and more expensive than when applied to the other three states. Much the most serious cause of friction, however, arose over Mediterranean passes. By treaties dating back to Charles II's reign with Tripoli and Algiers, British ships, whose captains held such passes, were immune from seizure by Barbary cruisers. These were valuable documents and despite the mutual interest of the British government and the Barbary states in limiting the issue of them to genuine British ships, all sorts of abuses soon developed. Apart from innumerable cases of outright fraud, passes were granted to foreigners settled in Gibraltar and Minorca and engaged in carrying provisions for the British garrisons in ships usually manned by Italian crews. The Barbaresques may reasonably have suspected abuse when none was intended and this coloured their whole approach to what was, apart from local and temporary crises, the most thorny problem which faced British consuls in North Africa.

After Stanhope's death his successors had to work out the details of the Mediterranean settlement which had been outlined in the Quadruple Alliance. An international congress, meeting at Cambrai, failed in this task. The Emperor tried to postpone the reintroduction of a Bourbon prince into Italy. Spain insisted upon guarantees, e.g. immediate control by Spanish garrisons of the duchies destined for Don Philip on the deaths of the reigning rulers. Even the short-lived alliance of Spain and the Emperor by the first treaty of Vienna (1725) did not achieve a definitive settlement of this troublesome problem, although it was accompanied by a futile Spanish attack upon Gibraltar and an equally futile British attempt to blockade Porto Bello and capture the Spanish annual treasure fleet.

A second international congress at Soissons had to wrestle with these new problems arising out of the Anglo-Spanish war, as well as with the old ones connected with the Italian duchies. Finally Britain, partly helped and partly hindered by Fleury, obtained what she wanted by direct negotiation with Spain. By the treaty of Seville, Britain was to recover her rights to supply negro slaves and send an annual ship to Spanish America, while the privileges offered by Spain to the Ostend Company[1] were cancelled. Nothing was said about Gibraltar; but Spanish garrisons were to be admitted to the duchies destined for Don Carlos, and Britain and France gave a guarantee that these duchies would eventually be transferred to him. Elizabeth Farnese had sacrificed once again the national interests of Spain to gain advantage for her own family.

[1] See chapter 5, p. 120.

It proved easier to make the treaty of Seville than to carry it out. Walpole had to guarantee the Pragmatic Sanction, and thus weaken his already uncertain alliance with France, before Charles VI would admit Spanish garrisons to the Italian duchies. Then and only then could a British Mediterranean squadron convoy Don Carlos and the Spanish garrisons to Italy.

Owing to the prominence of dynasticism in the history of eighteenth-century Europe, the question of the Italian duchies bulked large in Anglo-Spanish relations. It was obvious that Don Carlos, once established in Italy, would become the standard-bearer of Spain, indeed of the whole house of Bourbon, in the peninsula. Charles VI's qualms soon proved well founded. France and Spain drew together in the first Family Compact of 1733, which transferred Don Carlos from the north to the south of Italy and conferred on him the title of king of the Two Sicilies. Walpole refused to take part in this war; and the Bourbon courts, having secured their immediate ends on the Continent, proceeded to put into force the clauses of the first Family Compact which were directed against Britain.

Historians have argued fiercely over the consequences for Spain and for Europe of the establishment of the Bourbons in Spain. Obviously the new dynasty had undertaken large schemes for internal reforms, few of which had actually been carried out. Even more clearly the Bourbons had tried to strengthen control over Spanish America and to exploit their colonial empire to the greater profit of the dynasty. But both of these policies were subsidiary to foreign policy. A Spain with flourishing industries and large and fully occupied dockyards and naval arsenals, drawing substantial supplies of bullion and colonial produce from her colonies, could hope to play once again the role of a Great Power in world politics. Even the recovery of Spain's position as an Italian power was valued as a step towards this position almost as much as a gratification of Elizabeth Farnese's private ends. Even though Spain's ambitions had been very imperfectly realized and pursuit of them had proved costly, Spain had not, on balance, suffered by the substitution of Bourbon for Hapsburg kings.

This conclusion is reinforced by what was happening in the neighbouring kingdom of Portugal under the Braganza rulers. The bull-fighting king, Peter II, who had made the alliance with England died in 1706. His successor, John V, spent much of his income, derived mainly from Brazil, in purchasing privileges, such as the title of 'His Most Faithful Majesty', from the Pope. Since taxation in Portugal was minimal, the *Cortes* had not met since 1697. The Anglo-Portuguese alliance continued and there were flurries of interest in Portugal when Britain was at war with Spain in 1727–9 and 1739–48. For the rest Portugal was left in happy obscurity, so far as international politics were concerned, until the accession of Joseph I in 1750.

The more strained political relations between Britain and Spain had been in the 'twenties and 'thirties, the greater had been the restrictions imposed upon British trade both in Old and New Spain. During the cold war of 1727–9 all British consuls had been withdrawn from their posts in Spain and the annual ship of the South Sea Company had been arrested. What Spain most resented was the trade persistently carried on by the British colonists in Jamaica and other West Indian islands with Spanish America. The Spanish governors of Cuba, Porto Rico, and other Spanish West Indian islands organized coastguards to stop this illegal trade. Owing to the prevailing winds and currents, British ships trading from the Windward islands to the American mainland, or returning home to England, normally passed close by the shores of Cuba, Porto Rico, or Hispaniola.

Finding it difficult to catch British interlopers in Spanish ports the coastguards began to stop and search ships at sea. If they found on board any produce which could conceivably have come from Spanish America, the ship was confiscated, its cargo immediately sold and its crew often maltreated. Most of the coastguards were volunteers who expected to make a profit for themselves as professional privateers. Part of the trouble was that the home government of Spain could exercise very little effective authority over its local agents in the West Indies, even when it wished to pacify British merchants and improve thereby its relations with Britain.

While often conciliatory on individual cases, the Spanish government firmly maintained that the king of Spain owned not only the mainland and islands of Spanish America but also the surrounding oceans. No foreign ship could legally sail on these seas except directly to and from territories ceded by Spain to other sovereigns. These claims were anathema to the West Indian interest in London which had spokesmen in the house of Commons and soon effected a junction with the official Opposition which was intent on overthrowing Walpole and not at all particular in its choice of methods to achieve such a desirable end. To make matters worse, Newcastle, the secretary of state for the southern department, was personally timorous and liable to seek popularity by yielding to the self-interested clamour of commercial and political cliques.

Walpole himself threatened naval preparations and active retaliation for the misdeeds of Spanish sailors in the West Indies. The South Sea Company directors demurred when Walpole told them that as part of his settlement with Spain they must pay their accumulated debt under the terms of the Asiento treaty to the king of Spain, who then threatened to annul the Asiento. Finally, agreement was reached between the two governments by the convention of the Pardo (January 1739), but its terms were at once attacked so violently by the Opposition and by the West Indian interests, backed by the South Sea Company, that Walpole dared not implement it. By a formal declaration clearly drafted and published with the idea of recovering the support they had lost by continuing to negotiate with Spain, the British government declared war in 1739. To defend the illicit trade of her colonists, Britain had sacrificed the interests of the English merchants who traded with Old Spain and, through Cadiz, with her American colonies.

Within a year this colonial and maritime war had become merged in a great continental struggle over the Austrian succession. Spain joined France in attacking Austrian power in Italy, while Britain subsidized Austria, supported her as far as possible with a Mediterranean fleet and won for her the military aid of Sardinia, without which she must have lost her Italian provinces.

The death of Philip V in 1746 cost Elizabeth Farnese her control of Spanish foreign policy. Her stepson, Ferdinand VI, succeeded his father and soon showed a wish to withdraw from an expensive and unprofitable war. His wife Barbara was a Portuguese princess, and Keene was sent to Lisbon to try to arrange a direct and separate peace between Britain and Spain. This negotiation failed, but in 1748 Spain was included in the general peace at Aix-la-Chapelle.

The opposition complained bitterly that the British government had lost sight of the original causes of the war with Spain during its course and indeed they are hardly even mentioned in the Aix-la-Chapelle treaty. The Asiento was to be continued for four more years and then to lapse finally. No settlement was reached on the depredations and freedom of navigation issues. Gibraltar was completely ignored. The commercial treaty of 1715, which had been hailed as a British triumph, was not renewed, whether by accident or design on the part of Spain was not at first clear.

After much hard bargaining with Carvajal, the principal adviser of Ferdinand VI, the new king of Spain, a commercial treaty was signed in 1750. This ended the Asiento, and the South Sea Company ceased to trade. It incorporated the clauses in previous treaties which the British merchants valued mostly highly, such as most-favoured-nation treatment, which was to be reciprocal, and the stipulation that British merchants should not be required to pay higher duties than native Spaniards. Even more objectionable to Spain was the stipulation that the rates chargeable on British goods should not exceed those paid in the reign of Charles II.

Carvajal believed that Portugal, if fairly treated by Spain, would become her best ally. He was also prepared to give Britain a moderate degree of economic privilege, provided she would use her naval strength to stop the smuggling of other nations in Spanish America. Secure in Europe behind the frontier of the Pyrenees and with the backing of Britain and Portugal, he hoped to exploit Spain's colonial empire and to use the profits for economic development in Old Spain. He looked forward to the day when Spain would recover her seventeenth-century position as a Great Power. Ceasing to fear Britain, she need no longer be the humble satellite of France. Carvajal, almost alone of Spain's eighteenth-century ministers, saw that the promises he had made on paper were carried out in practice; and, as long as Ferdinand VI lived, Anglo-Spanish trade was carried on in what was for the eighteenth century a remarkably harmonious manner. Even Spanish sharp practice after 1748 in procuring the services of British technical experts, mainly weavers and dockyard workers, which had caused so much bad feeling in Alberoni's time, did not provoke the British government to formal protests.

Nowhere is the changed atmosphere clearer than in Carvajal's treatment of claims after 1748 for depredations suffered by British merchants and shipmasters in the West Indies. Ferdinand VI in 1752 agreed to repay out of his own purse the compensation agreed to be due for British ships taken in error and ordered that in future captors of British ships charged with illicit trading in the West

Indies should not receive any payment until the case had been determined in Spain. It was however Carvajal's successor, Wall, who secured actual execution of these orders by the Spanish authorities in the New World. It was under Wall's auspices that British merchants for the only time in the eighteenth century were fully satisfied with the Spanish government's attitude to their claims for compensation. When Britain and Spain again went to war in 1762, depredations by coastguards in the West Indies had no place in its causes.

Some credit for improved relations between Britain and Spain must be allowed to the British ambassador at Madrid, Sir Benjamin Keene, who had served in various capacities in Spain from 1721. When Ripperda had taken refuge in the British embassy at Madrid in 1727, it was Keene who had escorted him to London. Keene had negotiated the abortive settlement of British claims in the great depredations crisis of 1737-9 and had even been threatened with impeachment for his pains to avert an Anglo-Spanish war. Though he failed to make a separate peace with Spain at Lisbon in 1745, he returned to Madrid on the conclusion of a general peace in 1748 and founded a working partnership with Carvajal, of which the commercial treaty of 1750 constituted the first fruits.

Keene then discovered that Austria was making approaches to Spain for a mutual guarantee of Hapsburg and Bourbon possessions in Italy. This approach was inspired by the conviction at Vienna that Austrian major interests in Germany and against the Turks would make it very difficult to defend her remaining Italian provinces should a general war break out. It was linked also with the simultaneous approach being made by Kaunitz himself to the French Bourbons. The neutralization of Italy and the Netherlands and preservation of peace in the Balkans would enable Austria to concentrate her available forces against Prussia.

Carvajal, intent on domestic reconstruction and colonial development, welcomed the overtures. They fitted in well with his own dominant idea in foreign policy—that Spain's interests required her to act neither as a satellite of France nor of Austria but as a balancing power between them. This made him up to a point a natural ally for Britain. Newcastle indeed would have liked to secure the admission of Britain to what was regarded, not quite justly, as an alliance which implied the separation of France from Spain and the end of the second Family Compact. Keene failed to secure the inclusion of a non-Italian power in a league intended to preserve peace in Italy; but it was pressure from Newcastle and Keene which did obtain admission for Britain's Italian client, Sardinia.

The treaty of Aranjuez (1752), which was the outcome of these negotiations, changed its character with the Diplomatic Revolution of 1756, but by freezing Hapsburg–Bourbon rivalry in Italy it kept peace amongst the Italian states until the last decade of the eighteenth century. When in 1759 Don Carlos became Charles III, king of Spain, Austria allowed the Spanish Bourbons, contrary to previous international treaties, to retain their territories both in north and south Italy as secundogenitures. Freed from the constant preoccupations with securing and retaining territories in Italy which had largely determined her foreign policy in the first half of the eighteenth century, Spain could concentrate upon internal reconstruction and colonial development.

The death of Carvajal in 1754 and the Diplomatic Revolution destroyed the foundations of British influence at Madrid. Keene won a momentary triumph when he secured the dismissal of Ensenada, the advocate of alliance with France, and the appointment of an Irish exile, Richard Wall, as successor to Carvajal. But the apparent aggression of the British government in the colonies and on the seas revived Spanish fears and gave a fresh lease of life to the old idea that co-operation with France afforded the best chance of preserving her own empire. Spanish colonial governors and their agents began to seize British ships and confiscate their cargoes, while the British logwood cutters in Honduras, who had been tolerated by Carvajal, again became a source of grievance to his successors.

Byng's failure and the consequent French conquest of Minorca might have been expected to convince Spain that her fear of Britain was excessive, had France not promptly offered to cede the island to her. In addition France was prepared to help Spain to recover Gibraltar and settle, once and for all, her long-standing controversies with Britain in Spanish America. After Pitt had taken over the control of British foreign policy, he tried to recover Spanish co-operation. His offer to exchange Minorca, now held by France, for Gibraltar, and to renounce all British claims to trade or settle on the Gulf of Mexico, was not even submitted by Wall to Ferdinand VI.

The death of Ferdinand VI without issue brought to the throne of Spain his half-brother, Charles III. Although the new king of Spain owed his original establishment in Italy as much to Britain as to France, he had become the Bourbon standard-bearer in the peninsula. Consequently during the Austrian Succession war he had more than once been opposed, even humiliated, by British sea-power. His foreign policy after his accession in Spain was however guided more by consideration of Spain's future than by past resentments.

Hesitant at first, he was unnerved by the fall of Quebec. Pitt's world-wide victories alarmed him while he was tempted by a string of offers from Choiseul to support France actively in the Seven Years war. The crushing defeat of France might even be followed by a renewed Anglo-Austrian alliance against the Bourbons in Italy. Charles III signed the third Family Compact on 15 August 1761.[1] Pitt, knowing that the diplomatic battle was already lost at Madrid, was prevented by his colleagues in the Cabinet from declaring war upon Spain in October 1761 and promptly resigned.

Spain's declaration of war upon Britain in January 1762 in accordance with her obligations under the Family Compact came too late to affect the course of the colonial and maritime war. France was already beaten: Charles III merely placed his territories in actual instead of potential danger of seizure by Britain. In finally deciding to join forces with France he seems to have been as much influenced by fears of British economic domination as of her political ascendancy.

The outbreak of Anglo-Spanish war and the threat of a Spanish invasion of Portugal brought about a crisis in British relations with Portugal. While Ferdinand VI reigned at Madrid (1746–59) his Portuguese wife Barbara had helped to preserve good relations between the Iberian kingdoms and to secure Keene's momentary triumphs. When the Lisbon earthquake of 1755 devastated large parts of Lisbon, the British Parliament voted half a million sterling for the relief of distress. But in 1750 John V had been succeeded as king of Portugal by Joseph I. The new king soon gave his complete confidence to his chief minister, Pombal, whose reforms were avowedly based to some extent on the lessons he had learned while

---

[1] See D. Osanam, 'Les Origines du troisième pacte de famille (1761)' in *Revue d'histoire diplomatique* 75 (1961), 307–40.

serving as Portuguese ambassador at London and were at first welcomed by British agents at Lisbon.

The political and financial powers of the church were overthrown and the Jesuit order expelled in 1759. Noble privileges were curtailed and some nobles who opposed the reforms were executed. Pursuing the fashionable aim of self-sufficiency, Pombal soon attacked the dominant position which British traders had established and maintained in the Portuguese economy. He reverted to the old seventeenth-century plans of industrial development and state monopolies. The Oporto Wine Company was established with an exclusive right to purchase the wine produced in this area at a fixed price. When riots occurred Pombal blamed the British merchants.

Much of the good feeling between Britain and Portugal had been dissipated, but even in the mid-eighteenth century the free use of the port of Lisbon was of value to Britain in carrying on a naval war against the Bourbon courts. Pombal's encroachments on British economic privileges were tolerated in view of the continuing strategic value of the Portuguese ports and the profits that were still being made from indirect participation in Portugal's colonial trade. The importance attached by the British government to maintaining good relations with Portugal was clearly shown when British warships, operating against a French fleet in the naval battle of Lagos, violated Portuguese territorial waters. A special envoy was immediately sent to offer the amplest of apologies to the Portuguese court.

Choiseul regarded Portugal as a British colony and Charles III's declaration of war upon Britain carried with it an express threat to the independence and integrity of European Portugal as well as to her colonial empire. France and Spain agreed that an invasion of Portugal was a necessary step to the overthrow of British commercial ascendancy and denounced Portuguese connivance at British smuggling to the detriment of Spanish America. Once again, as in the war of the Spanish Succession, considerable British forces had to be spared from other theatres of war for the defence of Portugal against Spanish invasion. Indeed this extension of the field of operations, already almost world-wide, was one of the arguments used by the peace party in Britain to end British participation in the war in Germany.

Before joining in the war Charles III had toyed with the idea of damaging British commercial interests by organizing a league of neutrals in defence of their rights and—this was more of a novelty —by excluding British exports from states ruled by Bourbons and their allies. The actual invasion of Portugal followed upon Portuguese refusal to join with the Bourbons in the second objective and foreshadows therefore, in a sense, the later Napoleonic invasion and the Peninsular War. While Charles III planned to substitute native Spanish products for English imports, Choiseul hoped to secure larger openings in Spain for French trade.

Charles III in the negotiations leading to the peace of Paris in 1763 was still intent on reducing, if he had failed in war to destroy, British commercial predominance in Spain. Here again he met with total failure, mostly owing to the military, naval, and economic weakness of Spain but also to the clear conflict of interest between France and Spain. Choiseul saw no advantage in reducing British commercial influence in Spain and Spanish America unless France inherited the position held by Britain, whereas Charles III was determined by reviving Spanish industry to exclude France as well as Britain and made only minor and grudging commercial concessions to his French ally.[1] Although the Bourbon courts concluded a commercial treaty in 1768 its practical importance was slight.

Charles III's intervention in the Seven Years war had been based on more than one miscalculation; but the third Family Compact survived the end of the war. France did her best to compensate Spain for her war-losses by surrendering to her the French colony of Louisiana. Charles III now realized that to recover Florida, which gave Britain secure access to the Gulf of Mexico, and to drive the British logwood cutters from his American dominions were not, however, desirable, practicable objectives in the 1760's. Although he gave France diplomatic support in finally acquiring Corsica in 1768, and thus endangering British ascendancy in the western Mediterranean, he in fact failed to secure from France the support to which he considered himself entitled in the Falkland Islands crisis with Britain.

In June 1770 the governor of Buenos Aires had dispatched an expedition to take possession of the British settlement at Port Egmont in the Falkland Islands, which had always been regarded at Madrid as part of her far-flung empire. There were howls of

[1] A. S. Aiton, 'Spanish Colonial Reorganization under the Family Compact' in *Hispanic American Historical Review* 12 (1932), 269, 275–6.

protest from London against what was regarded there as the unprovoked aggression of Spain. Both sides prepared for war and Charles III appealed to Louis XV for help. Choiseul tried his hand at the thankless task of mediation between Britain and Spain: had he remained in office France would almost certainly have given Spain enough encouragement to bring about a war of revenge between the two Bourbon courts and Britain. But Louis XV dismissed Choiseul and made it plain to Charles III that there was no immediate prospect of active French support in a colonial war against Britain. Spain had then to give way and agreed to restore Port Egmont to Britain. This could be represented as a British victory but, as the parliamentary Opposition were not slow to point out, it was an incomplete one since Spain evaded a formal renunciation of its claims to sovereignty over the Falkland Islands.

Even before Louis XV had thus let him down, Charles III had learned his lesson and was much less ready to act as a knight errant for the Bourbon cause after 1763. Yet the years between 1763 and the fall of Choiseul have often been regarded as the high-water mark of cordiality between France and Spain. The two leading Bourbon powers agreed that they must concert defensive measures against Britain, and make themselves stronger, by a policy of internal and colonial reforms, if they were to stand a chance of emerging successfully from the next struggle with Britain.[1]

Even in the 'sixties there were clear divergencies between the policies of Choiseul and Charles III and his ministers. Contrary to Choiseul's wishes, Charles III persisted in attempts to include Austria, Sardinia, and even at one stage Portugal, in the Family Compact. Choiseul was obviously impatient with the rate at which Charles III's attempts to increase the number and efficiency of his troops and to build up a fleet produced practical results. During the earlier years of the American war of Independence Charles III's basic anti-British attitude was accompanied by caution and by considerable independence of France.

When France openly allied herself with the colonists in 1778, Spain adopted a mediatorial attitude and tried to recover Gibraltar from Britain as a reward for her continued neutrality. When this line of policy failed, Charles III then extracted from France an undertaking that France would help Spain to besiege Gibraltar and not make peace with Britain until Gibraltar had been secured for

[1] A. S. Aiton, op. cit., 270, 273.

Spain. Even after he had entered the war, Charles III continued to negotiate separately and secretly with Britain for the surrender of Gibraltar in exchange for his withdrawal from the anti-British coalition.[1] He consistently refused to recognize the independence of the American colonies until the end of the war and there was little effective military or naval co-operation against Britain by France and Spain during the war.

Britain lost Minorca in 1781, but Gibraltar held out until the end of the war. Though the war had demonstrated what ought to have been obvious in any case that the withdrawal of British fleets from the Mediterranean rendered Minorca indefensible, British opinion on the whole preferred to sacrifice Gibraltar rather than Minorca, if one of these outposts was the price of peace. A British surrender of Gibraltar, approved by the British Cabinet in 1782 on conditions which would have been acceptable to Spain, was blocked by Vergennes.

Like some of his distinguished predecessors, Vergennes believed that it was in France's best interests for Britian to retain Gibraltar, since this would go far to secure continued Spanish support for France in any future war or diplomatic crisis between France and Britain. Thus Britain by the peace of 1783 surrendered Minorca and Florida to Spain and retained Gibraltar. The younger Pitt would have been ready to surrender it to Spain in exchange for some compensation and a definitive breach between France and Spain—a price which the Spanish minister, Floridablanca, had no intention of paying.

The importance of Gibraltar in Anglo-Spanish relations had certainly increased during the eighteenth century. Yet it was by no means the only stumbling-block to better relations between the two countries after 1763. Charles III felt humiliated by the failure of his troops to make headway in their invasion of Portugal. He was as eager as Philip II had been to gain control of the whole Iberian peninsula; and once again the conquest of Portugal would have given Spain useful territories overseas, especially in South America, where there were long-standing boundary disputes between the two colonial empires. If after 1763 Portugal could be occupied by a sudden stroke, these advantages could be secured without a general war; and the prospect was the more attractive because it would be an obvious victory over Britain.

[1] See for details Stetson Conn, *Gibraltar in British Diplomacy*, chapters 8–10.

Portugal had not been admitted to the peace treaty of Paris (1763) as a principal contracting party and this was resented at Lisbon. Moreover, the actual terms of the treaty, which included a clause by which France and Spain undertook to evacuate and restore all Portuguese territories occupied by them in Europe and overseas, led to long and bitter disputes between Spain and Portugal. As early as 1764 there was a war-scare and a Spanish invasion of Portugal was believed to be imminent. Yet when there was rioting at Madrid in 1766, Portugal offered to send troops to help to restore order.

Portugal blamed Britain for the humiliating and unsatisfactory peace of 1763, while Pombal's economic nationalism led to bitter recriminations with British merchants and diplomatists. British exports to Portugal in the late 'sixties were less than half their value in the preceding decade, while Portuguese exports to Britain showed little change. Consequently the balance of trade in Britain's favour was much less substantial. Other causes than Pombal's economic nationalism contributed to this change—the cessation of British exports of grain, the end of the long period of Brazilian prosperity about 1760, and a protracted depression in Portuguese trade which lasted from 1762 to 1780 and was due partly to wars and threats of wars with Spain. Portugal's foreign trade picked up again in the 'eighties, but British exports to Portugal did not revive appreciably until the late 'nineties. England was now importing large quantities of Brazilian cotton and Portugal sometimes achieved a visible surplus of trade with England in the 'nineties.[1]

The relaxation of the bonds of trade was not the only cause of the perceptible cooling of Anglo-Portuguese friendship. Common hostility to the Jesuit order also tended to bring together France, Spain, and Portugal. Though France and Spain would have been satisfied with a promise of Portuguese neutrality in their next war against Britain, the Spanish-Portuguese *rapprochement* was prevented from ripening into alliance by a new crisis over their possessions in South America. Yet when Pombal demanded immediate help from the British navy, the secretary of state merely offered British 'good offices' for the settlement of these disputes. France and Britain, moved by a mutual desire to avoid the outbreak of a general European war over colonial problems in which

---

[1] This paragraph is based on H. E. S. Fisher, 'Anglo-Portuguese Trade 1700-70' in *Econ. Hist. Rev.* 16 (1963), 219-33.

they took no interest, brought pressure on their respective allies. A formal disavowal by Spain of any intention to attack Portugal in Europe averted war, but failed to procure a colonial settlement. When Britain became involved in difficulties with her American colonists, Spain took up once again a scheme for an invasion of Portugal. When she asked for a contingent of French troops, France vetoed the proposal. The death of Joseph and the consequent dismissal of his favourite minister, Pombal, at last made possible a settlement of Spanish-Portuguese colonial conflicts by the treaty of 1777, which also included a mutual guarantee of their territories in South America. This proved to be a compromise acceptable to both parties. Spain made no attempt to threaten European Portugal during the later years of the war of American Independence. Portugal did not merely remain neutral, but allowed her flag and her ports to be used by Spain to continue her trade with Spanish America, which would otherwise have suffered much more at the hands of British sailors.

Though active Portuguese participation in the war against Britain was unlikely, the Portuguese government issued a new book of rates, imposed restrictions upon imports of British and Irish woollens and in 1783 concluded a commercial treaty with France. These restrictions, which coincided with the sudden rise in British imports of Brazilian cotton in the later 1780's, markedly reduced the balance of trade in Britain's favour. Attempts to resolve these differences by concluding a new commercial treaty were conducted rather half-heartedly on both sides and finally bogged down.[1]

By this time the Methuen treaties were coming to be regarded in a new light in both countries. Adam Smith believed that they had on balance proved advantageous to Portugal and disadvantageous to Britain. Some Portuguese writers believed that by giving an adventitious aid to the export of wine from the Douro vineyards they had destroyed the Portuguese woollen industry and were damaging agriculture.

Charles III was not content to deprive his chief enemy of the advantages she had formerly derived from a close alliance with Portugal. He turned his attention in 1765 to the Barbary states. Failing to intimidate them by a military demonstration, he resorted with much greater success to the weapons of diplomacy. He made

[1] J. Ehrman, *The British Government and Commercial Negotiations with Europe 1783–93, passim.*

peace with Morocco in 1767 and henceforth Spanish diplomacy was directed to cutting off supplies to Gibraltar and closing Moroccan ports to British ships in the event of an Anglo-Spanish war. These attempts culminated during the American war of Independence when the British consul, George Logie, and the British colony at Tangier were expelled by the Emperor. But the successful resistance of Gibraltar, without any help from Morocco, restored British prestige and for the rest of the eighteenth century Britain held the upper hand over Spain at the Moroccan court.

Charles III's political understanding with France had surprisingly little effect upon British economic interests in Spain. Choiseul had vainly tried to secure concessions for French trade during the negotiation of the third Family Compact and he persisted in the 'sixties in trying to use Spain's need for French political support to undermine Britain's trading pre-eminence in Spain. Charles III had undertaken by the treaty of Paris to renew all English commercial privileges under former treaties and not to allow any privilege, favour, or indulgence to subsist contrary to their terms. Though British merchants were slow to return to Spain after the war, trade revived rapidly. Much of it was now conducted by native Spanish merchants and this reduced xenophobia, which, earlier in the eighteenth century, had been stimulated by the existence at the chief Spanish ports of prosperous British merchants organized in privileged factories. It should also be remembered that the decline in the British balance of trade with Portugal made Spain even more important than before in British eyes as almost the only remaining source of bullion imports.

Choiseul continued to press the claims of France and secured by the commercial agreements of 1768 and 1769 Charles III's undertaking to grant to the French every advantage possessed under previous treaties by English traders. This secret promise made Charles III more eager than ever to stop the smuggling of silver out of Spain by British subjects and led to much friction between the British and Spanish governments. On the plea of giving encouragement to infant industries in Spain, the import of printed linens, and in 1771 of cotton goods, was prohibited. When Britain protested, Spain replied that France would be more affected by the new regulations than Britain. In 1772, when the Spanish government for a time prohibited the export of any foreign goods from Cadiz to Spanish America with the annual *flota*, it was found that although more British than Spanish goods were dispatched, French goods substantially exceeded in value the combined totals of Spanish and British commodities included in the cargo.

Yet Britain still retained her superiority in trade with Old Spain after the end of the American war, though the balance of trade was no longer as greatly in her favour as it had been earlier in the century. Once again in 1783 the peace settlement, in spite of Spanish pleas that reciprocity was in practice worthless to Spain since 'England sends a thousand ships to Spain for every Spanish one that goes to England', renewed the ancient treaties. According to the Spanish minister in London, English exports for 1784 to Spain were valued at £589,887 and Spanish imports to England at £419,462. France, he stated, exported to Spain goods worth £98,106 and took from Spain commodities valued at £84,639.[1]

It was not merely Spanish conservatism which enabled Britain to retain the lion's share of foreign trade with Old Spain, even although British merchants had practically disappeared from the country. Charles III's radical but mercantilist programme for the development of the Spanish economy could be reconciled more readily with the interests of British than with those of French merchants trading to Spain. French efforts to draw economic advantage from her political connexions with Spain continued after Choiseul's fall; but, at least partly owing to French failure to support Spain in the Falkland Islands crisis, they produced singularly little result.

Pitt's policy towards Spain after the end of the American war had been conciliatory. As provided by the peace treaty of 1783 Spain recovered Minorca and Florida. Attempts were made to negotiate a new commercial treaty. Britain promised to evacuate the logwood cutters from the Moskito shore and formally recognized Spanish sovereignty over the areas in Yucatan and Honduras where British subjects were to continue their operations. When the outbreak of the French Revolution undermined the international position of France, the Spanish foreign minister, Floridablanca, was prepared to substitute alliance with Britain for the French alliance to which Spain had consistently adhered since the conclusion of the third Family Compact. Though there was no

[1] These figures are taken from Vera Lee Brown, *Studies in the History of Spain in the Second Half of the Eighteenth Century*, p. 61. The preceding paragraphs are also based on this work.

disposition at London to join Spain in a crusade against the French Revolution, her support of the Triple Alliance, in its ill-starred attempts to impose peace in eastern Europe, was welcomed.

Such harmony as existed was speedily broken by the arrival of news that the Spanish government had arrested a British trading ship, which had been seeking to establish a shore base for the fur trade at Nootka Sound. Once again Spain asserted unequivocally her right to possess the whole American continent under the papal bull of 1493, except in so far as it had been modified by valid international agreements. This claim was unhesitatingly rejected by Carmarthen, the British foreign secretary. Naval mobilization followed as an indication to Spain that the British government was prepared to go to war to protect the right of its subjects to trade and settle on the Pacific coast of North America. Spain must abandon once and for all her antiquated claims to sovereignty over all territory in America the occupation of which by other powers she had not formally recognized.

Whereas the Dutch with an eye to their own commercial advantage supported Britain with vigour and Prussia gave at least nominal support, Spain found herself completely isolated. Revolutionary France was preoccupied with much more pressing problems than the support of another Bourbon power in America: in any case the growing hostility to the Bourbons in France was undermining the very basis of the Family Compacts. Instead of a declaration of Franco-Spanish solidarity against Britain there came from the French National Assembly a declaration on behalf of the French nation that it would refuse to take part in what was regarded as a war of conquest.

There has been argument on the motives of the British government and the legal basis of British claims. One authority describes British action as 'a ruthless act of expropriation' and denies that it was based on any 'new principle of colonial sovereignty';[1] but it certainly opened up the Pacific coast of North America to Anglo-Saxon and even Russian trade, occupation, and settlement. Nor did memories of the crisis of 1790 prevent the *rapprochement* of Britain and Spain and the somewhat ineffective co-operation of these two powers in the First Coalition against republican France.

In March 1793 Britain and Spain joined in a defensive alliance, which included clauses regulating the conduct and protection of

[1] J. N. Norris in *English Historical Review* 70 (1955), 580.

their trade in war-time, but made no attempt to settle the long-standing commercial and colonial disputes between the two countries.[1] Indeed these disputes, as previously in the reign of Ferdinand VI, became insignificant when there was political harmony between Britain and Spain. The threat of the French revolutionaries to overthrow the established order in Europe dwarfed the petty conflicts over the Moskito shore and Nootka Sound which had seemed so important to both countries a few years earlier.

While the Anglo-Spanish alliance of 1793 was a diplomatic revolution it was not destined to endure. The Anglo-Spanish attempt jointly to hold Toulon as a base for anti-Revolutionary activity caused much friction between the two courts. The British occupation of Corsica as the ally of Paoli gave offence at Madrid and revived long-standing and deep-seated Spanish fears of British dominance in the western Mediterranean. When British troops took over control of parts of the French colony of Haiti in the West Indies, Spain, which had once owned the whole island of Hispaniola, of which Haiti occupied the western part, reasserted her claims to the island. The military fiascoes on the European continent of the First Coalition and a French threat to Catalonia led not only to the withdrawal of Spain from the coalition in 1795 but also to the co-operation of Spain and the French Republic to control the western Mediterranean. As part of the Franco-Spanish peace of 1795 Spain yielded her share of Hispaniola, the colony of Santo Domingo, to France; in exchange France restored her conquests in northern Spain and agreed to accept Spanish mediation between herself and Portugal.

In the following year Spain declared war on Britain and although the declaration was accompanied by soothing words from the all-powerful Spanish minister Godoy, it contributed to the British abandonment of the Mediterranean and the temporary concentration of her naval forces in the Atlantic and the Channel. Though Admiral Jervis won an important naval victory early in 1797 at Cape St. Vincent over a numerically superior Spanish fleet, British sea-power was soon immobilized by the great naval mutinies of 1797. Soon Nelson's victory of the Nile restored British ascendancy in the Mediterranean in 1798 and made possible

---

[1] J. Ehrman, *British Government and Commercial Negotiations with Europe 1783–93*, p. 173.

the Second Coalition against France. Yet Spain continued to give ineffective support to the French republic and suffered appreciable naval and colonial losses.

By the treaty of San Ildefonso (1800) Spain returned to France Choiseul's gift of Louisiana in exchange for secret promises of territory in Italy for Charles IV's son-in-law. Partly to revenge himself for Britain's defeat of his Egyptian expedition, Bonaparte now determined to attack Portugal, which had been at war with France since 1793. Spain became his involuntary ally on land as well as at sea and a joint Franco-Spanish army advanced against Portugal. The Portuguese had to make peace at the cost of surrendering some territory in Europe to Spain and part of Portuguese Guiana to France (1801).

The threat to Portugal was one of the factors which persuaded the British government to make the unsatisfactory truce of Amiens with France (1802). By one of the clauses of this treaty Britain undertook to return to Spain the overseas conquests she had made during the war. After the rupture of the truce Spain continued to support France; and her breaches of neutrality provoked the British government, without a previous declaration of war, to seize Spanish treasure-ships by way of retaliation. Nelson's crowning victory at Trafalgar annihilated what was left of the naval power of Spain as well as of France, and forced Napoleon to try his only remaining weapon against Britain—the continental blockade. To be effective this had to be complete. Portugal, with its political dependence on and economic links with Britain, was one of the most obvious leaks in the projected Continental System. Napoleon used French troops, which were ostensibly intended to reinforce the army seeking to conquer Portugal, to gain complete control of Spain. He forced Charles IV to renounce his crown and coerced his heir, Ferdinand, to surrender his claims to the succession in favour of Napoleon's brother Joseph (1808).

Not for the first nor for the last time Napoleon had over-reached himself. A furious Spanish national revolt broke out. Spanish guerrillas and Portuguese loyalists were soon backed by British regulars—the Peninsular war had begun. Henceforth the rivalry of France and Britain in the Iberian peninsula was to be linked, as it had not been in the eighteenth century, with domestic party strife in both Iberian kingdoms. The nineteenth century, with its basic conflicts between liberalism and nationalism, dynasticism and democracy, clericalism and anti-clericalism, was to transform the Iberian political scene, without however eliminating the rivalry of France and Britain for influence which had been the constant factor in the eighteenth-century international situation of the Iberian kingdoms.

A. *Primary Sources*

An Account of the Court of Portugal by John Colbatch (1700)
Coxe, W., *Memoirs of the Kings of Spain* [1700–1788] (5 vols., 2nd ed. 1815)
Eden, William (Lord Auckland), *Journal and Correspondence* (4 vols., 1861)
Lodge, Sir R., ed. *Private Correspondence of Benjamin Keene* (Cambridge, 1933)
Spain under Charles II, ed. Lord Mahon (1840, privately printed)

B. *Secondary Authorities*

Aiton, A. S., 'The Asiento Treaty as reflected in the Papers of Lord Shelburne' in *HAR* 8 (1928), 167–77
Albrecht, Johannes, *Englands Bemühungen um den Eintritt Portugals in die Grosse Allianz (1700–1703)* (Bremen, 1933)
Anderson, M. S., 'Great Britain and the Barbary States in the Eighteenth Century' in *BIHR* 29 (1956), 87–107
Batchelor, Lilian E. M., 'The South Sea Company and the Assiento' in *BIHR* 3 (1925–6), 128–30
Bemis, S. F., *The Hussey–Cumberland Mission and American Independence* (Princeton, New Jersey, 1931)
Brazão, E., *The Anglo–Portuguese Alliance* (ed. S. G. West) with texts of the Methuen treaties (1957)
Brown, Vera Lee (Mrs. Holmes), 'Anglo-Spanish Relations in America in the Closing Years of the Colonial Era' in *HAR* 5 (1922), 325–483
— 'The South Sea Company and Contraband Trade' in *AHR* 31 (1925–6), 662–78
Castries, duc de, 'Le Pacte de Famille et la Guerre d'Independance Américaine' in *RHD* 75 (1961), 254–306
Christelow, A., 'Economic Background of the Anglo-Spanish War of 1762' in *JMH* 18 (1946), 22–36
— 'Great Britain and the Trades from Cadiz and Lisbon to Spanish America and Brazil 1759–1783' in *HAR* 27 (1947), 2–29
Conn, Stetson, *Gibraltar in British Diplomacy in the 18th century* (New Haven, 1942)
Donnan, Elizabeth, 'The Early Days of the South Sea Company' in *Journal of Economic and Business History* 2 (1930), 419–50
Fisher, Sir Godfrey, *Barbary Legend* (Oxford, 1957)
Fisher, H. E. S., 'Anglo-Portuguese Trade 1700–1770' in *EcHR* 16 (1963–4), 219–33

Francis, A. D., *The Methuens and Portugal 1691–1708* (Cambridge, 1966)
Furber, H., 'An abortive attempt at Anglo-Spanish commercial co-operation in the Far East in 1793' in *HAR* 15 (1935), 448–63
Gipson, L. H., 'British Diplomacy in the Light of Anglo-Spanish New World Issues 1750–57' in *AHR* 51 (1945–6), 627–48
Goebel, Julius, *Struggle for the Falkland Islands* (New Haven, 1927)
Gómez Molleda, Señorita D., *Gibraltar* (Madrid, 1953)
Hildner, E. G., 'The Role of the South Sea Company in the Diplomacy leading to the War of Jenkins' Ear 1729–39' in *HAR* 18 (1938), 322–41
Kendrick, T. D., *The Lisbon Earthquake* (1956)
Lee, Hilda I., 'The Supervising of the Barbary Consuls 1756–1836' in *BIHR* 23 (1950), 191–9
Lodge, Sir R., 'The Treaty of Seville' in *TRHS* 4th series, 16 (1932), 1–43
— 'Sir Benjamin Keene' in *TRHS* 4th series, 15 (1932), 1–43
— 'The Treaties of 1703' in *Chapters in Anglo-Portuguese Relations*, ed. E. Prestage (Watford, 1935)
— 'The English Factory at Lisbon' in *TRHS* 4th series, 16 (1933), 211–47
Lokke, C. L., 'St. Domingue in Anglo-Spanish Diplomacy 1795' in *HAR* 16 (1936), 250–7
McLachlan, Jean, *Trade and Peace with Old Spain 1667–1750* (Cambridge, 1940)
— 'The Seven Years Peace and the West Indian Policy of Carvajal and Wall' in *EHR* 53 (1937), 457–77
— 'The Uneasy Neutrality. A Study of Anglo-Spanish Disputes over Spanish Ships prized 1756–59' in *CHJ* 6 (1938–40), 55–77
Manning, W. R., *The Nootka Sound Controversy* (Washington D.C., 1905)
Nelson, G. H., 'Contraband Trade under the Asiento 1730–39' in *AHR* 51 (1945–6), 55–67
Nettels, Curtis, 'England and the Spanish American Trade, 1680–1715' in *JMH* 3 (1931), 1–32
Norris, J. M., 'The Policy of the British Cabinet in the Nootka Crisis' in *EHR* 70 (1955), 562–80
Pares, R., *Colonial Blockade and Neutral Rights 1739–63* (Oxford, 1938)
— *War and Trade in the West Indies 1739–63* (Oxford, 1936)
Parnell, A., *The War of Succession in Spain* (1905)
Parrel, C. de, 'Pitt et l'Espagne' in *RHD* 64 (1950), 58–98 [deals with the Nootka Sound episode]
Prestage, E., *Portugal and the War of the Spanish Succession* [a bibliography] (Cambridge, 1938)
— 'The Anglo-Portuguese Alliance' in *TRHS* 4th series, 17 (1934), 69–99
Reese, T. R., 'Georgia in Anglo-Spanish Diplomacy [1736–9]' in *WMQ* 15 (1958), 168–90
Shillington, V. M., and Chapman, A. B. W., *Commercial Relations of England and Portugal* (1907)
Simon, A., *History of the Wine Trade* (1906)

Sutherland, Lucy S., 'The Accounts of an Eighteenth-century Merchant [The Portuguese Ventures of William Braund]' in *EcHR* 3 (1931–2), 367–87

Temperley, H. W. V., 'Causes of the War of Jenkins' Ear, 1739' in *TRHS* 3rd series, 3 (1909), 197–236

Walford, A. R., *The British Factory in Lisbon and its Closing Stages* (Lisbon, 1940)

Wheeler, G. C., 'The "Discours Politique" attributed to Pombal' in *EHR* 19 (1904), 128–31 [discusses Pombal's attitude to Britain]

Addendum

McGuffie, T. H., *The Siege of Gibraltar 1779–1783* (1965)

CHAPTER 11

Great Britain and Switzerland

I T was the accession of William III, the need to defend the Protestant succession, and the long wars with France, which established regular diplomatic contact between Britain and the Swiss cantons. These cantons and their dependencies were the nearest equivalent on the diplomatic chessboard to the Sovereign republics of the United Provinces and like them were linked by a federal assembly. But whereas all seven United Provinces were of equal status, Switzerland was composed of three distinct categories of states—cantons, associates, and allies. Exactly equivalent to the Dutch provinces were the thirteen Swiss cantons, which alone were full members of the Swiss Confederation. Each canton, individually and in conjunction with other cantons, ruled dependent states of lower status, described as 'subjects' or 'associates' which had been conquered by force of arms. All these territories were recognized by the thirteen cantons as forming part of the Helvetic body. The third category of 'allies' were attached to either the Roman Catholic or the Protestant cantons, but they were not recognized by the other group of cantons as forming part of the Swiss Confederation. In addition to formal meetings at which all thirteen cantons were represented and in which the Catholics had a permanent majority of one, the Roman Catholic and Protestant sections often met separately. While the Protestants met at Aarau, the Catholics usually assembled at Lucerne.

It follows from this that not all British diplomatists accredited to the Helvetic body were in fact accredited to them all. Since William III was not recognized by the Roman Catholic cantons as king of Great Britain, his first agent in Switzerland, Thomas Coxe, was received only by the Protestant cantons. This was also the case under Queen Anne;[1] and it offers a marked contrast to the position in the United Provinces. No British diplomatist, in the period with which we are concerned, was accredited to part only of the constituent republics of the United Provinces but always to the States General, which contained them all.

[1] M. Meier, *Die diplomatische Vertretung Englands in der Schweiz*, p. 30.

Another difference was that in Switzerland there was not only a regular series of diplomatic representatives accredited to the Helvetic body and normally resident at Berne or Zürich, but also two other categories. The British government, for reasons to be explained later on, thought it worth while to maintain also regular diplomatic contact with the republic of Geneva, one of the 'allies', down to 1774. It also sent, during some wars and international crises, very occasional missions to another 'ally', the Grison leagues, which controlled an important military route between Austria and Italy.

The three Grison leagues were even weaker and less capable of combined action than Switzerland itself. The Grey or Upper league, the league of God's House, and the league of the Ten Jurisdictions which together made up the Rhaetian Free State had a constitution so complicated, so loose and so dominated by checks and balances that it was almost incapable of reaching firm decisions on matters of foreign policy. Upon the whole, however, Austria held the leading place. When the Austro-British alliance broke apart in 1756, the rather languid and spasmodic interest taken by the British government in Grison affairs came to an end. No British diplomatist seems to have been accredited to them after the end of the Austrian Succession war, although the renewal of war between France and Austria both in Italy and in Germany after 1792 led to a short-lived revival of British interest.

One factor which enabled Britain to retain for long a foothold in Swiss politics was the change in the balance between Protestant and Roman Catholic cantons. Whereas the Catholic cantons remained rural and economically backward, Berne and Zürich became flourishing cities with highly developed industries and trade. The shift in economic power was partly responsible for, and was clearly revealed in, the change of fortune in the two Villmergen wars. Beaten in the first in 1656, the Protestants triumphed in the second (1712) and at the peace of Aarau the cantons of Zürich and Berne retained most of their territorial conquests and came near to securing actual parity between the two religions in the common lordships. In spite of French and Austrian backing for the Catholic cantons, Zürich and Berne retained the fruits of this victory for the rest of the eighteenth century. Their increasing strength made it clear that only with French military and economic support could the Catholic cantons hope to reverse the verdict of 1712.

In 1715, in exchange for Louis XIV's promise of support in reversing the Aarau settlement, the Catholic cantons undertook not to supply mercenaries to any power other than France. This secret treaty, known as the *Trücklibund*, was never formally ratified by Louis XIV; but it illustrates the breach between Swiss Roman Catholic and Protestant and the extent of the authority exercised over the Catholic cantons by France in the eighteenth century. In practice French influence was almost as great over the Protestant cantons.[1]

The long-standing alliance between all the cantons and France was renewed in 1723 and again in 1777.[2] Throughout the century the Protestant cantons supplied France with large numbers of mercenary soldiers, who would otherwise have found it difficult to secure remunerative employment. Even the commercial and industrial development of Zürich and Berne, which provided for some of their inhabitants an alternative to service abroad, ultimately increased their dependence on France. Many officials and other influential persons continued to receive pensions and gratifications from Louis XV. Swiss subjects enjoyed a privileged position in trading with France, especially at Lyons. Swiss mercenaries often sold wine as a sideline. In 1777 however, as Louis XVI's price for a renewal of the general alliance of the Swiss cantons, both Roman Catholic and Protestant, with France, Berne and Zürich had to surrender some of these privileges and immunities.

In these circumstances it was not unnatural that the importance attached by the British government to the Berne legation declined during the century. Envoys extraordinary gave way to ministers and the last British minister before the French Revolution treated his post as a sinecure. From 1769 to 1792 Britain was represented at Berne by a mere chargé d'affaires. Since the British government was developing a regular network of missions and taking a much more active interest than ever before in her relations with central and eastern Europe, the weakening of her contact with the Swiss cantons was all the more marked. Not until the outbreak of the French Revolutionary war which brought about a new situation was the eighteenth-century trend of Anglo-Swiss relations reversed.

[1] W. Ganz, 'Französisch-eidgenössische Bündnisverhandlungen 1725–1733' in *Zeitschrift für Schweizerische Geschichte* 20 (1940), 298–391.

[2] H. Mercier, 'Histoire du renouvellement de l'alliance générale entre la Couronne de France et les Ligues suissse et leurs alliés (1764–77)' in *Zeitschrift für Schweizerische Geschichte* 16 (1936), 167–202.

Another complication which did not affect British relations with the United Provinces was important in contacts with Switzerland. Whereas their High Mightinesses of the United Provinces were uniformly Protestant, there was a division in the Helvetic body between Protestant and Roman Catholic cantons, which inevitably affected their foreign policy and occasionally led to war, actual or threatened, between rival religious factions. Cromwell had sought to include the Protestant cantons in a league to coerce the duke of Savoy, who had massacred the Vaudois and driven the survivors from their homes. Though he was disappointed by lack of Swiss co-operation, when the first Villmergen war broke out between the Roman Catholic and Protestant cantons in 1656, he was prepared to subsidize the Protestants. Once the war had ended in the defeat of his allies and he had himself made an alliance with France, Cromwell withdrew his diplomatic agent from Switzerland. His action provided a precedent for Whig statesmen after the Utrecht settlement and the Triple Alliance of 1717, though it seems unlikely that it was in their minds at this time.

While the Roman Catholic cantons were already economically dependent on trade with France and dared not risk a tariff war with their only important customer, the leading Protestant cantons, Zürich and Basel, were not only nearer to self-sufficiency but had developed trade with Germany. The total lack of interest shown by Charles II and James II in the Swiss Confederation helped Louis XIV to reduce most of the cantons to the position of satellite states of France. He exploited his economic control of the Catholic cantons, built up a French party by generous bribes, and erected at Hüningen a fortress which threatened Basel. On one of the guns of Hüningen was engraved the words 'Si tu te remues, Bâle, je te tue'. By advancing the French frontier to the line of the Jura and revoking the edict of Nantes he alarmed the Protestants. The threat of French domination was now reinforced by what seemed to be a real danger of death or at least exile for the Swiss Protestants. Securely in control, Louis XIV treated even the Roman Catholic cantons in a way which aroused bitter resentment. He had failed to keep his promise never to employ the Swiss in offensive warfare.

The Swiss Protestants turned to William III for help in their predicament. This seemed to make possible one of his favourite schemes—an attack on France from the south-east, where there were no strong fortresses to be besieged and taken before an advance into the interior of France was practicable. If William could involve Switzerland in his plan, war would inevitably result between Louis XIV and some of the Swiss cantons, and it was William III's hope that Louis XIV's economic, political, and military domination of the Helvetic body might be finally overthrown. While the Protestant cantons would have been ready to hire a body of mercenaries for defensive duties with William III, participation in an offensive against the French, and the use of their territory for such a purpose, ran counter to the whole tradition of Swiss neutrality, already well established in the seventeenth century.

It was a minor difficulty that William's plan for invading France depended upon the co-operation of the Swiss mercenaries with the duke of Savoy, a neighbour with a long tradition of enmity to the Helvetic body. The duchy of Savoy, unsupported by Switzerland, was occupied by a French army in the summer of 1690; and the republic of Geneva, surrounded by French troops, lay at the mercy of Louis XIV. William III then sent a diplomatic agent to Geneva to stiffen internal resistance and, if possible, to involve Berne and Zürich, whose 'ally' Geneva was, in the war against France. Since it was by this time clear to the Protestant cantons that the object of William III in his Swiss negotiations was to involve Zürich and Berne in an offensive war against France they broke off the negotiation. Coxe's Dutch colleague succeeded in making a bargain with Berne and other cantons for the supply of Swiss mercenaries purely for defensive war.

In many ways Coxe's unsuccessful mission foreshadows the later relations between Britain and Switzerland. Britain's basic interest in Switzerland was to limit as far as practicable the predominant influence of France or at least prevent it being transformed into unquestioned domination. It is significant that when Britain and France were on good terms the British government allowed its diplomatic representation at Berne to lapse from 1722 to 1734. British hopes obviously centred on the Protestant cantons, to which alone, until later in the eighteenth century, successive British ministers at Berne were accredited.

Just as the opening of the war of the English Succession produced Coxe's mission, so did Queen Anne's government send William Aglionby to try to secure assistance from Berne at the beginning of the Spanish Succession war. Savoy's defection to the anti-French camp and the victories won by Eugene in Italy increased the importance attached to Switzerland by the British government. In Marlborough's view 'an active stirring minister in Switzerland would be capable of doing more service than anywhere else, both in supporting and encouraging the Protestant cantons, and in furnishing the quickest intelligence from all parts'.[1]

In practice during the war of the Spanish Succession the activity of British diplomatic agents was limited to the Protestant part of the Swiss Confederation, since the Roman Catholic cantons were so firmly wedded to France that they recognized the Old Pretender as legitimate king of Great Britain right up to the end of Anne's reign. Even Berne was bound by financial and commercial ties to France which were skilfully used by French diplomacy, whereas Britain's ally Austria treated the leading Protestant cantons of Berne and Zürich with an *hauteur* which was liable to be mistaken for hostility. Both Leopold I and Joseph I tried by economic pressure to force Zürich and Berne to support them. So far from helping Britain to encourage opposition to French domination in the Protestant cantons, Austria's attitude, and in particular her preference for a policy of economic sanctions and her pressing of territorial and other Hapsburg claims against the cantons, almost forced the Swiss Protestants to concur in the measures of the Francophil party.

When the duke of Savoy joined the coalition against France in 1703, the position of Geneva between France and Savoy became critical. Britain exerted such influence as she had to preserve its integrity. At the same time the question of the succession to Neuchâtel (Neuenburg) became acute and Britain committed herself to support the claims of Prussia against the French candidate. This question was settled in favour of the king of Prussia in 1707 —another Protestant victory. Then the Emperor demanded British support in securing free passage through the Grisons for troop movements from Austria to take part in the Italian campaign.

Marlborough's anticipation of the service to be rendered in Switzerland to the anti-French coalition had been fully realized by the work of Abraham Stanyan during the war years. If he had not secured any Swiss mercenaries for his own country, he had helped to obtain them for the Dutch and other allies. During the war 16,000 Swiss mercenaries were fighting for the United Provinces,

[1] *H.M.C. Bath MSS.* I, 63.

5,000 helping to defend Savoy and another 5,000 taking part in the protection of Austria's outlying territories in south-western Germany. France and Spain between them employed 31,000; but even so the Swiss had made a respectable contribution to allied manpower. Allied generals paid tribute to the quality as well as to the number of Swiss mercenaries. And just as William III had been careful to secure the inclusion of the Protestant cantons in the treaty of Ryswick, so Anne's Tory ministers looked after their interests in negotiating the treaty of Utrecht and saw that the territorial gains they had made during the civil war with the Roman Catholic cantons in 1711–12 were retained by Zürich and Berne.

The end of the Spanish Succession war and the inclusion of Switzerland in the treaty of Baden (1714) was a turning point in Anglo-Swiss diplomatic relations. It was not merely that the restoration of peace automatically reduced the interest taken in Swiss politics during the war by the British government. Britain in 1716 became the ally of France, while the Emperor was pressing the territorial claims of the Abbot of St. Gall against the Protestant cantons and trying to force them to compliance by a tariff war. While France seized the chance of alienating Protestant Switzerland from the Hapsburgs for ever, Britain took so little interest in the questions at stake that she convinced the Protestants that she neither could nor would give them effectual help. In 1719, for example, Stanhope urged Dubois to recruit Swiss mercenaries for the French service and to conclude an alliance with Switzerland.[1] Although the Catholic cantons at last recognized George I, as they had refused to recognize his two predecessors, as legitimate king of Great Britain in 1716, some well-known Jacobites were allowed to reside in Switzerland. Even this failed to arouse Townshend's interest and the diplomatic post at Berne was closed down in 1722. So long as the Triple Alliance survived, the British government was prepared to acquiesce in French domination of Switzerland.

The formation of a Franco-Spanish-Sardinian coalition to attack Austria in Italy in 1733 once again, as in 1689 and 1701, directed British attention to Switzerland. Walpole in 1734 offered to hire Swiss mercenaries or even to conclude a defensive alliance with the Protestant cantons. These suggestions were much less likely to bear fruit than similar proposals made by Walpole's pre-

[1] S.P. 78/164, f. 279.

decessors in earlier wars. Zürich and Berne could not but be suspicious of British motives. British lack of interest had strengthened
the position of France in the Protestant cantons. Walpole's refusal
to support the Emperor in the Polish Succession war did not encourage other powers to make defensive alliances with Britain.
Walpole was obviously trying to keep a foot in both camps and the
Protestant cantons would have been extremely foolish to disoblige
France without any real assurance of active and effective British-
Austrian diplomatic and military backing.

Seeing themselves threatened by Spanish troops operating
against Savoy in the early years of the Austrian Succession war, the
Protestant cantons declared their neutrality, but as a precautionary
measure they also appealed for help to the United Provinces,
France, Britain, and Prussia. Once again a British diplomatic
agent was sent to counteract French domination of the Helvetic
body and if possible conclude an alliance with the Protestant cantons. Under existing conditions such ideas were utterly unrealistic,
especially as Austria failed to give support to the British agent in
attempting to organize an anti-French party. Indeed the operations of Charles of Lorraine in Alsace in 1743-4 caused more
alarm to the Protestant cantons than had Spanish occupation of
Savoy in the previous year.

Though Burnaby's mission which lasted from 1743 to 1750 was
a total failure, the Berne legation was not closed down at the end
of the Austrian Succession war. Unlike Stanhope and Townshend,
Newcastle was determined to oppose the influence of France
everywhere in Europe by diplomacy after he had had reluctantly
to conclude with her the truce of Aix-la-Chapelle. But in Switzerland at least France held all the trumps. Newcastle's bright idea
that Savoy might be neutralized and linked with the Helvetic body
to provide an effective barrier in the south-east to French aggression was anathema to France and unpopular in Protestant Switzerland where Savoy was regarded as an intolerant and aggressive
power which had exterminated or expelled the Vaudois Protestants and whose designs on the Protestant city of Geneva had
caused trouble for two centuries. Even less promising was the suggestion of Villettes, the new minister at Berne, that Austria should
be invited to bring economic pressure upon the Swiss Protestants
by threatening to cut off the grain trade.

If Villettes was even further from success in the principal object of his mission than any of his predecessors, the nearer the approach of war between Britain and France the greater became his importance in the secondary role attributed by Marlborough to the Berne legation—that of supplying quickly reliable information from all parts of Europe to the British government. Newsletters in print were supplemented by secret intelligence of the strength of the French forces, rumours of French mobilization, and her plans for descents on England or Scotland. Once the war had started, it ran its course far from the Swiss frontiers and there was therefore less likelihood than ever of the Swiss being induced or forced to abandon their profitable neutrality. The classical role of Switzerland in the wars of the nineteenth and twentieth centuries was foreshadowed during the Seven Years war. Rival diplomatic agents organized spy rings on its territories, while their governments sought to use Switzerland in their war propaganda or to sound out the possibility of restoring peace on terms they were prepared to accept.

The end of the war reduced the usefulness of the Berne legation almost to zero. Even at the beginning of the war in 1757 Sir Benjamin Keene had written to his friend and colleague Abraham Castres: 'How often have I told you, and you agree to it, that *Swisserland* is the country to be employed in, where there are no admirals, no privateers, no trade, nor navigation.'[1] George III had no more desire for an alliance with the Swiss Protestants than they had for an alliance with him. Britain's need for subsidiary troops had never been satisfied from Switzerland: all the mercenaries that she required—and she had used many more in the Seven Years war than in previous wars—could be readily obtained from the German princes.

None the less when a new British diplomatist, William Norton, was sent to Berne in 1765 he was given instructions which differed little from those given by William III to Coxe in 1689. He was to keep alive and organize resistance to France and make inquiries about the possibility of an alliance between the Protestant cantons and Britain. Halifax attached more importance to his ability to supply information about Swiss politics, the strength of her defences and the state of her trade; and the British government maintained in the 'sixties the completely detached role of a mere observer. After 1769 Norton was allowed to treat his post as a

---

[1] *Private Correspondence of Sir Benjamin Keene*, ed. Sir R. Lodge, p. 511.

sinecure: two chargés d'affaires, Catt and Braun, successively occupied the position at Berne. They kept up the outward forms of diplomatic representation and filled their dispatches with extracts from the gazettes.

Norton's case is almost unique in the British diplomatic service of the eighteenth century: it was a fixed principle that the duties of foreign service posts were not to be discharged by deputy. That Norton was allowed to do this, and even to substitute one deputy for another when Catt died in 1776, until his own dismissal in 1783, is sufficient proof of the lack of interest taken in Switzerland by Lord North and his colleagues. When, on the outbreak of the war of American Independence, a group of Swiss Protestant officers wished to offer their professional services to the British government, they did not approach the Berne legation but tried to negotiate with Lord North through a Scottish visitor to Switzerland, James Francis Erskine.[1]

The outbreak and course of the French Revolution caused a revival of British interest in Switzerland. Hugh Cleghorn, a non-resident professor at the University of St. Andrews, as early as 1790, called the attention of the British foreign Secretary to the position in Switzerland, and the openings available for British diplomacy there. Troops could be recruited, capital raised for war loans, and a spy ring organized on Swiss territory. Joseph Ewart, the influential British diplomatic agent at Berlin, supported Cleghorn whom he had known during their student days at Edinburgh. The canton of Berne and the city of Geneva formally appealed to the British government for help. Neither Leeds nor his successor Grenville was much impressed in 1790–1, but when the French Revolution began to influence the internal politics of the Swiss cantons and to intensify the deep-seated differences between them, the British government took alarm. Louis Braun died in 1792 and a new agent of more exalted rank and functions, Lord Robert Stephen Fitzgerald, was dispatched to gain Swiss help. Pitt had now been converted to Cleghorn's ideas, but the favourable moment had already passed. No Swiss canton was willing to take part in the war against France. Fitzgerald's successor, William Wickham, though active and enterprising at his post until 1797, was as unable as his predecessors had been to make headway

---

[1] Ernest Giddey, 'J. F. Erskine et son Régiment Suisse' in *Schweizerische Zeitschrift für Geschichte* 4 (1954), 238–59.

against the traditional domination of France, now reinforced by the ideological influences exerted on Swiss democrats by the Revolution.[1] By 1792 it was already clear that the French revolutionaries would be a greater menace to the Helvetic body than Louis XIV had ever been.

With the actual outbreak of war the Berne legation became once again an invaluable observation post and source of information not only for France but for all the neighbouring states, although diplomatic relations were suspended from 1797 to 1814. British statesmen and diplomatic agents played in the early years of the war a much more active role in Switzerland than they had done since the end of the Spanish Succession war and the establishment of the Triple Alliance with France in 1717.

Though resident in Switzerland, Wickham's primary object was to send news of what was happening in France and comment upon it. But it was hoped that he would be able to make contact with the various groups which wished to overthrow the republic, mediate between them, and help them to create an organized opposition which might be strong enough to arrest or even reverse the revolutionary process.[2]

The French Revolution split Switzerland, already divided against itself by religion, into political parties. A few extremists, mostly in the west, were enthusiastic supporters of the Revolution and wished to ally themselves with France and extend its democratic doctrines into their own states, by force if necessary. The right-wing extremists, led by Nicolaus Friedrich von Steiger, chief magistrate of Berne, advocated the opposite policy of joining in the crusade against the Revolution, provided that the coalition would undertake to protect Switzerland against French attack. He was supported by the Roman Catholics and most of aristocratic Switzerland, although his policy ran counter to the strongest of Switzerland's political traditions—the maintenance of its neutrality. The middle party, led by Zürich and Basel and including most of eastern Switzerland, held firmly to the tradition of neutrality, which had served Switzerland well in the past and might be reckoned on to save her once again from the imminent dangers,

---

[1] Ernest Giddey, 'Quelques aspects des relations anglo-suisses à la fin du XVIIIᵉ-siècle' in *Zeitschrift für Schweizerische Geschichte* 29 (1949), 47–64: Ch-D. Bourcart, 'William Wickham, britischer Gesandter in der Schweiz' in *Basler Zeitschrift* 7 (1908), 1–18.

[2] Wickham's mission is also discussed above, chapter 3, pp. 73–4.

which would merely be intensified by participation on either side in the impending European crusade against France.

Under changed conditions, British diplomacy again had a political role to perform in Switzerland. The British ambassador Sir William Wickham negotiated, this time successfully, for Swiss mercenaries and started a propaganda campaign to induce the Swiss to break off relations with France. At the same time he kept in touch by secret-service agents with the French royalists and sought to organize and subsidize the Counter-Revolution within France. Not unnaturally the triumph of the revolutionaries in France and the advance of the revolutionary armies into Italy and Germany was followed by a formal demand for Wickham's expulsion from Swiss territory. His activities merely added a minor provocation to the determination of the French Directory and Napoleon to occupy Switzerland and make it in form what it already was in reality, a satellite of France.

From 1689 to 1774, with gaps totalling twenty-five years, Britain maintained diplomatic representation at Geneva as well as at Zürich or Berne. This was not an official tribute to the respect with which many British Protestants regarded the city of Calvin and the part that it had played in the Reformation. French in speech and habits, but linked by religion to the Swiss Protestants, though geographically isolated from them, its constant aim was to preserve its neutrality. Only thus could it hope to remain independent of its aggressive and powerful neighbours, France and Savoy.

Had Savoy followed a consistent policy of alignment with either France or Austria, Geneva would necessarily have depended on the support of the other. This resource was denied her by the notorious fluctuations in Savoyard policy between 1689 and the middle of the eighteenth century. Thus the situation of Geneva was always dangerous and became critical when France and Savoy took the same side in a general war. Her only hope of maintaining a shadow of independence lay in the backing of the Protestant Swiss cantons and their not entirely effective attempts to throw over the threatened city of Geneva the cloak of Swiss neutrality. They were hampered by the fact that the Catholic cantons would recognize no obligation towards Geneva.

A distant power such as Britain, even after its military reputation had been enhanced by Marlborough's successes on the Continent, could hardly expect to exert much influence in Geneva. The best that could be anticipated from the British point of view was that Geneva would continue to pursue a policy of wavering neutrality and of avoidance at almost any cost of a quarrel either with France or Savoy. The mere presence of William III's first diplomatic agent in the city was believed to endanger its position by causing annoyance to France. At Geneva, in distinction from Berne and Zürich, there was not even a limited prospect of rousing opposition to the dominant influence of France. In spite of this, Sir Luke Schaub succeeded in 1754 in arranging the treaty of Turin between Savoy-Sardinia and Geneva which gave some assurance that Genevan independence, such as it was, would be maintained and thus afforded a respite to the Genevan Protestants which in fact lasted for a quarter of a century. Successive British governments also took an interest in the Protestant Waldenses (Vaudois) who were under the rule of the house of Savoy. Cromwell and Milton had established a tradition and British ministers at Turin did their best to preserve the rights of this Protestant minority, though they were somewhat hampered by their primary duty at Turin, i.e. the advancement of British political and economic interests in Italy.[1]

The *raison d'être* of diplomatic representation at Geneva was the collection of news and, much more rarely, the dissemination of propaganda. For these purposes Geneva was almost ideal. It was a polyglot, international city, full of French and Italian refugees, many of whom maintained close connexions with their home country, as well as a natural centre of communications. The one restriction imposed was that the activities of the British agents must not afford provocation to France. Indeed, for this reason, few of them were formally recognized by the city of Geneva and under the laws of the city could not be given the outward distinctions allowed to foreign ministers. When the post was closed down in 1774, it was on the pretext that it was by no means consistent with the dignity of the king of Great Britain 'to keep a minister at Geneva or at any other state, who is not admitted to every honour and privilege to which he is justly entitled'.[2]

The limited recognition granted to British agents at Geneva was an additional reason for the ineffectiveness of their attempts— usually confined to periods of civil disturbance—to intervene in local politics. As a rule the British agents were instructed to support the aristocratic Establishment of Geneva and to damp down

---

[1] See chapter 12, p. 337.   [2] S.P. 96/52, dispatch of 22 April 1774.

democratic protests. One of the British agents, Colonel Pictet, was dismissed in 1767 because he openly took the Opposition side, associated with Jean-Jacques Rousseau, in Genevan party politics. Even the argument that the Opposition were opposed to France failed to move the secretary of state from support of the Genevan aristocrats.

While there was a regular succession of British diplomatic agents at Geneva as well as at Berne down to 1774, missions to the Grison leagues (*Graubünden*) were always *ad hoc*. There were only four of them in the period with which we are concerned. Two were designed to keep open communications between Italy and Austria during the Spanish Succession war and another with the same problem during the war of the Austrian Succession.

In each case Britain was the ally of Austria and as a Protestant power her intervention carried weight with the Grison leagues, which were somewhat suspicious of Austrian intentions in the Valtelline. A British guarantee of Austrian promises might make it easier for Austria to reach agreement with the leagues; but in practice it is clear that British intervention had little influence on the course of Austria's negotiations.

During the war of the Austrian Succession the position was rather different. This time Newcastle proposed to conclude an alliance with the Grisons, which would give Britain a corps of mercenary troops to be used in the war. But Austria made difficulties, better offers were received from other quarters and the Grisons finally proclaimed their neutrality. So long as the treaty of Aranjuez kept Italy at peace, Britain took no further interest in the Grison leagues. Forty years later, when a British diplomatist reappeared at Coire, he too was concerned almost exclusively with the strategic problems of a European war—this time the war against revolutionary France.

It is an indication of the comparative lack of interest in Swiss politics taken by the British government after 1714, that foreigners played a leading role in our diplomatic representation at all three missions. Of all the native British diplomatic agents in Switzerland only one, Abraham Stanyan, made a significant contribution to the cultural relations between the two countries. Until it was superseded in the 1780's by the work of Archdeacon William Coxe, Stanyan's *Account of Switzerland* was regarded as the standard guide to all aspects of Swiss life. Most British travellers to

Switzerland, and the number steadily increased during the century, slipped a copy of Stanyan's book into their baggage before setting out from London.

While the political connexions of Britain with Switzerland weakened during the eighteenth century, the cultural contacts between the two countries gained in strength. The works of Bishop Burnet and Abraham Stanyan laid a sound, but not uncritical, foundation for British appreciation of the merits of the Swiss way of life and a steady stream of British youths spent part of their Grand Tour amongst the Swiss. The story of William Tell was already well known in Britain where it was taken as a symbol of the age-long freedom and independence of the Swiss Confederation. In exchange Swiss scholars like Johannes von Müller and publicists like de Lolme were directly influenced by the works of David Hume, Adam Smith, and Adam Ferguson. Professor Bonjour goes so far as to say that the educated Swiss of the later eighteenth century took 'die britische Freiheit zum Idol'.[1]

The relations between Britain and Geneva were particularly close.[2] Several royal dukes, including Queen Victoria's father, stayed at Geneva during their travels on the Continent. The third Earl Stanhope founded in the city, where he resided from 1764 to 1774, a debating club which continued after his departure to conduct its debates in English. Many other visitors were of less exalted rank. Paul Priestley, son of the famous dissenting minister, and James Watt, son of the developer of the steam engine, were both sent to Geneva to 'perfect their French without risk to their Protestantism'. Prominent among the Genevan Anglophils were the two brothers du Luc. The elder brother, Jean-André, gave up a business and political career at Geneva, migrated to England and was appointed in 1774 reader to Queen Charlotte. The younger, Guillaume-Antoine, remained at Geneva; and his family continued to welcome English visitors to the city, including the illustrious family of Stanhope.

Earlier in the century most English visitors to Switzerland were young milords, usually accompanied by a tutor, and merely passed through the country on their travels between France and Italy.

---

[1] 'Johannes von Müllers Verhältnis zu England' in *Schweizerische Zeitschrift für Geschichte* 6 (1956), 289–314.

[2] See especially Claire Engel, 'Genève et l'Angleterre' in *Zeitschrift für Schweizerische Geschichte* 26 (1946), 479–504.

But with the change in the prevailing attitude to mountains, Switzerland began to attract admirers in its own right. Whereas Horace Walpole on the Grand Tour had been terrified by a simple crossing of the Alps, later travellers often came to revel in mountain scenery. More often they were attracted by a rudimentary acquaintance with the tradition of Swiss freedom. Others had a scientific bent and concerned themselves with such things as examining the glaciers and determining the height of hills by boiling water on the summits or experimenting with primitive aneroid barometers. The first ascent of Mont Blanc in 1786 is the great landmark here, although it was not until after the Napoleonic wars that the flood of British tourists, interested in climbing mountains, really began. Gibbon, who lived for fifteen years in Switzerland, was no Alpinist. Characteristically his incomplete sketch of Swiss history, which was not intended for publication, shows that he fully accepted the 'debunking' of the William Tell legend. He was lucky to escape marriage with the Swiss miss, Suzanne Churchod, later Madame Necker.

Though Swiss artists and architects found employment all over Europe, few of them, except Fuseli, found their way to Britain. De Lolme, himself active in Genevan local politics, wrote a celebrated work on the English constitution. The Swiss scientist, Jean André du Luc, stimulated certain lines of scientific inquiry in Britain, while the Basel mathematicians, the Bernoullis and Euler, had some influence upon English mathematics. Though Thomas Jefferson at the very end of the century spoke of the Academy of Geneva and the University of Edinburgh as 'the two eyes of Europe in respect of the exact sciences' there seems to have been little contact between the two institutions.

A. *Primary Sources*

Coxe, William, *Sketches of the natural, civil and political state of Swisserland* (1779)
— *Travels in Switzerland* (1789)
Stanyan, Abraham, *Account of Switzerland* (1714)

B. *Secondary Authorities*

Beer, G. R. de, *Travellers in Switzerland* (1949)
Bonjour, E., *Die Schweiz und England* (Berne, 1934)

Bonjour, E., 'Johannes von Müllers Verhältnis zur England' in *Schweizerische Zeitschrift für Geschichte* 6 (1956), 289–314

Bourcart, Ch.-D., 'William Wickham, britischer Gesandter in der Schweiz' in *Basler Zeitschrift* 7 (1908), 1–18

Chopard, A., *Die Mission des englischen Gesandten Philibert Herwarth in der Schweiz* (Berne, 1932)

Engel, Claire, 'Genève et l'Angleterre' in *Zeitschrift für Schweizerische Geschichte* 26 (1946), 479–504

Gagnebin, B., *Les Relations entre Genève et l'Angleterre* (Atlantis, Zürich, 1946)

Giddey, A., 'Quelques Aspects des Relations Anglo-Suisses à la fin du XVIIIe siècle' in *Zeitschrift für Schweizerische Geschichte* 29 (1949), 47–64

Kilchenmann, F., *Die Mission des englischen Gesandten Thomas Coxe in der Schweiz* (Zürich, 1914)

Massini, R., 'Der Vertrag von Turin (1754) zwischen dem Königreich Sardinien und der Republik Genf nach englischen Documenten' in *Basler Zeitschrift für Geschichte und Altertumskunde* 47 (1948), 85–104

Meier, M., *Die diplomatische Vertretung Englands in der Schweiz im 18 Jahrhundert* (Basel, 1952)

Robertson, L. A., 'The Relations of William III with the Swiss Protestants 1689–97' in *TRHS* 4th series, 12 (1929), 137–62

Rovillain, 'L'Angleterre et les troubles de Genève en 1766–67' in *Zeitschrift für Schweizerische Geschichte* 7 (1927), 164–207

Saussure, César de, *Lettres et voyages . . . en Angleterre 1725–9* (Lausanne, 1903)

Singer, G., *Die Bedeutung der Schweiz für England während der ersten Koalitionskriege* (Zürich, 1956)

Stelling-Michaud, S., *St.-Saphorin et la politique de la Suisse 1700–10* (Villette-les-Cully, 1935)

Zeerleder, A., 'Die politische und literarische Mission des englischen Gesandten Abraham Stanyan in der Schweiz' in *Berner Zeitschrift für Geschichte und Heimatkunde* (1942), 87–102

CHAPTER 12

Great Britain and the States of Italy

ONE of the most celebrated aphorisms attributed to Metternich about the time of the congress of Vienna was that Italy was not a political but merely a geographical expression. No one would deny that a hundred years earlier the peoples who occupied the Italian peninsula were cut off from other Romance peoples by the Mediterranean and separated from northern and eastern Europe by a mountain barrier, which was almost as difficult to cross in the days of Horace Walpole as in those of Hannibal. Isolation forced the states of Italy into much closer and more continuous cultural, political, and economic contacts with each other than was the norm in medieval Europe. It was not by accident that the idea of a political balance and the practice of regular diplomatic representation first emerged in fifteenth-century Italy and spread slowly to the rest of Europe during succeeding centuries.

If however we look more closely at the peninsula in early modern times, it soon becomes obvious that this geographical oneness is more apparent than real. The Italian peninsula divides itself into a number of regions which differ from each other as widely as they do from neighbouring countries across the Mediterranean or beyond the Alps. The Apennines were not much less of a natural barrier than the Alps: the desolate and sparsely populated uplands of Apulia contrasted with the rich valley of the Po and its flourishing cities.

Such concepts of Italian nationality as existed were confused and ineffective. They failed to draw together peoples of very mixed origins, varied historical development, and diverse political tradition and economic interests. At the most the upper classes in church and state continued to despise the barbarians from beyond the mountains; but it became more and more difficult to reconcile this inherited tradition with political and economic realities. In practice their first loyalty was always to their own state—recent attempts to push the Risorgimento back to the early eighteenth century fail to carry conviction. So far as the lower classes were concerned no Italian state recognized them as having political

327

rights. In the unlikely event of a Calabrian peasant meeting a farm labourer from the Po valley, they would have found it very difficult, if not entirely impossible, to converse intelligibly with each other, far less to reach agreement on the outstanding political issues of the day.

Even in the Middle Ages and early modern times the Mediterranean had linked Italy with other Mediterranean countries as well as dividing them. Arabs, Moors, and Turks had raided the mainland coasts of Italy and even established themselves in some of the islands. Aragonese and Provençals had waged war upon each other in Sicily. Ferdinand of Aragon and his general, Gonsalvo de Cordoba, had firmly established Spain in Naples as well as in Sicily where the house of Aragon had reigned since 1442. The Alps had not prevented the Holy Roman Emperors from waging wars in Italy and exercising well-founded claims, some of which were still politically important at the beginning of the eighteenth century, to feudal superiority over Italian provinces. Following in the footsteps of the medieval Emperors, but with all the resources of the first modern state behind them, the kings of France had ended Italian political isolation and brought Italian problems into the main stream of current international affairs during the sixteenth and seventeenth centuries.

Yet at the beginning of the eighteenth century Spain was still the dominant power in Italy. The Spanish Hapsburgs had used the toe-hold in the south, bequeathed to them by Ferdinand of Aragon, and the claims to feudal superiority over northern Italy, inherited by their Austrian cousins from the Holy Roman Emperors of the Middle Ages, to extend their territories from the south to the north of the peninsula. From 1535 they ruled the duchy of Milan, which not only enabled them to dominate the valley of the Po but gave them ready access to southern Germany where their Austrian cousins held sway. In view of the dominance of dynastic concepts at this time, the extent of foreign political control and the differences between the geographical regions which together made up modern Italy, it seems doubtful whether many contemporaries would have recognized the underlying geographical oneness of the peninsula.

There was certainly no close correspondence between political and geographical frontiers in the north. Savoy straddled the Alps, and, without abandoning its original French stamp, was already playing a significant role in Italian politics. Some of the Italian mountaineers who lived on the southern slopes of the Alps had linked their fortunes with those of the Swiss confederates, but because they controlled the passes between Italy and Germany could still play an important part in any Bourbon–Hapsburg war. Venice did not merely depend for its prosperity and prestige upon its international trade which had reached its highest point in the later Middle Ages. It had as an imperial power extended the territory under its control in north-eastern Italy to include much of the coast-line of the eastern Adriatic, with far-flung outposts in the Morea and the Greek islands of the Archipelago.

Much the most important influence exerted by Italy beyond its geographic frontiers was due to the supremacy of the Popes over the Catholic Church. The papal curia made and confirmed appointments, issued orders to secular rulers and decided disputes all over Europe. Even before the Reformation had set clear limits to the geographical area within which the papal curia could make its authority felt, secular sovereigns had succeeded to some extent in reducing the effective exercise of its authority within their dominions. Philip II of Spain, the eldest son of the Church, had been particularly successful in carrying out this line of policy within the Spanish empire. The Gallican tendencies of Louis XIV of France are even better known, if less consistently applied.

The Reformation limited the geographical area under the curia's jurisdiction, and the policy of secular rulers, intent on centralizing power in their own hands, diminished its actual control even in the reduced area which still acknowledged the authority of Rome. As a result of the Counter-Reformation the Roman Catholic Church was encouraged to develop its centralizing policies; but the more effective the authority of the Papacy the greater was the inducement to secular sovereigns of Roman Catholic countries to model their own administrations upon that of the Papacy and use such strengthened organizations to reduce, if not to exclude, papal authority within their dominions. In resisting such widespread tendencies one of the most effective papal weapons was the institution of new religious orders, above all the Society of Jesus, designed to bring all Christendom under the effective rule of the Papacy.

Medieval kings of England had followed, indeed occasionally led, their continental contemporaries in resistance to papal claims and a kind of *modus vivendi* had been reached in the fifteenth century. Not content with this, Henry VIII had broken the bonds of Rome, and his daughter, Elizabeth, had securely established a Protestant state-church in England. The echoes of this sixteenth-century controversy reverberated through the whole story of Britain's subsequent diplomatic relations with Italy. They have not yet completely died away.

The other major influence exerted by Italy beyond her own frontiers in early modern times was in the sphere of culture-contact. Concepts of the Renaissance change so rapidly and so violently that it is hard to generalize without arousing the ire of some specialist or other, but Italy was certainly the first European region to be seriously influenced by the new learning and the ideas about man and society which were its concomitant and fulfilment. The Renaissance was inevitably influenced by local conditions in the Italian peninsula; but many of its ideas and practices proved congenial in the north of Europe where painters, writers, and moralists had been slowly moving towards the new attitudes first fully developed in Italy.

France was the first of the northern countries to drink the heady draughts of Italian humanism. England soon followed the example of her rival: Scotland, partly owing to her traditional alliance with France, was not far behind. No British diplomatist's library was complete without a copy of Machiavelli's *Prince*. Aspiring country gentlemen in England studied the precepts of Castiglione's *Courtier* and tried to apply them in practice to the English way of life and political institutions. There may have been some justification for the sixteenth-century proverbial saying that an Englishman Italianate was the Devil incarnate; but from the sixteenth to the eighteenth centuries English gentlemen went to Italy for manners as well as to finish their education.

Though it is possible that the Italian Renaissance was most influential through translations, many Englishmen, and even Englishwomen, acquired a sound reading knowledge of Italian, if not a complete mastery of the language. At least until the heyday of Romanticism in the early nineteenth century, there were in Britain far more readers of Italian than of any other modern foreign language save French.

While Italian literature reached its peak and the language soon became merely one of the vigorously developing vernaculars spoken and written in western Europe, Italy long retained her artistic pre-eminence. This was partly owing to her possession of the material remains of Roman civilization, which made a particular appeal to scholars and gentlemen whose education was still dominated by the Greek and Roman classics. But it may be conjectured that Italian influence over the development of the arts in western Europe owed even more to the achievements of the artists who lived and worked in Italy in the sixteenth and seventeenth centuries. Not until well on in the eighteenth century could other national schools of painting, sculpture, and architecture hope to compete on level terms with the output of Italian studios and drawing offices. Long after Italian pre-eminence had actually become a thing of the past, the most successful and influential leaders of European intellectual and artistic movements in the eighteenth century drew much of their inspiration from the achievements of classical and Renaissance Italy.

Whereas the masterpieces of Italian literature could be studied at home and if necessary in translation, a personal visit to Italy was indispensable to gain acquaintance with the masterpieces of Italian art, whether they survived from classical times or were created by contemporaries. Even if reproductions and drawings would have been acceptable, there was nothing in the eighteenth century to take the place of Medici prints and Messrs. Thames and Hudson. This was not the only reason why the Grand Tour, usually heavily weighted towards Italy, came to be regarded as a normal stage in the education of English and Scottish gentlemen and the artists and architects whom they patronized; but it was certainly one of the important factors. Instead of visiting Italy as suitors to the papal curia or pilgrims to the shrines of Rome, Englishmen began to travel leisurely from one Italian capital to another, to visit the sights, to mix with native nobles, scholars, and artists and thus to acquire some superficial knowledge of Italian ways of life.[1]

As long as the Grand Tour survived, most Englishmen of the governing class had some knowledge of Italy. A few made friendships with like-minded Italians and continued to take an interest in the affairs of Rome, Florence, or Naples. Even if they failed to

---

[1] See A. Lytton Sells, *Paradise of Travellers, passim.* Chapters 2 and 3 of this work give an admirable account of British diplomatic contacts with Venice and other Italian courts in the first half of the seventeenth century.

make use of their opportunities and, as so many did, consorted solely with their fellow-countrymen, they could not avoid learning something about the material civilization which surrounded them and the forms of government which prevailed in the Italian states. Italian exports to Britain were not limited to works of scholarship, art, and antiquities. 'Italian gardens' became fashionable amongst the few who could afford the expense, while the earl of Rochford, returning from his mission to Turin, is supposed to have introduced into Britain the Lombardy poplar.

Some widening of their political as well as of their cultural horizons usually took place. It is hard to trace the practical influence of Anglo-Italian exchanges upon British policy towards the eighteenth-century states of Italy, but rather easier to observe the reverse action of British visitors upon Italian upper-class views of Britain as a liberal state from which useful political and social lessons could be learned. Even fragmentary knowledge and one-sided judgements offer a sounder basis for the conduct of foreign policy than the total ignorance and blind prejudice shown by most eighteenth-century Englishmen about, say, Russia or Spain.

It must however be admitted that the Grand Tour, in at least one respect, left the traveller as prejudiced as when he set out. The massive papal contribution to the wonders of the Renaissance entirely failed to remove Protestant antipathy to Rome. No British government of the eighteenth century could recognize officially the existence of the Papal states. It is true that the seventeenth century had witnessed a marked decline in the international position of the Popes: the peace treaties signed in 1648 at Westphalia were the last examples of successful papal mediation between warring Great Powers; and even in 1648 the part taken by the Papacy in the negotiation of the treaties was a comparatively minor one.

No longer could the Popes deceive themselves into thinking that they were *ex officio* arbiters of all international disputes. Still the Pope continued to be an important international figure with a large and well-organized diplomatic service, which some experts believe may have been the prototype of the diplomatic services of the national states of Europe. What made impossible English diplomatic contact with the Papacy after the Revolution of 1688 was the consistent support granted by successive Popes to the Jacobites. James III was unhesitatingly recognized by the Pope on the death of his father in 1701 as the legitimate king of Great Britain.

After the making of peace at Utrecht, and the grudging execution of the anti-Jacobite provisions of the treaty by the French government, the Jacobite court resided normally at Rome. While seeking help from any state which showed hostility to George I, the Jacobites' dependence upon the Papacy increased as time went on. The Pope used his influence with other Italian states to make difficulties for the house of Hanover. As other sources of supply dried up he contributed generously to Jacobite party funds. He helped to support missionaries to Ireland and the Scottish Highlands, who were as active in keeping alive the Jacobite embers in both countries as in educating the young, confirming old believers in their faith, and winning converts for the Roman Catholic church. James III had even to invoke the help of his papal protector to facilitate his marriage and to secure the continuance of his line.

In the hope of securing prompt and reliable intelligence from the enemy headquarters at Rome, George I employed Baron Philip von Stosch, a much-travelled antiquary and collector of medals and gems. Born in Brandenburg and educated partly in the Low Countries, Stosch soon settled in Rome under the protectorship of the powerful Albani family. From 1722 to 1731 Stosch, signing his reports 'John Walton', recorded in minute detail for the benefit of his employers the daily activities of the king over the water, his followers and his political associates attached to the papal curia. In 1731, after several incidents, Stosch either lost his nerve or was intimidated into leaving Rome by a Jacobite demonstration. Although he continued to send reports from Florence about what was happening at Rome until his death in 1757, his value as a spy soon became minimal.

In 1735 the appointment of a British consul in the Papal states to take Walton's place at Rome was rejected by the British government, which preferred to depend for information and, when required, active help for British subjects in Rome, upon Cardinal Alessandro Albani. The cardinal had close family ties with the exiled Stuarts as well as official contacts with both Austria and Sardinia, powers allied to the Hanoverian kings of England. As part of his duties as honorary British consul, Albani welcomed to Rome a stream of British collectors of antiques, artists, architects, &c.[1] Much of the information which he transmitted to London

[1] The two preceding paragraphs are based on my review in *English Historical*

passed through the hands of Horace Mann, the friend of Horace Walpole and British diplomatic representative at Florence. He continued to discharge his duties as what would now be called a double agent until well into the 1770's. He died in 1779.

The revival in 1772 of the British plan to send a consul to the Papal states may indicate a certain dissatisfaction with the service provided for so long by the ageing cardinal. By this time Jacobitism was dead and buried: its surviving standard-bearer became the protégé of George III. Even earlier the Pope had allowed the Hanoverian king of England's titles to be publicly displayed in Rome— for the first time since the Reformation, if Horace Mann is to be believed.[1] Sir William Hamilton took the risk of being received by the Pope in the course of his mission to Naples.

In the changed political atmosphere and with the slow growth of religious tolerance or indifference, the old projects of consular representation in the Papal states were revived in 1787,[2] 1789, and again in 1791, but without reaching fruition.[3] The idea of consular representation was presumably based not merely on the idea that the duties of any British agent in the Papal states would be largely concerned with commercial and social intercourse, but on the technicality that a consul could be appointed by a unilateral royal commission, whereas a diplomatic agent would need a credential letter from George III addressed to the Pope as the sovereign of these states. In the conditions prevailing in the second half of the eighteenth century contact at the higher diplomatic level was no longer needed and there was little inducement to run counter to Protestant and conservative feeling.

British contacts with the Papacy have been taken first, since the Papacy was *sui generis* amongst Italian sovereigns and English visitors usually exaggerated the influence of the Roman court on the other Italian states. The Stuart kings of England had probably been in closer contact with the lay rulers of Italy than with the

---

Review 78 (1963), 388–9, of Lesley Lewis, *Connoisseurs and Secret Agents in Eighteenth-Century Rome*, a book which gives an entertaining picture of the Roman scene.

[1] L. Lewis, *Connoisseurs and Secret Agents in Eighteenth-Century Rome*, p. 234.

[2] J. Ehrman, *British Government and Commercial Negotiations with Europe 1783–1793*, p. 1n.

[3] The preceding paragraphs are based mainly on Horn, *British Diplomatic Service*, p. 29.

German electors. This was not at first altered by the Revolution
of 1688. Italy as much as Germany was the battlefield upon which
Bourbon and Hapsburg fought for supremacy in Europe. The
more active foreign policy of William III and the reluctant participation of England in continental wars increased the *tempo* of English diplomacy in Italy as much as in Germany.

Down to the 1750's, from the political point of view at least,
Savoy-Sardinia was much the most important of the Italian states
to Britain. This was inevitable as long as Britain was the enemy of
France and the ally of Austria. Savoy's geographical position made
it either a bulwark of Italy against French penetration of the Lom-
bard plain or a French bridgehead for the subjection of northern
Italy. Moreover, with the acquisition of Sardinia and the status of
a kingdom, Piedmont became important and powerful enough to
play the risky role of buffer state between France and Austria.

British statesmen in the first half of the eighteenth century consistently encouraged Savoy. Bolingbroke meant to check Austrian
power in Italy by raising up Savoy and the addition of Sicily to
Savoy-Piedmont by the treaty of Utrecht was deliberately intended to make Britain a Mediterranean power. 'May I not add',
Bolingbroke continued, 'that there arises a prospect of changing
the scene of future wars, and removing them to a greater distance
from our Island, to a part of the world where we cannot well intervene, unless by our fleets, instead of running into the extravagant,
ruinous scheme of maintaining armies on the Continent?'[1] It was
at this time and for these purposes that Peterborough was given a
commission to all the princes and states of Italy. Savoy was as
important to Stanhope as she had been to Bolingbroke. His plan
to restore peace in the Mediterranean depended on the exchange
of Sicily, assigned to Savoy by the Utrecht settlement, for Sardinia, which Austria did not want. Even after this exchange had
been effected, the schemes of Elizabeth Farnese kept Italy in
uproar and forced the British government to take account of
Sardinian views in framing its Italian policies. The king of
Sardinia tried to use British support as a fulcrum which gave him
leverage in extracting territorial and other concessions from the
Hapsburgs.

Again in the 1730's Savoy was able to bring pressure on Britain
by threatening to join with France in an attack on Austria; and

[1] *Bolingbroke Corresp.* i. 583.

when Britain failed to secure adequate concessions from Austria to Savoy, Charles Emmanuel III did in fact fight on the French side in the war of the Polish Succession. In the next war the treaty of Worms by which Carteret secured Sardinian assistance for Maria Theresa (at a price) was hailed as his greatest triumph and did in fact contribute to the preservation of most of Austria's Italian lands. Soon afterwards, the end of active Bourbon–Hapsburg conflict in Italy by the treaty of Aranjuez cut the ground from under Sardinia's feet and greatly reduced, in Britain's eyes, her political value. Yet at the beginning of the Seven Years war Pitt wrote of the court of Turin 'from a situation and connection so essential to any plan that concerns Italy' and mentioned the king of Sardinia as 'a firm and affectionate ally' with a part to play in the future system of Europe.[1]

It should be noted that throughout the period Britain attached commercial value to her good relations with Sardinia. British naval vessels made some use of Villefranche, and Sardinia attempted to develop it as a free port. Particularly in the first three decades of the eighteenth century British diplomatists at the court of Savoy-Sardinia devoted much of their time to increasing direct British trade and especially exports of cloth to Piedmont. Peterborough with his usual lack of finesse stated bluntly that with 'a king of our own making' England was entitled to expect favourable treatment of her commerce. Chetwynd took the same line but less offensively: he was particularly attracted by the prospect of transferring to Britain much of the trade in manufactured goods which Piedmont conducted with France. He advocated a commercial treaty with the intention of facilitating this transfer. Another attraction was the prospect of securing directly from Piedmont supplies of raw silk. In the 1720's English cloth exports balanced raw silk imports.

Soon the king of Sardinia tried to develop the native woollen industry, especially as some of the leading nobles were anxious to raise the price of the wool produced on their estates by securing effective tariff protection for the home cloth industry. In 1731 the import of foreign cloth was prohibited. Nominally English manufactured cloth was excepted from this prohibition, but the heavy duties on imported English cloth reduced the value of this concession. Lord Essex, the British envoy to Turin, failed to persuade

[1] *Chatham Corresp.* i. 253–4.

the Sardinian government to reduce these duties. When Sardinia threw in her lot with France and Spain in the Polish Succession war the Sardinian frontiers were closed to British imports and some British merchants found themselves in difficulty.

Another, though much less important, source of conflict between Britain and her Italian protégé was due to differences of religion. Successive British envoys to Turin were instructed to look after the interests of the Vaudois Protestants who were included in the kingdom of Sardinia. Molesworth was particularly active in this matter and, owing to the bad relations between the Pope and the Sardinian king in the 1720's, had hopes of success which were not destined to be fulfilled. The settlement of 1725 which he had negotiated was soon more honoured in the breach than in the observance. Complaints started almost immediately both from the Vaudois and from the Protestant English merchants of Turin. Professor Venturi concluded that the results of British diplomacy at the court of Turin in this period were negative both in commercial development and Protestant protection.[1]

One thing that Sardinia really needed for commercial development was control of the port of Genoa. Britain in the 1740's was prepared to support Sardinian claims to Finale if not to Genoa itself, with the inevitable result that the Genoese were driven into the French camp, and the island of Corsica which was held by Genoa gradually passed under the control of France—a change which was completed in 1769 and was regarded by many contemporaries as an alteration of the Mediterranean balance of power which might well prove disastrous to Britain.

That Sardinia played a significant part in the preliminary peace negotiations at the end of the Seven Years war was due rather to the personal contacts between Sardinian diplomatic agents at London and Paris and British ministers, especially Newcastle, than to Sardinia's careful preservation of her neutrality during the war. As his enemies closed with his diminished armies, Frederick the Great planned to involve not only the Turks but the king of Sardinia in the war. He offered Charles Emmanuel the duchies of Milan, Parma, Piacenza, and Guastalla. The Sardinian king was much too wily to be tempted by such offers. Still less was he

---

[1] F. Venturi, 'Il Piemonte dei primi decenni del Settecento nelle Relazioni dei diplomatici inglesi' in *Bollettino Storico-Bibliografico Sub-Alpino* 54 (1956), 227–71.

attracted by British hints that he should join with the king of the Two Sicilies to seize a substantial part of the Papal states. Henceforth, it was suggested Sardinia would be the dominant power in northern Italy and the Bourbons would control the centre and south of the peninsula.

While Pitt was well aware of the rivalry between Sardinia and Naples and would do nothing to antagonize either, Frederick's desperation made him eager to extend the war to Italy and the only possible way of doing this was to bribe Sardinia to start a war there. As long as Austria and France had to detach troops from Germany to Italy, Frederick did not care whether Naples joined in the struggle or not: Pitt regarded good relations with the Two Sicilies as one of the bases of British power in the Mediterranean. He openly told the king of Sardinia that his ally's approaches were inopportune and untimely and thus confirmed Charles Emmanuel in his decision not to commit himself to Prussia.

That the rank of the British diplomatic agents accredited to Sardinia was higher in the second half of the eighteenth century than in the first does not indicate an increase in official business, but merely that a short residence at Turin had become not unattractive to peers and influential politicians of the calibre of James Stuart Mackenzie.[1] The Turin legation after 1763 showed the characteristic symptoms of frequent periods of non-residence and gaps between the appointments of heads of the mission.

The outbreak of the French Revolutionary wars ended the Bourbon–Hapsburg truce, which had kept Italy at peace for forty years and deprived Sardinia of much of her political importance in British eyes. Turin at once became one of the outlook points from which intelligence could be collected and the progress of the Revolution in France observed. Sardinia was inevitably drawn once again into the war between France and Austria and in 1793 became Britain's ally in the First Coalition. In exchange for an annual subsidy of £2,000,000, 20,000 Sardinian troops would serve against France. Some of them took part in the ill-fated attempt to hold Toulon against the Revolutionaries. The spread of Jacobinism in Piedmont and traditional and well-justified suspicion of the ultimate aims of Sardinia's Austrian ally soon ended her participation in the war; but Pitt and his successors followed

---

[1] The preceding paragraphs are quoted with minor changes from Horn, *British Diplomatic Service*, pp. 26–28.

a hundred years later the same policy towards Sardinia as Boling-broke and Stanhope. An independent and aggrandized Sardinia must be maintained as a barrier against French domination of Italy and as a restraint upon Austrian overlordship of the whole peninsula.

Judged by the test of continuous diplomatic representation, the only other Italian states in which Britain took an active interest during the whole of the eighteenth century were Venice and Tuscany. Venice was the only Italian town in which Britain consistently maintained both a diplomatic and a consular agent. This is perhaps less significant than it would appear at first sight, since the line drawn between diplomatic and consular functions was far from clear at the time. The British government, if there was no consul on the spot, had no hesitation in ordering its diplomatic agent to undertake duties which would normally have been discharged by consuls. On the other hand consuls were often appointed as *chargés d'affaires* and some of them, even without such formalities, felt quite competent to discharge the functions of a non-resident diplomatist.

So stringent were the limitations imposed by Venetian law and custom upon the normal functions of diplomatic agents that British representation there can hardly have been worth while. The more exalted the rank of the agent, the more stringent the restrictions. It was for this reason that Lord Holdernesse, originally sent as ambassador to Venice in 1744, was allowed to take formal leave of the republic in 1745 and try to secure the objects of his mission unhampered by the rigid restrictions on ambassadorial activities which Venice was supposed to have inherited from the Byzantine emperors. One of his predecessors had complained bitterly that almost his only contact with the Venetian nobles was through music. Any noble who showed a disposition to fraternize with a foreign diplomatist was at once ostracized by his fellows and might even suffer pecuniary fines or actual loss of privileges.

French influence was traditionally strong at Venice. Not until the treaty of Ryswick was being negotiated and Louis XIV was reluctantly recognizing William III as king of England were diplomatic relations, broken off by the Revolution of 1688, resumed. All attempts to secure help from Venice during the Italian campaigns of the Spanish Succession war failed. Holdernesse was no more successful in hiring Venetian troops in exchange for British subsidies during the Austrian Succession war. The republic of St. Mark continued to show that its sympathies lay not only with France but also with France's clients, the Jacobites. Diplomatic relations were broken off for this reason in 1737 and not resumed until 1744.

After 1714 Austria was the dominant power in Italy. She controlled the duchy of Milan to the west of Venice as well as the Alpine passes through which Austrian troops could enter Venetian territory from the north-east. Militarily impotent, Venice saw herself beset on both sides by Austria. Chronic suspicion of Austria's intentions confirmed her traditional tendencies towards France. As Turkish power declined and Venice lost her hold on the Levant the common danger which had made Austria and Venice uneasy allies against the Turks ceased to be effective. Austria and Venice openly became rivals for political and economic mastery of the eastern Adriatic coast and islands. The closer Britain's alliance with Austria the less likely Venice was to accept British offers of subsidy. In seeking to develop her Adriatic ports, Trieste and Fiume, Austria depended partly on British experts and offered terms so favourable for British imports that they aroused the antagonism of all the other Maritime Powers with interests in the Mediterranean. It was partly to compete with Austria that Venice became a free port in 1735.[1] Attempts during the Austrian Succession war to overcome or at least reduce economic conflicts between Britain and Venice failed owing to Venetian conservatism and the influence of French vested interests. Half a century before it happened Chesterfield had predicted the disappearance of the republic of St. Mark.

If Venice feared Britain's Austrian ally she despised and distrusted the upstart king of Sardinia. The fact that Sardinia was usually the protégé of the British government would in itself have been enough to make difficult and distant the relations between Britain and the Venetian republic. Carteret's obvious favouritism for Sardinia and the conclusion of the treaty of Worms evoked fears that sooner or later, with British backing, the king of Sardinia would become the master of Italy. Britain's patronage of the Barbary states, which preyed upon Venetian trade and occasion-

---

[1] A. Anderson, *An Historical and Chronological Deduction of the Origin of Commerce* (London, 1764), II, 355.

ally ravaged the coasts of the Adriatic, also caused offence at Venice.

No sooner had the final collapse of Jacobitism removed one stumbling block between Venice and Britain than the conclusion of the treaty of Aranjuez in 1752 ended for more than a generation the active intervention of Britain in the politics of Italy. The Bourbons and the Hapsburgs put Italy in cold storage and deliberately excluded, so far as they could, British influence from the peninsula. Venice, suffering from economic decline and political paralysis, asked for nothing better than immobility. The British diplomatists and consuls at Venice in the second half of the eighteenth century—above all Consul Smith—ceased to play a political role and busied themselves with other affairs. Lady Mary Wortley Montagu remarked of one of them that smuggling was his original profession. During their residence at Venice they collected pictures and books, smuggled antiques out of Italy in the diplomatic bag, and supplemented their incomes by dealing in *objets d'art*. The British Museum and the Royal Collection of pictures owe much to their leisure activities.

Whereas the outbreak of the French Revolutionary wars led to a renewal of political contact between Britain and several of the more important Italian states, notably Sardinia and the Two Sicilies, which became British allies against France, the republic of St. Mark was one of the first casualties of these wars. Caught between French revolutionary hostility on the one hand and long-matured Austrian projects of expansion on the other hand, the republic of a thousand years disappeared from the political map of Europe in 1797, exactly one hundred years after the renewal of diplomatic contacts between Britain and Venice. The record of diplomatic relations between the two states in the intervening century suggests that Britain had no particular reason to regret the end of the Venetian republic, although the dominant conservative and Romantic trends of the age led to some protests.

Early in the eighteenth century the British government had frequently entrusted to a single agent simultaneous missions to Florence and Genoa and at least once to Modena and Parma as well. When this arrangement ceased in 1722 no further diplomatic representatives were sent to Genoa, unless we include in the list three eccentric naval missions in the 1760's, which were much more concerned with the naval balance of power in the western

Mediterranean than with particular Genoese problems. After 1722 such business as Britain had with the Genoese republic was discharged by British consuls at Genoa or occasionally by extraordinary ambassadors sent to London from Genoa.

Since Genoa owed the original recognition of its international status to France, and had depended on Louis XIV's countenance and support against Imperial claims of suzerainty and Austrian hostility, Britain found it difficult to gain a foothold at Genoa. When Britain showed clearly her preference for Sardinia, the deadly rival of Genoa, all hope of good relations had to be abandoned. Carteret's treaty of Worms in 1743 led directly to Genoese participation against Britain's Sardinian and Austrian allies in the war of the Austrian Succession and ruined any chance there might otherwise have been of a successful allied invasion of southern France. French support of the Genoese in Corsica during the 1730's was followed in the 'sixties, and despite violent British paper protests, by French occupation of the island. As in the case of Venice, previously discussed, Britain's association with the Barbary states also militated against her diplomatic success at Genoa. Napoleon's setting up of the Ligurian republic as a French satellite was the natural outcome of a continuing process against which Britain had long struggled perfunctorily and in vain.

The closing down in 1722 of the legation at Genoa meant that Britain was to be represented continuously at only three Italian courts during the whole of the eighteenth century. Sardinia and Venice have been discussed earlier. The other Italian state was the grand duchy of Tuscany with its capital at Florence. When, after the Revolution of 1688, William III dispatched Sir Lambert Blackwell as his agent to the grand-duke, Blackwell was refused audience as envoy but allowed to reside at Leghorn as consul. As in the case of most other Italian states diplomatic relations with England were not restored until France had shown her willingness to recognize the new régime in England by the treaty of Ryswick.

Ruled at this time by the last and degenerate descendants in the male line of the once great house of Medici, Tuscany became by the third treaty of Vienna in 1738 a Hapsburg secundogeniture. But for nearly a generation the Tuscan inheritance had kept Europe in uproar and a succession of British agents at Florence had sought to give effect to the fluctuating policies of their government. Once Tuscany had succeeded in preserving its neutrality in the Italian campaigns of the Austrian Succession war, in spite of Horace Mann's attempt to direct British naval operations from his post at Florence, and Bourbon–Hapsburg conflicts in the peninsula had been reconciled by the treaty of Aranjuez, the political importance of Tuscany to Britain rapidly declined.

The British agent at Florence from 1738, the date of his appointment as chargé d'affaires, until his death in 1786 was Sir Horace Mann. Already 'well-known and esteemed to the [Tuscan] ministers' in 1738, Mann was appointed resident in 1740 and envoy extraordinary in 1765; and finally, owing to his friendship with Horace Walpole and not to the importance of the official business he had to transact at Florence, envoy extraordinary and minister plenipotentiary in 1782. According to Gibbon, Mann's 'most serious business was that of entertaining the English at his hospitable table'.

The Archduke Leopold succeeded his father, the Emperor Francis I, as ruler of Tuscany in 1765. Because he did not rush to impracticable extremes like his brother the Emperor Joseph II, the grand-duke's liberal administration made Tuscany a prosperous and contented state. No longer was Florence troubled by wars and rumours of wars. Leopold disbanded his army and sold his navy, consisting of two corvettes, to Russia.[1] Free trade, equality of taxation, judicial reforms all proved his enlightenment and added to the happiness of his subjects. In spite of the Bourbon–Hapsburg alliance French influence was less in Tuscany than in most other Italian states. Partly for this reason many English visitors, anticipating Victorian spinsters, lived in Florence for long periods. An English duke in the last days of the Medici had founded a Freemasons' Lodge at Florence and some intellectuals, notably the Della Cruscan poets, became members of the Tuscan academies and forged new literary links between Italy and England.

But the main factor in the friendly relationships between Tuscany and Britain in the second half of the eighteenth century was undoubtedly economic. The Medici grand-dukes, notably Ferdinand I, had created a city at Leghorn and endowed it with extensive and up-to-date port facilities. In contrast to his rivals elsewhere in the Mediterranean, Ferdinand I also offered the bait of complete religious toleration to any merchants who established themselves in the new town. Finally in 1593 he made Leghorn a free port.

[1] A. J. Whyte, *Evolution of Modern Italy*, p. 6.

Already endowed with a prosperous hinterland, it developed rapidly an extensive entrepôt trade. Goods sold at Leghorn by the trading nations of northern Europe were distributed not only to other ports in Italy but throughout the Mediterranean. At the same time much of the valued produce of the Levant and Middle East was channelled through Leghorn to its destinations in the western Mediterranean and beyond the Straits of Gibraltar.

The rise of Leghorn damaged the position of Marseilles and also contributed to the decline of Genoa and Venice, both of which were allied to France and consistently put obstacles in the way of expanding English trade in the Mediterranean. The facilities offered by Leghorn on the other hand enabled English textiles to compete successfully with the old-fashioned products of Venice and Lombardy and even to undercut the looms of Tuscany itself. As well as textiles England imported at Leghorn tin, lead, salt fish, and some colonial produce. When English war-ships began to appear in the Mediterranean they found at Leghorn a ready source of essential supplies.

The English were only one of many nationalities which frequented the port to their mutual advantage; but the English factory was certainly one of the largest and best organized national communities. In the seventeenth century the Dutch had been almost as prominent as the English and both competed with traders from Hamburg and the Baltic countries. Italian merchants came to make their purchases and sell their wares in a flourishing international market, well equipped with international credit and exchange facilities.

These were the speciality of the prosperous Jewish colony, mostly by origin refugees from Spain and Portugal. The Jews also largely controlled the extensive trade between Leghorn and the Barbary states and were always ready to negotiate for the ransom of Christian captives in the hands of the Moors. Merchants from the east as well as from the west found it worth their while to settle at the port—Levantine Greeks and Armenians, even the occasional Persian and Indian merchant, were to be seen in the streets of Leghorn.

In the eighteenth century much of the increasing trade between Britain and the Mediterranean was conducted through Leghorn. Indeed the Levant Company, privileged and conservative, complained bitterly that they were being ruined by the facilities available at Leghorn for selling and trans-shipping exports to and imports from the Levant. What the Levant Company lost other English merchants seem to have gained. According to official figures Italy in 1784 was the sixth and, eight years later, the fifth largest customer in Europe for British exports. When British imports from Italy are examined for the years from 1783 to 1792 they too rose markedly. By 1791 both exports and imports exceeded £1,000,000 in value. Italy by this time was second only to Russia as a source of British imports.[1] In time of war the loss of Minorca in 1782 made Leghorn even more useful than before as a source of supplies for British squadrons in the Mediterranean.

When the French Revolutionary wars broke out Tuscany tried to preserve its neutrality. Lord Hervey, the British envoy at Florence, in a well-intentioned attempt to preserve the use of Leghorn for his country's war-ships, tried to break off diplomatic relations between the grand-duke and the French revolutionary government. He was dismissed by his own government for his excess of zeal; but his successor, Wyndham, was no more successful. Threatened by French occupation in 1796, the British factory put to sea with the archives of the Tuscan legation, their own families, servants, and movable property, and accompanied by a number of *émigrés* and a large supply of fresh meat for victualling the British Mediterranean fleet. They found a temporary refuge in Elba until the withdrawal of French troops from Tuscany in 1797 enabled the British merchants to return to Leghorn and the envoy to resume his operations at Florence.

Tuscan neutrality was soon compromised by a Neapolitan army which landed at Leghorn as part of an allied operation against France. In 1799 French troops again occupied the grand-duchy. The grand-duke took refuge in Vienna and the attempts of Wyndham to organize Tuscan resistance to France in opposition to the wishes of the grand-duke speedily collapsed. Napoleon's victories over Austria at Marengo and Hohenlinden left Tuscany, indeed all Italy, defenceless at his feet.

It remains to say something of Naples and Sicily. They had formed part of the Spanish empire in the seventeenth century, although they had enjoyed a certain amount of self-government under Spanish viceroys. The Utrecht settlement of the problem of

[1] J. Ehrman, op. cit., 203–4 and Appendix 2. Separate figures are not available for Leghorn but much of the increase must have been with this port.

the succession to Charles II of Spain had awarded Naples (and Sardinia) to Austria and Sicily to the house of Savoy. Philip V, the new king of Spain, firmly refused to accept these arrangements and tried by force to recover both Sardinia and Sicily for Spain. The destruction of the Spanish fleet at Cape Passaro by a British squadron put paid to Philip V's hopes of overthrowing this part of the Utrecht settlement; but Spain's intractability made it essential for Britain to conciliate the Emperor Charles VI at the expense of the house of Savoy. Naples and Sicily were reunited under the Austrian Hapsburgs, while Savoy had to give up Sicily and accept the much inferior prize of Sardinia.

Unable to resist a combined attack by France, Spain, and Sardinia upon his Italian territories, Charles VI had to purchase peace at the end of the war of the Polish Succession by the surrender of his kingdom of the Two Sicilies to the elder son of Philip V and Elizabeth Farnese, Don Carlos. As long as the Two Sicilies had been ruled in turn by Spain, Savoy, and Austria, there was no need for British diplomatic representation at Naples. A good deal of trade was however being conducted with the kingdom of the Two Sicilies and a succession of British consuls, with vice-consuls under them at other ports, resided at Naples.

When it became apparent that the Bourbon kingdom of the Two Sicilies was likely to maintain its independent existence, Britain established a legation at Naples in 1753. From 1764 to 1800 this was tenanted by Sir William Hamilton, a member of the ducal family of that name and the complaisant husband of the celebrated Emma. 'Poor dear Emma,' he was once heard to remark, 'she has so much taste and all of it bad.' Hamilton devoted himself mainly to the study of the local antiquities, the collection of coins and medals, and the publication of works on volcanic erruptions and other natural phenomena. When there was not much official business to report from Naples, he filled his despatches to the secretaries of state with disquisitions upon natural philosophy and classical antiquities. Even so, according to Gibbon, he corresponded more with the Royal Society than with the king's ministers. He was tolerant not only towards his wife but towards the Pope and, while on a private visit to Rome, risked being received by His Holiness.

The commercial treaty of 1667 between England and Spain had given to English merchants most-favoured-nation privileges in the Two Sicilies as well as in Spain itself. As early as 1675 the English consul at Naples informed his government that English ships had the lion's share of Neapolitan trade. They purchased substantial supplies of oil, mostly used in the woollen industry, and raw silk, wine, and materials used in soap manufacture, and since their exports of textiles and salt fish to Naples were insufficient, made up the balance by payments in cash or bills of exchange. Their main rivals were the Genoese who distributed oil and corn from the Two Sicilies to other Mediterranean ports. With the transfer of the Two Sicilies to the house of Bourbon attempts were naturally made to expand trade between Naples and France.

The Bourbon kings, though hesitant to denounce the treaty of 1667 on which English trade was founded, took administrative action to make English privileges less advantageous in practice and there was a good deal of bickering in the second half of the eighteenth century. This was accentuated by the programme of industrial development, which the Bourbon kings adopted for their new kingdom in accordance with current ideas of enlightened despotism. There was some decline in local demand for British manufactures, but this seems to have been surmounted by price-cutting. Naples continued to be one of Britain's commercial strongholds in the Mediterranean until the Napoleonic wars.

There were however obvious weaknesses in the British trading position in the Two Sicilies in the later eighteenth century. Practically no British merchants or factors resided at Naples and there was no British factory there. Goods were shipped from England and sold on commission by local merchants while return cargoes were purchased by the supercargoes, no doubt with some local help. British ships had no share in the coasting trade of the Two Sicilies. If we can believe their French rivals, British ships scandalously abused their trading privileges and not only by clandestine smuggling. Prohibited imports were sold on board English ships in the harbour of Naples, printed circulars were distributed to all and sundry, while local boatmen plied a brisk trade between the English vessel and the shore. Finally whenever Britain became involved in war there was a steep drop in her trade with all Mediterranean ports, although during the war of American Independence British trade with Naples continued to be carried on in neutral shipping.

After the war the new cotton manufactures of Lancashire found

a ready sale at Naples. More important at the time, the loss of
Minorca increased the usefulness of Naples as a source of supplies
for British war-ships and an alternative entrepôt and quarantine
station to Leghorn for trade with the central and eastern areas of
the Mediterranean. Negotiations began in 1786 for a commercial
treaty between Britain and Naples, designed mainly to open the
Neapolitan and Sicilian markets even more effectually to British
manufactures and to enable the Two Sicilies to compete more
easily with Spain in producing raw materials used for industrial
processes in Britain, especially oil, raw silk, and ingredients required in the production of soap. It would appear that the main
reason for the failure of this promising and mutually advantageous
project was the dilatoriness of the Foreign Office, which spun out
negotiations until the attention of the Bourbon king and his
advisers was concentrated upon the political problems which followed upon the outbreak of the French Revolution.[1]

To these we must now turn to show their effect upon the
relations between Britain and the Two Sicilies. Ferdinand IV
had married a daughter of Maria Theresa and the fall of the
French Bourbons markedly increased Austrian influence. The
chief minister of Ferdinand and his wife was General Acton,
English by birth and well disposed to his ancestral country. On
the other hand the kingdom of Naples was already honeycombed
by subversive elements in sympathy with the French Revolution.

A French fleet threatened to bombard Naples in 1792, forced
Ferdinand to proclaim his neutrality, and encouraged the populace
of Naples to organize themselves in Jacobin clubs. Ferdinand soon
broke his promise, made an example of some of his opponents and
in 1798 marched on Rome as the self-appointed leader of a monarchical crusade against the French Revolution. Soon he was a
refugee in Sicily and Naples became the Parthenopean republic
under French control; but the overthrow of French rule in
northern Italy by the Austrians and Russians in 1799 enabled
Ferdinand and his queen, Maria Caroline, to overthrow the republic, execute, exile, and imprison hundreds of its leaders, and
establish, with some help from the English admiral, Nelson, a
royalist reign of terror.

---

[1] The preceding paragraphs are based on R. Romano, *Le Commerce du
Royaume de Naples avec la France*, and so far as the commercial negotiations are
concerned on J. Ehrman, op. cit.

Not until 1806 did Napoleon overthrow Ferdinand and set up his own brother Joseph as king in Naples. Ferdinand retired once again to Sicily, where he was protected by British sea-power until the downfall of Napoleon and the favour of Metternich allowed him to recover his mainland possessions and resume his reactionary rule over both the Sicilies. It was a successful rising against the restored monarch in 1820 that provided the occasion for Castlereagh's classic statement of the principle of British non-intervention in continental politics. The conduct of Ferdinand's heirs converted Gladstone, the greatest non-interventionist of them all, to a policy which took account of political realities in Italy and contributed essentially to the ultimate unification of the whole peninsula.

One result of the French Revolution was therefore a marked revival of British interest in the politics of Italy. From the middle years of the eighteenth century to 1793 Britain had been more concerned with Italy as a market for her manufactures and a source of raw material for her industries than as an element in the European balance of power. British consulates[1] greatly outnumbered legations in Italy. Whereas in eighteenth-century Germany there was a considerable strengthening of the British diplomatic network, the only new diplomatic post to be created in Italy was at Naples. The mission which had existed at Genoa in the early years of the century was closed down in 1722 and no ministers were sent to Parma after 1731.

So far as the stream of English milords was concerned an English consul was not much less serviceable than a resident. It was not always certain that a resident would belong to a higher social class than a consul and some consuls were much more prosperous than the lower ranks in the diplomatic service. Consul Dick lived at Leghorn, as one of his visitors put it, 'with the splendour of a minister'. Since consuls rarely left their posts and diplomatists in the second half of the century showed a tendency to non-residence, or at least to protract their absences on leave, the amount of official work undertaken by the consuls increased. When under George III the government showed a periodic interest in trade statistics, the consuls responded much more readily to its exhortations than most of the diplomatic agents in Italy.

[1] Mention should perhaps be made here of the rather anomalous consulate in Malta, through which intermittent relations with the Knights of St. John were maintained (M. S. Anderson, in *Mariner's Mirror* of May 1954).

This was natural since most British consuls were themselves engaged in trade and others had had a mercantile training. These connexions made them better purchasing agents of wine, modern works of art, or even antiques. They were much better acquainted with customs regulations and more experienced in evading them. As the stream of genuine milords became progressively adulterated by writers, artists, architects, and professional purchasing agents, they preferred to do business with the consuls rather than with a diplomatist who grudged having them at his table and suspected that their activities might involve him in trouble with the government to which he was accredited.

Whereas in Germany many Britons in the first half of the eighteenth century would have welcomed an increase in the Imperial authority because they saw in this the only hope of re-establishing an effective counterpoise to French domination of Europe, hardly any British voices were raised during the eighteenth century in favour of the unification or consolidation of Italy. Leaving out of account the eccentric earl of Peterborough, one of the few exceptions was Dr. Henry Newton, envoy to Genoa and Tuscany from 1706 to 1711, who sent to the secretary of state a project for forming a league of Italian princes to liberate Italy. The contrast in British attitudes can be readily explained. While the final emancipation of the German electors from the Imperial authority was sufficiently recent to be remembered in England in the latter years of the seventeenth century, Italy had for centuries already been divided into *de facto* sovereign states. So far from being a single unit in international relations, Italy had exported in the fifteenth century from its own local politics the conception of a balance of power which could be and was internationally applied.

Patriotic attempts by some Italian historians to trace the basic ideas of the Risorgimento back to the early eighteenth century find no echo in contemporary eighteenth-century British views on Italy. Even Newton considered the 'sacred egoism' of the princes of Savoy and the suspicion and aversion with which that house was regarded in Italy as a basic difficulty which stood in the way of creating an Italy free from the domination of Bourbons and Hapsburgs and therefore a suitable ally for his own country. Palmerston would not have disapproved of Newton's ideas.

A. *Primary Sources*

Blackley, Rev. W. (ed.), *Diplomatic Correspondence of Rt. Hon. Richard Hill* (1845)

Cole, Christian, *Historical and Political Memoirs* (1735)

Manchester, duke of (ed.), *Court and Society from Elizabeth to Anne* (1864)

Walpole Horace, *Correspondence with Sir Horace Mann*, ed. W. S. Lewis and others, vols. 1–6 (1955–60)

B. *Secondary Authorities*

Baudi de Vesme, C., *La Politica Mediterranea Inglese nelle relazioni degli inviati italiani a Londra 1741–48* (Turin, 1952)

Contessa, C., 'Aspirazioni commerciali intrecciate ad alleanze politiche della Casa di Savoia coll' Inghilterra' in *Memorie dell' Accademia delle Scienze di Torino* 2nd series, 64 (1913–14), No. 3

Fieldhouse, H. N., 'St. John and Savoy in the War of the Spanish Succession' in *EHR* 50 (1935), 278–84

Gutteridge, H. C. (ed.), *Nelson and the Neapolitan Jacobins* (1903)

Hale, J. R., *England and the Italian Renaissance* (1954)

Jollivet, M., *Les Anglais dans la Mediterranée: un royaume anglo-corse 1794–97* (Paris, 1896)

Jones, G. H., 'English diplomacy and Italian silk in the time of Lombe' in *BIHR* 34 (1961), 184–91

Lewis, Lesley, *Connoisseurs and Secret Agents in Eighteenth-Century Rome* (1961)

Marini, R. A., 'La politica Sabauda alla Corte inglese dopo il trattato di Annover' in *Rassegna Storica del risorgimento italiano* (1948), fasc. I

Martin, Abbé J., 'Les Stuarts et le Saint-Siège' in *RHD* 26 (1912), 446–71

Prato, 'L'espansione commerciale inglese nel primo Settecento' in *Miscellanea in onore di A. Mammo* (Turin, 1912)

Quazza, G., *Il problema italiano e l'equilibrio Europeo 1720–38* (Turin, 1965)

Sclopis, F., *Delle relazioni politiche tra dinastia di Savoia ed il governo britannico* [1240–1815, but devoted almost entirely to 18th century] (Turin, 1853)

Scrosoppi, P., 'Il porto di Livorno egli inizi della attività inglese nel Mediterraneo' in *Bollettino storico Livornese* 1 (1937)

Venturi, F., 'Il Piemonte dei primi decenni del Settecento nelle relazioni dei diplomatici inglesi' in *Bollettino Storico-Bibliographico Subalpino* 54 (1956), 227–71

Viora, M., 'Notizie e documenti sugli interventi diplomatici dell' Inghilterra in favore dei Valdese durante il regno di Vittorio Amedeo II' in *Studi Urbinati* (1928)

Wyndham, H. A., *A Family History* (1950) [W. F. Wyndham's mission to Tuscany 1794–1807], pp. 261–80

CHAPTER 13

Great Britain, Turkey, and the Eastern Question

IN any discussion of Britain's relations with Europe in the nineteenth century, it would be impossible to treat Russia and Turkey separately. In so far as Palmerston and other directors of British foreign policy can be described as Turcophils, this was a consequence of their Russophobia. Their attitude to Russia conditioned, if it did not entirely determine, their approach to all the emergent problems of the Near East. Even Palmerston, usually regarded as a foreign minister who wished to export to the Continent the blessings of the British constitution, preferred to retain in Turkey the autocracy of the Sultan, since he believed that any approach to a parliamentary system would weaken Turkish resistance to Russia and thus imperil the vital interests of Britain in the Near East.

It is true that the beginning of this attitude can be traced back into the eighteenth century, even occasionally into the early part of that century. When Peter the Great and George I were intent on pursuing a personal vendetta during the Great Northern war, Britain did everything in her power to make use of the Turks to annoy Russia and distract her attention from the Baltic. Later in the eighteenth century, when Britain was anxious to conclude a political alliance with Russia, the most constant, if not the most important obstacle to co-operation between Britain and Russia was Russia's insistence that Britain must commit herself to Russia's hostility to Turkey.

But, at least down to the middle of the century, the British government usually treated with Russia and Turkey not as factors in an eastern question, but as unrelated states operating in watertight compartments. It was indeed encouraged to do so by the fact that geographically Russia was 'tail-end Charlie' in the northern province, while Turkey occupied the same position in the southern province. Distance, with consequent divergence of interest and outlook, and the material difficulties of communication and co-operation, made the political contacts of Britain with both slight and unimportant, except at times of crisis. Largely owing to the German interests of George I, Russia's importance was however realized in London long before Turkey's became manifest.

Until the importance of Russia came to be appreciated, albeit imperfectly, by British statesmen in the course of the Northern war, there was a curious parallelism between Britain's relations with both countries. Britain regarded the Tsar and the Sultan as non-European potentates ruling over realms where political and social conditions made the 'factory system' of trading, and consequently the establishment of a monopolistic company, essential. In each case Britain was the active, Russia and Turkey the inactive or passive partners. All that the British government wanted was trading privileges: any attempt of the Tsar or the Sultan to conclude a political alliance was rejected or politely evaded. Elizabeth may generously have offered Tsar Ivan the Terrible a refuge in England if driven out of Russia by his outraged subjects, and she certainly represented herself at Constantinople as the enemy of the Sultan's enemy, Philip of Spain; but of actual political co-operation, there was none.

The early ambassadors to Turkey were themselves merchants and were paid by the Levant Company. Their main preoccupation was to secure from successive sultans a grant of privileges essential for carrying on English trade in competition with the older and more securely established colonies of French and Venetian merchants. The opening of direct trade to India by the Cape route and increasing competition from Dutch merchants did not prevent the Levant company from prospering in the first half of the seventeenth century.

Mercantilist theorists approved of its trade since it exported large quantities of cloth and colonial produce to the Mediterranean and, unlike the East India Company, made comparatively small demands upon scanty English stocks of bullion. Another reason for favouring the Levant Company was exactly parallel to one of the arguments used by supporters of the Muscovy Company. Since Turkey and Russia controlled alternative overland routes to Persia and India, it was constantly hoped that the companies concerned would be able to open up direct trade with the Middle East and thus secure a more ample supply of raw silk without paying either to Russia or Turkey the customary middleman's profits. Though the Sultan and the Tsar could hardly be expected to view this development with favour, failure of spasmodic and recurrent attempts by British adventurers must be attributed more to local difficulties and cost of transport overland than to the opposition of the Russian and Turkish governments.

Just as the Civil wars and disturbances of the Commonwealth period had completely destroyed the prosperity of the Muscovy Company in Russia, so did they, but for different reasons, damage the position of the Levant Company in Turkey and the Mediterranean. The Turkey merchants found it difficult to secure cloth for export and the Barbary corsairs preyed upon their ships, since the English navy was too much preoccupied to afford adequate defence in the Mediterranean. The French and Dutch exploited the opportunity to oust the English altogether from the Levant trade. After Cromwell had made an alliance with France, Spain also fitted out privateers and attacked the English convoys as they sought to enter and navigate the Mediterranean. Still worse was the relaxation of control by the Company over its agents and factors and intestine strife between consuls and factories. An ambassador appointed by the king refused to yield his position to an agent sent out by Cromwell. So great were the difficulties that the Company seriously considered the abandonment of its trade with the Levant and the surrender of all its privileges.

Helped by a new charter of 1661 from Charles II, which remained in force until the company was dissolved in 1825, and by the fair treatment given by the able and enlightened grand vizier, Fazil Ahmed Köprülü, to all foreign merchants, English trade revived. Venice had now fallen upon evil days and the Dutch were unable to supply the large amount of cloth exported annually from England. The French however continued to be dangerous competitors, especially after the mercantilist reforms successfully enforced by Colbert and the organization of an efficient consular service in the Levant under the control of the minister for the Marine. By the 1680's France could export cloth, which may have been less durable but looked at least as good as English cloth, in quantities adequate to meet Turkish demands. Heavily subsidized by the state, and exported only from Marseilles under the inspection of the intendant of Provence in ships especially built for the Levant trade with government subsidies, French cloth steadily undermined the sale of the basic English export to the Levant.

Almost as serious was the competition of the English East India Company, which under Crown patronage used the Cape route to bring silks to England more cheaply than the Turkey Company could buy and import them from the Levant. Worst of all, the grand vizier, Kara Mustapha (1676–83) forced the English merchants to contribute large sums to the Sultan's coffers in preparation for his attack upon Austria and the famous siege of Vienna in 1683. Since France alone of the European powers took the side of Turkey in this war, while England and Holland hailed the relief of Vienna with joyful demonstrations, the Turks had strong political reasons for favouring France at the expense of English and Dutch merchants. Successive French ambassadors to the Porte exploited this argument to the full.

The decline of English cloth exports had commenced before the Revolution of 1688: it was consummated by the outbreak of the war of the English Succession. With a French navy at large in the Channel and French privateers scouring the high seas, no English vessel could hope even to reach the Mediterranean except under convoy. At first the Admiralty was too busy fighting the French to think of protecting commerce. When it did attempt to do so in 1693 a gigantic convoy of over 400 English and Dutch vessels was intercepted, scattered, captured, sunk, or otherwise destroyed by a French fleet in the bay of Lagos. With the decline of French naval power, and the temporary ascendancy of Britain in the western Mediterranean in 1694–6, some British ships got through to the Levant but losses from privateers remained heavy.

Since Britain and the Dutch were now the principal allies of the Emperor, the arch-enemy of the Sultan, against France, French political influence was completely in the ascendant at Constantinople. Sir William Trumbull, the English ambassador, complained that his countrymen were 'looked upon almost as enemies, so all advantages are improved against us by the French ambassador'.[1] In particular, exercise by English ships of 'belligerent rights', such as attempts to prevent French ships entering Turkish ports, or the actual seizure of Turkish goods found on board a French vessel, evoked protests from the Turks whereas similar actions by the French were allowed to pass unremarked by Turkish officials.

Competition between the Turkey and East India Companies had been continuous since their foundation. The Turkey merchants

---

[1] Quoted by A. C. Wood, *History of the Levant Company*, p. 109. My indebtedness to this standard work will be visible to the informed reader of this chapter.

urged that their trade deserved support because they exported large quantities of cloth, whereas the East India Company could only stay in business by draining England of precious bullion. Partly as a result of this dispute, the government inserted a clause in the East India Company's charters that they must export woollen goods equal to one-tenth in value of their exports. By selling this compulsory export in Persia in exchange for silk, the East India Company neatly turned the tables on their critics. The Turkey Company lost a good market for its cloth and a means of securing adequate supplies of silk for import to England even if their prices could hardly be competitive with those of the rival company. The importance of wool and silk in English trade with Turkey is shown by official figures at the end of the seventeenth century. In 1697–8, for example, out of £172,000 exports cloth accounted for £144,000; and in the same year imports of silk amounted to £86,000 out of £162,000 total imports.[1]

In the end it was French competition which proved most disastrous to the Turkish merchants. During the war, French trade with the Ottoman empire advanced by leaps and bounds. It developed even further in the years of peace between 1697 and 1702, although English trade revived once the war was over. In the next war—that of the Spanish Succession—English naval supremacy was so manifest, not only in the Channel and the Bay of Biscay but also in the Mediterranean, that it was French trade with Turkey which suffered much more severely than British.

The years following the peace of Utrecht witnessed the triumph of France over Britain in the Levant trade. French cloth was thinner and lighter and therefore more suited to the local climate. It was dyed in bright colours, which suited the tastes of oriental customers. Natural and artificial advantages combined to enable French merchants to sell this attractive commodity at a price at which their English rivals could not profitably compete. Much English cloth lay unsold in the factories, but the British government refused to subsidize exports in order to lower prices.

In 1740 the French government, as a reward for mediating peace between Turkey and her Austro-Russian enemies, was granted a new set of capitulations, which exempted French imports from the *Misteria* duty and thus gave French cloth tariff reductions which were not extended to British imports until more than forty years

[2] Quoted in A. C. Wood, op. cit., p. 120.

later. French commercial ascendancy in the Levant remained un-
challengeable until almost the end of the eighteenth century. In
1789 France had three-fifths and Britain only one-fifth of the total
European trade with Turkey.[1]

Although French ascendancy, like that of Britain in the previous
century, was based on cloth exports, it was buttressed by trade in
other commodities. The capitulations of 1740 allowed French colonial products, notably coffee, indigo, and sugar, to enter the Ottoman empire at competitive prices. A gap in the defensive mecha-
nism of the British Navigation Acts enabled French and Dutch
merchants at the free port of Leghorn to buy English exports and
use them in trade with the Levant: at the same time they brought
back silks, cottons, drugs, and dyes from the Levant and sold them
to Italian merchants at Leghorn for export to Britain. It is significant that goods from the Levant imported into England via Leghorn by the French and Dutch rivals of the Levant Company could
be sold in England at lower prices than the same goods imported
directly from the Levant by the Company.

Critics of the Company throughout the eighteenth century, including Adam Smith, asserted that the decline of British trade with
the Levant was due more to the various restrictive practices of the
Turkey Company than to foreign competition.[2] The inner ring of
London merchants who controlled the Company's affairs deliberately made regulations to hamper the out-ports and make difficult
profitable participation in the Turkey trade by less specialized
merchants. They preferred to make large profits by maintaining
prices on a limited exchange of commodities conducted in accordance with an established routine rather than to scramble for profits
with energetic and enterprising competitors intent on expanding
trade by competitive prices and lower percentage profits. Though
the Company succeeded in maintaining its nominal monopoly
against British interlopers, it is not surprising that it steadily lost
ground to foreign competitors. The French and Dutch made use
of Leghorn to undermine effectively the Company's monopoly of
Turkish trade with Britain.[3] By this time also much of the coasting

---

[1] Quoted by P. Masson, *Histoire du Commerce français dans le Levant*,
pp. 412–16, 476–8.

[2] The arguments used by the Company and its critics are conveniently summarized in A. Anderson, *An Historical and Chronological Deduction of the Origin
of Commerce* (London, 1764), II, 373–4.

[3] See above, chapter 12, pp. 344–5.

trade of the Levant, which had been almost monopolized by Venice in the seventeenth century, had fallen into French hands.

The wars of the middle-eighteenth century between 1739 and 1763 temporarily damaged British trade, but once British naval ascendancy in the Mediterranean was restored, France lost much more than Britain because she had so much more to lose. She cut her losses by admitting neutrals to take part in trade between Marseilles and the Levant. When British privateers seized these vessels and refused to recognize the usual argument of the neutral that his ships and goods were immune from seizure under international law, conflict with the Turkish authorities inevitably followed. The American war of Independence, when the British fleet had to be withdrawn from the Mediterranean and Gibraltar was cut off for years from England, caused an almost complete suspension of direct trade between England and the Levant.

Even before the outbreak of the American war, the Turkey Company was unable any longer to pay its ambassador and consuls in the Levant without the aid of occasional grants from parliament. But the clearest evidence of decay is the continued decline in the number of British factors at the main establishments in the Levant. The flourishing factories with thirty or forty resident factors at the beginning of the eighteenth century were reduced to five at constantinople, six at Smyrna, and two at Aleppo by its closing years. Indeed the consulate at Aleppo was officially closed in 1791. The reduction in direct exports of cotton goods to the Ottoman empire was largely responsible for continued decline in the 'eighties. On the other hand some progress was made in developing trade through Salonica; and, thanks to the persistence of George Baldwin and his defiance of the wishes both of the Turkey merchants and the Turkish government, a beginning was made in opening the Suez route between Britain and India through Egypt. Baldwin's experiments had no appreciable effect upon British commerce at the time, but were to prove significant later. More immediately important was the exemption of British imports from the *Misteria* duty, secured by Sir Robert Ainslie in 1784, which removed one advantage the French had enjoyed under the capitulations of 1740.

The outbreak of the Revolutionary war with France, followed by the withdrawal of the British fleet from the Mediterranean and the uncontrolled activity of French, Spanish, and other privateers, once again gravely damaged the Turkey Company's trade. Something was saved from the wreck by the renewal of permission to the Turkey Company, first granted during the war of American Independence, to carry on the Levant trade indirectly and even by the use of foreign shipping. Napoleon's expedition to Egypt and the restoration of British naval supremacy in the Mediterranean not merely made possible the resumption of direct trade with the Levant, but brought about, in 1799, a political alliance between Britain and Turkey with the object of driving the French out of Egypt. Britain thus assumed for the first time the normal eighteenth-century role of France as protector of the Ottoman empire. It was this which secured for the Turkey Company in 1802 the right to navigate the Black Sea and trade directly with its ports as France and Russia had been allowed to do earlier. It is indeed curious that Pitt had thought it worth while to challenge Russia during the Ochakov crisis of 1791 without any assurance from the Turks that British ships would be allowed access to Poland via the Straits.

Even before the outbreak of the French Revolution French cloth had declined in quality and English shalloons were beginning to make some impression on the Levant markets. The Sultan, provoked by Napoleon's attack upon Egypt, promptly imprisoned all the subjects of France in his dominions and laid an embargo upon trade with France. British privateers annihilated what was left of it. As French domination extended over Italy and the United Provinces, the Italians and the Dutch were treated as enemies and their merchant fleets also were driven from the Mediterranean Sea. The prosperity of the Turkey merchants was temporarily interrupted by the Russo-Turkish war into which Britain was dragged as Russia's ally in 1807. But the Turks made peace with Britain in 1809 and trade boomed until the dissolution of the Turkey Company in 1825. The staple British export was no longer woollen cloth but cotton goods produced in the Lancashire factories. In exchange Turkey exported as before large quantities of raw silk but also increasing quantities of raw cotton and madder roots used for dyeing cotton goods, which were then exported largely to the Levant. Vast as the flow of trade had become between the countries included in the Levant Company's monopoly and Britain in the early years of the nineteenth century, British relations with Turkey were now regulated much more by political considerations than by economic contacts. It is necessary therefore to trace how the exclusively trading nexus of the seventeenth century developed into a political alliance soon to be hallowed by the diplomatic achievements of Palmerston.

The suggestions occasionally made in the reign of Queen Elizabeth of a political understanding between England and Turkey against their common enemy, the king of Spain, never produced any practical result. The appearance of the Commonwealth and Protectorate navies in the Mediterranean made this practicable for the first time, especially as France was now the ally both of Cromwell and the Sultan. One thing which stood in the way was the interference of the Barbary corsairs with English Mediterranean trade and their capture and enslavement of English sailors. It was not yet realized in England that the Barbary states were for all practical purposes independent of the nominal suzerainty which the Porte still affected to retain over Algiers, Tunis, and Tripoli, though not over the independent empire of Morocco.

Until the Revolution of 1688 at least the British diplomatic representative at Constantinople remained a commercial agent masquerading as an ambassador. One of Charles II's secretaries of state summed up the lack of any political contact when he wrote of Constantinople as a place 'so remote as any intelligence from hence hither (it's conceived) can be of little use here'. Yet Charles II's ex-minister Danby, writing in the year after the Revolution of 1688, foreshadowed the new approach which was to dominate the British political attitude to Turkey for the next two generations. The defeat of the Turks 'might be of infinite advantage to us and the rest of Christendom if our allies in Germany and in the House of Commons would agree to improve this advantage the next summer to that degree which will certainly be in their power'.[1]

The relief of Vienna only a few years earlier had evoked in England an outburst of religious enthusiasm almost unaffected by political calculation and this attitude survived well into the nineteenth century. Alexander Somerville, author of *The Autobiography of a Working Man*, on hearing the news of the battle of Navarino in 1827, 'wondered why any body should doubt the right or propriety of Sir Edward Codrington destroying the Turkish fleet. The claims of the Greeks, or the principles of international law we knew nothing of. It was enough to us that the enemy which the English had fought and vanquished was the Turks, and that the Turks

[1] *H.M.C. Finch MSS.* II, 247.

were Mahommedans, and not believers in the same religion as ours.'[1]

The attitude of most eighteenth-century politicians to Turkey foreshadowed by Danby was based on two assumptions: (1) that France was the natural enemy of England and (2) that Britain needed the alliance of Austria if she was to resist French aggression with any hope of success. The first assumption made them suspicious of Turkey, which had been the political ally of France for two centuries, and had granted to the French a position of clear pre-eminence amongst the foreigners who resided in or visited the Ottoman empire for trade and other purposes.

English resentment was sharpened when the period of good relations between Britain and France ended in 1731. At the same time, as we have seen, British trade languished and French trade flourished in the Levant, partly because of the award to France of further privileges by the capitulations of 1740. Instead of abandoning the unequal struggle with France at Constantinople, Britain persisted in ineffectual opposition to French domination in the hope of retaining the remnants of her Levant trade.

The second assumption, though dormant during the period of Franco-British friendship, ultimately reinforced the first. Austria, during the war of the English Succession, persisted in fighting France and the Turks simultaneously. The experience of this war convinced English statesmen that Austrian resources, even when supplemented by English and Dutch support, were inadequate to carry on a double continental war with any prospect of success. Henceforth Britain, although herself for long uninterested in the eastern question, had a powerful indirect interest in it. Unless she could settle the chronic disputes between the Turks and Austria, which were liable to lead to war at any moment, she could expect little assistance from her Austrian ally in a war against France. And if an Austro-Turkish war did break out in spite of British endeavours, British interests imperatively required that it should be brought to an end before France seized the chances it offered her in western Europe.

The Revolution of 1688 by making Britain the irreconcilable enemy of France and the ally of Austria pretty well determined the British attitude to Turkey until the Diplomatic Revolution of 1756. William III dispatched a special ambassador, William Harbord, in

[1] Op. cit., p. 110.

1691 to mediate between the Emperor and the Porte, but he died at Belgrade before accomplishing his task. Later British ambassadors to the Sultan were more successful and their mediation contributed to the conclusion of the important peace treaties between Austria and the Turks at Carlowitz in 1699 and at Passarowitz in 1718. One criticism of Walpole's foreign policy during the war of the Polish Succession is that he so antagonized Austria that Charles VI asked France, and not Britain, to mediate peace between himself and the Porte. Villeneuve, the French ambassador at Constantinople, succeeded in this task and his success damaged British prestige in Europe as well as British trade in the Levant.

The British role of mediator was an ungrateful one and led to complaints from both sides. The treaty of Carlowitz was the first treaty of peace, as distinct from a temporary truce, to be concluded by the Sultan with Christian powers and was therefore abhorred by fanatical Moslems. Taken along with the peace treaty of Constantinople between Russia and the Turks which was concluded in 1700, it cost Turkey territories which were 'important from the strategic, economic, and political point of view [and . . .] indeed the very existence of the empire was imperilled'.[1] So violent was the reaction at Constantinople that the Sultan was deposed; but his successor Ahmed III rejected French proposals that he should again try the fortunes of war against Austria and Russia. When Charles XII of Sweden and the Cossack hetman, Mazepa, took refuge in Turkey after the battle of Poltava, a protracted crisis followed.

The Turks were quick to realize that Russia had become as dangerous an enemy as Austria. The grand vizier, Tchorlulu Ali Pasha, who had agreed to Russian demands for the expulsion of Charles XII from Turkey, was denounced as a traitor and overthrown. A Russo-Turkish war followed in which Peter the Great was unexpectedly and disastrously defeated on the Pruth. French influence was exerted to stir up the Turks to join with Charles XII in an all-out attack upon Russia and Austria, while the British ambassador, Sir Robert Sutton, exerted himself successfully to mediate peace between the Turks and the Russians and to prevent war breaking out between Austria and Turkey. In the opinion of the Russian vice-chancellor, Shafirov, who was sent to the Turkish camp to negotiate peace with the Turks, Sutton 'worked strenu-

[1] *Despatches of Sir Robert Sutton*, ed. A. N. Kurat (Camden Series, 1953), p. 1.

ously by day and night to persuade the Turks to preserve peace and used hard words to [the Turks]; in consequence the Turks were annoyed and grumbled at him; even your natural slave [i.e. one of your subjects] could not do more for your majesty [Peter the Great]'.[1]

Sutton was acting without instructions from his government, if not in opposition to them; but he would hardly have dared to do what he did unless he had had some reason to believe that his activity would be acceptable to his superiors. Britain had not the same urgent need to preserve or restore peace between Russia and Turkey as she had between Austria and the Turks, but a Russo-Turkish war was likely to include Austria sooner rather than later. The reason for British hesitation to intervene officially between Russia and the Turks seems to have been delicacy towards Charles XII of Sweden and the desire not to make an enemy of him. Even the Tory government in the last years of Queen Anne realized the danger which Peter the Great represented to major British interests in the Baltic: if peace were concluded between Russia and Turkey this would enable Peter to concentrate his forces in the Northern war; and official British intervention in the peace negotiations with Turkey might antagonize Charles XII, who was now coming to be regarded as the best hope of thwarting the ambitions of Russia in the Baltic. Sutton's unofficial mediation secured for the Turks all they could reasonably expect from Russia at the price of abandoning Charles XII. It was therefore bitterly resented by Charles XII, whose agents combined with the French ambassador to impugn the impartiality of Sutton's mediation. This task was made easier by Sutton's acceptance of presents or bribes from Russia, in accordance with the customs of the time, as a reward for his services. In spite of these attacks Sutton remained on good terms with the Porte for the rest of his embassy and was mainly responsible for mediating peace, this time between Austria and Turkey, at Passarowitz in 1718.

In his despatches Sutton showed no interest in the Turkey Company or British trade in the Levant. As a career diplomat, he preferred to confine himself to the political functions of the Constantinople embassy and leave trade to his subordinates. He and his predecessor, Paget, who mediated the treaty of Carlowitz in 1699, set the pattern for the rest of the eighteenth century. Though the ambassadors to Turkey continued to be paid wholly or, after 1768,

[1] Ibid., p. 8.

partly, by the Turkey Company, their successors were all 'servant[s] of the Crown sent primarily for political and diplomatic business'.[1] At last in 1804 the forms were brought into accordance with the facts: the Crown's nominees as ambassadors ceased to be formally elected by the company and their salaries were paid entirely by the Crown. At the same time a commercial agent was chosen by the Company to look after commercial business and received a commission from the Crown as consul-general. Whether or not the new arrangement contributed to the vast expansion of British trade with Turkey in the following decades, it removed a long-standing grievance of the eighteenth-century ambassadors at Constantinople, who resented having to take orders from a trading company. Paget was typical in his complaint that the Company treated him 'more like a footman than an ambassador'.[2] Though the decline of British trade in the Levant during the eighteenth century was due to deeper causes, the unsatisfactory relationship between the Company and its chief agent in the Levant may well have contributed to it.

The decade following the mediation of the treaty of Passarowitz, because of its eccentricity, stands out in the story of British relations with Turkey. Britain had become the ally of France in 1716. Britain and Hanover were already on the brink of war with Russia in the Baltic. This made George I more dependent on the Regent Orleans, especially as he in his electoral capacity was already on bad terms with the Emperor. For a short time therefore the British government deliberately adapted to its own needs the policy traditionally followed by France at Constantinople of invoking Turkish intervention to distract her main enemy from pursuing a war against her. Failing to secure safeguards for British trade in the Baltic and for the political balance of power in that area by the treaty of Nystad, Townshend attempted to involve the Turks in George I's quarrel with Russia.

Peter the Great after 1721 had transferred his armies from the Baltic to the Caspian and was engaged in occupying territories, which it was feared would give Russia a monopoly of the coveted trade in silks with Persia, alike to the detriment of Britain and Turkey. A Turkish conquest of Astrakan, Townshend suggested, 'would free them [the Turks] for ever from all apprehensions from the Muscovites'. That such an idea could seriously be advanced by a secretary of state reflects upon Townshend's competence to

---

[1] A. C. Wood, *History of the Levant Company*, p. 130.   [2] Ibid., p. 132.

hold this office, even if he reveals later in the same dispatch his real object. This was 'by giving the Tsaritsa so much occupation on the side of Asia that she may be less attentive and less enterprising to create trouble and uneasiness to the King [George I] on this side'.[1]

Any chance that the Turks would be attracted by British proposals was destroyed by the attitude of France at Constantinople. The French ambassador received instructions to damp down Russo-Turkish hostility in Asia, since a war there would leave the Hapsburg Emperor free to pursue his ambitious projects in Europe. Townshend on the other hand expressly warned the British ambassador that in stirring up the Turks he must direct their wrath solely against Russia and not 'say or do anything that may look like incensing them against the Emperor'.[2] He added that Peter the Great's use of the Jacobites justified any reprisals against Russia. Thus Britain without offering any help urged the Turks to involve themselves in a distant and difficult war, while France advised them to remain uncommitted in Asia and ready to face the Emperor on the Danube. There could be no doubt which line of action would seem preferable to the Turks. Not until Russia was on the point of joining with the Emperor in the league of Vienna did France abandon her efforts to preserve peace between Russia and Turkey and come into line with the policy advocated for years by British statesmen. By then it was too late: the union of Russia with Austria in a close alliance intimidated the Turks.

Britain's reconciliation with Austria by the second treaty of Vienna in 1731 shattered her alliance with France and restored the British ambassador to his old position as the opponent of French influence at Constantinople. Yet when Austria and Russia made war upon Turkey in 1736 it was the French ambassador at Constantinople who mediated peace in 1739. Walpole's non-interventionist policy had made France the arbiter of Europe and it was the resentment of Charles VI at Walpole's failure to support him in the Polish Succession war, rather than any change in the attitude of the Turks to Great Britain, that gave the task of mediation to the French ambassador at Constantinople and its profits to his court.

Had the Turks joined with Maria Theresa's other enemies to prevent her succession to the Hapsburg lands, her position would

---

[1] Ilse Jacob, *Beziehungen Englands zu Russland und zur Türkei in den Jahren 1718–1727*, pp. 148–9.

[2] Ibid., p. 149.

have been much more dangerous than it actually proved to be. The British ambassadors at Constantinople during the Austrian succession war thus rendered substantial but little-regarded services to her cause. British determination to keep a foothold at the Porte made it difficult for her to conclude an alliance with Russia, since Russia's price included a British promise of assistance against the Turks. By insisting on her self-appointed role of 'honest broker' Britain hoped to remain on good terms with both Russia and Turkey. She was beginning also in the 'fifties to take some interest in Polish affairs with a view of checking French influence there and giving support to the Czartoryski princes, who had close links with Russia and were regarded as the opponents of French influence.

When the old alliance of Britain and Austria broke down and Britain became the ally of Prussia in the Seven Years war her attitude to Turkey changed once again. When the French ambassador officially informed the grand vizier of the conclusion of the alliance between France and Austria, which consummated the Diplomatic Revolution, he was told with some *hauteur* that the Porte did not concern itself with the union of one hog with another.[1] In fact the reversal of alliances was bound to weaken the position of the French at Constantinople. France had now become the ally of Turkey's arch-enemy, Austria, as well as of Russia. During the war Russian troops, in violation of ancient treaties with the Turks, occupied Poland and France had to exert such influence as she retained at Constantinople to persuade the Turks that a Russian army in occupation of Poland was not a danger to the Ottoman empire.

Britain's ally, Frederick the Great, was the first Hohenzollern to take an interest in the eastern question: the successive defeats inflicted upon him by Russian troops convinced him that his only hope of escaping ruin was to persuade the Turks to attack Russia and divert her attention from the German war. Britain was press-ganged by Frederick to support him at Constantinople, and Turkish doubts about the reliability of her old friend France gave more weight to Prussian and British representations. But the Turks had little inclination to take on the three great powers of the Continent, France, Austria, and Russia; and they remained obstinately neutral. This proved fortunate for Frederick. Had he gained the alliance of the Turks, even Peter III on his accession could hardly have added Russia to a Prusso-Turkish combination. It was fortunate also for

[1] *H.M.C. Finch MSS.* I, 406.

Britain that Frederick's intrigues failed, since had they succeeded Bute would have found the problem of making a general peace even more intractable than it actually was.

After the end of the Seven Years war the primary political function of the British ambassador at Constantinople continued to be opposition to the dominant influence of France. His task was easier than before to the extent that French policy during the war and the continuance of the French alliance with Austria kept alive Turkish suspicions of French motives and made the Porte less amenable to French influence. These suspicions found confirmation in French failure either to give adequate support to the Turks in the war against Russia (1768–74) or to secure a favourable peace for them. Russia's ability to impose her own terms at Kutchuk-Kainardji in 1774 taught the Turks a salutary lesson. They had rushed into war to protect Poland and found themselves unable to defend themselves. Choiseul and his successors had pursued towards Poland, France's other ally in south-eastern Europe, a wavering and ineffectual policy which might well have broken off completely the Franco-Turkish alliance. That it did not do so was largely due to the persistent neglect by the French ambassadors at Constantinople of their official instructions, and the determination of influential people at Versailles not to sacrifice the traditions of French policy in eastern Europe to the demands of a temporary and at best unsatisfactory and unpopular alliance with Austria. In any case France's position in eastern Europe had been so undermined before 1763 that several French statesmen were sceptical of the ability of efforts to restore it.

In practice Britain failed to seize the chances offered by the decline of French influence, and indeed interest, in eastern Europe. The Whig governments which succeeded each other rapidly in the 1760's, so far as they concerned themselves with foreign policy at all, were intent on making an alliance either with Austria or occasionally with Russia and Prussia. Whether the advocates of the old system or the devotees of a new Northern System of alliances were predominant in British governing circles, there was no basis for political co-operation between them and the Turks. In the 'seventies the British reaction to the first Partition of Poland was even more discouraging to the Turks than that of France: it amounted to a formal disavowal of any political interest in south-eastern Europe and a public admission that even had such interest existed

Britain had no means of effective intervention. Moral disapproval of the action of Russia and Austria was of no use to the Turks, increasingly aware of their own decadence and alarmed by the developments which were giving superior political strength and more technical expertise to their enemies. In spite of the inherent weaknesses of her foreign policy and its dangerous dependence upon Austria, France had much more to offer the Turks than Britain in the later eighteenth century.

Apart from such general considerations, two special factors further reduced British influence at Constantinople after the end of the Seven Years war. The first was the spasmodic attempts of British statesmen, usually made at times of crisis, to gain the alliance of Russia against France or at least to secure the use of a corps of Russian troops. It is true that down to the despairing effort to secure Russian intervention on the British side in the war of American Independence by offering Catherine II Minorca as a Mediterranean base, Britain firmly refused to commit herself to Russian hostility towards Turkey. Britain also argued that, since he that pays the piper calls the tune, the hiring of Russian auxiliary troops by payment of a subsidy was an entirely different proposition from a defensive alliance. But every British approach to Russia was magnified and misrepresented to the Porte by the French ambassador at Constantinople.

When Britain pointed out to the Turks that as long as France was Austria's ally she could not be their true friend, France retorted that Britain in her persistent pursuit of the Russian alliance would readily sacrifice to this end the vital interests of the Ottoman empire. The British ambassador at Constantinople ought properly to be regarded merely as the Russian chargé d'affaires. The help afforded by the British government to the Russian Baltic fleet, when it sailed to attack the Turks in the eastern Mediterranean during the war of 1768–74, certainly went beyond what was permissible for a neutral power. British help had enabled Russia to appeal effectively for the first time to what was to become in the nineteenth century her strongest weapons against the Turks—the overt religious antagonism and dormant feelings of nationalism amongst her Christian subjects in the Balkans. Britain's anti-Turkish acts were the more regarded because they accorded with the avowal of Burke that he did not wish well to the Turks[1] and Chatham, who in 1773

[1] He added that 'any people but the Turks so seated as they are, would have

publicly professed himself 'quite a Russ'. It is fair to point out that if Britain certainly facilitated this Russian naval attack upon Turkey's territories and trade in the Levant, she genuinely tried to help Turkey to escape from the war on terms not justified by the diplomatic and military position. Here at least there was some convergence in French and British policies at Constantinople. It is a measure of the decline of the west after 1763 that even in agreement Britain and France could no longer impose their mediation and thus end wars in eastern Europe.

The other special factor which impaired British influence at Constantinople from the 1770's was the persistent attempts of James Bruce and George Baldwin to open up the Suez route to India. This ran counter to the traditional Turkish prohibition of navigation of the northern half of the Red Sea by Christian vessels. Russian pressure to force open the Black Sea no doubt made the Turks more determined to shut out the infidel from the Red Sea. Moreover to open this sea threatened loss to the Turkish merchants, who controlled the normal overland route to India through Mesopotamia to the Persian gulf. Since the mamelukes governed Egypt in virtual independence of the Sultan, the new route lay beyond his effective control. He would lose the income derived from customs duties on silk, coffee, and other goods imported from Persia and India to Turkey and then re-exported to Europe.

Once established by agreement with the governors of Egypt, the route could be used for the rapid transit of passengers between Britain and India. In particular, important dispatches could be carried to and from India much more quickly than by the long voyage round the Cape. Warren Hastings considered that the opening of this route would be of 'great public utility' and his agents negotiated a formal treaty of navigation and commerce with the Egyptian authorities in 1775. The East India Company, however, reluctantly decided that it would be better to confine themselves to the sea-route of which they had an effective monopoly, rather than risk opening a new route which they might have to share with the Levant Company. When the Sultan protested against the use by East Indian ships of the Suez route and formally proclaimed the closure of the northern Red Sea to Christian navigation the Company readily accepted this decision.

been cultivated in three hundred years; but they grow more gross in the very native soil of civility and refinement' (*Works* (ed. 1852), I, 399–403).

The British government however asked the Sultan to make an exception in favour of packet-boats which would carry no merchandise but solely urgent dispatches from the East India Company. Attempts to make use of this privilege before it was granted led to incidents when messengers were arrested and not allowed to proceed and their baggage was searched. In defiance of the Sultan's edict, British merchant vessels continued to trade with Egypt and when France joined the American colonists in war against Britain it was by Suez that the news was transmitted to India with the result that Pondicherry was captured and French operations in India forestalled.[1]

Baldwin's persistence in using the route for commerce in spite of reiterated prohibitions from the Porte led to inevitable disaster. In 1779 a valuable caravan on its way overland from Suez was pillaged by Bedouins, while the traders in charge of it were left to die of thirst and exhaustion. The Egyptian beys sequestrated the vessels which had brought the goods and arrested Baldwin to serve as a hostage in the event of reprisals. Messengers officially sent by the East India Company were arrested and their dispatches intercepted both by Egyptian and Turkish officials. By 1780 Britain realized that 'trade to Egypt had become more dangerous than profitable'[2] and that the Suez route was too uncertain as a means of speedy communication with India. From 1775 to 1780 repeated incidents in Egypt kept up tension between Britain and Turkey, while France exploited them to the utmost at Constantinople.

After the end of the American war the situation altered and it was France which sought to develop the Suez route by agreement with the Egyptian beys in 1785. The British ambassador at Constantinople protested and received assurances that the Sultan had no intention of lifting in favour of the French the ban imposed upon Christian navigation of the northern Red Sea. These inspired so little confidence at London that a new post of agent and consul-general at Cairo was established in 1786 and George Baldwin was appointed to it. His instructions were to watch closely all the proceedings of the French and to try to secure freedom of communication between Britain and India through Egypt for British subjects authorized to make the passage either by the East India Company or the government.

[1] H. L. Hoskins, *British Routes to India*, p. 18.
[2] H. L. Hoskins, op. cit., p. 25.

Baldwin arrived in Egypt in 1786 to find a Turkish army supported by a powerful fleet in control of the Mediterranean coast. When Egyptian resistance was crushed in the course of 1787 Baldwin tried to obtain from the victorious Turkish capitan pasha what he had hoped to gain, in despite of the Porte, from the Egyptian beys. Encouraged by this local success the Turks plucked up courage to declare war on Russia. The French ambassador at Constantinople seized the chance to spread rumours that Britain was preparing to do what she had done in the previous Turkish-Russian war to help Russia and perhaps even to supply ships and crews to support Russian naval action in the Mediterranean. Though the Turks still refused to grant the formal right of passage via Suez either to France or to Britain, the ineffectiveness of their renewed control of Egypt and their need for diplomatic and naval support from one or both of these powers against Russia, compelled them to connive from 1788 at use of the Suez route not only for official messengers but also for a limited amount of commercial traffic.

While the French republic was resolute to maintain communications and trade with India by way of the Red Sea, the British government and the East India Company showed little interest in the 'nineties. In 1793 Baldwin was dismissed and the Egyptian consulate-general closed. Even the use of the Suez route to carry to India news of the outbreak of war between Britain and France in 1793 and the consequent capture of Pondicherry failed to persuade Lord Grenville, the foreign secretary, to change his attitude. Baldwin however remained at his post and actually concluded in 1794 a treaty with the Egyptian beys which granted to Britain the position of most-favoured nation in Egypt and the other privileges which had been granted by their predecessors to France in 1785. The Foreign Office remained unimpressed and made no attempt to secure from the Porte the formal ratification of the treaty required to make it legally effective. Nor did the East India Company show any eagerness either to establish a regular line of communication through Egypt or to develop a transit trade by this route.

The French government on the other hand continued to take an active interest in Egypt. As French trade with other parts of the Ottoman empire declined, Egypt became more important commercially. If France could gain exclusive commercial use of the Suez 'the colossus which the English have raised in Bengal would be thrown down'.[1] If to this she could add effective domination of Egypt with a French garrison to hold it against all comers, she would have the best military base for the reconquest of her eastern empire. Other Frenchmen valued Egypt chiefly for its own sake and believed that it could be developed as a great tropical colony which would more than compensate France for actual or potential losses in Louisiana and the Caribbean. These ideas, already influential but clearly impracticable in the closing years of the Bourbon régime, were eagerly taken up by the French revolutionaries. The French consulate-general in Egypt, closed since 1777, was reopened in 1793 at the very moment when the British consulate-general was officially suppressed. In India Tippoo Sahib, the ruler of Mysore, and other princes in alliance with France were preparing to join with a French expeditionary force from Egypt in driving the British out of India.

In this as in other respects, Bonaparte made himself the supreme executant of the ambition and aggression inherent in the French Revolution. Realizing that a straightforward conquest of Egypt would irretrievably antagonize the Turks, the French Directory claimed that Egypt under the rule of the beys had become a British satellite and that French troops would restore the legitimate authority of the Sultan. The Porte was not deceived by this bare-faced pretence: the long tradition of Franco-Turkish amity and co-operation was never fully restored. The success of Nelson in annihilating the French fleet at Aboukir bay, the subsequent defeat of the French army in Syria by Sir Sidney Smith, and its final expulsion from Egypt by Sir Ralph Abercromby gave the Turks some indication of the services which Britain was now in a position to render to the Porte.

Britain had belatedly awakened to the immediacy of her own interests in a transformed eastern question. Pitt had failed to raise Britain to action against Russia during the Ochakov crisis in 1791: his determined intervention against France in the Levant won him almost universal approbation a decade later. Most Britons at the very end of the eighteenth century found it difficult to think of Russia as a national enemy: they had no such inhibitions about France. The defence of Egypt against all comers, but particularly against the French, gave Britain and Turkey at last a mutual interest apart from trade. The Francophil tendencies of Mehemet Ali con-

[1] Quoted in H. L. Hoskins, op. cit., p. 51.

solidated this mutual interest. On the other hand, the Turks were as jealous of British as of French influence in Egypt and this weakened the cordiality of the Turco-British alliance even in its heyday under Palmerston and Disraeli. If the original French occupation of Egypt by Bonaparte in 1798 irretrievably damaged the Franco-Turkish alliance, the final establishment of Britain as the controlling power in Egypt, did as much to end Anglo-Turkish co-operation in the last years of the nineteenth century.

The changing British attitude to Turkey in the closing years of the eighteenth century can be illustrated elsewhere than in Egypt. In the first Russo-Turk war of Catherine II's reign, Britain had helped Russia to launch an attack upon Turkey in the Mediterranean and had made no serious attempt to moderate Russian peace terms at the end of the war. In the second war, which continued from 1787 to 1792, she fulfilled her obligations as a neutral power. Russia's behaviour towards Britain and in particular her organizing of the Armed Neutrality of 1780 during the war of American Independence had done something to kill the prevalent idea that Russia was still Britain's natural ally. Britain in 1790 warned the Turks of an impending attack upon their Red Sea ports by Russia's Baltic fleet which would sail under the Dutch flag round the Cape of Good Hope. Even if this *canard* was manufactured for propaganda purposes by British intelligence and propagated by the Foreign Office, it indicates that Henry Dundas and other ministers were becoming alarmed at Russian advances and aware of the strategic threat they presented to British control of India.

One of the objects of the Triple Alliance of 1788 between Britain, Prussia, and the Dutch was to intervene in favour of the Turks in the war between Turkey and the Austro-Russian allies. The temporary eclipse of France made it easier for Britain, both practically and psychologically, to take over the former role of France; but the divergences between the three partners made successful intervention highly unlikely from the beginning. Relying upon her armed might, Prussia detached Austria from Russia and forced the Emperor Leopold II to make a separate peace with Turkey at Orsova in 1791; but Prussia's disregard of her western allies and selfish territorial schemes in eastern Europe put a tremendous strain upon the alliance. Pitt tried to restore confidence by coercing Russia to follow Austria's example and make peace with the Turks on terms dictated by the Triple Alliance.

When this failed, the Triple Alliance broke up. Prussia ceased to oppose Russia and Austria and became for a time their jackal. The union of the three eastern monarchies placed Turkey in great jeopardy and undoubtedly increased the cordiality of what was already a marked *rapprochement* between Britain and Turkey. But what really saved Turkey was the involvement of both Austria and Prussia in war with revolutionary France and the feeling that, in spite of Turkish decline, Poland was a much easier nut to crack. Indeed, to paraphrase Burke, once the eastern powers had breakfasted off Poland, they were constantly tempted to dine on the remains. By the time they had dined, the course of the French Revolutionary wars and Bonaparte's expedition to Egypt had transformed the eastern question as it had existed in the eighteenth century. What had hitherto been an unimportant political problem for Britain, one in which her interest was indirect, through her successive alliances with Austria and Prussia, her intermittent desire for an alliance with Russia, and her constant determination to thwart France, had become basic for British imperial strategy and foreign policy. And so it continued for more than a century. Whether it still is so today must be left for some future historian to determine.

The British diplomatists, consuls, and factors who resided for long periods in Turkey did little to promote culture-contact or even to contribute to a better appreciation of the Turkish way of life. Paul Rycaut, who had served as secretary to a British ambassador to the Porte, published *The Present State of the Ottoman Empire* in 1688 and *The History of the Turks* [from 1679] in 1700. Translated into various continental languages, the first of these works was not superseded until a century later, when a British ambassador, Sir James Porter, published in 1768 his *Observations on the Religion, Law, Government and Manners of the Turks*. This was highly approved by the historian, Principal William Robertson, when it was published as the work of a man who had observed the government of the Turks with attention and described it with ability. When the outbreak of the Crimean war led to renewed interest in Turkey, Porter's work was reissued almost a century after publication as the best available book on Turkish government and society.[1]

Since the Levant trade was mostly in the hands of Jews, Greeks, and Armenians, the foreign factors as a rule had considerably less

[1] Larpent, *Turkey: its History and Progress* (2 vols., London, 1854).

contact with the governing class of Turks than the ambassadors and consuls. And even the relatively few British traders who returned home with ample fortunes to dabble in politics did little to affect prevalent British opinions about the Ottoman empire. There never was a Levant Company lobby comparable, in its political and social influence, to the West Indian planters or the East Indian nabobs.

A greater contribution to British understanding of Turkey was certainly made by the travellers who journeyed widely in the Ottoman empire in the second half of the eighteenth century. Whereas the officials and factors tended to shut themselves up in their residences and avoid any unnecessary contact with the natives, travellers were bound to meet all sorts and conditions of Turks from provincial pashas downwards; and in the course of their travels they acquired first-hand knowledge of many parts of the empire which were quite unknown to British officials and traders. Richard Pococke, later to be an Irish bishop, travelled extensively in the Levant as early as the 1730's. James Bruce was a pioneer in opening up the Red Sea and its western hinterland. About the turn of the century two later travellers, William Eton and Thomas Thornton, published valuable surveys of the Turkish empire. The diversity of their interests, ranging from Orthodox religion to classical archaeology and from oriental languages to economic development, and in particular opportunities for trade, gave their works additional value and wider circulation.

It is only fair to add that one of the latest eighteenth-century ambassadors, Sir Robert Ainslie, made in several illustrated works a massive contribution to the study of the scenery and architecture of the Levant, and that Lady Mary Wortley Montagu, wife of an earlier ambassador, introduced into England the practice of inoculation against smallpox. Her attitude to the Turks, eccentric at the time, foreshadows the fascination felt by many later Englishwomen, such as Lady Hester Stanhope, in face of the inscrutable east. While Ainslie amassed a large collection of ancient coins, the earl of Elgin bought the Elgin marbles.

If the British were still, at best, superficially acquainted with Turkish society at the end of the eighteenth century, the Turks knew much less about Britain. Occasional diplomatic missions were sent from Constantinople to France but never to Britain. Trade was carried on entirely by British merchants in British ships: no

Turkish merchants resided at London and no Turkish sailors visited British ports. The Turks in their own country remained convinced that theirs was the only true religion. Their secular ruler was also their Caliph—both emperor and pope. No alteration was possible either in government or society without destroying the way of life prescribed by Mohammed.

All 'Franks' were Christian dogs and even the ambassadors never walked in the streets unless accompanied by janissaries who formed part of the staff of the embassy. Otherwise they would have been continually insulted, if not actually injured, by a mob of Moslems. It is significant that the janissaries employed to protect the foreign ambassadors were known in Turkish slang as 'swineherds'.[1] Turkish law forbade, under the penalty of death, the marriage of Christian and Moslem.

Under such conditions almost the only influence which could conceivably have led to some adoption of western ideas was the presence of occasional Christian renegades—converts of course to Mohammedanism—in the higher ranges of the Turkish government; but these were relatively few and knew well that even cautious attempts to westernize Turkey would lead to their deposition and death. Thus fossilized, the Turkish political, military, and social system, which had probably been superior in efficiency to that of early modern European states, ceased to be competitive with the powerful centralized monarchies which were being established by her enemies and labelled enlightened despotisms. A few sophisticated Turks could now argue that the Turkish governmental system was more akin to that of Britain than to absolutism. The limitations enforced upon George III by the powers of Parliament were similar to those imposed upon the Sultan by the doctors of the sacred law in Turkey. Such sophisms were unlikely to impose upon British opinion. At the end as at the beginning of the eighteenth century, Turkey was almost invariably regarded as a typical oriental despotism, camping amidst the ruins of classical civilization, and oppressing without mercy the descendants of the classical Jews and Greeks, whose achievements formed the indispensable basis of Christian and Western civilization.

[1] W. Eton, *Survey of the Turkish Empire* (London, 1801), p. 112.

A. *Primary Sources*

Baldwin, G., *Political Recollections relative to Egypt* (1801)
[*The*] *Despatches of Sir Robert Sutton Ambassador in Constantinople 1710–14*, ed. A. N. Kurat (Camden Series, 1953)
Eton, W., *Survey of the Turkish Empire* (2 vols., 1799)
Montagu, Lady Mary Wortley, *Complete Letters*, ed. Halsband, vol. I (Oxford, 1965)

B. *Secondary Authorities*

Ambrose, G., 'English Traders at Aleppo (1658–1756)' in *EcHR* 3 (1932), 246–67
Anderson, M. S., 'Great Britain and the Russo–Turkish War of 1768–74' in *EHR* 59 (1954), 39–58
Charles-Roux, F., *L'Angleterre et l'Expédition française en Égypte* (2 vols., Cairo, 1925)
— *L'Angleterre, l'isthme de Suez et l'Égypte au XVIIIᵉ siècle* (Paris, 1923)
Gibb, H. A. R., and Bowen, H., *Islamic Society and the West in the Eighteenth Century*, vol. I, parts 1 and 2 (1950 and 1957)
Halsband, R., *The Life of Lady Mary Wortley Montagu* (Oxford, 1956)
Hoskins, H. L., *British Routes to India* (New York, 1928)
Jacob, Ilse, *Beziehungen Englands zu Russland und zur Türkei [1718–27]* (Basel, 1945)
Sorel, A., *The Eastern Question in the Eighteenth Century* (Engl. transl., 1898)
Stavrianos, L. S., 'Antecedents to the Balkan Revolutions of the Nineteenth Century' in *JMH* 29 (1957), 335–48
Wood, A. C., *History of the Levant Company* (1935)
— 'The English Embassy at Constantinople 1660–1762' in *EHR* 40 (1925), 533–61

Note. The sectional bibliography for Russia and Poland should also be consulted.

CONCLUSION

THE study of the diplomatic relations between Britain and the other states of Europe enables one to draw certain conclusions about British foreign policy, in general, during the eighteenth century. At the beginning of the century Britain's primary objective was clearly self-defence. She entered the Spanish Succession war, after concluding the Grand Alliance with the Dutch and the Emperor, neither to maintain Imperial claims to the Spanish inheritance nor to support abstract conceptions of the balance of power, but to defend (1) the Revolution settlement and the Protestant succession, (2) the national security which seemed to be endangered by French control of the Spanish Netherlands, and (3) her commercial interests in Europe and overseas. Marlborough's co-operation with Heinsius and Eugene of Savoy sufficed to secure all three aims, despite Tory mishandling of the peace negotiations at Utrecht.

In the disturbed years that followed the Utrecht settlement Britain's main aim continued to be self-defence. Indeed internal disunion and the insecurity of the newly settled Hanoverian dynasty made this traditional basis of the country's foreign relations more prominent than ever. The dominant factor was fear of a Jacobite restoration engineered by France or some other continental power such as Spain, Sweden, or Russia. This meant that for the next thirty years home and foreign policy were inextricably interwoven. It was partly for this reason that foreign policy attracted more attention than had been normal in the seventeenth century.

At the same time it is undeniable that commercial ambitions played a much larger part than they had done in the history of English diplomacy in the seventeenth century. This was perhaps most obvious in the Mediterranean where military garrisons were now maintained at Gibraltar and Port Mahon, naval squadrons were regularly seen, the Barbary pirates were overawed or bribed, and the merchant navy, aided by a network of consulates, did a brisk trade. Similarly in the Baltic there was a great expansion of British mercantile activity. To keep watch on ships entering the Sound, a consulate was established at Elsinore. Others were instituted at Riga and St. Petersburg. During the Northern war the

British government did not hesitate to send fleets into the Baltic to defend the extending commercial activity of its subjects, though defence of commercial interests was sometimes merely a cloak for other designs which were unlikely to be relished by Parliament. In two other areas British commercial and political interests were closely linked. Portugal was not only a valuable market for woollen exports and a source of bullion imports, but even after the acquisition of Gibraltar and Port Mahon its ports were useful in time of war to British war-ships and merchant vessels. If necessary, as it was in the closing stages of the Seven Years war, the British government was prepared to undertake military measures for the defence of 'our oldest ally'. The British Parliament voted £100,000 for the relief of distress after the Lisbon tidal wave of 1755. The defence of Portugal was one of the factors which induced the British government to begin the Peninsular war: without his Portuguese base Wellington's Spanish campaigns would have been impossible. An even keener interest was taken in the Low Countries, the defence of which was entrusted mainly to our allies, the Austrians and the Dutch, by the Barrier treaty of 1715. When Austria almost immediately betrayed the trust reposed in her by seeking to revive the commercial prosperity of the Netherlands, Britain and Austria came within measurable distance of war over the Ostend Company. After the collapse of the Barrier in the Austrian Succession war and the rupture of the old system of alliances between the Maritime Powers and Austria in 1755, Britain was no longer in a position to control the Netherlands.

British interest in the remaining areas of Europe was much less close and active. As yet she had no political preoccupations in the Eastern Question, being intent merely on her trade with the Ottoman empire, and that declined markedly in the early eighteenth century. It is significant that the treaties of Carlowitz and Passarowitz between Austria and Turkey were mediated by the Maritime Powers, who objected to their ally Austria involving herself in a Balkan war when they wished her to keep her hands free to assist them in western Europe. Even in Germany comparatively little interest was taken, provided that British merchants were allowed to sell their goods freely and that Protestant fanaticism was not aroused by Roman Catholic proselytism or persecution. Beyond Europe Britain already had commercial and colonial interests in America, Africa, and India, but apart from embittering relations with Spain, these exerted little direct influence on foreign policy for nearly a generation after 1714.

Such was the geographical extension of the British system in 1701, and surprisingly little change took place before the end of the eighteenth century. Undoubtedly the main alteration was the much greater importance which came to be attached to extra-European problems. This manifested itself clearly in the causes of the Anglo-Spanish war of 1739 and the Seven Years war—the first large-scale war in which British participation is to be explained primarily by colonial ambitions. In western Europe the principal centres of interest were still the Low Countries and Portugal, though in both areas, and especially in the Netherlands, there was some decline of British influence. The Dutch even joined the anti-British coalition during the war of American Independence, although British influence was restored by the conclusion of the Triple Alliance. It was largely to defend Holland that Britain became involved in the French Revolutionary war. Britain was still vitally concerned in the Mediterranean and the Baltic, though in the former, the alliance of France and Spain, and in the latter, the first Armed Neutrality, both during the war of American Independence, weakened her position. France and Spain continued in the main to co-operate during the French Revolutionary war, and the attempts of Britain and Russia to combine in opposition to the French revolutionaries speedily broke down in mutual recriminations which made difficult co-operation in the future. Even earlier Russian determination to exploit her political ascendancy in the Baltic was shown by the markedly less favourable terms secured for British merchants in the commercial treaty of 1766 as compared with those gained in the previous commercial treaty of 1734.

On the other hand there was for a time some extension of interest in central and eastern Europe. In Germany during the middle years of the century Britain had subsidized a number of the princes in the hope of organizing an anti-French league or at least of securing some military aid in war against France. When after 1783 national revival came under Pitt, Britain emerged from isolation by alliance with Prussia. This alliance proved ineffective and short-lived; but the French Revolutionary war made it essential for Britain to secure German manpower by bargains with the German princes, not only with Austria and Prussia but with minor states. For a time too, in close conjunction with the ambitious power of

Sardinia, Britain had played a part in Italian politics and wars, but the treaty of Aranjuez in 1752 ended this activity and Italy remained at peace in the following generation. As in Germany, so also in Italy war with revolutionary France led Britain to conclude alliances with Italian princes designed to secure their active help against revolutionary France. Sardinia took part in the First Coalition. Naples, backed by British sea-power, for a short time during the Second Coalition attempted to take over the leadership of the anti-revolutionary forces in Italy.

Even with Poland in the 'fifties and early 'sixties there had been a certain tendency to closer ties, seen for example in the proposal of the Czartoryski party to place Ferdinand of Brunswick on the Polish throne. But when the news of the first Partition of Poland broke upon an astonished world the British government washed its hands publicly of the whole transaction on the avowed ground that Poland lay beyond the British sphere of interest and that it had no means of intervening effectively in Poland. British public opinion was much more excited by the second and third than it had been by the first Partition of Poland. Similarly until the time of the Triple Alliance of 1788 the British government dissociated itself from the Eastern Question. British politicians in the 'sixties and 'seventies at the most privately avowed an academic sympathy with the Russians against the Turks either, like Burke, on humanitarian and religious grounds, or, like Chatham, because they asserted that British interests required an understanding with Russia. The transition to the nineteenth-century preoccupation of British statesmen with the Eastern Question, foreshadowed by the Ochakov crisis, only became a dominant factor in British foreign policy with Bonaparte's occupation of Egypt.

If one asks what were the factors which shaped British foreign policy in the century, a variety of answers may be offered. The most obvious of these are commercial and colonial expansion on the one hand and the balance of power on the other. It is easy to show that neither of these was dominant throughout the period. The former was probably most influential in the middle section, but was comparatively weak in the early years when the main factor was probably fear of Jacobitism, intensified by Louis XIV's threat to overturn the Revolution settlement, and weak again in the later years when Britain on the whole regarded herself as a satiated state. No government ever went to war with greater reluctance than Pitt's in 1793. The French Revolution was believed to threaten the established order in Britain only less immediately than in Europe. It was only very slowly that hopes of commercial and colonial expansion infiltrated British war-aims and down to the treaty of Amiens their influence was limited and always subsidiary.

Similarly although the secretaries of state continually wrote of the need to preserve 'the Protestant cause and the liberties of Europe' they hardly lived up to this statement of policy. Within two years of the accession of the house of Hanover Britain was in close alliance with France, undoubtedly, in spite of her recent defeats, the strongest power in Europe. For the next twenty years this alliance was maintained by Townshend and Walpole until too late Walpole realized that he had made France the arbiter of Europe. Alike to Carteret and Pitt, and even Newcastle, the maintenance of the liberties of Europe meant antagonism to France if not to the whole house of Bourbon. Carteret and Newcastle struggled in vain to find an effective counterpoise. Pitt was luckier as well as abler; and the failure of his successors to maintain his system was responsible for the worst disasters of the American Revolutionary war. So far from being able to act as the balancing power of Europe after 1763, Britain virtually dropped out of European politics altogether for a whole generation. A continental league was organized against her by France. By 1783 the wheel had turned full circle since the opening of the century and the dominating idea until its closing years was again self-defence, complicated now by a great extension of the area to be defended and by a massive and final breach within the empire itself owing to the recognition of American independence.

The nearest approach to a single dominant idea running right through the century would probably be found in hostility to France, which was detested by the average Englishman equally in 1701 and in 1800. It was not merely that France was Britain's most dangerous commercial and colonial rival beyond Europe. From her proximity, her much larger population, and her alliance with other Bourbon states, she was a standing threat to the security of Britain. France was detested equally as the patron of the Pretenders and the leading Roman Catholic power in Europe. Contemporary Englishmen, proud of the free institutions bequeathed to them by their ancestors, affected to despise, and certainly hated, the absolutism which Louis XIV had established in France and propagated in

Europe. Only in the days of the Spanish Armada did internal security, religious zeal, political prejudice, and economic advantage designate so clearly a natural and national enemy. The more one considers these truths the more one must be impressed by the willingness of the government to sign the Triple Alliance with France in 1717 and to make the Tory peace settlement of 1713 the basis of Whig foreign policy for two decades.

What made it possible was the long survival of the tradition that foreign policy was a mystery of state with which Parliament, let alone the common man, had no right to meddle, and about which they had almost as little right to be informed. In the days of the Stuarts, Parliament had vainly asserted claims to control of foreign policy: even the victory of Parliament over the monarchy at the Revolution was not followed by any sensational advance in this direction. William III was notoriously his own foreign minister and even after 1714 the powers of the executive were at their widest and were least supervised when dealing with foreign relations.

Just as much in foreign as in home affairs practical advantages, and not ideological concepts, dominated British politics in the eighteenth-century. Many of Britain's prime ministers looked upon foreign politics from the point of view attributed to one of their nineteenth century successors—how simple foreign policy would be if it were not for 'these demned foreigners'. Walpole, North, and the Younger Pitt were alike in their basic approach. They usually adopted a line in foreign policy which they hoped would fit in with, or at least cause as little disturbance and damage as possible to, what they regarded as the more important policies they were anxious to follow at home. To them the 'Protestant interest' had become a meaningless shibboleth and the 'balance of power', on the lips of an eighteenth-century British politician, was merely designed to secure support from other states for British antagonism to France. And as British power rose by fits and starts, foreigners were less and less impressed. France and Austria joined forces in the Diplomatic Revolution in the conviction that this was the only way to repress British meddling and dictation on the European continent. The leading European powers combined against Britain in the American war of Independence in the belief that in so doing they were not merely serving their own particular interests but also cutting down to size the upstart British empire.

The French Revolution ushered in a new period of ideological warfare and revived in foreign politics the influence of ideological concepts, which had been declining since the treaties of Westphalia. French success in exploiting these, and Pitt's deficiencies as a war minister, enabled her to conclude the triumphant treaty of Amiens with the intention of excluding Britain from any say in continental affairs. Belatedly convinced that Napoleon was a menace to the established order and the several interests of the Great Powers, which could be resisted only with active British support, they formed with her a new Grand Alliance, which, after repeated defeats, was to prove as successful as the Grand Alliance of 1701 had been in securing the overthrow of Louis XIV. Whatever else it did or failed to do the Congress of Vienna set up a durable system of balance among the leading European states.

GENERAL BIBLIOGRAPHY

Note. The distinction between works included in the general bibliography and some of those listed in sectional bibliographies at the end of
each chapter is somewhat arbitrary. A few titles have been included in
more than one list; but, to save space, such works as the *Malmesbury
Diaries* which record the diplomatic career of a British diplomatist
accredited to several courts are often listed only in the general bibliography. Works dealing mainly with domestic politics are normally ignored,
although many contain material of value for diplomatic relations between
Great Britain and one or more continental states. Specialized works
whose primary concern is with colonial problems beyond Europe are, in
general, excluded. Few works not written in English, French, German,
or Italian are included. Place of publication, unless otherwise indicated,
is London.

A. *Reference Works*

British Diplomatic Representatives [1689–1852], ed. D. B. Horn, S. T.
    Bindoff, and others (Royal Historical Society, Camden Series, 1932
    and 1934)
Bromley, J. S., and Goodwin, A. (edd.), *Select List of Works on Europe
    and Europe Overseas 1715–1815* (Oxford, 1956)
Calendar of Home Office Papers [1760–75], ed. J. Redington and R. A.
    Roberts (4 vols., 1878–99)
Chalmers, G., *Collection of Treaties between Great Britain and Other
    Powers* (2 vols., 1790)
Jenkinson, C., *Collection of all the Treaties of Peace, Alliance and Com-
    merce between Great Britain and Other Powers* (3 vols., 1785)
Materials for English Diplomatic History 1509–1783 [included in B.M.
    MS. Collections and *H.M.C.* Reports], ed. Frances G. Davenport
    (*H.M.C. 18th Report* (1917), part 2, pp. 357–402)
Pargellis, S., and Medley, D. J., *Bibliography of British History* [1714–89]
    (Oxford, 1951)
Recueil des Instructions Données aux Ambassadeurs et Ministres de France
    [1648–1789] (Paris, 1884–)
Repertorium der diplomatischen Vertreter aller Länder [1648–1815], vols.
    1–3 [various editors and places of publication, 1936–65]

B. *Primary Sources*

Nearly all political diaries and memoirs and collections of correspondence
include material relevant to the study of diplomatic relations between
Great Britain and other states. They are listed in the bibliographies mentioned in Section A. The list that follows includes only a few important

works on foreign policy published in the eighteenth century and subsequent publications of diplomatic correspondence. For material published by the Historical Manuscripts Commission, see *Materials for English Diplomatic History* and Pargellis and Medley's *Bibliography*, both listed in Section A.

Campbell, J., *Present State of Europe* (5th ed., 1757)
Diaries and Correspondence of the first earl of Malmesbury, ed. by the third earl (4 vols., 1844)
Journal and Correspondence of William Eden, Baron Auckland (4 vols., 1861–2)
The Lexington Papers, ed. H. Manners Sutton (1851)
Mauduit, I., *Considerations on the present German War* (4th ed., 1761)
Memoir of Hugh Elliot, ed. Lady Minto (Edinburgh, 1868)
Memoirs and Correspondence of Sir Robert Murray Keith, ed. Mrs. Gillespie Smyth (2 vols., 1849)
Memoirs of Horatio, Lord Walpole, ed. W. Coxe (2 vols., 1820)
Memoirs of the Secret Services of J. Macky [often said to have been written by Bishop Burnet] (1733)
Piggott, F. T., and Ormond, G. W. T. (edd.), *Documentary History of the Armed Neutralities of 1780 and 1800* (1919)
Postlethwayt, M., *Britain's Commercial Interest explained and improved* (2 vols., 1757)
The Present State of Europe: or the Historical and Political Monthly Mercury (1690–1714)
Reports of Committees of the House of Commons, vol. I (1803) [for the official inquiry into the negotiation of the treaty of Utrecht, pp. 44 ff.]
Spencer, F. (ed.), *The fourth Earl of Sandwich Diplomatic Correspondence 1763–65* (Manchester, 1961)
Vernon Correspondence [1696–1708], ed. G. P. R. James (1841) [on which see Mrs. Dorothy H. Somerville, 'The dates in the Vernon correspondence' in *EHR* 48 (1933), 624–30]
Wentworth Papers [1705–39], ed. J. J. Cartwright (1883)

C. *Secondary Authorities*

Adams, E. D., *Influence of Grenville on Pitt's Foreign Policy* (Washington, 1904)
Antheunis, L., 'Thomas Strickland evêque de Namur, au service de la couronne d'Angleterre' in *Bulletin de la Commission Royale d'Histoire* 122 (1957), 239–59 [Strickland was a secret agent both of George I and George II]
Bamford, P. W., 'French Shipping in North European Trade' in *JMH* 26 (1954), 207–19
Barbour, Violet, 'Consular service in the reign of Charles II' in *AHR* 33 (1927–8), 553–78
Baudi de Vesme, C., 'L'influenza del potere marittimo nella guerra di successione d'Austria' in *Nuova Rivista Storica* 37 (1953), 19–43

Browning, O., 'Foreign Policy of Pitt to the outbreak of the war with France' in *Cambridge Mod. Hist.*, vol. 8 (1904)
— 'The Triple Alliance of 1788' in *TRHS* New Series, 2 (1885), 77–96
Butterfield, H., 'British Foreign Policy' in *H Journal* 6 (1963), 131–40
— *The Reconstruction of an Historical Episode: the history of the enquiry into the origins of the Seven Years War* (Glasgow, 1951)
Carillo, Elisa A., 'The Corsican kingdom of George III' in *JMH* 34 (1962), 254–74
Chance, J. F., *The Alliance of Hanover* (1923)
— *George I and the Northern War* (1909)
Clapham, J. H., *Causes of the War of 1792* (Cambridge, 1899)
— 'Loans and Subsidies in time of war 1793–1914' in *Econ. Journal* 27 (1917), 495–501
Clark, Sir G., 'The Character of the Nine Years War 1688–97' in *CHJ* 11 (1953–5), 168–82
Coombs, D., 'Dr. Davenant and the Debate on Franco-Dutch Trade' in *EcHR* 10 (1957–8), 94–103
Corbett, J. S., *England in the Mediterranean* [1603–1713] (2 vols., 1904)
— *England in the Seven Years War* (2 vols., 2nd ed., 1918)
Dalzel, A., *History of the University of Edinburgh*, vol. I (Edinburgh, 1862) [for the diplomatic career of Sir Robert Liston]
Davis, R., 'English Foreign Trade 1660–1700' in *EcHR* 7 (1954–5), 150–66
— 'English Foreign Trade 1700–1774' in *EcHR* 15 (1961–2), 285–303
Ehrman, J., *The British Government and Commercial Negotiations with Europe 1783–93* (Cambridge, 1962)
Eldon, C. W., *England's subsidy Policy towards the Continent during the Seven Years War* (Philadelphia, 1938)
Fayle, C. E., 'Economic Pressure in the War of 1739–48' in *Journal of the Royal United Service Institution* 68 (1923), 434–46
Fieldhouse, H. N., 'Bolingbroke and the D'Iberville Correspondence [1714–15]' in *EHR* 52 (1937), 673–82
— 'A Note on the Negotiations for the Peace of Utrecht' in *AHR* 40 (1934–5), 274–7
Gibbs, G. C., 'Britain and the Alliance of Hanover' in *EHR* 73 (1958), 404–30
— 'Parliament and Foreign Policy in the Age of Stanhope and Walpole' in *EHR* 77 (1962), 18–37
Glover, R., 'Arms and the British Diplomat in the French Revolutionary Era' in *JMH* 29 (1957), 199–212
Goebel, J., *The Struggle for the Falkland Islands* (New Haven, 1927)
Hautala, K., *European and American Tar in the English Market* (Helsinki, 1963)
Henderson, W. O., *Britain and Industrial Europe 1750–1870* (Liverpool, 1954)
Horn, D. B., *The British Diplomatic Service 1689–1789* (Oxford, 1961)
— *Sir Charles Hanbury Williams and European Diplomacy* (1930)
— 'The Board of Trade and Consular Reports' in *EHR* 54 (1939), 476–80

Horn, D. B., 'The Cabinet Controversy on Subsidy Treaties in time of peace' in *EHR* 45 (1930), 463–6
— 'The Diplomatic Revolution' in *New Cambridge Mod. Hist.* VII (1957), 440–64
— 'The Origins of the proposed election of a king of the Romans' in *EHR* 42 (1927), 361–70
John, A. H., 'War and the English Economy 1700–63' in *EcHR* 7 (1954–5), 329–44
Jusserand, J. J., 'The School for Ambassadors' in *AHR* 27 (1922–3), 426–64
Lachs, Phyllis S., *The Diplomatic Corps under Charles II and James II* (Rutgers U.P., 1965)
Lätt, A., 'Zwei schweizerische Diplomaten im Dienste Grossbritannien' in *Basler Zeitschrift für Geschichte und Altertumskunde* 21, p. 127
Lane, Margery, 'The Diplomatic Service under William III' in *TRHS* 4th series, 10 (1927), 87–109
— 'Lighter Side of Diplomacy under William III' in *Nineteenth Century* 102 (1927), 558–64
Lodge, Sir R., *Studies in Eighteenth-Century Diplomacy* (1930)
— 'English Neutrality in the War of the Polish Succession' in *TRHS* 4th series, 14 (1931), 141–73
— 'The Continental Policy of Great Britain 1740–60' in *History* 38 (1930–1), 246–51
— 'The Hanau Controversy' in *EHR* 38 (1923), 509–31
— 'The so-called Treaty of Hanau' in *EHR* 38 (1923), 384–407
— 'The Spanish Succession' in *History* 12 (1927–8), 333–8
McKendrick, N., 'Josiah Wedgwood: an eighteenth century entrepreneur in salesmanship and marketing techniques' in *EcHR* 12 (1959–60), 408–33
Massini, R., *Sir Luke Schaub: ein Basler im diplomatischen Dienst Englands* (Basel, 1953)
Michael, W., *Englische Geschichte im 18. Jahrhundert* (5 vols., Hamburg &c., 1896–1955) [English translation of vols. 1–2]
Morgan, W. T., 'Economic aspects of the negotiations at Ryswick' in *TRHS* 4th series, 14 (1931), 225–49
Murray, J. J., 'Baltic Commerce and Power Politics in the early eighteenth century' in *HLQ* 6 (1942–3), 293–312
Newton, A. P., 'The West Indies in international politics 1550–1850' in *History* 19 (1934–5), 193–207, 302–10
Pares, R., 'American versus Continental Warfare 1739–63' in *EHR* 51 (1936), 429–65
Parry, E. J., 'Undersecretaries of state for foreign affairs 1782–1855' in *EHR* 49 (1934), 308–20
Patterson, A. T., *The Other Armada* (Manchester, 1960)
Penson, Lilian, *Colonial Background of British Foreign Policy* (1930)
Poston, L., 'Defoe and the Peace Campaign 1710–13' in *HLQ* 27 (1963–4), 1–20

Rauch, G. von, 'Zur baltischen Frage im 18. Jahrhundert' in *JGO* 5 (1957), 441–87

Richmond, Sir H., *Navy in the War of 1739–48* (3 vols., Cambridge, 1920)

— *Statesmen and Sea Power* (Oxford, 2nd ed., 1947)

Robinson, E., 'Boulton and Fothergill 1762–82, and the Birmingham Export of Hardware 1762–82' in *Univ. of Birmingham Historical Journal* 7 (1959–60), 60–79

— 'Eighteenth-century Commerce and Fashion: Boulton's marketing techniques' in *EcHR* 16 (1963–4), 39–60

— 'The international exchange of men and machines 1750–1800' in *Business History* 1 (1958), 3–15

Rodger, A. B., *War of the Second Coalition* (Oxford, 1964)

Rose, J. H., *William Pitt and the National Revival* (1911)

— *William Pitt and the Great War* (1912)

— 'The Missions of William Grenville to The Hague and Versailles in 1787' in *EHR* 24 (1909), 278–95

Salomon, F., 'The Foreign Policy of William Pitt [1783–93]' in *TRHS* New Series, 10 (1896), 111–20

Sherwig, J. M., 'Lord Grenville's plan for a concert of Europe 1797–99' in *JMH* 34 (1962), 284–93

Skrine, E. H., *Fontenoy and Great Britain's share in the War of the Austrian Succession* (1906)

Smith, E. M., *British Diplomacy in the Eighteenth Century* (1937)

Somerville, Mrs. D. H., 'Shrewsbury and the Peace of Utrecht' in *EHR* 47 (1932), 646–7

Swedenborg, H. T., 'George Stepney, My Lord Dorset's Boy' in *HLQ* 10 (1946–7), 1–33

Thomson, M. A., *The Secretaries of State 1681–1782* (Oxford, 1932)

— 'Louis XIV and the Grand Alliance 1705–10' in *BIHR* 34 (1961), 16–35

— 'Louis XIV and the Origins of the War of the Spanish Succession' in *TRHS* 5th series, 4 (1954), 111–34

— 'Parliament and Foreign Policy 1689–1714' in *History* 38 (1953), 234–43

— 'The Safeguarding of the Protestant Succession 1702–18' in *History* 39 (1954), 39–53

Walker, J. C., 'The duke of Newcastle and the British envoys at the Congress of Cambrai' in *EHR* 50 (1935), 113–19

Ward, A. W., and Gooch, G. P. (edd.), *Cambridge History of British Foreign Policy*, vol. I (Cambridge, 1922)

Williams, Basil, *Carteret and Newcastle* (Cambridge, 1943)

— *Stanhope* (Oxford, 1932)

— *William Pitt, Earl of Chatham* (2 vols., 1913)

— 'Carteret and the so-called Treaty of Hanau' in *EHR* 49 (1934), 684–7

— series of articles on Walpole's foreign policy in *EHR* 15 and 16 (1900–1): vol. 15, 251–76, 479–94, 665–98, and vol. 16, 67–83, 308–27, and 439–51

Wilson, C. H., 'Cloth Production and International Competition in the Seventeenth Century' in *EcHR* 13 (1960–1), 208–21

Addendum. Some articles in *The New Cambridge Modern History*, vols. VIII and IX (1965), make incidental mention of relations between Britain and Continental states.

LIST OF ABBREVIATIONS
used in bibliographies

AHR	= *American Historical Review*
BIHR	= *Bulletin of the Institute of Historical Research*
CHJ	= *Cambridge Historical Journal*
EHR	= *English Historical Review*
EcHR	= *Economic History Review*
FBPG	= *Forschungen zur brandenburgischen und preussischen Geschichte*
HAR	= *Hispanic American Historical Review*
HJ	= *Historisches Jahrbuch*
H Journal	= *Historical Journal*
HLQ	= *Huntington Library Quarterly*
JCEA	= *Journal of Central European Affairs*
JGO	= *Jahrbücher für Geschichte Osteuropas*
JMH	= *Journal of Modern History*
MIOG	= *Mitteilungen des Instituts für österreichische Geschichtsforschung*
OSP	= *Oxford Slavonic Papers*
RH	= *Revue historique*
RHD	= *Revue d'histoire diplomatique*
SEER	= *Slavonic and East European Review*
TRHS	= *Transactions of the Royal Historical Society*
WMQ	= *William and Mary Quarterly*

INDEX

Carmarthen, Francis Godolphin Osborne, marquess of (later 5th duke of Leeds), regards Cabinet's views as decisive on foreign policy, 13; relationship of, to Pitt, 15; foreign policy of, in the 'eighties, 65; wishes to oppose French control of the United Provinces, 66; makes approach to Prussia for common action in the United Provinces, 164; Austrophil tendencies of, 166; expresses dissatisfaction with Hertzberg's acquisitive policy, 168; resignation of, 227, 230; and Nootka Sound, 304; and Switzerland, 319

Caroline Matilda, wife of Christian VII, king of Denmark, 197, 256, 258, 260, 263

Carteret, John, Lord (later Earl Granville), political heir of Sunderland 48; his German policy, 55; policy of, in Austrian Succession war, 126–128, 194; attitude of, to Prussia, 149–150, 154; driven from office, 150–1; speaks German, 178; advocates alliance with Russia, 210; mission of, to Stockholm, 248–9; and the treaty of Worms, 336, 340, 352; and the 'liberties of Europe', 382

Carvajal, y Lancaster, Don José de, 292–4

Castiglione, Baldassarre, count, 330

Castlereagh, Robert Stewart, viscount (2nd marquess of Londonderry), 28, 176, 233, 349

Castres, Abraham, 318

Catalans, 115, 285

Catherine I, tsaritsa, 50, 207–8, 250

Catherine II, tsaritsa, 1st Russo-Turkish war of, 38; organizes Armed Neutrality, 103, 163, 203, 219, 262–3, 373; alliance of, with Joseph II, 139, 222; and the Northern System, 162; attitude of, to the Bavarian Exchange scheme, 164; commercial negotiations of, with Britain, 204, 231; as grand duchess, opposes French influence at Petersburg, 211–12; policy and outlook of, 212–13, 216, 221–2; defeats Turks at Chesmé, 216; political negotiations of, with Britain, 218–222; and Poland, 216, 229; sends fleet to Mediterranean, 216,

230; alliance of, with Prussia, 218; growth of merchant navy under, 220; and Charles James Fox, 221–2; advance of, towards Black Sea, 225; and the Ochakov crisis, 225–8, 230; concludes Treaty of Verela, 227, 264; and 2nd and 3rd partitions of Poland, 231; inactive against France in 1st coalition, 232; Corsica offered to, 232; and Schleswig-Holstein, 258–9; and the Swedish crisis of 1772, 261–2; supported by the Danes, 264; Minorca offered to, 368; Turkish wars of, 373

Catherine of Braganza, wife of Charles II, king of Great Britain, 271

Catt, Jean Gabriel, 319

Celle, duke of, 8, 144

Ceuta, 287

Ceylon, 80, 104

Cevennes, Protestant revolt in, 31

Chalmers, George, quoted, 215

Chamber of Manufactures, 39

Chancellor, Richard, 201

Charles V, Holy Roman Emperor, 50, 120

Charles VI, Holy Roman Emperor, over-rated by contemporaries, 22–23; becomes French satellite, 23; as archduke Charles, candidate for throne of Spain, 41, 115; accession of, as Emperor, 44; concludes defensive treaty with England, 44; disputes of, with Philip V, 45–46, 50–51, 115, 119, 283; and the Ostend Company, 50; British opposition to, 52; claims British support in Polish Succession war, 54, 209; and the Netherlands, 96, 105; his power weakened in 1730's, 114; influenced by 'the Spanish Council', 115, 122; tries to overturn Treaty of Utrecht, 116; accepts Netherlands, 116; indignant at Triple Alliance, 117; on bad terms with Elector of Hanover, 117–18, 249, 252; joins Triple Alliance, 118; and the Pragmatic Sanction, 119–20; and the 1st Treaty of Vienna, 119–20; break-up of his alliance with Spain, 121–3; suspends and abolishes Ostend Company, 123, 251; and the Polish Succession, 123–4, 365; his contacts with British Opposition re-

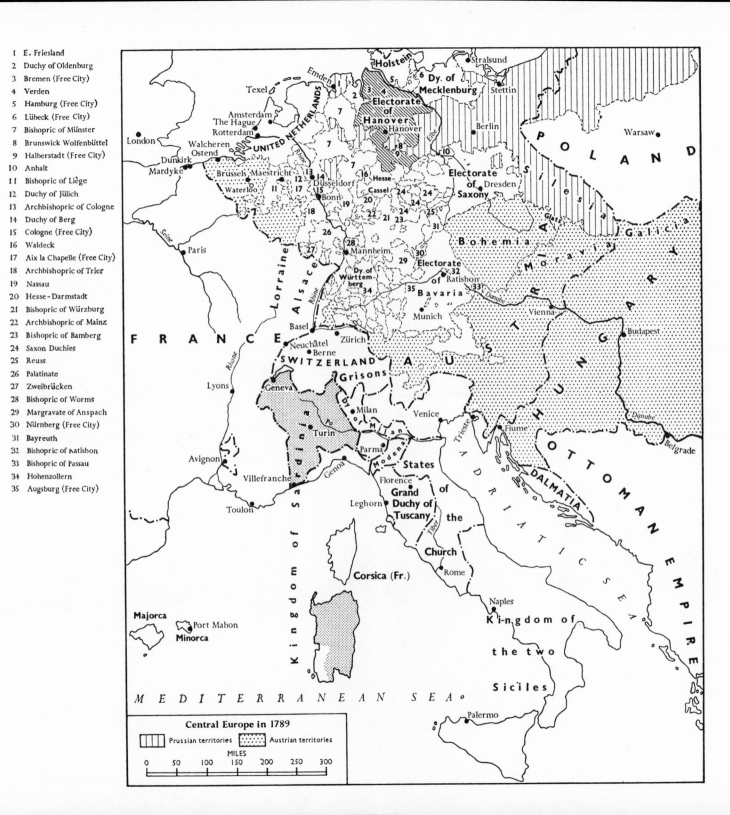

1 E. Friesland
2 Duchy of Oldenburg
3 Bremen (Free City)
4 Verden
5 Hamburg (Free City)
6 Lübeck (Free City)
7 Bishopric of Münster
8 Brunswick Wolfenbüttel
9 Halberstadt (Free City)
10 Anhalt
11 Bishopric of Liège
12 Duchy of Jülich
13 Archbishopric of Cologne
14 Duchy of Berg
15 Cologne (Free City)
16 Waldeck
17 Aix la Chapelle (Free City)
18 Archbishopric of Trier
19 Nassau
20 Hesse-Darmstadt
21 Bishopric of Würzburg
22 Archbishopric of Mainz
23 Bishopric of Bamberg
24 Saxon Duchies
25 Reuss
26 Palatinate
27 Zweibrücken
28 Bishopric of Worms
29 Margravate of Anspach
30 Nürnberg (Free City)
31 Bayreuth
32 Bishopric of Ratisbon
33 Bishopric of Passau
34 Hohenzollern
35 Augsburg (Free City)

Central Europe in 1789

▯▯▯ Prussian territories   ⦂⦂⦂ Austrian territories

MILES
0   50   100 150 200 250 300

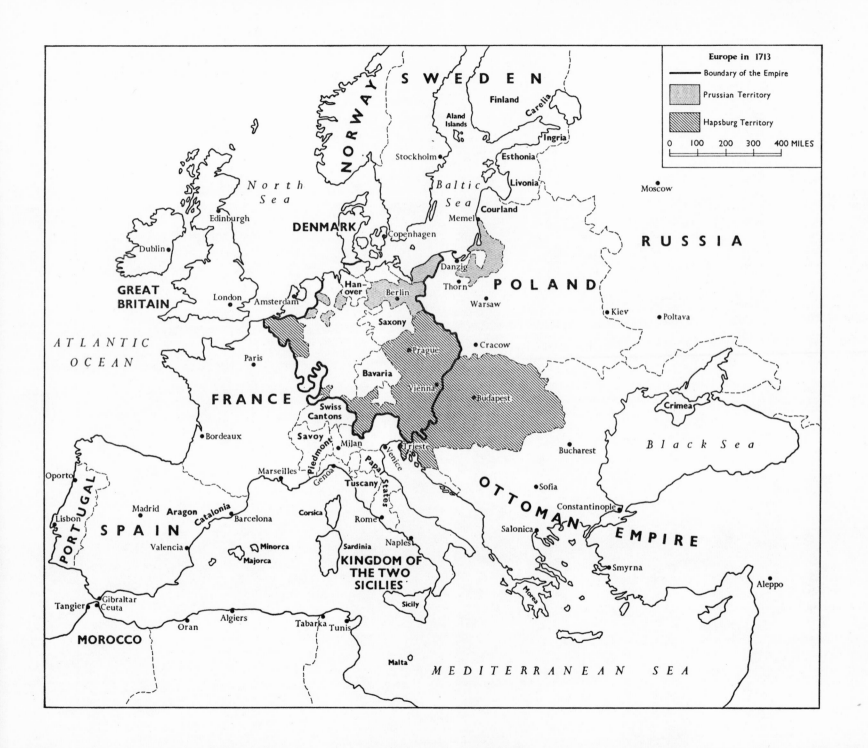

Europe in 1713

Boundary of the Empire

Prussian Territory

Hapsburg Territory

0 100 200 300 400 MILES

NORWAY

SWEDEN

Finland

Aland
Islands

Stockholm

Carelia

Ingria

Esthonia

Livonia

North
Sea

Baltic
Sea

Moscow

DENMARK

Copenhagen

Memel

Courland

RUSSIA

Edinburgh

Danzig

Dublin

Han-
over

Berlin

Thorn

POLAND

Warsaw

Kiev

Poltava

GREAT
BRITAIN

London

Amsterdam

Saxony

ATLANTIC
OCEAN

Paris

Prague

Cracow

FRANCE

Bavaria

Vienna

Budapest

Bordeaux

Swiss
Cantons

Savoy

Milan

Piedmont

Venice

Trieste

Black Sea

Bucharest

Marseilles

Genoa

Papal
States

Tuscany

OTTOMAN

Oporto

Corsica

Rome

Sofia

PORTUGAL

Lisbon

Madrid

Aragon

Catalonia

Barcelona

Constantinople

Salonica

SPAIN

Valencia

Minorca

Majorca

Sardinia

Naples

KINGDOM OF
THE TWO
SICILIES

EMPIRE

Smyrna

Tangier

Gibraltar
Ceuta

Algiers

Tabarka

Tunis

Morea

Sicily

Aleppo

MOROCCO

Oran

Malta

MEDITERRANEAN   SEA